THE JUDICIAL MIND

This collection of essays is a tribute to Lord Kerr of Tonaghmore, who died aged 72 on 1 December 2020 after having retired from the UK Supreme Court just two months earlier.

Brian Kerr was appointed as a judge of the High Court of Northern Ireland in 1993. He became the Lord Chief Justice of Northern Ireland in 2004 before being elevated to a peerage and appointed as the last Lord of Appeal in Ordinary in June 2009. Four months later, as Lord Kerr, he moved from the Appellate Committee of the House of Lords to the UK Supreme Court where, after exactly 11 years, he concluded his distinguished judicial career as the longest-serving Justice to date. During his career he established an exceptional reputation for independence of thought, fairness and humanitarianism.

Lord Kerr's judicial mind has inspired and influenced a significant number of scholars and jurists throughout the UK and beyond. In this book, his unique brand of jurisprudence is examined alongside a catalogue of broader issues in which he displayed a keen interest during his lifetime. The volume includes topical contributions from a range of legal experts in Britain and Ireland. Lord Kerr's particular interests in public law, human rights law, criminal law, and family law are featured prominently, but so too is the importance of his dissenting judgments, some influential jurisprudence of the Judicial Committee of the Privy Council (where he sat on many occasions), the legacy of his influence on the law and legal system of Northern Ireland and the significance of his place in the development of judicial roles and responsibilities more generally.

The Judicial Mind

A Festschrift for Lord Kerr of Tonaghmore

Edited by
Brice Dickson
and
Conor McCormick

•HART•
OXFORD • LONDON • NEW YORK • NEW DELHI • SYDNEY

HART PUBLISHING
Bloomsbury Publishing Plc
Kemp House, Chawley Park, Cumnor Hill, Oxford, OX2 9PH, UK
1385 Broadway, New York, NY 10018, USA
29 Earlsfort Terrace, Dublin 2, Ireland

HART PUBLISHING, the Hart/Stag logo, BLOOMSBURY and the Diana logo are trademarks of Bloomsbury Publishing Plc

First published in Great Britain 2021

A catalogue record for this book is available from the British Library.

Library of Congress Cataloging-in-Publication data

Names: Kerr, Brian, 1948–2020, honouree. | Dickson, Brice, editor. | McCormick, Conor, editor.

Title: The judicial mind : a festschrift for Lord Kerr of Tonaghmore / edited by Brice Dickson and Conor McCormick.

Description: Oxford ; New York : Hart, 2021. | Includes bibliographical references and index.

Identifiers: LCCN 2021042766 (print) | LCCN 2021042767 (ebook) | ISBN 9781509944781 (hardback) | ISBN 9781509944828 (paperback) | ISBN 9781509944804 (pdf) | ISBN 9781509944798 (Epub)

Subjects: LCSH: Law—Great Britain. | Law—Northern Ireland. | Kerr, Brian, 1948–2020. | Judges—Great Britain—Biography. | Judges—Northern Ireland—Biography. | LCGFT: Festschriften.

Classification: LCC KD354 .J83 2021 (print) | LCC KD354 (ebook) | DDC 349.41—dc23/eng/20211014

LC record available at https://lccn.loc.gov/2021042766

LC ebook record available at https://lccn.loc.gov/2021042767

ISBN: HB: 978-1-50994-478-1
ePDF: 978-1-50994-480-4
ePub: 978-1-50994-479-8

Typeset by Compuscript Ltd, Shannon
Printed and bound in Great Britain

FOREWORD

It was a privilege to know Brian Kerr; still more, to be able to count him as a friend. He was a friend as well as a colleague to most of his fellow justices. His death on 1 December 2020, two months after his retirement, was a shock to everyone at the court, and to his former colleagues in retirement. He was the most popular of the justices with the staff and the judicial assistants and is sadly missed by us all.

Many of Brian's qualities as a man were apparent in his work as a member of the court. He was warm and approachable in his dealings with the court's staff, and especially with the judicial assistants, for whom he had responsibility. They in turn were inspired by his liberal approach to the law, his readiness to take the side of the underdog, and his adventurousness in developing the law. Those were characteristic features of his judgments, although it should also be remembered that he was in agreement with his colleagues more often than not.[1]

He was not especially interested in the commercial and chancery work which forms a large part of the court's list, to the extent that in one case I remember, where the other members of the court were divided 2:2 on an issue in the law of insolvency, we agreed to leave the point undecided, rather than have it depend on Brian. On the other hand, he greatly enjoyed cases in public law, human rights law, immigration and asylum law, criminal law, family law, employment law and tort, and wrote important judgments in those fields. If, in judicial review cases, he sometimes appeared to apply a presumption that the government was in the wrong, he was unfailingly courteous and good-humoured towards Crown counsel. I remember Sir James Eadie QC, appearing for the government, saying to him, 'I fear that I have not persuaded your Lordship on this point', to which Brian responded, with a glint in his eye, 'I fear, Sir James, that you have never persuaded me of anything', to which Sir James replied, with equal good humour, 'I live in the hope that I may, one day, persuade your Lordship of something'.

Brian wrote a relatively high proportion of dissenting judgments, particularly in his later years, when he became increasingly reluctant to allow orthodox legal thinking to stand in the way of doing justice as he saw it. He also wrote interestingly, extra-judicially, about the value of dissenting judgments.[2] The view he then

[1] For example, although he and I might be regarded as taking different approaches, we were usually in agreement, and found ourselves dissenting together in a number of cases, eg *Mohammed v Secretary of State for Defence* [2017] UKSC 2, [2017] AC 821, *R (Hallam) v Secretary of State for Justice* [2019] UKSC 2, [2020] AC 279 and *R (Maughan) v HM Senior Coroner for Oxfordshire* [2020] UKSC 46, [2021] AC 454.

[2] 'Dissenting judgments – self indulgence or self sacrifice?', The Birkenhead Lecture 2012, available on the Supreme Court website at www.supremecourt.uk/docs/speech-121008.pdf.

expressed, that judges 'should feel entirely uninhibited by anything more than their conscience and their conviction of what is the right and just legal outcome', was characteristic. All of his dissenting judgments were of value in compelling the majority of the court to consider and address a contrary argument in greater depth than they might otherwise have done. This important aspect of dissenting judgments is explored in some of the essays in this collection.[3]

Nevertheless, his most important judgments, so far as it is possible to make an assessment at the present time, seem to me to be those where he was speaking for the majority of the court. He naturally played a central role in most appeals from Northern Ireland, and derived particular satisfaction from his judgment in the Northern Ireland abortion case.[4] But his contribution to the law was far from being confined to the law of Northern Ireland. I would mention, in no particular order, as other examples of important judgments which he wrote, his judgment in a defamation case concerned with social media, where he showed robust common sense and an understanding of the nature of the medium in issue;[5] his judgment in a criminal appeal to the Judicial Committee of the Privy Council concerned with expert evidence, where he set out a clear and principled approach to the role of such evidence;[6] and the judgment which he and I wrote together on informed consent to medical treatment, where he showed his sensitivity to social change and his sympathy for a victim of high-handed and unfeeling behaviour.[7]

Brian's influence on the court was not confined to his judgments. In his later years, as one of the four most senior justices, he presided over a quarter of the panels considering applications for permission to appeal, with the result that the size and composition of the court's list was (and has, until recently, continued to be) significantly influenced by his interests and concerns. Latterly, as one of the three most senior justices, he was a member of the panel which considered many of the most urgent and sensitive applications for permission to appeal: something which resulted in a rare example of one member of the panel being overruled by the other two, when Brian wished to have the question of a right to assisted suicide re-argued but Lady Hale and I considered that the appeal would not have sufficient prospects of success.[8] Brian also presided in a large number of appeals from 2011 onwards, particularly but not only in the Judicial Committee of the Privy Council, where he demonstrated great skill in managing hearings efficiently, and was able, as presider, to choose the person whom he would prefer to draft the majority judgment.

[3] Most fully in Rachel Cahill-O'Callaghan (ch 4).

[4] *In the matter of an application by the Northern Ireland Human Rights Commission for Judicial Review* [2018] UKSC 27, [2019] 1 All ER 173.

[5] *Stocker v Stocker* [2019] UKSC 17, [2020] AC 593.

[6] *Pora v The Queen* [2015] UKPC 9, [2015] Crim LR 884.

[7] *Montgomery v Lanarkshire Health Board* [2015] UKSC 11, [2015] AC 1430.

[8] The decision in *R (Conway) v Secretary of State for Justice*, 27 November 2018, is available in the News section of the Supreme Court website at www.supremecourt.uk/news/permission-to-appeal-determination-on-r-on-the-application-of-conway-v-secretary-of-state-for-justice.html.

Brian's commitment to equal treatment of the sexes, and of different ethnic groups, has also had a lasting influence on the court. He was keen to see more women appointed as justices and demonstrated that the selection of judicial assistants on merit was consistent with a high level of diversity. He also instigated the court's connection with Bridging the Bar, an organisation devoted to providing students from under-represented groups with equality of access to opportunities in the legal profession. Since Brian's retirement, this connection has resulted in the court's offering paid internships for students from under-represented groups: an initiative which some other courts are now following. Brian's commitment to equality is, in this respect as in others, likely to be of enduring benefit to the court.

The present collection of essays is a sign of the respect in which Brian was held in the wider world beyond the court. It was intended, as Brice Dickson and Conor McCormick explain in their Preface, as a Festschrift to mark Brian's retirement from the Bench. Sadly, it has also become a Gedenkschrift: a commemoration. The title, *The Judicial Mind*, reflects the linking element of the essays as a whole. Written by authors drawn from a range of different backgrounds, including the judiciary, government, and universities in the UK and Ireland, they examine judicial decision-making both in the particular case of Brian Kerr and more widely. The essays in the first part of the book focus on Brian's own work and reflect his commitment to the rule of law and to the legal system of Northern Ireland, his service on the Judicial Committee of the Privy Council and his interests in family law, gender equality, other aspects of human rights law, and EU law. The second part of the book addresses wider issues connected to Brian's life and work, relating to constitutional law, criminal law, family law, human rights law and legal history.

Brian would have enjoyed reading these essays. They are a fitting tribute to the memory of an outstanding judge and a remarkable man.

Robert Reed
July 2021

PREFACE

A Festschrift is defined by the Oxford English Dictionary as 'a collection of writings forming a volume presented to a scholar or savant on the occasion of his attaining a certain age or period in his career'. True to that definition, our original plans for this volume entailed a book launch at which Lord Kerr of Tonaghmore would be presented with an academic tribute to him on the occasion of his judicial retirement. Sadly, Lord Kerr's unexpected passing in December 2020 has meant that the book must now serve not just as a Festschrift but also as a Gedenkschrift, namely a commemorative collection published posthumously in his memory.

It is a testament to Lord Kerr's influence on the legal academy, particularly but certainly not exclusively in Northern Ireland, that all of the contributors to this volume have shared their thoughts so willingly and timeously. We are indebted to each of them for doing so, just as we are indebted to Lord Reed of Allermuir for his Foreword to the volume. Similarly, we wish to thank the editorial team at Hart – particularly Kate Whetter, Rosie Mearns and Linda Staniford – for facilitating the book's production with such great efficiency and understanding. We are also grateful to Colin Davidson for permission to use his portrait of Lord Kerr on the cover, and to Dr Marek Martyniszyn, Head of the School of Law at Queen's University Belfast, for his support in this respect. Likewise, we thank Kevin Leighton, the UK Supreme Court and Lord Kerr's family for their permission to use the photograph included in the opening pages of the book.

Lastly, we feel it is important to record our gratitude to Lord Kerr himself for inspiring and supporting us in our academic endeavours to promote a better understanding of the law and legal system of Northern Ireland, and for giving his imprimatur to this volume at the early stages of its development. We hope above all that the contributions within it will remind readers of the various qualities which made his judicial mind so inspirational to so many.

Brice Dickson and Conor McCormick
Queen's University Belfast
September 2021

CONTENTS

NOTES ON CONTRIBUTORS

Gordon Anthony is Professor of Public Law in the School of Law at Queen's University Belfast and a Barrister-at-Law. He teaches and researches almost exclusively in the field of judicial review, and his books include *Textbook on Administrative Law*, 8th edn (Oxford, OUP, 2016, with Peter Leyland) and *Judicial Review in Northern Ireland*, 2nd edn (Oxford, Hart Publishing, 2014). He is the Director of the Academy of European Public Law in Athens, Greece, and an Academic Tenant at Francis Taylor Building.

Claire Archbold is the Deputy Departmental Solicitor for Northern Ireland, that is, a senior government lawyer responsible for advising the devolved Northern Ireland Ministers and Departments. She is Honorary Professor of Practice in Public Law at Queen's University Belfast, a Deputy Statutory Officer and a member of the Irish Judicial Conduct Committee. Her extensive public sector experience includes time spent in the Department of Justice, as Legal Secretary to Sir Brian Kerr when he was Lord Chief Justice of Northern Ireland, and in the Office of Law Reform. Formerly, Claire was a legal academic and a barrister in independent practice.

Rachel Cahill-O'Callaghan is a Reader at Cardiff School of Law and Politics (Cardiff University, Wales). She moved into the study of law from a successful career in academic science and her research combines both specialities by drawing on theories from psychology to understand judicial decision-making. Her monograph, *Values in the Supreme Court: Decisions, Division and Diversity* (Oxford, Hart Publishing, 2020) was short-listed for the Birks prize.

Brice Dickson is Emeritus Professor of International and Comparative Law at Queen's University Belfast and was Chief Commissioner of the Northern Ireland Human Rights Commission from 1999 to 2005. His main research interests are human rights law and judicial activism. He is the author of *Human Rights and the United Kingdom Supreme Court* (Oxford, OUP, 2013), for which Lord Kerr wrote the Foreword. His latest books are *The Irish Supreme Court: Historical and Comparative Perspectives* (Oxford, OUP, 2019) and *Writing the United Kingdom Constitution* (Manchester, Manchester UP, 2019).

Baroness Hale of Richmond DBE retired as President of the Supreme Court of the United Kingdom in January 2020, after a varied career as an academic lawyer, law reformer, author and judge. Lady Hale has always taken a special interest in women, children, welfare and equality. She served with Lord Kerr throughout his career as Lord of Appeal in Ordinary and Justice of the Supreme Court.

Sarah Hansen is a PhD candidate at Queen's University Belfast completing her thesis on post-adoption contact. She specialises in family law and was previously a practising barrister at the Bar of Northern Ireland.

John Jackson is Professor of Comparative Criminal Law and Procedure at the University of Nottingham, a qualified barrister and a Parole Commissioner for Northern Ireland. He was previously Dean of the School of Law at University College Dublin from 2008 to 2011 and Professor of Public Law at Queen's University Belfast from 1995 to 2008. His numerous books and articles in the areas of criminal procedure and evidence include (with Sarah Summers) *The Internationalisation of Criminal Evidence* (Cambridge, CUP, 2012) and *Obstacles to Fairness in Criminal Proceedings* (Oxford, Hart Publishing, 2018). His latest book is *Special Advocates in the Adversarial System* (Abingdon, Routledge, 2019).

Imelda Maher is Sutherland Full Professor of European Law at the UCD Sutherland School of Law. Her most recent book, co-authored with Dermot Hodson, is *The Transformation of EU Treaty Making: The Rise of Parliaments, Referendums and Courts Since 1950* (Cambridge, CUP, 2018). Her current research is on implementation of EU Law in Irish courts (with Rónán Riordan). She is a member of the Royal Irish Academy, an Honorary Bencher of Middle Temple and a former President of the Society of Legal Scholars of the UK and Ireland.

Conor McCormick is a Lecturer in Law at Queen's University Belfast. He specialises in constitutional and administrative law, with a particular focus on developments in the law and legal system of Northern Ireland. Conor has a strong interest both in the application and development of human rights law and in the work of law officers like the Attorney General. He is Deputy Editor of the *European Human Rights Law Review* and his first monograph, *The Constitutional Legitimacy of Law Officers in the United Kingdom*, will be published by Hart Publishing in 2022.

Aileen McHarg is Professor of Public Law and Human Rights at Durham University. Amongst other things, she is joint general editor of *Public Law* and co-chair of the British-Irish Chapter of the International Society for Public Law (ICON-S). She has published widely in the areas of UK and Scots public law, and her most recent book is *The Brexit Challenge for Ireland and the United Kingdom: Constitutions Under Pressure* (Cambridge, CUP, 2021), co-edited with Oran Doyle and Jo Murkens.

Gráinne McKeever is a Professor of Law and Social Justice at Ulster University's School of Law. She has published widely on social security and access to justice, focusing on how individual citizens access their legal entitlements, particularly those who experience difficulties in accessing state systems of support. She is the Joint Editor for the *Journal of Social Security Law*, a member of the Social Security Advisory Committee, a member of the academic panel advising the UK Administrative Justice Council, and a former Chair and Executive Director of the Law Centre (Northern Ireland).

Kathryn McNeilly is a Senior Lecturer at the School of Law, Queen's University Belfast. She has published widely in the area of human rights law theory and practice. In 2019, Kathryn was awarded a Leverhulme Research Fellowship to undertake research on international human rights law monitoring practices. Her monograph, *Human Rights and Radical Social Transformation* (Abingdon, Routledge, 2017) was one of two books shortlisted for the 2018 Hart-SLSA Early Career Award. Kathryn is a member of the Editorial Boards of leading international journals *Human Rights Law Review* and *Feminist Legal Studies.*

John Morison is Professor of Jurisprudence in the School of Law at Queen's University Belfast, a former Head of School and an elected Member of the Royal Irish Academy. He was a Commissioner in the Northern Ireland Judicial Appointments Commission from its establishment in 2005, serving two terms until 2012. He has published extensively in the area of constitutional law and theory. He currently leads a Leverhulme Interdisciplinary Network on Algorithmic Solutions, which is a doctoral training programme funded by the Leverhulme Trust exploring the interaction of technology with law and society, and is an Assessor for the Law Panel in the Research Evaluation Framework (REF) 2021.

Derek O'Brien is a Reader in Public Law at Oxford Brookes University. He previously taught at the Truman Bodden Law School in the Cayman Islands. He is the author of *Constitutional Systems of the Commonwealth Caribbean* (Oxford, Hart Publishing, 2014) and a co-editor of the *Oxford Handbook of Caribbean Constitutions* (Oxford, OUP, 2020).

Rory O'Connell is Professor of Human Rights and Constitutional Law at Ulster University. He has written extensively on human rights, constitutional law and equality law. His most recent book is *Law, Democracy and the European Court of Human Rights* (Cambridge, CUP, 2020). He has been the Research Director for Law since 2017 and was the Director of the Transitional Justice Institute from 2014 to 2020. Prior to joining Ulster he was a lecturer at the School of Law, Queen's University Belfast, where he was a member of the Human Rights Centre. Rory tweets @rjjoconnell.

Éamon Phoenix is a political historian, journalist and broadcaster. A former Principal Lecturer in History and Head of Lifelong Learning at Stranmillis University College, Queen's University, Belfast, he was also a Research Fellow of the Institute of Irish Studies at Queen's. Among his publications are *Northern Nationalism: Nationalist Politics, Partition and the Catholic Minority in Northern Ireland 1890–1940* (Belfast, 1994) and *A Century of Northern Life: The Irish News and 100 Years of Ulster History* (Belfast, 1995). He is a member of the Taoiseach's Expert Advisory Committee on Commemorations and a daily columnist for the *Irish News.*

TABLE OF CASES

TABLE OF STATUTES

TABLE OF STATUTORY INSTRUMENTS

TABLE OF INTERNATIONAL AND EU LEGISLATION

United Nations

TABLE OF NATIONAL LEGISLATION

Trinidad and Tobago

1

The Development of Lord Kerr's Judicial Mind

BRICE DICKSON AND CONOR McCORMICK

Introduction

When this book was first conceived and contracted for in the summer of 2020, we were delighted that Lord Kerr had not only acquiesced in its production but also agreed to contribute a concluding chapter based on his perusal of the preceding offerings. Ever modest, he was surprised that a book in his honour was called for, but he was clearly pleased that it had been commissioned and was relishing the opportunity to be involved in its development. It is all the sadder, therefore, that the book has had to be brought to fruition without an overview from the man at the heart of it. His death on 1 December 2020 was a great shock to everyone,[1] not least because he had retired from the Supreme Court just two months earlier and was planning a host of future activities within legal circles, such as practising as an arbitrator and mediator through the chambers of Francis Taylor Building[2] and taking up an Honorary Professorship at Queen's University Belfast.[3] This chapter offers a rounded view of the roles and accomplishments

[1] An encomium by Lord Reed, the President of the Supreme Court, can be accessed at www.supremecourt.uk/news/lord-kerr-rip.html. For further tributes see Lady Arden in *Royal Mencap Society v Tomlinson-Blake* [2021] UKSC 8, [2021] ICR 758, [76] and the recording of a Human Rights Lawyers' Association event on 23 March 2021, available at https://hoganlovells.qumucloud.com/view/SZGzSoV5nFt. A podcast on 'Lord Kerr – the "Provocative Judge"', produced by Anurag Deb at the School of Law of Queen's University Belfast and featuring three of the contributors to this book, is available at http://lawpod.org/?name=2021-04-20_lord_kerr_provocative_judge.mp3.

[2] Further details of Lord Kerr's association with FTB can be read at www.ftbchambers.co.uk/news/lord-kerr.

[3] The University's tribute to Lord Kerr is available at daro.qub.ac.uk/tribute-to-lord-kerr-honorary-professor-of-law-at-queens. Moreover, details of The Lord Kerr Scholarship – which was recently launched 'to encourage the very best home and international students to pursue their postgraduate legal studies at Queen's' – are available at www.qub.ac.uk/Study/funding-scholarships/ahss/SchoolofLaw/LordKerrScholarship.html.

which punctuated Lord Kerr's rise to the top of the UK's judicial hierarchy, with his seemingly insatiable drive for new challenges and opportunities in mind.

The Barrister

Born in County Armagh in 1948, Brian Kerr attended St Colman's College in Newry, County Down.[4] He claimed to have fallen into a law degree almost by accident, but he took to the subject like a duck to water and was called to the Northern Ireland Bar in 1970. As was common at the time, he was called to the English Bar a few years later, although he never practised there. From 1978 to 1983 he served as Junior Crown Counsel, in which role he appeared for the UK Government at the European Court of Human Rights (ECtHR) in Strasbourg, most notably in the famous case of *Dudgeon v UK*, where his duty was to try to defend the criminalisation of homosexuality in Northern Ireland.[5] In 1983 he took silk.

From 1988 Brian Kerr served as Senior Crown Counsel and he was called to the Bar of Ireland in 1990. In *Kelly v Ministry of Defence* he persuaded both the High Court and the Court of Appeal of Northern Ireland that the Ministry of Defence was not liable for the fatal shooting of a 17-year-old youth who, while 'joy-riding', had crashed through an army checkpoint in Belfast,[6] a conclusion which the European Commission of Human Rights later ruled was consistent with the European Convention on Human Rights (ECHR).[7] He also acted for the government when Gerry Adams unsuccessfully claimed compensation for the injuries he suffered in a gun attack on his car in 1984,[8] but a year later he represented Glor na nGael, an umbrella body for Irish language organisations in Belfast, which unsuccessfully challenged the government's decision to deny it further funding, allegedly based on a suspicion that its West Belfast branch was supporting a proscribed organisation.[9] Although his work for the Crown was mainly on the civil side, he did occasional criminal work too: in 1992 he prosecuted a notorious loyalist, Brian Nelson, who allegedly supplied intelligence to the British army about planned attacks on republicans.[10]

[4] We are grateful to Oswyn Paulin for help with some of the information in this section.

[5] *Dudgeon v UK* (1982) 4 EHRR 149, and see the text below at n 101. See too *Fox, Campbell and Hartley v UK* (1995) 19 EHRR 193.

[6] *Kelly v Ministry of Defence* [1989] NI 341.

[7] *Kelly v UK* (1993) 16 EHRR CD20 (a decision that the claim was inadmissible).

[8] *Adams v Secretary of State for Northern Ireland* [1990] NI 183 (CA). The court held that the state did not need to give reasons for deciding that Mr Adams was not deserving of compensation.

[9] *Re Glor na nGael's Application* [1991] NI 117 (Carswell J). Again the court ruled that the state was not obliged to disclose documents lying behind its decision.

[10] Nelson finally pleaded guilty to 20 charges, including five of conspiracy to murder. He was sentenced to 10 years' imprisonment and a number of other charges against him were dropped. For more details, see the website of Madden and Finucane, solicitors: madden-finucane.com/1997/12/21/collusion-british-military-intelligence-and-brian-nelson-a-case-for-an-independent-public-inquiry.

Brian's years at the Bar coincided almost exactly with the years of the troubles in Northern Ireland. As a lawyer who often acted for the Crown, he inevitably had to confront difficult legal challenges, but as a judge he also had to be constantly aware of the security threat, especially as he came from a Catholic background. In 1973 and 1974 two Resident Magistrates and a County Court Judge were murdered. In 1982 Lord Chief Justice Lowry was shot at while attending a function at Queen's, but the gunman missed his target. The barrister and law lecturer Edgar Graham was not so lucky: he was summarily executed as he walked down University Square in 1983. County Court Judge William Doyle was murdered in the same year. On that occasion the IRA issued a statement saying it was irrelevant that Doyle was a Catholic: he was killed because he was 'a key figure in Britain's oppressive occupation … [h]e was a member of the loyalist judiciary'. Four years later Lord Justice Maurice Gibson was blown up by an IRA bomb just South of Newry. Loyalist paramilitaries were not averse to killing Catholic lawyers too: in 1989 solicitor Pat Finucane was gunned down in his home and as late as March 1999, nearly a year after the Belfast (Good Friday) Agreement had been reached, solicitor Rosemary Nelson was killed by a bomb placed under her car.

Such was the environment within which Brian was working. His wife and children were at risk too. When, in 1984, the IRA shot Resident Magistrate Tom Travers five times he miraculously survived, but his daughter Mary did not. When Lord Justice Gibson was blown up, so was his wife Cicely. Several judges and their families had to move home because of the threat level against them. The impact of living with the thought that you and your family are constantly at risk of assassination should not be underestimated. To maintain a deep commitment to the rule of law in the midst of such fear is difficult indeed. But Brian Kerr, like all his Bar and judicial colleagues in Northern Ireland, never flinched from fulfilling his legal duties.

The High Court Judge

In 1993 Brian was metaphorically tapped on the shoulder by the then Lord Chief Justice, Sir Brian Hutton, and asked to let his name go forward for a seat on the High Court. He was duly appointed, on the recommendation of the then Lord Chancellor, Lord Mackay. During his 11 years as a High Court judge Sir Brian had spells as the lead judge in family law matters and also in judicial review applications. In the latter role he rejected an application lodged by Martin McGuinness, the former IRA commander who was elected as a Sinn Féin MP for Mid-Ulster in 1997. Even though Mr McGuinness had no intention of taking his seat at Westminster he complained that as an MP he was required to take an oath of allegiance to the Queen. Sir Brian had no choice but to rule that he had no discretion to disapply provisions in the Parliamentary Oaths Act 1866.[11] The European Commission of Human Rights, perhaps surprisingly, later held that no breach of human rights was involved.[12] When Lord Kerr visited Queen's University to open a new School of Law building in 2016, Martin McGuinness also attended in his then role as Deputy First Minister. While Arlene Foster, who also attended as First Minister, was able to say what a great time she had had at Queen's when studying law there two decades after Brian Kerr, Martin McGuinness joked that he too knew a lot about the legal system, but from the point of view of a defendant and failed litigant. The event captured just how far Northern Ireland had progressed since the Belfast (Good Friday) Agreement in 1998.

His work as a High Court judge inevitably required Brian Kerr to grapple with many other contentious issues.[13] In 1995 he dismissed a claim by a man who alleged he had been denied a position as a junior civil servant because he was supposedly a security risk – an allegation he was barred by statute from challenging. Kerr J was simply applying the existing law, but in due course the ECtHR ruled that the law itself was in breach of Article 6 of the ECHR, which guarantees the right to a fair trial.[14] In a case on the provision of transport to an Irish medium primary school he suggested that when the Human Rights Act 1998 came into force the relevant legislation might be deemed incompatible with the Act's non-discrimination provision, coupled with the guaranteed right to education.[15] Soon afterwards he did in fact issue Northern Ireland's first ever declaration of incompatibility under the Human Rights Act in a case where a man had been prosecuted for engaging in anal intercourse;[16] a decision which was not appealed against and which soon led to repeal of the offending legislation.[17] In *Re Jacqueline Lynch's Application* he rejected the argument that a statutory prohibition on granting legal aid for libel claims was a breach of Article 6 of the ECHR[18] and in the course of applying the jurisprudence of the ECtHR to that issue, he said:

> [T]he area of discretionary judgment on matters such as the deployment of public funds must be recognised and courts should be appropriately reluctant to substitute their views as to the disbursement of those funds for those of the legislators. This is particularly so where acceptance of the validity of the right claimed would require the state to take positive measures.[19]

[11] *Re McGuinness's Application* [1997] NI 359.

[12] *McGuinness v UK*, App No 38511/98, decision of 8 June 1999.

[13] See Conor McCormick (ch 13) 230–231 and Gordon Anthony (ch 5). One of the cases, *Re De Brún and McGuinness's Application* [2001] NIQB 3, again involved Mr McGuinness. This is examined in detail by Gordon Anthony (ch 5) 95–7.

[14] *Devlin v UK* (2002) 34 EHRR 43.

[15] *Re Martin's Application* [2000] NIQB 8. The legislation in question was the Education and Libraries (NI) Order 1986, SI 1986/594 (NI 3), art 52, as amended by the Education (NI) Order 1997, SI 1997/866 (NI 5), art 23.

[16] *Re McR's Application* [2002] NIQB 55.

[17] The Sexual Offences Act 2003, s 140 and Sch 7, repealed s 62 of the Offences Against the Person Act 1861.

[18] *Re Jacqueline Lynch's Application* [2002] NIQB 35.

[19] ibid, under the heading 'The area of discretionary judgment'.

His decision in *Lynch* was not subsequently challenged in the ECtHR, but another decision, in *Re McKay's Application*,[20] was. He had held that it was not a breach of Article 5 of the ECHR (the right to liberty) to prohibit persons accused of 'scheduled offences' (those likely to be committed by members of proscribed organisations) from applying for bail when initially appearing before a magistrates' court: a statutory provision allowed only a higher level judge to grant bail. By 16 votes to 1 the judges of the ECtHR's Grand Chamber upheld Kerr J's interpretation of the ECHR.[21]

Mr Justice Kerr also had frequent encounters with judicial review applications relating to a particular killing: that of an IRA member, Pearse Jordan, by a police officer in 1992. In 2002 the ECtHR found that this killing had not been investigated in accordance with the standards set by Article 2 of the ECHR.[22] Four months after that finding, however, Sir Brian held that it was not a violation of Article 2 for the police to agree to release documents to the deceased's family only if the family first undertook not to disclose those documents to a third party.[23] In 2002 he rejected an application from the Jordan family challenging the Lord Chancellor's failure to introduce legislation ensuring that Northern Ireland's inquest system was compliant with Article 2[24] and he also rejected a challenge to the coroner's decision to conduct the inquest into Pearse Jordan's death on the basis of existing law and practice and not to leave to the jury the option of returning a verdict of unlawful killing.[25] The Court of Appeal dismissed appeals against both of those rulings[26] and in turn the House of Lords dismissed a further appeal on the latter point, albeit by a decision of three to two.[27] Finally, in 2003 Kerr J held, in yet another judicial review application brought by the Jordan family, that the Human Rights Act could not be applied retrospectively so as to permit challenges to decisions taken by the Director of Public Prosecutions in 1993 and 1995 not to prosecute the police officers involved in the killing of Pearse.[28] While that particular decision was not appealed, the retrospectivity point was considered by the High Court and Court of Appeal in a similar case not involving Kerr J.[29] The Court of Appeal held that the Human Rights Act *could* be applied retrospectively

[20] *Re McKay's Application*, decision of 3 May 2002 (unreported).

[21] *McKay v UK* (2007) 44 EHRR 41.

[22] *Jordan v UK* (2003) 37 EHRR 2, judgment of 4 May 2001. For further details of Lord Kerr's engagement with Arts 2 and 3 of the ECHR see Brice Dickson (ch 6).

[23] *Re Jordan's Application* [2001] NIQB 32.

[24] *Re Jordan's Application* [2002] NIQB 7, [2002] NI 151.

[25] *Re Jordan's Application* [2002] NIQB 20.

[26] *Re Jordan's Application* [2004] NICA 29, [2005] NI 144.

[27] *Jordan v Lord Chancellor* [2007] UKHL 14, [2007] 2 AC 226. Lady Hale and Lord Mance dissented.

[28] *Re Jordan's Application* [2003] NIQB 1, upheld at [2003] NICA 54. There are numerous other cases connected with Pearse Jordan's death. In *Re Jordan's Applications* [2014] NICA 76, Morgan LCJ pointed out (at [122]) that there had been, by that stage, 24 judicial reviews, 14 appeals to the Court of Appeal, two hearings in the House of Lords and one hearing in the European Court of Human Rights.

[29] *Re McKerr's Application*, Campbell LJ (26 July 2002, unreported); [2003] NICA 1 (Carswell LCJ, McCollum LJ and Coghlin J).

but the House of Lords held unanimously that it could not.[30] When a further appeal relating to Mr Jordan's death reached the Supreme Court in 2019 Lord Kerr did not sit in it, no doubt because of his repeated involvement in previous applications relating to the same incident.[31]

One of the few occasions on which a decision by Kerr J was overturned by the Court of Appeal was in *Re the Family Planning Association's Application*, where he rejected a request that he should order the Department of Health, Social Services and Public Safety to issue guidance about the circumstances in which an abortion could be obtained in Northern Ireland and to investigate the difficulties women were facing in obtaining services for the termination of pregnancy.[32] Read in the light of his Supreme Court judgment on abortion law in Northern Ireland many years later,[33] it is surprising that his conclusion in the Family Planning Association case was that 'having carefully reviewed all the available evidence, I am not satisfied that it has been shown that there is any significant uncertainty among the medical profession as to the principles that govern the law on abortion in this jurisdiction'.[34] The Court of Appeal unanimously disagreed with his stance and issued a declaration requiring the Department to provide the guidance asked for.[35]

The Lord Chief Justice

In 2004 the then Lord Chief Justice of Northern Ireland, Sir Robert Carswell, was appointed to fill the shoes of Lord Hutton in the Appellate Committee of the House of Lords, thereby continuing the tradition which was beginning to emerge whereby one of the judges on the nation's top court needed to be an expert in the law of Northern Ireland. It might have been expected that the vacancy thus created for the top judicial position in Northern Ireland would have been filled by one of the three members of the Court of Appeal, all of whom had several more years of judicial experience than Mr Justice Kerr.[36] At the time there was still

[30] *Re McKerr* [2004] UKHL 12, [2004] 1 WLR 807.

[31] *In the matter of an application by Hugh Jordan for Judicial Review* [2019] UKSC 9, [2020] NI 570. By then an Art 2 compliant inquest had taken place but Horner J, serving as a coroner, concluded that it was impossible to say with certainty what had happened on the day of the killing: [2016] NICoroner 1. Leave to bring an application for judicial review challenging the verdict was refused: [2017] NIQB 135 and, on appeal, [2018] NICA 34. The 2019 UKSC case was about the family's claim for damages for the delay in holding an Art 2 compliant inquest.

[32] *Re the Family Planning Association of Northern Ireland's Application* [2003] NIQB 48. See too Lady Hale (ch 2) 40.

[33] *In the matter of an application by the Northern Ireland Human Rights Commission for Judicial Review* [2018] UKSC 27, [2019] 1 All ER 173. See also Lady Hale (ch 2) 42–44 and Kathryn McNeilly (ch 3) 52.

[34] *FPANI* (n 32) [29].

[35] *Family Planning Association of Northern Ireland v Minister for Health, Social Services and Public Safety* [2004] NICA 37 (Sheil LJ), 38 (Campbell LJ) and 39 (Nicholson LJ).

[36] These were Nicholson, McCollum and Campbell LJJ.

no open competition for such posts. Instead, soundings were taken from those who were familiar with the track record and personality of the likely contenders. Brian Kerr was the one eventually chosen by the Lord Chancellor, Lord Falconer, to take on the mantle of Lord Chief Justice. This was an indicator not only that Brian had excellent legal skills but also that he would be well able to perform the extensive administrative duties of the Chief Justice and to navigate carefully the political sensitivities of the position. In the same year Sir Brian became an Honorary Bencher of King's Inns in Dublin.

Brian was the first appointee to the top judicial post in Northern Ireland since the Belfast (Good Friday) Agreement and the first since the Human Rights Act came fully into force in 2000. He was also only the second person from a Catholic background to serve as Lord Chief Justice of Northern Ireland; the first, Sir Denis Henry, served from 1921 to 1925.[37] After he moved to the top post he occasionally sat alone to hear judicial review applications[38] but mostly he sat with one or two fellow judges in the Divisional Court or Court of Appeal, always as the presider and more often than not as the judgment writer. However, more so than any of his predecessors in the role, he was frequently content to let his fellow judges write the judgment of the court so that he could devote his energies to his onerous administrative responsibilities. Even so, a good deal of his time as Lord Chief Justice was spent on appeals against convictions and sentences in criminal cases.

He did take time out to sit on one occasion as an ad hoc judge in a case before the European Court of Human Rights, *Hatton v UK*. This was a claim made by eight applicants who lived close to Heathrow Airport that government policy on night flights at the airport was so disruptive of their sleep as to amount to a violation of their right to a private life under Article 8 of the ECHR. At the Chamber level it was held by five votes to two that Article 8 had indeed been violated.[39] Lord Kerr was one of the dissenters. To him the evidence did not show that there was a significant interference with the right to a private life; rather it strongly favoured the conclusion that there would be considerable adverse effect to the economy if night flights were curtailed. Besides, 'those who claim sleep disturbance from night flying have a genuine choice as to whether to remain or to move elsewhere'.[40] He struck a distinctly deferential tone to the government's position:

> when, as here, a substantial proportion of the population of south London is in a similar position to the applicants, the Court must consider whether the proper place for a discussion of the particular policy is in Strasbourg, or whether the issue should not be left to the domestic political sphere.[41]

[37] See Eamon Phoenix (ch 11).

[38] eg, *Re E's Application* [2004] NIQB 35; *Re Teresa Kelly's Application* [2004] NIQB 72. Both of these cases are mentioned in Brice Dickson (ch 6) 115–116 and 100 respectively.

[39] *Hatton v UK* (2002) 34 EHRR 1.

[40] ibid 36.

[41] ibid 40.

Alone amongst the seven judges he even thought that the applicants' grievances were not 'arguable' enough to trigger their right to an effective remedy under Article 13 of the ECHR. The possibility of bringing a judicial review application was, to him, a sufficient remedy. The case was then referred to the Grand Chamber of the ECtHR, where Sir Brian was again sitting.[42] This time the majority (12:5) voted in line with his analysis, at least as far as Article 8 was concerned: he must clearly have been a convincing advocate during the judges' collective deliberations on the matter. But he remained a solitary dissenter on the Article 13 issue: the other 16 judges thought that the UK's judicial review procedures were inadequate to comply with Article 13, as they did not include a Convention-based approach to justifiability, the Human Rights Act not having been in force when the applicants lodged their complaint.

Appeals to the House of Lords or Supreme Court

Most of the cases decided by Sir Brian, whether civil or criminal, were not appealed against. It is instructive, however, to look at some of them which were. A survey of how his decisions fared when they were considered by the House of Lords or Supreme Court reveals a mixed record, as it would for any judge serving in a lower court. Four of his first instance decisions in the High Court were subsequently upheld first by the Court of Appeal and then by the House of Lords[43] and two of his decisions in the Divisional Court in a criminal cause or matter were upheld by the House of Lords.[44] In four other cases the views he expressed in the Court of Appeal were endorsed by the House of Lords, including a case in which he had dissented in the Court of Appeal.[45]

[42] *Hatton v UK* (2003) 37 EHRR 28. When a case is referred to the Grand Chamber the President of the Chamber and the national judge from the state in question are asked to sit alongside 15 other colleagues.

[43] *Robinson v Secretary of State for Northern Ireland* [2001] NIQB 49, [2002] NI 64 (Kerr J); [2002] NICA 18, [2002] NI 206; [2002] NI 390 (the election of the First and deputy First Ministers of Northern Ireland was lawful: see also Gordon Anthony (ch 5)); *In re McFarland* [2000] NI 403 (Kerr J); [2002] NICA 28, [2002] NI 337; [2004] 1 WLR 1289 (no compensation for a miscarriage of justice because no 'serious default' by the Resident Magistrate); *Jordan v Lord Chancellor* (n 27), upholding [2004] NICA 29, [2005] NI 144 (Kerr J's judgment is unreported) (coroners and juries at inquests in Northern Ireland cannot return verdicts of lawful or unlawful killing); *Re E's Application* [2008] UKHL 66, [2009] 1 AC 536, upholding [2004] NIQB 35 (Kerr J); [2006] NICA 37 (police did not breach the rights of child targets of 'protesters').

[44] *R v Chief Constable of the RUC, ex parte Begley* [1997] 1 WLR 1475, upholding the unreported judgment of MacDermott LJ and Kerr J (no right at that time for a suspect interviewed at a police station to have a solicitor present during the interview); *Re McE's Application* [2009] UKHL 15, [2009] 1 AC 908, upholding [2007] NIQB 101 (the Regulation of Investigatory Powers Act 2000 permits covert surveillance of communications between persons in custody and their legal or medical advisers).

[45] *Re Northern Ireland Human Rights Commission* [2002] NI 236, upholding Kerr J's dissent in [2001] NICA 17, [2001] NI 271 (on the powers of the NIHRC to apply to intervene in court cases); *Re Shields* [2003] UKHL 3, [2003] NI 161, upholding [2002] NICA 21, [2002] NI 301 (on the Chief Constable's

On the other hand, there were eight Court of Appeal decisions to which Kerr LCJ was a party which were *reversed* by the House of Lords. This reversal rate (8 out of 18 cases, or 44 per cent) is more or less in line with the average success rate for appeals to the House of Lords or Supreme Court, but no doubt Brian Kerr paid close attention to the instances in which his views were overturned. We can only speculate as to what effect these reversals had on his judicial mind, if any. At that high appellate level, when the legal questions involved are almost by definition complex and controversial, there is plenty of scope for judges to come to different conclusions as to what the appropriate solutions should be. On the other hand, as Brian Kerr would have been aware that there was a distinct possibility that he himself might one day be appointed to the top court, he probably took a keen interest in how its jurisprudence was developing.

The first of the reversals occurred in *Tweed v Parades Commission for Northern Ireland*, where the Law Lords, in particular Brian Kerr's predecessor as Lord Chief Justice, Lord Carswell, grabbed the opportunity, based on the principle of proportionality, to broaden the rules relating to disclosure of documents in judicial review proceedings across the UK.[46] Three more reversals occurred in 2007, two in conflict-related appeals[47] and one in a case raising a more general human rights issue. In this last case, *Belfast City Council v Miss Behavin' Ltd*,[48] Kerr LCJ and his Court of Appeal colleagues thought they were faithfully applying the Human Rights Act in holding that the Council's decision to deny the applicant a sex establishment licence was unlawful because the Council had not taken into account the applicant's rights to peaceful enjoyment of his possessions and freedom of expression.[49] The Law Lords, regrettably in our opinion, held that this omission did not matter so long as, at the end of the day, those rights had not been breached. The House was unanimous and clear on that point, but the stance does seem to run counter to an implicit aim of the Human Rights Act, which is that respect for human rights should become a core feature of the functions performed by all public authorities. Although the approach favoured by the House in *Miss Behavin'* has not since been expressly altered, it is surely hard to reconcile with the position

powers relating to promotion of officers); *R v Z* [2005] UKHL 35, [2005] 2 AC 645, upholding [2004] NICA 23, [2005] NI 106 (on whether the 'Real IRA' was a proscribed organisation); *SCA Packaging v Boyle* [2009] UKHL 37, [2009] 4 All ER 1181, upholding [2008] NICA 48, [2009] IRLR 54 (on what qualifies as an 'impairment' under disability discrimination law).

[46] *Tweed v Parades Commission for Northern Ireland* [2006] UKHL 53, [2007] 1 AC 650, reversing [2005] NICA 42, [2007] NI 66. See Gordon Anthony, *Judicial Review in Northern Ireland*, 2nd edn (Oxford, Hart Publishing, 2014) [3.54]–[3.56].

[47] *McCaughey v Chief Constable of the PSNI* [2007] UKHL 14, [2007] 2 AC 226 (dealt with alongside *Jordan v Lord Chancellor*), reversing [2005] NICA 1, [2005] NI 344; *Re Officer L* [2007] UKHL 36, [2007] 1 WLR 2135; [2007] NICA 8, [2007] NI 277. Both cases are discussed by Brice Dickson (ch 6) 100 and 105–106.

[48] *Belfast City Council v Miss Behavin' Ltd* [2007] UKHL 19, [2007] 1 WLR 1420. The Law Lord from Northern Ireland, Lord Carswell, did not sit in this case, presumably partly because there was no specifically Northern Irish dimension to the legal issues at stake.

[49] *Re Miss Behavin' Ltd's Application* [2005] NICA 35. The Court of Appeal overturned the first instance decision of Weatherup J, [2004] NIQB 61.

adopted by the Supreme Court three years later in *Manchester City Council v Pinnock*,[50] where nine Justices accepted that the right to respect for one's home meant that the council had to ensure that before evicting a tenant from his or her home it had taken account of the tenant's rights under Article 8 of the ECHR.

Kerr LCJ was again reversed on three occasions in 2008. In *In re Duffy*, another case involving the Parades Commission, the Law Lords found that the Court of Appeal had been mistaken in holding that two appointments to the Commission were lawful.[51] The appointees were members of the Orange Order and had obviously been appointed by the Secretary of State, Peter Hain, in an attempt to enhance the credibility of the Commission in the eyes of the unionist community in Northern Ireland (the Commission's commonest task is to decide what route Orange Order marches should take). Kerr LCJ held that, even if the appointments were politically motivated, the courts could not interfere with them.[52] He observed:

> It is perhaps right that I should say that the decision considered in this case was *par excellence* a political one. Regrettably, it appears that there is still a widespread misconception that the merits of such a decision fall under scrutiny where a judicial review challenge is made. It is important that this misconception be dispelled. The courts may only entertain a challenge to a decision such as that taken by the Secretary of State on well established judicial review grounds. I am not concerned with the wisdom of the decision made – either on political grounds or otherwise. The role of the courts is to examine the procedures by which the decision has been made and the rationality (in the legal context) of the decision. It goes no further.[53]

In the House of Lords all five judges, including Lord Carswell, thought that the majority in the Court of Appeal had been too restrained in their approach. The Secretary of State had failed to take into account the material consideration that two members of the seven-member Parades Commission would be unable to take part in much of the Commission's business because of their perceived conflict of interest and possible bias. Even if he had done so, appointing the two individuals in question was not something any reasonable Secretary of State would have done.[54] The House did not specifically address Kerr LCJ's point about 'political' decisions but its approach exposed another rare instance of judicial conservatism on his part. We wonder whether the terms in which the Law Lords' critique was framed might have prompted him, consciously or otherwise, to be more 'activist' in his subsequent judgments, especially when he reached the top echelon of the judiciary less than 18 months later.

[50] *Manchester City Council v Pinnock* [2010] UKSC 45, [2011] 2 AC 104. See also Anthony (n 46) 155.

[51] *In re Duffy* [2008] UKHL 4, [2008] NI 152.

[52] *Re Duffy's Application* [2006] NICA 28. At first instance Morgan J had held the appointments unlawful only on the ground that the Secretary of State had not also sought applications from people opposed to Orange Order marches: [2006] NIQB 31.

[53] ibid [40]. Campbell LJ agreed with Kerr LCJ, but Nicholson LJ dissented.

[54] *In re Duffy* (n 51), [26]–[28] per Lord Bingham; [31] per Lord Rodger; [33] per Lady Hale; [52]–[53] per Lord Carswell; [60] per Lord Brown.

A similarly united reversal of Kerr LCJ's views occurred in *In re Doherty*[55] and *In re P*.[56] The former was about whether a prisoner sentenced to life imprisonment but then released on licence could be returned to prison even if the Life Sentence Commissioners believed only on the balance of probabilities that he had committed another serious offence. The Court of Appeal, in a judgment penned by Kerr LCJ, decided that proof greater than on the balance of probabilities was required but the Law Lords, through judgments from Lord Carswell and Lord Brown, affirmed that the law knew of only two standards of proof – the civil and the criminal – and that in this instance the civil standard sufficed. Having been chided for not being activist enough in *Re Duffy*, here Brian Kerr was upbraided for being too activist! In *In re P* he and his colleagues in the Court of Appeal affirmed the High Court's decision that a provision in the Adoption (NI) Order 1987,[57] which allowed couples to adopt a child only if they were married, did not breach any Convention rights.[58] He did so not only because he did not think that unmarried couples, as a group, were in an analogous situation to that of married couples but also because this was a matter of social policy 'where choices on behalf of the country as a whole are properly left to Government and to the legislature'.[59] He was doubtless taken aback when, in the House of Lords, Lord Hoffmann, an arch sceptic of the Human Rights Act,[60] led the court in holding that the provision in question was irrational and disproportionate and should therefore be disapplied. This at a time when even the ECtHR had not yet declared that the ECHR confers on anyone a right to adopt.

Lord Kerr's final experience of being reversed on appeal was when he himself was already in the Supreme Court. This was in *In re JR17*,[61] where the question was whether a school principal had acted lawfully in suspending a boy from school because a girl at the school had alleged misconduct by him in relation to herself. The courts in Northern Ireland thought there was legal justification for the suspension,[62] but the Lords, unanimously, found that there was none, either within the statutory scheme or under the common law.

Of the top court's eight reversals of Kerr LCJ's views, it is fair to say that five of them displayed a more liberal attitude than he had done in the Court of Appeal

[55] In the House of Lords this case was dealt with under the name *In re D* [2008] UKHL 33, [2008] 1 WLR 1499, reversing [2007] NICA 33, which had itself reversed Girvan J, [2006] NIQB 33.

[56] In the House of Lords this case was dealt with under the name *In re G (Adoption: Unmarried Couple)* [2008] UKHL 38, [2009] 1 AC 173. Lord Walker dissented. See too Lady Hale (ch 2) 31–32.

[57] Adoption (NI) Order 1987, SI 1987/2203 (NI 22).

[58] *Re P (A Child)* [2007] NICA 20, [2007] NI 251.

[59] ibid [30]–[36] and [37]–[46]. The quote (at [45]) is from Lord Hope in *A v Secretary of State for the Home Dept* [2004] UKHL 56, [2005] 2 AC 68, [108].

[60] See his 'The universality of human rights' (2009) 125 *LQR* 416, where he castigated the ECtHR for imposing human rights standards on the UK which the country's law-makers had opposed.

[61] *In the matter of an application by JR17 for Judicial Review* [2010] UKSC 27, [2010] NI 105. Lord Kerr was obviously unable to sit in this appeal. None of the five Justices who did sit had any experience of practice in the law of Northern Ireland. The Constitutional Reform Act 2005, s 27(8), requires that at least one Supreme Court Justice must have that experience, but it does not mandate the participation of such a judge in an appeal from Northern Ireland.

[62] *Re JR17's Application for Judicial Review (Education)* [2009] NICA 14; [2007] NIQB 107.

(*Tweed*, *McCaughey*, *Duffy*, *In re P* and *In re JR17*), while three adopted a more conservative line, one which tended to restrict the protection of human rights (*Miss Behavin'*, *Officer L* and *In re Doherty*). Apart from the dissent of Lord Walker in *In re P*, all the reversals were unanimous, which suggests that judicial minds in London were working rather differently from those in Belfast. But naturally we should not read too much into this analysis, for in any court the outcome depends as much on the way the arguments are presented by counsel as it does on the independent thinking of the judges. Besides, the very raison d'être of an apex court is to allow a larger, more experienced, group of judges to re-assess the legal consequences of a lower court's decision. The higher court is less bound by precedent than the lower court and is also, especially in the UK, more conscious that it plays a constitutional role in settling the law for the whole of the nation, not just for part of it.[63]

The Supreme Court Justice

Sir Brian Kerr was appointed as the 112th, and last, Lord of Appeal in Ordinary in June 2009 and with that accolade went a life peerage. He sat in only two cases in the House of Lords before moving across Parliament Square with his fellow Law Lords to form the new United Kingdom Supreme Court in October 2009. He was always a strong supporter of the creation of that court and happily participated in two television programmes promoting it in 2012.[64] He was to serve there for precisely 11 years, the longest service on the Court of any Justice to date.[65] It is also a period longer than that served by any of his predecessors from Northern Ireland in the House of Lords. Lord Carswell served from 2004 to 2009, Lord Hutton from 1997 to 2004, Lord Lowry from 1988 to 1994, and Lord MacDermott from 1947 to 1951.[66] Although some of those judges also sat as *ad hoc* Law Lords before their appointment to that role, or after retirement from it, none of them issued anything like as many judgments as Lord Kerr did.[67]

Given the length of Lord Kerr's service, it may be helpful to present some statistical information. Table 1 indicates that he sat in 39 per cent of all the Supreme Court cases decided during his time on the Court and that in turn he delivered

[63] See, generally, Lady Hale, 'What is the United Kingdom Supreme Court for?', Macfadyen Lecture, Edinburgh, 28 March 2019, available at www.supremecourt.uk/docs/speech-190328.pdf.

[64] One of the documentaries was made for Channel 4 by Karen Hamilton but is unavailable for online streaming, while the other was produced by Nicola Stockley for BBC 4 and is available to view at www.youtube.com/watch?v=PZtYENfNa7k.

[65] Lady Hale served for 10 years and 3 months, but she had previously served in the House of Lords for a further 5 years and 9 months, so her total period of service in the nation's apex court was 16 years. Lord Reed, the current President of the Court, will exceed Lord Kerr's Supreme Court record if he remains in office until mid-February 2023.

[66] There were inexplicable gaps between 1951 and 1988 and from 1994 to 1997.

[67] The same statement could be made in relation to decisions taken in the Judicial Committee of the Privy Council.

substantive judgments in 38 per cent of the cases in which he sat. His appearance rate in Supreme Court cases is exactly in line with what it should have been, based on an average of five Justices sitting per case but also taking into account the number of cases in which three, seven, nine or 11 Justices sat.[68] In the Privy Council Lord Kerr sat in 42 per cent of the cases and delivered a judgment in 17 per cent of those cases: in the Privy Council there is a stronger convention that concurring judgments should be avoided if possible. His number of appearances in Privy Council cases (192) was higher than the average (180), though not by much.

Table 1 Lord Kerr's judicial work 2009–2020

	Supreme Court cases			Privy Council cases		
	Cases decided[a]	Cases in which Lord Kerr sat	Judgments given by Lord Kerr[b]	Cases decided	Cases in which Lord Kerr sat	Judgments given by Lord Kerr
2009	17	7	4	16	2	0
2010	58	27	11	33	10	2
2011	60	30	21	47	26	6
2012	62[c]	32	7	39	13	5
2013	81	33	7	31	18	7
2014	68	23	10	43	20	1
2015	79	18	9	48	17	2
2016	65	17	6	38	11	1
2017	82	34	10	45	30	4
2018	67	29	9	33	13	2
2019	60	18	9	48	18	1
2020	37	20	7	32	14	1
	736	288 (39%)	110 (38%)	453	192 (42%)	32 (17%)

Notes

a The figure for 2009 obviously relates only to cases from 1 October, when the Supreme Court began operating. The figure for 2020 covers the period up to 1 October, when Lord Kerr retired.

b These exclude instances where Lord Kerr delivered, or shared, a one-paragraph judgment concurring with one or more of his colleagues. In three of the cases in which he sat it appears that Lord Kerr had not confirmed his views on the questions at issue by the time he died. These were *In re an application by Anthony McIntyre for Judicial Review* UKSC 2019/0031, heard on 24 October 2019 and in which judgment remains pending; *Royal Mencap Society v Tomlinson-Blake* [2021] UKSC 8, [2021] ICR 758; and *X v Kuoni Travel Ltd* [2021] UKSC 34, which was decided by the UKSC only after the CJEU had issued its judgment on a preliminary reference on 18 March 2021.

c Although the last case of 2012 carried the neutral citation [2012] UKSC 63, no case was reported with the citation [2012] UKSC 43, so there were just 62 sets of judgment that year.

[68] In this period 6 of the cases were decided by 3 Justices, 93 by 7 Justices, 20 by 9 Justices and 2 by 11 Justices.

Lord Kerr's judgment rate in the Supreme Court was perfectly acceptable, but it was by no means the highest.[69] Table 2 compares his output with three other Justices who served on the Court for several years during Lord Kerr's time there but who, like him, did not become the Court's President or Deputy President. There is a remarkable similarity as regards the percentage of cases in which each of the four Justices sat: they each heard about two out of every five cases coming before the Court, thereby demonstrating that the Court's system for allocating Justices does result in an even distribution of workload. But there are differentials as regards the rate of judgment-writing by each Justice. Lord Kerr falls in the middle of the spectrum in that respect, some way behind the pace set by Lord Sumption, who delivered a judgment in almost one-half of the cases in which he sat. Conversely, a higher proportion of Lord Kerr's judgments were ones with which his fellow Justices in the case were happy to agree without making any further comment: this occurred in 25 per cent of the cases in which he gave a judgment,[70] while for Lord Sumption it occurred in only 19 per cent of the cases. Lord Carnwath's 'sole judgment' rate was even higher than Lord Kerr's, at 29 per cent.

Hearings in the Supreme Court are usually presided over by the President or Deputy President; if neither of them is available the Justice who has the longest period of service on the Court presides. Lord Kerr was in that position for the first time in May 2014.[71] In total he presided in 22 cases,[72] five of which were appeals from Northern Ireland, and he gave a judgment in eight of those 22 cases (36 per cent), including the five from Northern Ireland. When he became the fourth most senior member of the Supreme Court, in 2013, he began presiding in one of the four committees which consider applications for permission to appeal.[73] We know from Lord Reed's Foreword to this book that Lord Kerr was thereby able to wield significant influence over the composition of the Court's list.

In his 110 judgments Lord Kerr dissented wholly or partly from a majority of his fellow Justices on 33 occasions (30 per cent). A later chapter in this book looks at his dissents in more detail and a further chapter examines some of his judgments in the Privy Council.[74] We ourselves have drawn attention elsewhere to the centrality of Lord Kerr to the Supreme Court's decisions on appeals and references

[69] When measuring judgment rates for the period 2009 to 2013, Alan Paterson placed Lord Kerr 15th out of the 16 Justices involved: *Final Judgment: The Last Law Lords and the Supreme Court* (Oxford, Hart Publishing, 2013) 105 (Table 3.4).

[70] But for the period 2009–2013 Lord Kerr was again 15th out of 16 as regards the percentage of lead and single judgments he delivered: ibid, 161 (Table 4.4).

[71] *Henderson v Foxworth Investments Ltd* [2014] UKSC 41, [2014] 1 WLR 2600 (an appeal from Scotland). Lord Kerr first presided in the Privy Council in *Samuel Robie v The Queen* [2011] UKPC 43. For the role of the presiding judge more generally, see Rosemary Hunter and Erika Rackley, 'Judicial Leadership on the UK Supreme Court' (2018) 38 *Legal Studies* 191, 202–05.

[72] 1 in 2014; 1 in 2015; 1 in 2016; 2 in 2017; 6 in 2018; 4 in 2019; 7 in 2020.

[73] Paterson (n 69) 69.

[74] See, respectively, Rachel Cahill-O'Callaghan (ch 4) and Derek O'Brien (ch 9).

Table 2 Judgment rates in the Supreme Court

	Period of service	Cases decided during this period[a]	Cases in which the Justice sat	Cases in which the Justice issued a judgment[b]	Cases in which the Justice issued a sole judgment
Lord Kerr	Oct 2009 to Sept 2020	737	286 (38%)	110 (38%)	26 (24%)
Lord Wilson	May 2011 to May 2020	649	240 (37%)	75 (31%)	15 (20%)
Lord Carnwath	Apr 2012 to Mar 2020	599	222 (37%)	101 (46%)	29 (29%)
Lord Sumption	Jan 2012 to Dec 2018	552	207 (38%)	101 (49%)	19 (19%)

a This includes cases decided after the Justice retired but in which he sat before retiring. For Lord Kerr it includes *Mastercard Inc v Walter Hugh Merricks* [2020] UKSC 51, [2021] *Business Law Review* 25.

b These exclude instances where the Justice delivered, or shared, a one-paragraph judgment concurring with one or more of his colleagues.

reaching the Supreme Court from Northern Ireland.[75] Updating some of the statistics presented in that piece, we can now note that of the 127 three-Justice panels that were convened to consider applications for permission to appeal from Northern Ireland to the Supreme Court during Lord Kerr's time on the Court, he served on 96 of them (76 per cent). Only 32 of the 127 applications were successful (25 per cent). As regards the appeals and references from Northern Ireland which were heard and decided by the Supreme Court prior to Lord Kerr's death, there were 35 and four respectively. Lord Kerr participated in 32 of the appeals and in all of the references. He gave a substantive judgment in 31 of the appeals and in all of the references, including the two references from Northern Ireland dealt with in *R (Miller) v Secretary of State for Exiting the EU*, where we can reasonably assume that Lord Kerr was centrally involved in crafting the section of the joint judgment of the eight Justices in the majority which deals with the five devolution questions contained in the two references.[76] Clearly, as perhaps was only to be expected,

[75] Brice Dickson and Conor McCormick, 'Northern Ireland Dimensions to the First Decade of the United Kingdom Supreme Court' (2020) 83 *MLR* 1133. See also Lord Kerr's own lecture on 4 December 2019 marking the 10th anniversary of the Supreme Court, 'The Impact of the Supreme Court on the Law of Northern Ireland', available at www.supremecourt.uk/watch/ten-year-anniversary/lord-kerr.html and in Daniel Clarry (ed), *The UK Supreme Court Yearbook 2018–19, Vol 10* (Appellate Press, 2021) 86.

[76] *R (Miller) v Secretary of State for Exiting the EU* [2017] UKSC 5, [2018] AC 61, [126]–[151]. The three dissenting Justices in *Miller* did not dissent on the devolution issues: [242] per Lord Reed, [243] per Lord Carnwath, [282] per Lord Hughes.

Lord Kerr was the go-to judge as regards the Supreme Court's handling of cases emanating from Northern Ireland, regardless of the subject matter. The only plausible reasons for excluding him from either the petition stage or the hearing stage of such proceedings would have been because (1) he had had prior involvement in the case as a barrister or judge in Northern Ireland,[77] (2) he was required to recuse himself because his niece (Neasa Murnaghan QC) was appearing before the Court as counsel,[78] (3) the case was being heard alongside one or more cases from elsewhere in the United Kingdom and there was no particular aspect of the Northern Ireland case which required a judge with experience of the practice of law in that jurisdiction to participate in it, or (4) he was indisposed.[79]

It should not be thought, however, that Lord Kerr's contribution to the work of the Supreme Court was confined to his judgments in cases from Northern Ireland. His 35 judgments in those cases represent just 32 per cent of all his 110 judgments. The two chief features of the remaining 68 per cent of judgments (75 in number) are the number of dissents amongst them and the liberal approach he consistently displayed towards the human rights arguments they raised. He did not, of course, always accept the human rights arguments, but he accepted them more frequently than his colleagues did, including Lady Hale, and he also sought to develop the common law's approach to human rights rather than merely interpret legislation in accordance with human rights standards.[80] The chapters by Lady Hale, Kathryn McNeilly, Brice Dickson and Gráinne McKeever in Part I of this book set out many examples of how Lord Kerr demonstrated his liberal views in a variety of specific legal fields,[81] but here we can provide a more general overview of his record in delivering leading judgments. We would classify 12 of those judgments as principally concerned with human rights law (including discrimination law) and a further four with asylum law. He also issued leading judgments in the fields of civil procedure law, consumer protection law, employment law, family law and tort law. We will briefly summarise the impact of these judgments

[77] This was so as regards *JR17* (n 61) (where he had sat in the Court of Appeal in Northern Ireland) and also perhaps *Jordan* (n 31), where he had adjudicated on previous applications relating to the same death.

[78] Ms Murnaghan's appearance as senior counsel on behalf of the Dept of Justice explains Lord Kerr's absence from the panel in *In the matter of an application by Deborah McGuinness for Judicial Review* [2020] UKSC 6, [2020] NI 324.

[79] This may be why he did not sit in *In the matter of an application by JR55 for Judicial Review* [2016] UKSC 22, [2016] 4 All ER 779, which turned on the interpretation of Ombudsman legislation specific to Northern Ireland, though that case was heard on 8 March 2016 and he did sit in other appeals on both 7 March and 15–17 March. There was, however, a period between 28 July 2015 and 16 February 2016 when he did not sit in any appeals, and no appeals from Northern Ireland were heard during that time.

[80] Prime examples are his judgments in *Baker v Quantum Clothing Group Ltd* [2011] UKSC 17, [2011] 1 WLR 1003; *R (Keyu) v Secretary of State for Foreign Affairs* [2015] UKSC 69, [2016] AC 1355; and *Elgizouli v Secretary of State for the Home Dept* [2020] UKSC 10, [2020] 2 WLR 857. See too his important, and controversial, decision in *R v Adams* [2020] UKSC 19, [2020] 1 WLR 2077, discussed in detail by Claire Archbold (ch 14). That was primarily a case in administrative law but it also concerned the right to liberty.

[81] See Lady Hale (ch 2), Kathryn McNeilly (ch 3), Brice Dickson (ch 6) and Gráinne McKeever (ch 7).

in the following two sections of this chapter. They provide evidence, we suggest, that in the Supreme Court Lord Kerr was an activist,[82] even an interventionist,[83] Justice – much more so than he had been when serving as a judge in Northern Ireland, whether as a High Court judge or Lord Chief Justice. We would go so far as to say that he is probably the most liberal Justice to have served in the Supreme Court to date. He himself maintained, however, that, as a body, the Supreme Court was no more ready than the House of Lords to interfere in the decisions of the Government.[84]

It has to be added that during his time on the Supreme Court Lord Kerr also became known for his friendliness and approachability. He never let his position go to his head and was always particularly welcoming to lawyers from Northern Ireland who litigated in the Supreme Court. In the months following his passing, numerous tributes were paid to him for his kindness towards the Supreme Court's judicial assistants whose recruitment he was in charge of, to female lawyers who might have felt uncomfortable in the rather patriarchal atmosphere which the Supreme Court sometimes displays and to Supreme Court staff. He may have preferred to keep the room temperature very low in his own chambers, to the point that colleagues often asked to meet him elsewhere to avoid the cold, but the great warmth of his personality was undeniable.[85]

Supreme Court Judgments on Human Rights, Discrimination and Asylum

Whilst Lord Kerr was often sympathetic to claims based on human rights, he was also prepared to be more conservative in his approach when he felt there were powerful counter-arguments to the claim. That characterises his stance in *R (Keyu) v Secretary of State for Foreign Affairs*,[86] where he agreed with all but one of his colleagues (Lady Hale) that it was too late for an Article 2-compliant investigation to be conducted into the killing by British soldiers of 23 unarmed

[82] On activism more generally in the UKSC see Brice Dickson, 'Activism and restraint within the UK Supreme Court' (2015) 21 *European Journal of Current Legal Issues*, available at webjcli.org/article/view/399/515.

[83] On interventionism within the UKSC in the context of 'clashes of higher-order principles, for instance between parliamentary sovereignty and the rule of law' see Jo Murkens, 'Judicious review: the constitutional practice of the UK Supreme Court' (2018) 77 *CLJ* 349. See also the UKSC's momentous decision in *R (Miller) v Prime Minister* [2019] UKSC 41, [2020] AC 373, where it struck down the Prime Minister's decision to prorogue Parliament. Lord Kerr was one of the 11 Justices in that case.

[84] Interview with Owen Bowcott for *The Guardian*, 19 October 2000, 'UK needs judges to limit government power, says Lord Kerr', available at www.theguardian.com/law/2020/oct/19/uk-needs-judges-to-limit-government-power-says-lord-kerr.

[85] See, eg, the HRLA event and the QUB podcast, both referenced at n 1 above.

[86] *Keyu* (n 80).

civilians in Malaya in 1948: there was no 'genuine connection' between the deaths and the date on which the ECHR became binding on the UK, which he put at 1966 when the UK Government first recognised the right of individuals in the UK to lodge an application in Strasbourg against the Government.[87] In relation to Article 3 of the ECHR (the right not to be ill-treated), in *B (Algeria) v Secretary of State for the Home Department*[88] Lord Kerr found no violation in the Court of Appeal's refusal to remit a prison sentence to the Special Immigration Appeals Commission after it found that the Commission had wrongly rejected the evidence of two psychiatrists. On the other hand, in *R (EM (Eritrea)) v Secretary of State for the Home Department*[89] he ruled that if the state wished to deport an asylum-seeker to a supposedly safe state, in this case Italy, it must still verify that that state was likely to fulfil its Article 3 obligation not to ill-treat the asylum-seeker. And in a highly publicised case involving the 'black cab rapist', John Worboys, Lord Kerr was to the fore in holding that there can be a violation of Article 3 if there is a 'serious' flaw in the police's investigation into an assault: the flaw does not need to be 'systemic'. He also made it clear that, even though police forces do not owe victims of crime a duty of care under the common law, victims can still sue for damages in respect of a violation of their rights under the Human Rights Act 1998.[90]

In the context of the right to liberty Lord Kerr ruled in *Secretary of State for Foreign and Commonwealth Affairs v Rahmatullah* that a person handed over to the Americans by British forces in Afghanistan was entitled to a writ of habeas corpus, although surprisingly he then held, as part of the majority of 5:2, that it was a sufficient answer to the writ for the Americans to say that they were discussing the further handover of the detainee to the Pakistanis.[91] In *SXH v Crown Prosecution Service* Lord Kerr observed *obiter* that continuing the prosecution of a detained person beyond the date by which it should have been recognised that he had an answerable defence could constitute a violation of the right to liberty guaranteed by Article 5 of the ECHR.[92]

In relation to the scope of Article 6 of the ECHR (the right to a fair trial)[93] Lord Kerr contributed a short judgment in *Ali v Birmingham City Council*, which concerned the duties resting on a housing authority when deciding whether a homeless person had been provided with suitable accommodation.[94] Like his

[87] Alone amongst the five Justices who heard this case, Lady Hale put the date on which the ECHR became binding on the UK as 1953, the year in which it came into force at the international level, thereby allowing inter-state applications but not applications from individuals.

[88] *B (Algeria) v Secretary of State for the Home Dept* [2013] UKSC 4, [2013] 1 WLR 435.

[89] *R (EM (Eritrea)) v Secretary of State for the Home Dept* [2014] UKSC 12, [2014] AC 1321.

[90] *Commissioner of Police of the Metropolis v DSD* [2018] UKSC 11, [2019] AC 196, [66]–[72]. For more on this case see the text at n 153 below.

[91] *Secretary of State for Foreign and Commonwealth Affairs v Rahmatullah* [2012] UKSC 48, [2013] 1 AC 614 (Lady Hale and Lord Carnwath dissented on the second issue).

[92] *SXH v Crown Prosecution Service* [2017] UKSC 30, [2017] 1 WLR 1401, [43].

[93] See also John Jackson (ch 15).

[94] *Ali v Birmingham City Council* [2010] UKSC 8, [2010] 2 AC 39.

colleagues, Lord Kerr did not think that such decisions engaged Article 6(1) at all. This was a rare instance of Lord Kerr misjudging the reach of the Convention, for five years later the ECtHR ruled that Article 6(1) did apply to the circumstances of this case, although it then accepted that the applicant had in fact received a fair hearing when her request for accommodation was dealt with.[95] Lord Kerr also made it clear in *R (Ismail) v Secretary of State for the Home Department*[96] that merely serving on someone a foreign judgment asserting his or her criminal liability does not of itself engage Article 6 and that decision was not, it seems, challenged in Strasbourg.

It is in relation to Article 8 of the ECHR (the right to a private and family life) that Lord Kerr's influence is perhaps most marked. In *Norris v Government of the USA (No 2)* he agreed that in the context of extradition the consequences of any interference with Article 8 rights would need to be exceptionally serious before they could be viewed as outweighing the public importance of extradition,[97] and in *SXH v CPS*,[98] already referred to, he agreed that there was no authority to suggest that instituting criminal proceedings against someone when there is sufficient evidence that he or she may have committed a crime could amount to a breach of Article 8. Likewise, in *In re B (A Child)* he joined the majority (Lady Hale *contra*) in holding that on the facts of that case the conditions for placing a child under a care order had been satisfied and there would be no breach of the parents' Article 8 rights even if the care order was made with a view to the child's later adoption.[99]

In two later cases Lord Kerr delivered judgments upholding the right not to be discriminated against on the basis of sexual orientation. The first was *Walker v Innospec Ltd*, where a gay man won the right, after his death, to have his surviving spouse's pension paid to his civil partner or husband on the same basis that it would have been paid to his widow if he had been married to a woman.[100] After discussing this case at the inaugural 'Belfast Pride Law Lecture' in 2017, for which there is sadly no public transcript, an audience member welcomed Lord Kerr's talk as a 'small act of contrition' given that he had (unsuccessfully) argued the UK Government's case against the decriminalisation of homosexuality in *Dudgeon v UK*.[101] Lord Kerr memorably replied by describing his lecture as 'quite a large act of contrition!' and reminded those present that the personal views of a barrister do not always align with those of his or her client. The second case involving discrimination on the basis of sexual orientation was

[95] *Ali v UK* (2016) 63 EHRR 20.

[96] *R (Ismail) v Secretary of State for the Home Dept* [2016] UKSC 37, [2006] 1 WLR 2814.

[97] *Norris v Government of the USA (No 2)* [2010] UKSC 9, [2010] 2 AC 487.

[98] See *SXH* (n 92).

[99] *In re B (A Child) (Care Proceedings: Threshold Criteria)* [2013] UKSC 33, [2013] 1 WLR 1911. Lady Hale took the view that the mere possibility that the child would suffer psychological harm if not placed in care was not enough to override the parents' Art 8 rights.

[100] *Walker v Innospec Ltd* [2017] UKSC 47, [2017] 4 All ER 1004. Lords Carnwath and Hughes partly dissented in this case.

[101] *Dudgeon v UK* (1982) 4 EHRR 149.

R (Steinfeld and Keidan) v Secretary of State for International Development, where a heterosexual couple persuaded the Court that they had the right to enter into a civil partnership rather than a marriage – a choice which at that time was open only to homosexual couples.[102] Lord Kerr (for the Court) issued a declaration that sections 1 and 3 of Civil Partnership Act 2004 were to that extent incompatible with Article 14 of the ECHR, taken in conjunction with Article 8.

To complete Lord Kerr's contribution to the law on asylum we must refer to a clutch of further significant judgments, not all of which were decided in favour of the applicant. In *ZO (Somalia)*[103] he ensured that an asylum-seeker who makes a second application for asylum after an earlier application has been rejected is still entitled to benefits conferred by the EU Reception Directive, such as the right to work.[104] He did not think it was necessary to refer the matter to the Court of Justice of the EU for a preliminary ruling. In *Lumba* he powerfully, yet succinctly, explained that the detention in question constituted false imprisonment because it had not occurred in accordance with a *published* policy (but unlike three of his colleagues, he was in favour of awarding only nominal damages).[105] In *IA (Iran)* Lord Kerr explained that just because an asylum-seeker had already been granted refugee status by the UN High Commissioner for Refugees in both Iraq and Turkey this did not create a presumption in favour of granting him refugee status when he later made an application in the UK: all depended on what evidence was available to the UK authorities at that time.[106] This might seem a harsh approach, but it has the merit of trying to eliminate fraudulent claims and it was supported by all four of Lord Kerr's fellow Justices in the case, including Lady Hale. In *Hesham Ali* he delivered a long dissenting judgment in which he argued that, as regards when it would be lawful to deport a convicted criminal, the UK's Immigration Rules were incompatible with the balancing exercise that has to be undertaken in each case by virtue of Article 8 of the ECHR.[107] Citing the *Huang* case from 2007, he observed that a key feature of that decision was that:

> consideration of whether an individual's Article 8 rights will be infringed by a decision to deport her or to refuse her permission to reside in this country,

[102] *R (Steinfeld and Keidan) v Secretary of State for International Development* [2018] UKSC 32, [2020] AC 1. All four of the other Justices concurred with Lord Kerr. See also Kathryn McNeilly (ch 3) 55–56. It is regrettable that Lord Kerr did not give a judgment in the 'gay cake' case (*Ashers Baking Co Ltd v Lee* [2018] UKSC 49, [2020] AC 413), which had more than one dimension to it that were peculiar to the law of Northern Ireland: see Brice Dickson, 'The "Gay Cake" Case and the Scope of Discrimination Law' in Daniel Clarry (ed), *The UK Supreme Court Yearbook 2018–19*, Vol 10 (Appellate Press, 2021) 225.

[103] *R (ZO) (Somalia) v Secretary of State for the Home Dept* [2010] UKSC 36, [2010] 1 WLR 1948.

[104] Council Directive 2003/9/EC of 27 January 2003 laying down minimum standards for the reception of asylum seekers [2003] OJ L31/18.

[105] *R (Lumba) v Secretary of State for the Home Dept* [2011] UKSC 12, [2012] 1 AC 245. Lords Hope and Walker and Lady Hale favoured substantial damages.

[106] *IA (Iran) v Secretary of State for the Home Dept* [2014] UKSC 6, [2014] 1 WLR 384.

[107] *Hesham Ali v Secretary of State for the Home Dept* [2016] UKSC 60, [2016] 1 WLR 4799, esp [115]–[123]. None of the other six Justices in the case agreed with Lord Kerr, but his dissenting judgment was cited with apparent approval by the ECtHR in *Unuane v UK*, App No 80343/17, judgment of 24 November 2020, where the UK was found to have breached Art 8 in deporting a convicted

notwithstanding her Article 8 right, does not lend itself naturally to the application of a series of rules.[108]

Finally, in *Bashir*, Lord Kerr was a contributor to a judgment compiled by seven Justices which ruled that, while the 1951 UN Convention Relating to the Status of Refugees is in force in the military bases maintained by the UK in Cyprus, this does not of itself entitle asylum-seekers there to be resettled in the UK.[109]

In all of these cases on human rights, discrimination and asylum we see a liberal but realistic approach on the part of Lord Kerr. These are also features of his judgments in the troubles-related cases from Northern Ireland, which we have examined elsewhere.[110] When we turn to his dissenting judgments, in the next but one section, we will find many other cases where he adopted the same stance but was not able to persuade enough of his judicial colleagues to support his position. But first we must look briefly at some of his remaining assenting judgments.

Supreme Court Judgments on Other Issues

As previously noted, Lord Kerr has delivered influential judgments on civil procedure law, consumer protection law, employment law, family law and tort law. In the area of civil procedure he led the Court, comprising seven Justices, in *Takhar v Gracefield Developments Ltd*, which raised the question of what a person has to prove in order to have an earlier judgment set aside on the basis that it was obtained by fraud.[111] The answer given was that the person does *not* have to prove that the evidence of the fraud could not have been obtained with reasonable diligence before the earlier trial. In the area of consumer protection law, which is not often the object of Supreme Court attention, he led the Court in *Robertson v Swift* in ruling on the interpretation of a 1985 European Council Directive designed to protect consumers against the risks inherent in entering into a contract away from business premises.[112] At the relevant time the Directive was implemented in the UK by the Cancellation of Contracts made in a Consumer's Home Regulations 2008[113] and Lord Kerr made sure that these were interpreted

criminal to Nigeria. The Immigration Rules in question are Rules 396–399A, as amended in 2012. In an appeal from Northern Ireland heard alongside *Hesham Ali* but for which a separate set of judgments was issued (*Makhlouf v Secretary of State for the Home Dept* [2016] UKSC 59, [2017] 3 All ER 1), Lord Kerr led the Court in holding that there would be no breach of Art 8 if the applicant in question were deported. See also Lady Hale (ch 2) 35.

[108] *Hesham Ali* (ibid) [154], referring to *Huang v Secretary of State for the Home Dept* [2007] UKHL 11, [2007] 2 AC 167.

[109] *R (Bashir) v Secretary of State for the Home Dept* [2018] UKSC 45, [2019] AC 484.

[110] See Dickson and McCormick (n 75) 1138–44.

[111] *Takhar v Gracefield Developments Ltd* [2019] UKSC 13, [2020] AC 450.

[112] *Robertson v Swift* [2014] UKSC 50, [2014] 1 WLR 3438 regarding Council Directive 85/577/EEC of 20 December 1985 to protect the consumer in respect of contracts negotiated away from business premises.

[113] Cancellation of Contracts made in a Consumer's Home Regulations 2008, SI 2008/1816.

in a way which gave the consumer the benefit of any doubt concerning their effect. In this case this meant that Dr Robertson was allowed a longer period during which to cancel the contract he had entered into for the moving of furniture.

Lord Kerr issued two landmark judgments in employment law, firstly in *Gisda Cyf v Barrett*, stipulating that the effective date of termination of a person's employment is when the employee is informed of the dismissal or has had a reasonable opportunity of discovering the dismissal, and the behaviour of the employee can be taken into account when assessing whether he or she has had that reasonable opportunity.[114] The second judgment was in *Michalak v General Medical Council*, where he led the Supreme Court in holding that the fact that judicial review proceedings could be taken in respect of the employment decisions made by a disciplinary authority did not mean they were 'in the nature of an appeal' and so the jurisdiction of the Employment Tribunal was not thereby excluded by statute.[115]

In family law Lord Kerr reaffirmed, in a judgment of the Court, that where a child's custody or upbringing is in question the child's welfare is the paramount consideration.[116] In a subsequent case, one in which Lady Hale dissented, he joined the majority in upholding a care order with a view to the adoption of a child whose mother suffered from disorders causing her to raise fictitious medical issues.[117] Perhaps his most significant contribution in this field is his judgment in *R (Steinfeld and Keidan) v Secretary of State for International Development* which, as mentioned above, is where the Supreme Court declared that legislation precluding a different-sex couple from entering into a civil partnership was incompatible with the ECHR.[118] He observed that: 'to create a situation of inequality and then ask for the indulgence of time – in this case several years – as to how that inequality is to be cured is, to say the least, less obviously deserving of a margin of discretion'.[119]

In tort law Lord Kerr held in *McDonald v The National Grid Electricity Transmission plc*, alongside two colleagues, that the claimant should be allowed to claim compensation for her deceased husband's exposure to asbestosis, even though he had been only a 'casual visitor' to the defendant's premises more than 50 years earlier.[120] In *Montgomery v Lanarkshire Health Board* he and Lord Reed delivered the joint leading judgment, reaching the significant conclusion that, in situations where a doctor does not explain the risks of a procedure to a patient, the test for deciding if this is negligence is not the *Bolam* test[121] – which makes

[114] *Gisda Cyf v Barrett* [2010] UKSC 41, [2010] ICR 1475.

[115] *Michalak v General Medical Council* [2017] UKSC 71, [2017] 1 WLR 4193. The statutory provision in question was the Equality Act 2010, s 120(7).

[116] *In re B (A Child) (Residence: Biological Parent)* [2009] UKSC 5, [2009] 1 WLR 2496.

[117] *In re B (A Child) (Care Proceedings: Threshold Criteria)* (n 99).

[118] *Steinfeld and Keidan* (n 102).

[119] ibid [36].

[120] *McDonald v The National Grid Electricity Transmission plc* [2014] UKSC 53, [2015] AC 1128. Lady Hale dissented from the secondary decision taken by the other four Justices that the claimant was not entitled to claim compensation under the Factories Act 1937, s 47.

[121] *Bolam v Friern Hospital Management Committee* [1957] 1 WLR 582.

the outcome depend on what is accepted as proper by a responsible body of medical opinion – but whether the patient has been given enough information to decide for him- or herself whether to undergo the procedure.[122] Most recently, in the defamation case of *Stocker v Stocker*, Lord Kerr led the Court in finding unanimously that the phrase 'trying to strangle' should not be construed in the dictionary sense of trying to kill someone but rather in the more colloquial sense of grabbing someone by the neck with a view to putting him or her in fear of being killed.[123]

In this group of 'other' cases we again see Lord Kerr adjudicating in a predominantly pro-claimant fashion, protective of rights and freedoms, and being prepared to change precedent, or at least to go against received wisdom, in order to arrive at a more progressive legal position. These features are just as prominently displayed in his Lordship's dissenting judgments.

Dissenting Judgments in the Supreme Court

Lord Kerr was a staunch defender of the value of dissents.[124] As many as 33 of the 110 judgments he delivered during the Supreme Court's first decade were full or partial dissents (30 per cent),[125] and we know that of the 12 Supreme Court Justices sitting in 2015 he had dissented in a higher percentage of cases since the Court's creation in 2009 than any of his then colleagues (12.6 per cent).[126] His first dissent occurred in March 2010, in *Martin v HM Advocate*,[127] where he joined Lord Rodger, often a conservative judge, in disagreeing with the view of Lord Hope and two other judges that the Scottish Parliament had not exceeded its powers by enacting legislation extending the sentencing powers of sheriffs in road traffic cases. Fittingly, he also dissented in the very last judgment he delivered, in *R (Maughan) v Her Majesty's Senior Coroner for Oxfordshire*, where, along with Lord Reed, he held that if an inquest jury wishes to issue a short form verdict of suicide or unlawful killing it must be satisfied of that to the criminal standard of proof, that is, beyond reasonable doubt.[128]

[122] *Montgomery v Lanarkshire Health Board* [2015] UKSC 11, [2015] AC 1430. Lord Reed paid tribute to Lord Kerr for his contribution to that judgment in his encomium on 1 December 2020: see n 1 above. See too Lord Reed's Foreword to this book.

[123] *Stocker v Stocker* [2019] UKSC 17, [2020] AC 593.

[124] See his Birkenhead Lecture, delivered on 8 October 2012: 'Dissenting judgments – self indulgence or self sacrifice?', available' at www.supremecourt.uk/docs/speech-121008.pdf. In the Privy Council, where dissenting is more unusual, he issued dissenting judgments on four occasions. In each of them he was in favour of a position more sympathetic to the weaker party in a transaction or, in criminal appeals, the defendant.

[125] Between 2009 and 2013 he had the joint highest dissent rate (13%), alongside Lady Hale and Lord Rodger: see Paterson (n 69) 173.

[126] Hunter and Rackley (n 71) 210.

[127] *Martin v HM Advocate* [2010] UKSC 10, 2010 SC (UKSC) 40.

[128] *R (Maughan) v Her Majesty's Senior Coroner for Oxfordshire* [2020] UKSC 46, [2021] AC 454.

In *R (Smith) v Oxfordshire Assistant Deputy Coroner* Lord Kerr was one of three dissenters in a nine-judge court where the majority held that British soldiers serving abroad were not within the UK's jurisdiction for the purposes of the ECHR.[129] The minority view was later vindicated in *Smith v Ministry of Defence*, where a seven-judge Court decided not to follow the earlier *Smith* decision,[130] preferring instead the position set out in two more recent judgments of the Grand Chamber of the European Court of Human Rights.[131] Having clearly nailed his colours to the mast regarding the importance of a human rights approach to adjudication, Lord Kerr was to express it again in numerous subsequent judgments, although several of these were dissents, in some of which he was a lone voice[132] but in others he was joined by at least one other Justice, often Lady Hale[133] but occasionally Lord Reed or Lord Wilson.[134] In two of these cases Lord Kerr's dissents were later cited with apparent approval by the ECtHR when it found that the UK had breached Article 8 of the ECHR,[135] although in a third case the ECtHR declared inadmissible the application of the claimant whose argument on Article 6 Lord Kerr had accepted.[136]

[129] *R (Smith) v Oxfordshire Assistant Deputy Coroner* [2010] UKSC 29, [2011] 1 AC 1. See also Brice Dickson (ch 6) 102–104.

[130] *Smith v Ministry of Defence* [2013] UKSC 41, [2014] AC 52.

[131] *Al-Skeini v UK* (2011) 53 EHRR 589; *Hirsi Jamaa v Italy* (2012) 55 EHRR 627.

[132] *R (Morge) v Hampshire County Council* [2011] UKSC 2, [2011] 1 WLR 268 (on planning permission law; 1:4); *R (G) v Governors of X School* [2011] UKSC 30, [2012] 1 AC 167 (on the right to legal representation at a disciplinary hearing; 1:4); *Tariq v Home Office* [2011] UKSC 35, [2012] 1 AC 452 (on closed material proceedings in employment tribunals: 1:8); *Ambrose v Harris* [2011] UKSC 43, [2001] 1 WLR 2435 (on the right of access to a solicitor; 1:4); *McGowan v B* [2011] UKSC 54, [2011] 1 WLR 3121 (on the admissibility of evidence; 1:4); *Jude v HM Advocate* [2011] UKSC 55, 2012 SC (UKSC) 222 (on waiver of the right to a solicitor; 1:4); *R (Lord Carlile of Berriew QC) v Secretary of State for the Home Dept* [2014] UKSC 60, [2015] AC 945 (on the right to free speech; 1:4); *Gaughran v Chief Constable of the PSNI* [2015] UKSC 29, [2016] AC 345 (on police retention of biometric data; 1:4); *Beghal v DPP* [2015] UKSC 49, [2016] AC 88 (on detention at ports under the Terrorism Act; 1:4); *Hesham Ali* (n 107) (on the deportation of foreign criminals; 1:6; see the text at n 107 above).

[133] For seven cases where he and Lady Hale both dissented on a human rights point (differing from the more conservative view of their colleagues) see *A v Essex County Council* [2010] UKSC 33, [2011] 1 AC 280 (on the right to education); *R (Nicklinson) v Ministry of Justice* [2014] UKSC 38, [2015] AC 657 (on the right to assisted suicide); *Michael v Chief Constable of South Wales Police* [2015] UKSC 2, [2015] AC 1732 (on the right to sue the police); *R (SG) v Secretary of State for Work and Pensions* [2015] UKSC 16, [2015] 1 WLR 1449 (on whether the benefit cap was indirectly discriminatory on gender grounds); *R (A and B) v Secretary of State for Health* [2017] UKSC 41, [2017] 1 WLR 2492 (on whether women from Northern Ireland are entitled to NHS abortion services in England: see the next paragraph in the text above); *In the matter of an application by the Northern Ireland Human Rights Commission for Judicial Review* (n 33) (on abortion law in Northern Ireland, also with Lord Wilson); *R (DA) v Secretary of State for Work and Pensions* [2019] UKSC 21, [2019] 1 WLR 3289 (on the proportionality of benefit cap vis-à-vis children and lone parents).

[134] As in *Moohan v The Lord Advocate* [2014] UKSC 67, [2015] AC 901 (prisoners' voting rights in the Scottish referendum, with Lord Wilson); *Mohammed v Secretary of State for Defence* [2017] UKSC 2, [2017] AC 821 (on whether detentions in Iraq were lawful, with Lord Reed); *Khuja v Times Newspapers Ltd* [2017] UKSC 49, [2019] AC 161 (on the misuse of private information by newspapers, with Lord Wilson); *In re C (Children)* [2018] UKSC 8, [2019] AC 1 (on international child abduction, with Lord Wilson); *R (Hallam) v Secretary of State for Justice* [2019] UKSC 2, [2020] AC 279 (on compensation for a miscarriage of justice, with Lord Reed).

[135] See *Beghal v UK* (2019) 69 EHRR 28, paras 33–38; *Gaughran v UK*, App No 45245/15, judgment of 12 February 2020, at paras 17–19.

[136] *Tariq v UK* (2018) 67 EHRR SE2.

Amongst the most pertinent of Lord Kerr's dissents is that in *R (A and B) v Secretary of State for Health*,[137] a case taken in England by a mother and daughter who argued, unsuccessfully, that it was unlawful for the UK government to fail to allow a UK citizen usually resident in Northern Ireland to obtain an abortion free of charge in England under the National Health Service. Disagreeing with the majority, Lord Kerr, together with Lady Hale, thought that there was no legitimate aim for interfering in this way with the private life of women from Northern Ireland. A few weeks after the decision the then Minister for Women and Equalities, Justine Greening MP, announced that women from Northern Ireland would no longer have to pay to access abortion services in England, the Government Equalities Office having committed to provide funding for this.[138] Lord Kerr's preferred view as to what was permissible under existing law appears to have been influential on that change of policy.

In a further 10 cases which did not directly involve Convention rights but which were nevertheless about protecting a claimant's 'non-human' right (eg to sue for damages for personal injuries), Lord Kerr dissented because he favoured a more liberal outcome to the case.[139] Unfortunately, limitations on space prevent us from providing more details here.

In at least one judgment, and also in extra-judicial speeches, Lord Kerr was a consistent opponent of the so-called 'mirror principle', first enunciated by Lord Bingham (although he did not give it that name) in *R (Ullah) v Special Adjudicator*.[140] In Lord Bingham's famous phrase: 'The duty of national courts is to keep pace with the Strasbourg jurisprudence as it evolves over time: no more, but certainly no less'.[141] In *Ullah* itself Lady Hale did not object to what Lord Bingham said on this matter, but she later made it clear that she was not in full

[137] *A and B* (n 133). See also Lady Hale (ch 2) 41–42.

[138] Letter dated 29 June 2017, available at assets.publishing.service.gov.uk/government/uploads/system/uploads/attachment_data/file/623669/Letter_from_Justine_Greening_on_Abortion_in_England.pdf. Nevertheless A and B have lodged an application with the ECtHR, App No 80046/17; see hudoc.echr.coe.int/eng#{%22itemid%22:[%22001-189928%22]}.

[139] See eg *Baker* (n 80) (on the right to damages for hearing loss); *Edwards v Chesterfield Royal Hospital NHS Foundation Trust* [2011] UKSC 58, [2012] 2 AC 22 (on the right to damages for wrongful dismissal, with Lady Hale and Lord Wilson); *R v Gnango* [2011] UKSC 59, [2012] 1 AC 827 (on the law of murder); *AB v Ministry of Defence* [2012] UKSC 9, [2013] 1 AC 78 (on time limits for making a personal injuries claim); *Sharif v London Borough of Camden* [2013] UKSC 10, [2013] 2 All ER 309 (on housing rights); *Bank Mellat v HM Treasury (No 1)* [2013] UKSC 38, [2014] AC 700 (on closed material procedures in civil cases); *R (Bancoult (No 2)) v Secretary of State for Foreign and Commonwealth Affairs* [2016] UKSC 35, [2017] AC 300 (on whether fresh evidence meant that an earlier UKSC decision needed to be re-opened, with Lady Hale); *FirstGroup plc v Paulley* [2017] UKSC 4, [2017] 1 WLR 423 (on whether damages should be paid for disability discrimination, with Lady Hale and Lord Clarke); *R (Bancoult (No 3) v Secretary of State for Foreign and Commonwealth Affairs* [2018] UKSC 3, [2018] 1 WLR 973 (on whether the government's decision to impose a marine protected area around the Chagos Islands was improperly motivated, with Lady Hale); *In the matter of an application by Lorraine Gallagher for Judicial Review* [2019] UKSC 3, [2020] AC 185 (on the test for deciding whether a disclosure scheme was in accordance with law and proportionate).

[140] *R (Ullah) v Special Adjudicator* [2004] UKHL 26, [2004] 2 AC 323.

[141] ibid [20].

agreement with it.[142] Lord Kerr, on the other hand, never seems to have been content with it. He first made his position clear in a lecture delivered in 2009,[143] then in a set of references from Scotland considered by the Supreme Court under the name of *Ambrose v Harris* in 2011,[144] and once more in another lecture delivered in 2012.[145] In *Ambrose v Harris* he went out of his way to protect the right to a fair trial to an extent to which the ECtHR had never before stretched, declaring inadmissible as evidence answers given by a detained person to questions put to him by police officers before he had been taken to a police station and given access to a solicitor. Lord Kerr spoke pejoratively of '*Ullah*-type reticence'[146] and added:

> I believe that, in the absence of a declaration by the European Court of Human Rights as to the validity of a claim to a Convention right, it is not open to courts of this country to adopt an attitude of agnosticism and refrain from recognising such a right simply because Strasbourg has not spoken.[147]

Lord Kerr reaffirmed his position on *Ullah* nearly three years later, in *Surrey County Council v P*,[148] and in the following year he returned to it in *R (Keyu) v Secretary of State for Foreign and Commonwealth Affairs*, discussed above, where he noted that since his dissent in *Ambrose v Harris* 'judgments have been given in which a departure from a rigid application of the mirror principle is discernible'.[149] In support he cited Lord Neuberger's judgment in *Surrey County Council v P*[150] and also *Moohan v Lord Advocate*,[151] where Lord Wilson, having suggested that the Supreme Court had 'retreated' and 'substantially modified' the *Ullah* principle, added:

> where there is no directly relevant decision of the ECtHR with which it would be possible (even if appropriate) to keep pace, we can and must do more. We must determine for ourselves the existence or otherwise of an alleged Convention right.[152]

[142] Principally in '*Argentoratum locutum*: is Strasbourg or the Supreme Court Supreme?' (2012) 12 *Human Rights LR* 65, where she cited in support three House of Lords decisions in which she herself had participated in 2005 and 2008: *R (Limbuela) v Secretary of State for the Home Dept* [2005] UKHL 66, [2006] 1 AC 396; *In re G (Adoption: Unmarried Couple)* [2008] UKHL 38, [2009] 1 AC 173; *EM (Lebanon) v Secretary of State for the Home Dept* [2008] UKHL 64, [2009] 1 AC 1198.

[143] Lord Kerr, 'The conversation between Strasbourg and national courts – dialogue or dictation?' (2009) 44 *Irish Jurist* 1.

[144] See n 132 above and also John Jackson (ch 15) 274–275.

[145] 'The UK Supreme Court: the modest underworker of Strasbourg?' (The Clifford Chance Lecture, 25 January 2012), available at www.supremecourt.uk/docs/speech_120125.pdf. See too his contribution to the event held by the AIRE Centre marking the 70th anniversary of the ECtHR on 2 November 2020, available at www.gardencourtchambers.co.uk/events/echr-70-lord-kerr-of-tonaghmore-in-conversation-with-nuala-mole-founder-of-the-aire-centre-hosted-by-garden-court-chambers.

[146] See *Ambrose* (n 132) [126]–[130].

[147] ibid [127].

[148] *Surrey County Council v P* [2014] UKSC 19, [2014] AC 896.

[149] *Keyu* (n 80) [233]. See also Brice Dickson (ch 6) 106–107.

[150] See *Surrey County Council* (n 148) [62].

[151] *Moohan* (n 134).

[152] ibid [105]. Lord Kerr could also have cited Lady Hale in the same case, where she said, at [53]: 'I further agree that, if we are confronted with a question which has not yet arisen in the European Court, we have to work out the answer for ourselves, taking into account, not only the principles which have been developed in Strasbourg, but also the principles of our own law and constitution'.

In *Commissioner of Police of the Metropolis v DSD* Lord Kerr again mentioned *Ullah* but carefully explained developments in the ECtHR's case law before concluding that in his view that Court had already adopted 'clear and constant jurisprudence' to the effect that a state's duty to investigate incidents of ill-treatment was not limited to cases of ill-treatment by state agents.[153] This case is therefore not so much about going beyond where the ECtHR has already gone as about giving a generous interpretation to statements made by that Court about its current position.[154]

Lord Kerr also stuck his neck out by opposing the UK's strict adherence to a dualist approach to international law, according to which a treaty provision is binding in domestic law only if it has first been formally incorporated into that law by primary legislation. In *R (SG) v Secretary of State for Work and Pensions*,[155] where the compatibility with human rights of the so-called 'benefit cap' was under scrutiny, he called for 'open recognition' of Lord Steyn's suggestion in *Re McKerr*[156] that an exception should be made to the dualist approach when what is at issue is the applicability of an international human rights treaty. In the case before him Lord Kerr was unequivocally of the view that Article 3(1) of the UN Convention on the Rights of the Child should be directly enforceable in UK domestic law.[157] Even Lady Hale, who also dissented in the *SG* case and is a great proponent of children's rights, was not prepared to go so far, but she did accept that, given that the ECtHR often tries to align its judgments with standards set in international human rights treaties besides the ECHR, 'the Strasbourg court would look with particular care at the justification put forward for any measure which places the United Kingdom in breach of its international obligations under another human rights treaty to which we are party'.[158]

Conclusion

According to Alan Paterson, whose research covered the period 2009 to 2013, Lord Kerr was one of those Supreme Court Justices who made up their minds

[153] See *DSD* (n 90) a [17]–[43] and Brice Dickson (ch 6) 114.

[154] Lady Hale, Lord Neuberger and Lord Mance all endorsed Lord Kerr's approach in *DSD*, but Lord Hughes did not go so far. For the Supreme Court's most recent view on the status of *Ullah*, see *R (AB) v Secretary of State for Justice* [2021] UKSC 28, [2021] 3 WLR 494 [54]–[59].

[155] See *SG* (n 133) a [254], Lady Hale (ch 2) 36–38 and Gráinne McKeever (ch 7) 127–130. Also see Conor McCormick, 'Debating Constitutional Dualism' (*UK Constitutional Law Association Blog*, 24 November 2015), available at ukconstitutionallaw.org/2015/11/24/conor-mccormick-debating-constitutional-dualism/.

[156] *McKerr* (n 30).

[157] This provides: 'in all actions concerning children … the best interests of the child shall be a primary consideration'.

[158] See *SG* (n 133) [218]. For the Supreme Court's most recent view on the non-enforceability of the UNCRC, see *R (SC, CB and 8 children) v Secretary of State for Work and Pensions* [2021] UKSC 26, [2021] 3 WLR 428, [74]–[96].

relatively early in the hearing of a case and rarely shifted away from it.[159] If that is true it does not, of course, mean that Lord Kerr was pre-judging the outcome of cases but only that he had a pretty good idea of how he thought the case should be decided, having read the documents submitted by counsel prior to the hearing and listened to their opening arguments. At some point in his judicial career, however, Lord Kerr seems to have become more determined than previously to assert his support for an expansive approach to the protection of human rights and for greater judicial involvement in developing the law. That point may have been reached in 2011, when he delivered dissenting judgments in no fewer than nine cases. Thereafter he may have been aware that, in academic legal circles at least, which in the UK are generally left-leaning, he was becoming something of a darling of the liberal elite. We are not suggesting for one minute that he then began to 'play to the gallery', only that he may then have been bolstered in his own mind that his instincts for what would be a just and fair position to adopt in legal debates – always within the constraints of his judicial oath, naturally – were ones that he could follow with sincerity and integrity, especially as he was always able to support his conclusions with rigorous reasoning and reliance on 'authorities'. Had he still been with us, Lord Kerr's retirement from the Supreme Court might have prompted him to be more forthcoming about what motivated him to develop his judicial mind in the way that he appears to have done. We are all the sadder that that cannot now happen.

[159] See Paterson (n 69) 207; Paterson put Lord Wilson in the same category.

PART I

The Judicial Mind of Lord Kerr

2

Women and Children First

LADY HALE

'As I get older', said Lord Kerr in his lecture to mark the 10-year anniversary of the Supreme Court of the United Kingdom, 'I find that the chance to be provocative is not to be missed'.[1] He was, of course, speaking out of court. But there is little doubt that, the longer he spent in the highest court in the land, the more provocative he felt able to be, even in the court. There was little sign of this, however, when he first joined the House of Lords, as the last-ever person to be appointed a Lord of Appeal in Ordinary, in June 2009. His judgments as Lord Chief Justice of Northern Ireland had seemed to us to be models of judicial restraint, for understandable reasons, given the political sensitivities of the role. By the time he retired from the Supreme Court in 2020, his judgments were always carefully and properly argued, but models of judicial restraint they were not. The development of his judicial mind can clearly be seen in the cases about the rights and interests of women and children in which he was involved. They even provide further evidence that he was my ally in the techniques of feminist judging.[2]

Children First

In *In re G (Adoption: Unmarried Couple)*,[3] the issue was whether the Adoption (NI) Order 1987, which only provided for joint adoption by married couples, discriminated against unmarried couples in the enjoyment of their right to respect for family life, prohibited by Article 14, read with Article 8, of the European Convention on Human Rights ('the European Convention'). In both the High Court and the Court of Appeal in Northern Ireland, the answer was 'no'.[4] While Kerr LCJ had no doubt that the subject matter fell 'within the ambit' of Article 8, he found it difficult to recognise unmarried cohabiting couples as a 'status' for the

[1] Available on the website of the Supreme Court at www.supremecourt.uk/watch/ten-year-anniversary/lord-kerr.html (at 2'50").

[2] See Kathryn McNeilly (ch 3).

[3] *In re G (Adoption: Unmarried Couple)* [2008] UKHL 38, [2009] 1 AC 173.

[4] *Re P (A Child)* [2007] NICA 20, [2007] NI 251.

purpose of Article 14; but if he was wrong about that, their exclusion pursued the legitimate aim of 'securing the familial stability that a child needs' and was proportionate to that aim. This was quintessentially a matter of social policy on which the court should accord respect to the decisions of the legislature.

In the House of Lords, the answer was 'yes'. Being unmarried was a status. The aim of adoption was to promote the best interests of the child. Lord Hoffmann thought that it was irrational to exclude all unmarried couples, irrespective of whether allowing a particular couple to adopt a particular child would be in the best interests of that child. Lord Hope considered that, although matters of economic and social policy were usually best left to the legislature, this did not apply where the question was discrimination. Four of their lordships were therefore prepared to go beyond the jurisprudence of the European Court of Human Rights ('the Strasbourg Court') and hold that the Order was incompatible. Lord Walker alone thought that the matter should be left to the Northern Ireland Assembly, albeit with a clear warning that, if a clear consensus did emerge from Europe, something would have to be done. He was particularly conscious that public opinion in Northern Ireland appeared to be against the change.

Of course, if unmarried couples were to be eligible to apply to adopt jointly, this would have to include same sex as well as opposite sex couples: the cases on which we relied to indicate the direction of travel in Strasbourg involved same sex couples. Our prediction of the direction of travel was eventually proved correct, in *X v Austria*,[5] a case about adoption by a same sex partner. Public opinion in Northern Ireland may well have played some part in the thinking of Kerr LCJ that this was a matter best left to the legislature: as time went on, it would not have deterred Lord Kerr of Tonaghmore from finding a breach of the Human Rights Act 1998 had he felt it right to do so.

As the law was contained in delegated rather than primary legislation, the offending limitation could simply be ignored. The House declared that it was unlawful for the Family Division of the High Court to reject the applicants on the ground only that they were not married. Clearly, the decision was so controversial in Northern Ireland that it took time to sink in. Years later, the Supreme Court received an application for permission to appeal the decision of the Northern Ireland Court of Appeal that the law now was that both opposite and same sex unmarried couples had to be allowed to apply to adopt.[6] We had no hesitation in turning it down.[7]

But Lord Kerr's deep concern for the welfare of children emerged very early on in his career in the highest court. One of his first judgments in the Supreme

[5] *X v Austria* (2013) 57 EHRR 14. Austrian law allowed an opposite sex partner of a child's parent to adopt the child so as to share parenthood jointly with the birth parent, but this was not available to same sex partners. The Court held this to be unjustified discrimination against a same sex partner.

[6] *Re Northern Ireland Human Rights Commission's Application for Judicial Review* [2013] NICA 37, [2014] NI 263.

[7] UKSC 2013/0216, 22 October 2013.

Court was *In re B (A Child) (Residence: Biological Parent)*.[8] A little boy whom the court called Harry was born in December 2005. His parents had separated before he was born. From birth he had lived with his maternal grandmother. His mother was unable to look after him satisfactorily (there were mental health problems and substance abuse). She lived with them intermittently for about seven months but then left and did not return. The grandmother was granted an order that Harry should live with her. Harry also spent time visiting each of his parents. Then his father was sent to prison and, while there, he met the sister of another inmate. When he was released, they formed a relationship and married. She already had a daughter, about Harry's age, from another relationship. Together they had a baby born shortly before the hearing in the magistrates' court. The father applied for Harry to live with him. The magistrates heard the evidence, including a social worker's report recommending that Harry should stay where he was. They weighed up all the relevant factors and concluded that it was in Harry's best interests to continue to live with his grandmother and to visit each of his parents. The judge considered that this was plainly wrong and made an order in favour of the father, which the Court of Appeal upheld. The Supreme Court restored the magistrates' order. Lord Kerr gave the judgment of the court.

He began, generously, by saying that:

> The significance of parenthood in private law disputes about residence and contact has exercised many courts over many years but one might have thought that the final word on the subject had been uttered in the comprehensive and authoritative opinion of Baroness Hale of Richmond in *Re G (Children) (Residence: Same-sex Partner)* [2006] UKHL 43, [2006] 1 WLR 2305.[9]

Both the judge and the Court of Appeal had misunderstood the true import of that decision. When Lord Nicholls had said that 'in the ordinary way the rearing of a child by his or her biological parent can be expected to be in the child's best interests', he had set that comment 'firmly in the context of the child's welfare'.[10] The welfare of the child was the paramount consideration. It ruled on or determined the course to be followed.[11] Bluntly,

> It is only as a contributor to the child's welfare that parenthood assumes any significance. In common with all other factors bearing on what is in the best interests of the child, it must be examined for its potential to fulfill that aim.[12]

Harry had lived virtually all his young life with his grandmother and formed a strong bond with her. He was thriving in her care and at his current nursery. If that bond was broken, his stability would be threatened. Considerable disruption

[8] *In re B (A Child) (Residence: Biological Parent)* [2009] UKSC 5, [2009] 1 WLR 2496.
[9] ibid [2].
[10] ibid [34].
[11] ibid [36], citing Lord MacDermott in *J v C* [1970] AC 668, 711.
[12] ibid [37].

would be involved in moving to his father. His father's arrangements were untested when the magistrates made their decision.

I was extremely grateful to Lord Kerr, and the other members of the Court, for reaffirming so decisively what I had tried to say in *Re G* and for putting what might have seemed to be the contradictory remarks of Lord Nicholls into their proper context. Lord Kerr later confided in me that his own grandmother had played an important part in bringing him up. That explained why he was able to see things so clearly from the child's point of view.

This may have settled things in private law disputes between parents and other family members or friends, but where should the best interests of children come into the decisions of public authorities? Article 3(1) of the United Nations Convention on the Rights of the Child (UNCRC) states firmly that:

> In all actions concerning children, whether undertaken by public or private social welfare institutions, courts of law, administrative authorities or legislative bodies, the best interests of the child shall be a primary consideration.

The UNCRC has not been incorporated into UK law, although certain public authorities have a duty to make arrangements for ensuring that their functions are carried out 'having regard to the need to safeguard and promote the welfare of children who are in the United Kingdom'.[13] This includes the Home Secretary and immigration authorities when making decisions about immigration, asylum and nationality.[14] It was apparently intended to reflect the UK's obligations under Article 3(1), although it does not say exactly the same thing. Having regard to a need is not necessarily the same as making the child's interests a primary consideration.

In *ZH (Tanzania) v Secretary of State for the Home Department* the issue was the weight to be given to the interests of children who were British citizens, born and brought up here all their lives.[15] There was no power to deport or remove them from the country, but their mother was here illegally and had 'an appalling immigration history'.[16] Removing her to Tanzania would inevitably mean that they had to go too, as there was no-one else in the UK to look after them: their British citizen father was an alcoholic with HIV. Not only would their lives be seriously disrupted, they would lose all the benefits to which they were entitled as British citizens. The Supreme Court held that their best interests had to be factored into deciding whether the inevitable interference with their private and family lives was proportionate. Making their best interests a primary consideration did not mean that they were paramount – they could be outweighed by other considerations,

[13] Children Act 2004, s 11, which applies to local authorities, the health service, the police, prisons and probation.

[14] Borders, Citizenship and Immigration Act 2009, s 55.

[15] *ZH (Tanzania) v Secretary of State for the Home Dept* [2011] UKSC 4, [2011] 2 AC 160.

[16] ibid [5] and [33].

but they had to come first. Lord Kerr put it more strongly than I had done in my leading judgment:

> [I]n reaching decisions that will affect a child, a primacy of importance must be accorded to his or her best interests. This is not, it is agreed, a factor of limitless importance in the sense that it will prevail over all other considerations. It is a factor, however, that must rank higher than any other. It is not merely one consideration that weighs in the balance alongside other competing factors. Where the best interests of the child clearly favour a certain course, that course must be followed unless countervailing considerations of considerable force displace them. It is not necessary to express this in terms of a presumption but the primacy of the consideration needs to be made clear in emphatic terms. What is determined to be in a child's best interests should customarily dictate the outcome in cases such as the present, therefore, and it will require considerations of substantial moment to permit a different result.[17]

He also considered that the children's nationality was important, not only as a contributor to their best interests, but also as a factor in its own right. That may explain why he was able to agree with the rest of us in *Zoumbas (DRC) v Secretary of State for the Home Department*.[18] This was about removing a family to the Democratic Republic of Congo (DRC); their three children had been born here, but were not British citizens. There was no dispute about the applicable principles: the dispute was about whether the Secretary of State's decision letter had complied with them. We satisfied ourselves (perhaps optimistically) that the children's interests had indeed been carefully considered. Although born here, they were not British citizens and had no right to education and health care here. They were part of a close-knit family with well-educated parents and could be removed to the DRC without serious detriment to their well-being.

In *Makhlouf v Secretary of State for the Home Department*,[19] a case coming from Northern Ireland in which Lord Kerr gave the leading judgment, the family courts had decided that it was in the best interests of the appellant's children to have no contact with him: making their interests a primary consideration actually supported, rather than undermined, the Secretary of State's decision to remove him. There was no need for the Secretary of State to conduct her own inquiries to second-guess the family courts' conclusions. The case reinforces the principle that children are rights-holders in their own right, not simply an adjunct to the adults' rights or a passport to what the adults want.

The principle in *ZH (Tanzania)* applies to any action by a public authority which interferes with the Article 8 rights of children. But how does it apply to extradition? In *HH v Deputy Prosecutor of the Italian Republic, Genoa* Lord Kerr once again took a stronger line even than I.[20] In a brief concurrence with

[17] ibid [46].
[18] *Zoumbas (DRC) v Secretary of State for the Home Dept* [2013] UKSC 74, [2013] 1 WLR 3690.
[19] *Makhlouf v Secretary of State for the Home Dept* [2016] UKSC 59, [2017] NI 127.
[20] *HH v Deputy Prosecutor of the Italian Republic, Genoa* [2012] UKSC 25, [2013] 1 AC 338, grouping three cases involving European Arrest Warrants.

my leading judgment, he agreed that extradition and expulsion are different. Expulsion is performed unilaterally and designed to protect the national interest. Extradition involves international co-operation to further the suppression of transnational crime and the elimination of safe havens. It has greater weight. But the exercise of making the children's interests a primary consideration should be the same. He found the notion (which I had conceded) that there could be more than one primary consideration 'conceptually difficult'. He favoured a structured approach to decision-making. The importance to be attached to the children's interests should be considered first, followed by an assessment of the degree of interference with their rights, and finally addressing whether extradition justifies the interference. In that way, proper prominence would be accorded to the children's interests: considering them first avoided the risk that they might be undervalued in a more open-ended inquiry.

That has always seemed the correct approach to me (although failing to follow it is not necessarily fatal, as *Zoumbas* showed). Unfortunately, other Justices were resistant to the idea that a judge or other decision-maker should structure his thinking in any particular order. But, on the facts in *HH*, Lord Kerr agreed with the majority. One of the cases involved a Polish woman who was accused of offences of dishonesty committed before she and her family had come to the UK 10 years earlier. She and her husband had five children, two of them born here. The effect upon them all, but especially the two youngest children, would be devastating if she were extradited. We all agreed that their interests were not outweighed by the importance of extradition. The other case involved a married couple who had been involved in smuggling large qualities of drugs into Italy. Their three children would suffer serious harm if both parents were extradited: their whole lives would be severely disrupted. I would have put their interests above the public interest in extraditing their father, who was their primary carer, but unsurprisingly not even Lord Kerr agreed with me.

There was no equivalent statutory duty placed on the Department for Work and Pensions, but in 2010 there had been 'a clear commitment that the government will give due consideration to the UNCRC articles when making new policy and legislation'.[21] This was repeated in the Cabinet Office *Guide to Making Legislation* in 2013.[22] But this does not seem to have happened with the Welfare Reform Act 2012 or the regulations made under it which introduced the benefit cap.[23] This imposed a limit on the total benefits payable to a household, even though this would take them below the officially defined amount that they needed to live on. It operated particularly harshly against lone parents with several children living in high rent areas. In *R (SG) v Secretary of State for Work and Pensions*,[24]

[21] Minister of State for Children and Families, Written Statement to Parliament, 6 December 2010.
[22] *Guide to Making Legislation*, July 2013, para 11.30.
[23] Benefit Cap (Housing Benefit) Regulations 2012, SI 2012/2994.
[24] *R (SG) v Secretary of State for Work and Pensions* [2015] UKSC 16, [2015] 1 WLR 1449.

three single mothers and their children claimed that this discriminated against lone parent women in the right to the enjoyment of their possessions, contrary to Article 14 read with Article 1 of the First Protocol (A1P1) to the European Convention. The government admitted that their benefits were possessions for the purpose of A1P1[25] and that the cap was indirectly discriminatory against women, because the great majority of lone parents are women. At first, the government also admitted that Article 3(1) of the UNCRC was relevant to considering whether there had been a breach of Convention rights. The government claimed that it had been complied with, because it was fully aware of what the effect would be on the welfare of the children affected. However, as the majority of the Supreme Court agreed, it clearly had not been complied with:

> It cannot possibly be in the best interests of the children affected by the cap to deprive them of the means to provide them with adequate food, clothing, warmth and housing, the basic necessities of life. It is not enough that children in general, now or in the future, may benefit by a shift in welfare culture.[26]

So the government shifted tack and argued that, while Article 3(1) was undoubtedly relevant to interpreting the content of the Convention rights, it was not relevant to the justification and proportionality of interfering with them. Furthermore, the discrimination was not against the children but against their mothers. The children would suffer just as much from the cap if they were living with their lone fathers, so how could their interests be relevant to a claim of sex discrimination? It was this latter point which swung the majority away from finding in the claimants' favour. Lord Kerr and I dissented.

Lord Kerr began with the radical argument that human rights treaties are incorporated into UK law even without legislation to implement them. He agreed with Lord Steyn[27] that the rationale for the dualist theory, requiring legislation if a treaty is to change the law, is to protect the citizen against the risk of abuses by the executive. This does not apply to human rights treaties, which give rights to the citizenry against the executive. 'If the government commits itself to a standard of human rights protection, it seems to me entirely logical that it should be held to account in the courts as to its actual compliance with that standard.'[28]

Accepting that no-one else was going to agree with him, he went on to agree with me that Article 3(1) was relevant to whether there had been a breach of the Convention rights. He was particularly strong in his rebuttal of the argument that this was discrimination against the mothers but not the children:

> A mother's personality, the essence of her parenthood, is defined not simply by her gender but by her role and responsibility as a carer for her children, particularly when

[25] They had to do that because of the Strasbourg Grand Chamber decision in *Stec v UK* (2006) 43 EHRR 1017.

[26] *SG* (n 24), [226] per Lady Hale.

[27] In *In re McKerr* [2004] UKHL 12, [2004] 1 WLR 807, [49]–[50].

[28] *SG* (n 24) [256].

> she is a lone parent. Justification of a discriminatory measure must directly address the impact that it will have on the children of lone mothers because that impact is inextricably bound up with the women's capacity to fulfill their role as mothers. If you take money away from children which mothers would receive on their behalf, the discrimination that you perpetrate involves withholding resources necessary to fully discharge their maternal role. Because, therefore, one cannot segregate the interests of the deprived children from those of their mothers, the discrimination against the mothers and the children is of the same stripe. No hermetically sealed compartmentalisation of their interests is possible.[29]

Some might see this as painting an idealised picture of motherhood, but how I wish that I had said the same!

In *SG*, Lord Kerr accepted that the test for deciding upon the justification for a measure of socio-economic policy which interfered with Convention rights was whether the measure was 'manifestly without reasonable foundation'. This test, which was derived from *Stec v UK*,[30] had been accepted by the Supreme Court in a case about child tax credit[31] and reaffirmed in the 'bedroom tax' cases.[32] Lord Kerr had not taken part in either. By the time of the next benefit cap case, *R (DA) v Secretary of State for Work and Pensions*,[33] he had thought better of it. In 2016, the government lowered the ceiling, making the effect of the cap even worse than it had previously been. This time, instead of complaining of sex discrimination, two groups of claimants complained of discrimination against the lone parents of young children and their children. They should have been treated differently from dual parent families because their situation was significantly different: they were much less likely to be able to avoid the effect of the cap by finding work outside the home.[34] The majority of a seven Justice panel in the Supreme Court accepted that Article 3(1) was relevant to the children's claim, but held that it had not been 'breached': the government had evaluated the likely impact upon the children and taken it into account. Applying the 'manifestly without reasonable foundation' test, the government's belief that there were better long-term outcomes for children who live in households in which an adult works, though not 'the surest foundation', was a 'reasonable foundation'.[35]

Lord Kerr and I disagreed with the majority. I was content to continue to adopt the 'manifestly without reasonable foundation' test, because I thought that it had been met. The government's three declared aims – fairness between families in and out of work, incentivising work outside the home, and fiscal savings – had

[29] ibid [264]–[265].
[30] *Stec* (n 25) para 52.
[31] *Humphreys v Revenue and Customs Comrs* [2012] UKSC 18, [2012] 1 WLR 1545.
[32] *R (MA) v Secretary of State for Work and Pensions* [2016] UKSC 58, [2016] 1 WLR 4550.
[33] *R (DA) v Secretary of State for Work and Pensions* [2019] UKSC 21, [2019] 1 WLR 3289.
[34] A type of discrimination recognised by the European Court of Human Rights in *Thlimmenos v Greece* (2000) 31 EHRR 411.
[35] *DA* (n 33) [88] per Lord Wilson.

all been exploded by the evidence. Even if they had not, the government had not struck a fair balance between the benefits to the community and the interests of the children and their parents: this would have set the very limited benefits to the community against the damage done to the family lives of young children and their parents. It was not enough for the government to show that it was aware of others' concerns; awareness is not the same as taking the best interests of the children seriously into account.

Lord Kerr began by launching a wholesale attack upon the 'manifestly without reasonable foundation' test. It was the product of the margin of appreciation which the European Court of Human Rights accords to the national authorities in matters of social and economic policy. It was impermissible to import it into the national courts' consideration of the proportionality of a measure. The approach of the national courts to proportionality could not simply mirror the approach in Strasbourg.[36] The UK's four-stage scheme for assessing proportionality was well settled: was the objective of the measure sufficiently important to justify interfering with a fundamental right; was it rationally connected to that aim; could a less intrusive measure have achieved it; and, above all, did the measure strike a fair balance between the interests of the community at large and the rights of the individual?[37] That scheme should also be applied in this context. Even in Strasbourg, a distinction had been drawn between the aims of the measure and its proportionality, a distinction which the UK Supreme Court had followed elsewhere.[38] Therefore, certainly at the final, fair balance, stage of the analysis, the 'manifestly without reasonable foundation' standard should not be applied.[39] In striking a fair balance between the interests of the community and the impact on these children, it was not enough to show that notice had been taken of the representations made: the government had to show that it had weighed the interests of these particular children against what was likely to be achieved in their case. The government and Parliament were aware of the state's obligation under Article 3(1), but they had not discharged it by giving the impact on children's rights the 'primacy of importance which Article 3 requires'.[40]

There is indeed some reason to believe that the Supreme Court may have been too hasty in adopting the 'manifestly without reasonable foundation' test. Two of the bedroom tax cases went to Strasbourg, where one of them succeeded.[41]

[36] Citing Lord Reed in *Bank Mellat v HM Treasury (No 2)* [2013] UKSC 39, [2014] AC 700, [71].

[37] In several cases but beginning with *R (Quila) v Secretary of State for the Home Dept* [2011] UKSC 45, [2012] 1 AC 621, [45].

[38] *Recovery of Medical Costs for Asbestos Diseases (Wales) Bill* [2015] UKSC 3, [2015] AC 1016, [46].

[39] *DA* (n 33) [177]. It is fair to say that he rather dented the clarity of this by concluding the paragraph 'The proper test to apply in relation to the final stage of the proportionality assessment is whether the government has established that there is a reasonable foundation to the conclusion that a fair balance has been struck'; see also [179] and [194].

[40] ibid [196].

[41] *JD and A v UK* [2020] HLR 5. See too Gráinne McKeever (ch 7).

The Court (albeit only a Chamber) pointed out that 'even a wide margin of appreciation in the sphere of economic or social policy does not justify the adoption of laws or practices that would violate the prohibition of discrimination'. The 'manifestly without reasonable foundation' test had been limited to 'circumstances where an alleged difference in treatment resulted from a transitional measure forming part of a scheme carried out in order to correct an inequality'. That is certainly true of *Stec*, so perhaps Lord Kerr had correctly divined the direction of travel in Strasbourg.

Women First

Clearly then, Lord Kerr had no hesitation or difficulty in putting the interests of children first. But what about the interests of women? In the course of his time in the Supreme Court, he developed a keen understanding of the reproductive rights of women and an empathy for their situation which was perhaps not so apparent in his first instance judgment in *Family Planning Association of Northern Ireland v Minister for Health, Social Services and Public Safety*.[42] The Association wanted the minister to issue guidance on the circumstances in which abortion might be obtained in Northern Ireland and to investigate the avowed difficulties in obtaining services for the termination of pregnancy. Kerr J held that the law was clear: termination of pregnancy was only lawful where its continuance threatened the life of the mother or would adversely affect her mental or physical health; the adverse effect must be 'real and serious' and also 'permanent or long term'.[43] (The effect of this, when confirmed by the Court of Appeal, was to put an immediate stop to abortions where there was a fatal foetal abnormality, which had been readily available before.) Applying the law in individual cases was a matter of clinical judgment, not guidance. And there was no evidence that lawful abortions were not available, so there was no need to investigate. The tone of his judgment is noticeably different from the tone of his judgments in the two cases about abortion in Northern Ireland which reached the Supreme Court many years later.

Before coming to them, there was his landmark judgment, jointly with Lord Reed, in *Montgomery v Lanarkshire Health Board*.[44] A pregnant woman, small-framed and an insulin dependent diabetic, was not informed of the risks of shoulder dystocia: that the baby's shoulders would be wider than his head, so that his head might descend into the birth canal and his shoulders get stuck: this is a major obstetric emergency bringing with it risks to both the baby and the mother. Nor was she offered a choice between a vaginal delivery and a caesarian section.

[42] *Family Planning Association of Northern Ireland v Minister for Health, Social Services and Public Safety* [2003] NIQB 48.

[43] ibid [37]; he was endorsed by Sheil LJ in the Court of Appeal [2004] NICA 37, [2005] NI 188, [12].

[44] *Montgomery v Lanarkshire Health Board* [2015] UKSC 11, [2015] AC 1430.

The Court held that any patient has the right to decide on her own treatment and should be offered the information necessary to enable her to make a proper choice. The information depended upon medical knowledge and judgement, but the decision whether to tell the patient did not. The tone of the judgment of Lord Reed and Lord Kerr, rejecting the model of medical paternalism adopted by the majority of the House of Lords in *Sideaway v Governors of Bethlem Royal Hospital*,[45] is noticeably more empathetic to the position of the patient and her right to control what is done with her own body. No doubt the result would have been the same had the patient been a man, but the rejection of medical paternalism is all the more striking because it took place in the particular context of a pregnant woman.

Miss A became pregnant at the age of 15. She was unable to obtain an abortion in Northern Ireland where she lived. So she and her mother travelled to Manchester where she had an abortion at the Marie Stopes International Clinic. The total cost was £900. In *R (A) v Secretary of State for Health*,[46] Ms A and her mother claimed that the policy of the Secretary of State to refuse NHS abortions to women from Northern Ireland was unlawful both at common law and under the Human Rights Act 1998. The majority held that it was not unlawful. Lord Kerr and I dissented. He began his judgment in what had become a typical style:

> A woman from Northern Ireland visiting England who suffers an acute attack of appendicitis will have, if it proves necessary, her appendix removed in a National Health Service hospital, without charge. The same woman, if she travels to England in order to obtain an abortion, must pay for that procedure. How can this be right? The answer is that it cannot be, and is not, right.[47]

He then demonstrated that the Secretary of State's duty[48] to promote a comprehensive health service for the prevention, diagnosis and treatment of illness applied throughout the geographical area of England; it was only the duty to promote services to improve physical and mental health which was limited to the 'people of England'. He also demolished the Secretary of State's argument that the NHS should not fund services which the Northern Ireland Assembly had deliberately decided not to provide and which would be unlawful if provided in Northern Ireland. The Northern Ireland Assembly had expressed no view on whether women from Northern Ireland should be allowed to come to England for abortions and was perfectly well aware that they did so. 'The democratic decision-making in Northern Ireland simply does not impinge on the exercise by NI women of their rights in England'.[49] The Secretary of State's decision was

[45] *Sideaway v Governors of Bethlem Royal Hospital* [1985] AC 871.
[46] *R (A) v Secretary of State for Health* [2017] UKSC 41, [2017] 1 WLR 2492.
[47] ibid [50].
[48] National Health Service Act 2006, s 1.
[49] *A* (n 46), [76].

unlawful in conventional public law terms. Nor did it have any legitimate aim which might justify the discrimination against women from Northern Ireland in the enjoyment of their right to respect for their private lives. Like the majority, Lord Kerr recognised 'the plight into which many of these vulnerable women are cast'.[50] Unlike them, he would have done something about it.

Dissenting judgments are not always writ in water. They may indicate the direction in which the law is travelling.[51] They may even have concrete results. Within a few days of the judgment, the Scottish government announced that it would provide free NHS abortions for women from Northern Ireland, and the political pressure in England was such that the Secretary of State eventually followed suit.

The next stage, of course, was an attack upon abortion law in Northern Ireland. Lord Kerr regarded his judgment in *Re Northern Ireland Human Rights Commission's Application for Judicial Review*[52] (the *NIHRC* case) as the most significant of his career. It is easy to see why. It was a tour de force. The issue was whether the law in Northern Ireland was incompatible with the rights protected by Articles 3 and 8 of the European Convention because it prohibited abortion in cases of fatal or serious foetal abnormality, rape and incest. Lord Kerr gave the leading judgment on that issue. He began by doing something which Supreme Court judgments rarely do. He recounted the graphic evidence of the ordeals suffered by Ashleigh Topley, Sarah Jane Ewart and Denise Phelan when they discovered that their wanted babies were doomed to die but they were forced by the law of Northern Ireland to carry them to term and then give birth to them. He also recounted the evidence given by Marie Stopes International in Northern Ireland of the rape victims – one a child under 13 who had been raped by a family member – who had consulted them. Some of these women were able to go to England to have an abortion, itself a traumatic experience, but the evidence was that health care professionals in Northern Ireland were so afraid of being accused of aiding and abetting an abortion that they were reluctant to offer any advice and support. Admiration and sympathy for these women did not provide an answer to the legal questions, '[b]ut the nature of their suffering and the trauma of their experiences are by no means irrelevant to the unravelling and resolution of the issues to which this appeal gives rise'.[53] This was a very different tone from 15 years previously.

So too was the passage with which he concluded his discussion of Article 3:

> Binding the girls and women of Northern Ireland to that edict[54] means that they may not assert their autonomy in their own country. They are forbidden to do to their own

[50] ibid [52].

[51] See also Rachel Cahill-O'Callaghan (ch 4).

[52] *Re Northern Ireland Human Rights Commission's Application for Judicial Review* [2018] UKSC 27, [2018] NI 228.

[53] ibid [141].

[54] ie, the Offences against the Person Act 1861, ss 58, 59, and the Criminal Justice Act (NI) 1945, s 25.

> bodies that which they wish to do; they are prevented from arranging their lives in the way that they want; they are denied the chance to shape their future as they desire. If, as well as the curtailment on their autonomy which this involves, they are carrying a foetus with a fatal abnormality or have been the victims of rape or incest, they are condemned … to endure untold suffering and desolation. What is that, if it is not humiliation and debasement?[55]

He accepted that not all women and girls would suffer such profound psychological trauma, but the risk of their doing so was enough to trigger the state's positive obligation under Article 3 to take measures to prevent that happening. Hence, he (and Lord Wilson who agreed with his judgment) would have declared the law incompatible with Article 3. I sympathised with his view but found it unnecessary to decide the point, as we were agreed that the law was inevitably incompatible with Article 8.

Lord Kerr returned to the theme of women's autonomy when he discussed Article 8:

> A woman's right to respect for her private life, her right to exercise autonomy over her own body, her entitlement to make decisions as to her own welfare and happiness lie at the very centre of her existence.[56]

The interference had to be no more than was necessary to achieve its legitimate aim. But he had difficulty identifying the legitimate aim. How could the simple aim of protecting the life of the unborn child be a legitimate aim if that child was bound to die? And how could such an aim be reconciled with allowing the abortion of a healthy foetus where there was a serious threat to the long-term health of the mother? The Court of Appeal had seen the protection of the life of the unborn child as an aspect of the moral views of the people of Northern Ireland, but how could it be moral to permit abortion in those circumstances but forbid it when the pregnancy was the result of rape or incest? He also decisively dismissed the European Court of Human Rights' decision in *A, B and C v Ireland*,[57] which was heavily relied upon both by the respondents to NIHRC's appeal and the dissenting Justices. The Court had held that, although the existence of a European consensus in favour of abortion would normally narrow the state's margin of appreciation, it did not do so in that case, apparently because of the profound moral values concerning the nature of life held by the majority of the Irish people. Even if the Court had been right about the moral views of the Irish people, such evidence as there was did not support the view that those values were shared by the majority of the people of Northern Ireland. The Northern Ireland Assembly had quite recently voted to reject amendments which would have allowed abortion in the circumstances under discussion, but the two political parties whose members had

[55] *NIHRC* (n 52), [261].
[56] ibid [280].
[57] *A, B and C v Ireland* (2010) 53 EHRR 429.

opposed the change were neither of them implacably opposed to it: a majority of Assembly members were at least prepared to contemplate change. 'For that reason alone, *A, B and C v Ireland* cannot be regarded as a significant decision in the present case.'[58]

The judgment is redolent of some familiar themes to emerge from Lord Kerr's jurisprudence as a whole. One is rejection of the margin of appreciation: this was a principle 'applied on the pan-European plane by the supra-national court in Strasbourg'.[59] But:

> when it comes to the domestic superintendence by one institution (the judiciary) of another institution's (the executive's or the legislature's) decision in the field of human rights, there is no place for reticence on the basis of a margin of appreciation.[60]

There might be a place for reticence based on institutional competence or the view that the other institution was better equipped to make the decision. But the question of usurping the function of the decision-maker simply did not arise in this case. The Northern Ireland Assembly had not made a decision: 'The courts should feel no sense of inhibition … in the light of the absence of any firmly expressed view of the democratic institutions of Northern Ireland.'[61] There are echoes here of his willingness to take the bull by the horns in cases such as *R (Nicklinson) v Ministry of Justice*,[62] the assisted suicide case.

A related theme is proportionality. Lord Kerr was always firmly of the view that it is for the courts, as well as the primary decision-maker, to evaluate whether an interference with a qualified human right is proportionate. Lord Bingham had made it clear that this was the role of the immigration appellate authorities in *Huang v Secretary of State for the Home Department*,[63] but there was not always the same clarity when the government was the primary decision-maker. In *NIHRC*[64] Lord Kerr playfully cites Lord Sumption in *R (Lord Carlile of Berriew) v Secretary of State for the Home Department*,[65] who drew attention to criticisms of the notion of 'deference' before going on to display something remarkably similar. In *Carlile*, the issue was whether the Home Secretary had acted incompatibly with the free speech rights of a number of distinguished Parliamentarians and Mrs Rajavi, a prominent Iranian dissident, in denying her entry to this country in order to meet them in the Houses of Parliament. I believe that all the Justices

[58] *NIHRC* (n 52), [321].

[59] ibid [290].

[60] ibid [291].

[61] ibid [295].

[62] *R (Nicklinson) v Ministry of Justice* [2014] UKSC 38, [2015] AC 657. See also Rachel Cahill-O'Callaghan (ch 4).

[63] *Huang v Secretary of State for the Home Dept* [2007] UKHL 11, [2007] 2 AC 167.

[64] *NIHRC* (n 52) [294].

[65] *R (Lord Carlile of Berriew) v Secretary of State for the Home Dept* [2014] UKSC 60, [2015] AC 945, [22].

in *Carlile* accepted that it was the court's role, as a public authority bound by section 6(1) of the Human Rights Act 1998, to form its own view of whether the primary decision-maker had acted incompatibly with the Convention rights, but they took slightly different views of what might lead them to disagree with the government's assessment. Lord Kerr put it most trenchantly:

> Shortly stated, the court's role in deciding whether there has been an unjustified interference with a Convention right is to answer the four questions which are said to usually arise … In dealing with the latter two of these questions the court must indeed exercise its own judgment. Of course, it may defer to the Secretary of State's assessment of the risks involved and of the consequences should the risks materialise. But that does not relieve the court of the duty to confront frankly the stark questions whether, given those risks and consequences, it (as opposed to the decision-maker) has been persuaded that the measures are no more than required to achieve the stated object and that a fair balance has been struck.[66]

He accepted that the Home Secretary (taking the advice of the Foreign Secretary) was better placed to assess the risks to our 'fragile but imperative' relations with Iran if Mrs Rajavi were permitted to come to this country to share views with our Parliamentarians. But it was for us to assess the importance of the rights of Mrs Rajavi, and the Parliamentarians, to freedom of speech. In his assessment:

> Mrs Rajavi stands for values which this country has cherished and championed, some of them for centuries. To deny her the opportunity to express views and advance causes in this country that all right-thinking members of our society fervently support is a very significant step indeed.[67]

While the risks were 'a loosely expressed agglomeration of possible outcomes', the interference with freedom of speech was 'direct and immediate'. He would have required evidence of the most compelling kind to interfere with the Parliamentarians' right to have a face-to-face exchange with her.[68] I do not think it a coincidence that Mrs Rajavi was a prominent champion of women's rights in Iran: 'a true believer in gender equality'.[69]

A third theme is his understanding of and sensitivity to the social and political tensions in Northern Ireland. I am not sure that he would have been deterred from making a declaration of incompatibility in the *NIHRC* case even if the Assembly had decisively rejected any thought of changing the law. But he would have handled it differently. And he had no hesitation in holding that the NIHRC had standing to bring the case. If ever there were a pointless dispute, it was this. The NIHRC could easily have found women who undoubtedly had the

[66] ibid [137].
[67] ibid [168].
[68] ibid [180].
[69] ibid [130].

standing to bring the case and given them their support. What could possibly be gained by holding – when construing some very convoluted statutory provisions – that the NIHRC did not have standing? Yet that is what the majority of the Supreme Court did, rejecting the unanimous view of the High Court, the Court of Appeal and the Supreme Court Justice from Northern Ireland.

By the time that he retired, Lord Kerr had established himself as the most consistently liberal and forward-looking of the Supreme Court Justices.[70] He assured me that those who knew him well in Northern Ireland would have known that this was the real man. Once free of the burdens of office as Lord Chief Justice, he was able to let that spirit fly. That is one of the reasons why he always refused to contemplate becoming President or Deputy President of the Supreme Court. That is another thing that I have to thank him for, along with so much more.

[70] It is perhaps unlikely that the Supreme Court would have been unanimous in deciding in favour of the government in *R (SC, CB and 8 children) v Secretary of State for Work and Pensions* [2021] UKSC 26, limiting welfare benefits to two children despite the disparate impact upon women, and in *R (AB) v Secretary of State for Justice* [2021] UKSC 28, holding that unlawful solitary confinement of a child prisoner was not incompatible with Art 3 of the European Convention, had Lord Kerr been a member of the panel.

3

Human Rights, Gender Equality and the Judge's Toolbox in the UK Supreme Court

KATHRYN McNEILLY

Introduction

When considering how gender equality may intersect with the practice of judging, the concept of feminist judging soon comes to mind. Over recent years, this term has become familiar in legal scholarship and practice. Feminist judging was first developed by the Women's Court of Canada project, which in 2006 published six 'shadow judgments' supplementing Canadian Charter of Rights and Freedoms jurisprudence.[1] This aimed to demonstrate how a commitment to gender equality could be better integrated into this body of case law. Feminist judgment projects have since emerged in England, Northern/Ireland, Scotland, New Zealand, the United States, Australia, Africa, India, Mexico and in international law.[2] Across all of these projects, scholars and lawyers have undertaken a rewriting of court judgments in almost every area of law imaginable. Following the same conventions and parameters as judges themselves, this work 'provides a means of re-imagining the role of the judge … demonstrating that it is possible to decide even very difficult cases in ways which take proper account of feminist concerns'.[3]

[1] Special Issue (2006) 18(1) *Canadian Journal of Women and the Law.*

[2] Rosemary Hunter, Clare McGlynn and Erika Rackley (eds), *Feminist Judgments: From Theory to Practice* (Oxford, Hart Publishing, 2010); Máiréad Enright, Julie McCandless and Aoife O'Donoghue (eds), *Northern/Irish Feminist Judgments: Judges' Troubles and the Gendered Politics of Identity* (Oxford, Hart Publishing, 2017); Sharon Cowan, Chloe Kennedy and Vanessa Munro (eds), *Scottish Feminist Judgments: (Re)Creating Law from the Outside In* (Oxford, Hart Publishing, 2019); Elisabeth McDonald et al (eds), *Feminist Judgments of Aotearoa New Zealand: Te Rino: A Two-Stranded Rope* (Oxford, Hart Publishing, 2017); Kathryn Stanchi, Linda Berger and Bridget Crawford (eds), *Feminist Judgments: Rewritten Opinions of the United States Supreme Court* (New York, Cambridge UP, 2017); Heather Douglas et al (eds), *Australian Feminist Judgments: Righting and Rewriting Law* (Oxford, Hart Publishing, 2014); Loveday Hodson and Troy Lavers (eds), *Feminist Judgments in International Law* (Oxford, Hart Publishing, 2019). Projects in India, Mexico and Africa remain ongoing at the date of writing.

[3] Julie McCandless, Mairead Enright and Aoife O'Donoghue, 'Introduction: Troubling Judgment' in Enright, McCandless and O'Donoghue (ibid) 8.

Given the level of maturity this methodology has now reached, and its commitment to the connection between theory and practice, a natural extension for scholars involved in the projects above has been to move from writing judgments to considering feminist judging in practice. In other words, how judges in real world settings engage commitments to gender equality when deciding cases. This has included qualitative studies with judges on how they undertake their work,[4] case studies of the judgments written by individual judges,[5] and case studies of courts and their judgments.[6] In the last category, Rosemary Hunter and Erika Rackley have recently explored feminist judging on the UK Supreme Court (UKSC) between 2009 and 2017.[7] Two points from this recent investigation are interesting to note. First, Lady Hale, followed by Lord Kerr and Lord Wilson, appeared as the judges most frequently engaging feminist reasoning in their work.[8] Second, human rights case law – a significant area of expertise for Lord Kerr – emerged as the area offering the most fertile ground for feminist judging.[9] From these two points, the connection between gender equality and judging practice appears as a particularly pertinent topic to explore in the present collection dedicated to Lord Kerr's contribution to judicial life. As a human rights scholar, when invited to contribute toward this collection I was interested in exploring more of the specific form that judging compatible with gender equality in UK human rights cases has taken.

In the academic projects and in 'real world' analyses, a number of tools have been identified as employed by judges who are engaging in reasoning attentive to equality.[10] These tools are instructive in providing a means for scholars, students and practitioners to investigate the gender equality credentials of any judgment, and also as a way for judges to reflect on their own practice. However, little has been considered of the unique tools that may be developed within particular areas of law.[11] These tailored tools may draw from, adapt or modify the more generally

[4] Heather Douglas, 'Sexual Violence, Domestic Abuse and the Feminist Judge' (2016) 3 *Journal of International and Comparative Law* 317; Rosemary Hunter, 'Feminist Judging in the "Real World"' (2018) 8 *Oñati Socio-legal Series* 1275.

[5] Rosemary Hunter and Danielle Tyson, 'Justice Betty King: A Study of Feminist Judging in Action' (2017) 40 *UNSW Law Journal* 778; Rosemary Hunter, 'Justice Marcia Neave: Case Study of a Feminist Judge' in Ulrike Schultz and Gisela Shaw (eds), *Gender and Judging* (Oxford, Hart Publishing, 2013) 399.

[6] Rosemary Hunter and Erika Rackley, 'Feminist Judgments on the UK Supreme Court' (2020) 32 *Canadian Journal of Women and the Law* 85. See also smaller scale comments on the US Supreme Court in Bridget Crawford, Kathryn Stanchi and Linda Berger, 'Feminist Judging Matters: How Feminist Theory and Methods Affect the Process of Judgment' (2018) 47 *University of Baltimore Law Review* 186.

[7] ibid.

[8] ibid 90.

[9] Of the 114 cases Hunter and Rackley identified as engaging feminist/gender concerns across 2009–2017, almost 40 were cases involving human rights: ibid 97.

[10] These are explored further in the next section of this chapter.

[11] For one exception, see Douglas (n 4).

applicable feminist judging tools to fit the area of law at hand, and their identification offers enhanced possibilities for furthering judging cognisant of gender equality and justice in the legal area being considered. In this chapter, I seek to understand more of the tools employed in human rights judging in practice, considering the 'real world' judge's toolbox that may emerge. Examining recent human rights judgments delivered by the UKSC during Lady Hale's Presidency (2017–2020),[12] I uncover a set of identifiable judging tools that are unique to this area of law and that stand to be reflected on by those interested in human rights law and feminist judging alike. As will be explored, Lord Kerr's work provides significant instruction in this analysis.

My discussion proceeds in three sections. In the first, I introduce the general feminist judging tools that have been identified to date, outline the methods employed in the current study seeking to build on this work in the context of human rights case law, and present the unique human rights-focused tools identified in my textual reading of judgments from the UKSC. In the chapter's second section, I explore these tools and their use in more detail through examination of five human rights judgments that engaged gender equality concerns during the period under study.[13] I conclude the chapter by considering what can be learned from this analysis, including steps that might be taken to further strengthen judging attentive to gender equality in this area of law.

Identifying Judging Tools

For those interested in how awareness of gender equality might be integrated into everyday judging practice, a variety of responses to the question 'what makes a feminist judgment?' can be found in scholarship and the judgment projects. Each person donning feminist judging robes can be understood to take an individual approach influenced by their own reading of the facts and issues in front of them – similar to judges in practice – as well as their own interpretation of what the aims and goals of equality are. More generally, however, a set of tools

[12] I have taken this to span the first and last cases Lady Hale heard as President, from *O'Connor v Bar Standards Board* [2017] UKSC 78, [2017] 1 WLR 4833 to *XX v Whittington Hospital NHS Trust* [2020] UKSC 14, [2021] AC 275.

[13] These are: *Commissioner of Police of the Metropolis v DSD* [2018] UKSC 11, [2019] AC 196; *R (Steinfeld and Keidan) v Secretary of State for the International Development* [2018] UKSC 32, [2020] AC 1; *In the matter of an Application by Siobhan McLaughlin for Judicial Review* [2018] UKSC 48, [2018] 1 WLR 4250; *RR v Secretary of State for Work and Pensions* [2019] UKSC 52, [2019] 1 WLR 6430; *R (AR) v Chief Constable of Greater Manchester Police* [2018] UKSC 47, [2018] 1 WLR 4079.

has been identified which underpins and guides feminist judging in important ways. The English Feminist Judgments Project outlines these as follows:[14]

1. *Asking the woman question:* Drawing from legal scholar Katharine Bartlett,[15] it is necessary to notice 'the gender implications of apparently neutral rules and practices (as well as their implications for other traditionally excluded groups)'.[16]
2. *Including women*: This involves including the experiences and stories of women, as litigants but also more broadly, in judgments and bringing experiences that may be marginalised or invisible into view.
3. *Challenging gender bias*: This includes examining current legal constructions of 'woman', rejecting stereotyped accounts of behaviour or sexual difference, and challenging previous judgments which perpetuate such stereotypes or myths.
4. *Contextualisation*: It is essential to reason from context and be attentive to the reality of women's everyday lives. This often takes the form of 'retelling the story (the facts) of the case … in a very different way',[17] but also encompasses placing a case into its wider social or policy context.
5. *Remedying injustices and improving the conditions of women's lives*: This tool involves being attentive to social injustice and the need to advance material conditions to pursue gender equality.
6. *Promoting substantive equality:* In other words, advancing meaningful understandings of equality between men and women, and more widely.
7. *Drawing on feminist legal scholarship to inform decisions:* Alongside academic sources, wider 'non-legal' sources may be engaged, including what is often referred to as feminist 'common knowledge' about the world.[18]

These tools usually feature in some form in the introductory text of other feminist judgment projects.[19] Beyond these, additional tools identified include use of case law and statutory interpretation to advance equality,[20] approaching existing legal

[14] Rosemary Hunter, 'An Account of Feminist Judging' in Hunter, McGlynn and Rackley (n 2) 35. See also Rosemary Hunter, 'Can *Feminist* Judges Make a Difference?' (2008) 15 *International Journal of the Legal Profession* 10.

[15] Katharine Bartlett, 'Feminist Legal Methods' (1990) 103 *Harvard Law Review* 837.

[16] Hunter (n 14) 35.

[17] ibid 36.

[18] Julie McCandless, Mairead Enright and Aoife O'Donoghue, 'Introduction: Troubling Judgment' in Enright, McCandless and O'Donoghue (n 2) 8; Sharon Cowan, Chloe Kennedy and Vanessa Munro, 'Through the Looking Glass? Feminist Praxis, Artistic Methods and Scottish Feminist Judging' in Cowan, Kennedy and Munro (n 2) 7–10.

[19] Heather Douglas et al, 'Introduction: Righting Australian Law' in Douglas et al (n 2) 8; McCandless, Enright and O'Donoghue (ibid) 8–10; Kathryn Stanchi, Linda Berger and Bridget Crawford, 'Introduction to the US Feminist Judgments Project' in Stanchi, Berger and Crawford (n 2) 15–17.

[20] Cowan, Kennedy and Munro (n 2) 4–10.

concepts anew,[21] and use of *obiter dicta* to supplement analysis.[22] These general tools have also been discussed in 'real world' feminist judgment research. In Hunter and Rackley's investigation of the UKSC, the authors examine to what extent the tools listed above have been engaged by this court and identify 'two forms of feminist judicial approach: substantive and procedural'.[23] The former centres on employment of tools 5 and 6, seeking to 'achieve gender justice and/or to implement feminist theoretical or ethical commitments',[24] while the latter involves use of the rest of the tools above in various combinations. Hunter and Rackley conclude that procedural approaches were dominant in the UKSC during the period under study, meaning that tools 1–4 and 7 were those used with the most frequency.[25]

When it comes to investigation of judging in the context of human rights case law, the tools outlined above are a starting point, offering a roadmap for understanding and analysis. As a human rights scholar, however, I wonder whether more might be said on the specific toolbox used in 'real world' human rights judging to gain a richer understanding of how judges are engaging reasoning compatible with gender equality and justice – either directly or indirectly – in this area of law. This exploration does not seek to undermine or set aside those tools identified to date and used in construction of the feminist judgment methodology. Quite the contrary, it aims to bring these tools into further conversation with judging in practice and add to our understanding of the precise ways in which gender equality-focused judging occurs across different areas of law.

In approaching this study, I decided to remain with the UKSC, in particular given Lord Kerr's contribution to this court and its human rights jurisprudence. I sought to undertake an analysis of UKSC judgments that covered a recent time period and, ideally, that had not been the subject of feminist judging analysis before. This led me to determine Lady Hale's Presidency between 2017 and 2020 as offering the ideal parameters for my work. After compiling a list of all cases decided during this time (over 160 in total), I identified those cases that engaged some substantive element of human rights law. This led to a total of 44 cases. The next step in my analysis was to locate the human rights cases that engaged gender equality concerns. I defined this as relating to women collectively, or engaging individual litigants on issues of gender equality, including parental and familial issues that may incorporate men as litigants also.[26] This led me to cases that focused on criminal law and sexual offences;[27] legal recognition of relationship status;[28]

[21] This includes, importantly, the concept of equality: Rosemary Hunter et al, 'Introducing the Feminist and Mana Wahine Judgments' in McDonald et al (n 2) 38–41.

[22] Rosemary Hunter, Clare McGlynn and Erika Rackley, 'Feminist Judgments: An Introduction' in Hunter, McGlynn and Rackley (n 2) 14.

[23] Hunter and Rackley (n 6) 96.

[24] ibid.

[25] ibid 104.

[26] A similar approach was taken by Hunter and Rackley (n 6) 92–93.

[27] *DSD* (n 13); *AR* (n 13).

[28] *Steinfeld* (n 13).

access to welfare benefits and settings of care;[29] discrimination;[30] reproductive health;[31] and protection of family life in migration contexts.[32] There are 11 such cases in total. There is of course room for debate on whether further cases could be read as engaging gender equality concerns – indeed, as the feminist judgment projects demonstrate, almost any case can be approached in a gender-aware way – but on my reading the cases identified are those most obviously engaging such content. The final step was to undertake a close textual reading of the judgments delivered and identify any gender equality-attentive tools that were used.[33] From this reading, I observed such tools being deployed by one or more judges in seven of the 11 cases. Lord Kerr sat as a judge on five of these seven cases and, as will be explored below, often engaged these tools. These 11 cases can be further categorised into those that ultimately reached an outcome that can be read as compatible with gender equality and justice broadly conceived: five in total.[34]

Throughout textual analysis of this case law, a human rights-focused judging toolbox began to emerge. In other words, a set of tools used by judges in their reasoning which intersects with the original tools noted above, but is unique to human rights case law and tailored to the type of judging required within it. This toolbox contains the following main tools:

1. *Interpreting or deploying European Court of Human Rights (ECtHR) and domestic human rights jurisprudence to support analysis of gender equality issues or facilitate outcomes compatible with such goals:* Regional or domestic human rights case law can be read in a narrow or wide way, particular cases can be foregrounded, and facts either compared or distinguished from the case at hand to facilitate effective grappling with equality concerns.
2. *Understanding proportionality and justification in a way that is cognisant of gender equality*: Human rights case law often centres on determination of whether the violation in question is proportionate or justifiable. Here the general tool of approaching existing legal concepts anew in ways that support and render visible gender equality concerns appears engaged in a way that is unique to this area of law.
3. *Statutory interpretation of the Human Rights Act 1998 to support analysis of gender equality issues:* This coheres with the place of statutory interpretation

[29] *RR* (n 13); *McLaughlin* (n 13); *R (DA) v Secretary of State for Work and Pensions* [2019] UKSC 21, [2019] 1 WLR 3289.

[30] *O'Connor* (n 12); *Gilham v Ministry of Justice* [2019] UKSC 44, [2019] 1 WLR 5905.

[31] *In the matter of an application by the Northern Ireland Human Rights Commission for Judicial Review* [2018] UKSC 27, [2019] 1 All ER 173.

[32] *KO (Nigeria) v Secretary of State for the Home Dept* [2018] UKSC 53, [2018] 1 WLR 5273 and *Rhuppiah v Secretary of State for the Home Dept* [2018] UKSC 58, [2018] 1 WLR 5536.

[33] Here I undertook a discourse rather than doctrinal analysis, as has been employed in the feminist judgment methodology: Rosemary Hunter, 'Analysing Judgments from a Feminist Perspective' (2015) 15 *Legal Information Management* 8.

[34] Listed at nn 27–33 above and explored in detail in the section to follow.

as a key feminist judging tool, but is exclusive to this piece of legislation given its fundamental place in UK human rights law.

4. *Centring the human in human rights law*: Drawing on and modifying tool 4 of the general toolbox, human rights judgments can be delivered in a highly technical and doctrinal manner, engaging the intricacies of domestic and regional human rights law, or they can aim to bring the human aspect of the rights engaged to the fore.
5. *Use of alternative human rights sources to support reasoning*: Modifying and adding to tool 7 of the general toolbox, alternative human rights sources can be drawn upon, including not only scholarship but also international human rights law which may assist in reasoning and discussion of the equality issues arising.

It is important to note that observation of these tools emerges from my reading of the relatively small number of human rights cases engaging gender equality concerns that were heard by the UKSC between 2017 and 2020. Naturally, therefore, it cannot be taken as exhaustive and may be added to further. It does, however, offer a foundation for considering the unique tools employed by judges in this area of law and how they cohere with and modify the general equality-attentive tools already identified. In the following section, I turn to further unpack these unique tools in the cases where they were used. Due to the constraints of space, I will limit my analysis to the five cases where the overall outcome appears to be compatible with gender equality and justice.

Human Rights Case Law and the Judge's Toolbox in the UKSC

The first case to draw attention in consideration of the tools above is *Commissioner of Police of the Metropolis v DSD and another* (*DSD*).[35] Here the respondents – DSD and NBV – were two women who had been sexually assaulted by John Worboys, a London black cab driver who committed a range of sexual offences against women passengers in the early 2000s. DSD and NBV had initiated proceedings against the Commissioner of the Metropolitan Police Service (MPS) arguing that the police failed to carry out effective investigation of Worboys' crimes. Engaging sections 7 and 8 of the Human Rights Act 1998, they claimed that police failures in investigation had led to violation of their rights under Article 3 of the European Convention of Human Rights (ECHR). Following judgments in the respondents' favour at first instance and in the Court of Appeal, the MPS appealed to the UKSC. The central question before the Court related to the

[35] *DSD* (n 13).

nature of the duty to investigate ill-treatment constituting an Article 3 violation.[36] The crux of the issue was whether a duty existed towards individuals, as opposed to the public at large, to investigate ill-treatment perpetrated by a non-state actor, and whether in such circumstances the positive obligation is confined to putting structures in place which enable investigation to be carried out, or whether it extends to the operational conduct of investigation. The UKSC dismissed the appeal, determining that there is a positive obligation to conduct a proper inquiry into alleged behaviour violating Article 3, and that serious operational failures are sufficient to establish a claim, as opposed to structural/systemic failures. This conclusion facilitated state accountability for the litigants at hand and sharpens understanding of the nature of police duty and positive obligations when it comes to serious crimes, including sexual offences.

In the reasoning underpinning this judgment, one of the human rights-focused tools outlined above came particularly to the fore: interpretation or deployment of ECtHR jurisprudence in a way that supports an outcome compatible with gender equality concerns. This was particularly apparent in Lord Kerr's leading judgment, with which Lady Hale agreed. Lord Kerr foregrounded *MC v Bulgaria*[37] as authority for the proposition that Article 3 includes a duty pertaining to ill-treatment by non-state actors, and that operational errors will suffice to establish liability, and he cited subsequent cases supporting this proposition.[38] Rejecting the interpretation of *Assenov v Bulgaria*,[39] and the later cases of *Gäfgen v Germany*[40] and *El-Masri v The Former Yugoslav Republic of Macedonia*[41] offered by the appellant,[42] he concluded that on his reading the existing judgments 'amount to clear and constant case law of the Strasbourg court'.[43] Lord Kerr also rejected the narrower interpretation of the ECtHR case law advanced by Lord Hughes on the structural/operational failure point – Lord Hughes asserting that the latter will not suffice – and the associated public policy 'floodgates' argument.[44] When it came to Lord Neuberger, his judgment adopted a similarly wide interpretation of the ECtHR authorities, which he narrated as compatible with domestic case law in the area.[45] While Lord Hughes and Lord Mance – the latter also adopting a narrower approach albeit formulated slightly differently[46] – agreed that the appeal should be dismissed, the approach to case law authorities adopted by Lord Kerr and Lord Neuberger

[36] ibid para 6.
[37] *MC v Bulgaria* (2005) 40 EHRR 20.
[38] eg, *Vasilyev v Russia*, App No 32704/04, judgment of 17 December 2009.
[39] *Assenov v Bulgaria* (1998) 28 EHRR 652.
[40] *Gäfgen v Germany* (2010) 52 EHRR 1.
[41] *El-Masri v The Former Yugoslav Republic of Macedonia* (2012) 57 EHRR 25.
[42] *DSD* (n 13) [46]–[48].
[43] ibid [48].
[44] ibid [53]. Lord Hughes's summary on this point is outlined at [102].
[45] ibid [97].
[46] ibid [141]–[153].

appears particularly capable of recognising and responding to everyday failures that may occur in legal responses to serious crimes such as sexual assault.

In his judgment, Lord Kerr also briefly employed a second judging tool when it came to the argument that the question posed to the Court should be left to the ECtHR in Strasbourg: interpretation of the Human Rights Act in a way that facilitates analysis and grappling with gender equality concerns. Drawing support from recent domestic case law,[47] he asserted that 'reticence by the courts of the UK to decide whether a Convention right has been violated would be an abnegation of our statutory obligation under section 6 of [the Human Rights Act]'.[48] Understanding the Court as empowered by section 6 in this way was important to the overall outcome of *DSD*. Here, while certainly a secondary tool, we see an approach to the Human Rights Act which supports judicial scrutiny of state action and alleged rights violations in cases of this kind at the domestic level.

The second case we will look at is *R (Steinfeld and Keidan) v Secretary of State for the International Development* (*Steinfeld*).[49] This case focused on the absence of legal provision facilitating different-sex couples to enter into a civil partnership. The appellants were a couple who wished to enter into such a legal arrangement due to personal objections to marriage. Following adoption of the Marriage (Same Sex Couples) Act 2013, civil partnerships were not abolished, but neither were they extended to different-sex couples. The appellants argued that this constituted a breach of Article 14 of the ECHR, read in conjunction with Article 8. After no violation was found at first instance, the Court of Appeal determined that the rights in question had been breached, but that the government's 'wait and evaluate' policy – whereby further consultation and data-gathering was to be carried out before making a determination on reform – was justified. At the UKSC, it was held that the rights interference was not justified on policy grounds, nor did the government's approach fall within the margin of appreciation. A declaration of incompatibility was accordingly issued. *Steinfeld* thus found a need to extend legal recognition of different-sex relationships, declining to determine such social policy issues as lying outside the court's remit.

The main judging tool that can be detected in this case is an approach to justification of the human rights violation at hand that is cognisant of gender equality and related concerns, here those pertaining to legal recognition of relationship status and family forms. Interference with Convention rights was accepted by the time the case appeared before the UKSC, leaving the case to turn on the point of justification. Again delivering the leading judgment, Lord Kerr adopted an approach that differed from the Court of Appeal. Rejecting the respondent's reliance on ECtHR jurisprudence such as *Schalk and Kopf v Austria*[50] as offering a wide margin

[47] In particular Lord Wilson's comments in *Moohan v Lord Advocate* [2014] UKSC 67, [2015] AC 901.

[48] *DSD* (n 13) [78].

[49] See n 13 above.

[50] *Schalk and Kopf v Austria* (2010) 53 EHRR 20.

of appreciation in terms of the timing of legislative change,[51] he engaged in a detailed exploration of justification. Drawing comparison with *Vallianatos v Greece*,[52] Lord Kerr stated that what must be shown:

> is that it was necessary to exclude different sex couples from civil partnerships for an indefinite period, while inquiries, consultations and surveys were conducted and a decision based on these could be made. I consider that that necessity has not been established.[53]

Considering the four-stage test for justification established in *R (Aguilar Quila) v Secretary of State for the Home Department*,[54] he concluded that the case fell on the first limb: the government accepted that the difference in question did not pursue a legitimate aim. He stated: 'what it seeks is tolerance of the discrimination while it sorts out how to deal with it. That cannot be characterised as a legitimate aim'.[55] This approach to justification was facilitated in part by a different reading of ECtHR authorities – including the jurisprudence on margin of appreciation as well as the case of *Walden v Liechtenstein*,[56] which the Court of Appeal relied on – and so intersects with this tool also. In this respect, it is evident that the tools of ECtHR interpretation and an approach to justification that is attentive to concerns relevant to gender equality may overlap. Lord Kerr's reasoning demonstrates how justification may be examined in differing ways, shaping discussion of the equality issues in question.

The third case for consideration engages tools familiar from *DSD* and *Steinfeld*, but also introduces a new tool in the toolbox. This case is *In the Matter of an Application by Siobhan McLaughlin for Judicial Review* (*McLaughlin*).[57] The applicant was a woman who had lived with her partner for 23 years prior to his death. The couple had four children together. On her partner's death, Ms McLaughlin sought to claim bereavement payment and widowed parent's allowance (WPA), both of which were declined due to the fact that she was not married to her partner. A judicial review was undertaken on the basis of an asserted incompatibility with Article 14 of the ECHR, read with Article 8. The case was partially successful at first instance, a declaration of incompatibility being made in relation to WPA but not the bereavement payment. At the Court of Appeal, however, no incompatibility with Article 14 was found, whether read with Article 8 or with Article 1 of Protocol 1. The case before the UKSC focused on WPA, with the Court finding by a majority that there was incompatibility with Article 14 read alongside Article 8. Lord Hodge delivered a dissenting judgment grounded in a different reading of ECtHR jurisprudence. A declaration of

[51] *Steinfeld* (n 13), [26]–[29] and [36].
[52] *Vallianatos v Greece* (2013) 59 EHRR 12.
[53] *Steinfeld* (n 13) [40].
[54] *R (Aguilar Quila) v Secretary of State for the Home Dept* [2011] UKSC 45, [2012] 1 AC 621.
[55] *Steinfeld* (n 13) [42].
[56] *Walden v Liechtenstein*, App No 33916/96, judgment of 16 March 2000.
[57] *McLaughlin* (n 13).

incompatibility was made. Similarly to *Steinfeld*, this case found a need to extend legal recognition and entitlements to wider family forms and recognised the ongoing nature of parenting responsibilities following a partner's death.

In *McLaughlin*, four main judging tools can be observed as engaged by judges across the case. First, as with the previous two cases, ECtHR jurisprudence is interpreted or deployed by the majority in the UKSC in a manner that supports analysis of gender equality issues. A particular difference of opinion came to the fore in the case regarding *Shackell v UK*.[58] This involved a complaint submitted to the ECtHR regarding widow's benefits which was determined to be inadmissible. The issue arising was how *Shackell* should be read in relation to the case at hand. Lady Hale, delivering the leading judgment, distinguished the facts involved from those in Ms McLaughlin's case. Taking a different approach, Lord Mance asserted that *Shackell* should not be determined as correct, due to the fact that it did not address the purpose of widowed mother's allowance, namely, the interests of children. Lord Hodge, in contrast, determined in his dissenting opinion that *Shackell* should be followed. This interpretation led him to conclude that the appeal should be dismissed. Here it is possible to see the significant difference that ECtHR interpretation can make. The interpretations of *Shackell*, and its relationship to the facts in the present case, observable in the judgments of Lady Hale and Lord Mance, allowed them to consider the case substantively and grapple with the gender equality concerns arising.

The second tool detectable in *McLaughlin* is also familiar from the discussion above: an interpretation of proportionality and justification which helps to achieve equality outcomes. Following identification of the legitimate aim of promoting marriage in society, Lady Hale concluded in her reasoning that declining Ms McLaughlin the benefit in question was not a proportionate means of achieving that aim.[59] Her understanding was outlined as follows: 'the allowance exists because of the responsibilities of the deceased and the survivor towards their children. Those responsibilities are the same whether or not they are married to or in a civil partnership with one another'.[60] In particular, Lady Hale noted that the facts of the case – a long-term partnership where both parties were parents of all children – made this conclusion on the absence of justification straightforward to reach.[61] Again a contrasting approach was taken by Lord Hodge, who did not see a disproportionality that could not be objectively justified.[62] In elaborating on her approach to proportionality, Lady Hale engaged a third tool: use of alternative human rights sources to support understandings of equality. Specifically, she made reference to the United Nations Convention on the Rights of the Child. While it was not directly binding on the Court, Lady Hale used this treaty to place

[58] *Shackell v UK* App No 45851/99, decision of 27 April 2000.
[59] *McLaughlin* (n 13) [38]–[39].
[60] ibid [39].
[61] ibid [42].
[62] ibid [87].

the concerns of the case in a wider human rights context. This involves drawing attention to the fact that an international obligation exists to protect the best interests of children, and that 'denying children the benefit of social insurance simply because their parents were not married to one another is inconsistent with that obligation'.[63]

The fourth tool deployed in *McLaughlin* is one that also has not been encountered so far: centring the human aspect of human rights. In her judgment, Lady Hale outlined the facts of Ms McLaughlin's case before engaging in a socio-legal history of bereavement benefits from the early 1900s to the present day.[64] In this narration, she brought into view the changing position of women in society and of family life more generally. She concluded that

> in essence, therefore, what began as a long-term replacement of a wife's and children's loss of a breadwinning husband's income, moved to a long-term replacement of a breadwinner's income while children were growing up, and is now a transitional compensation for the immediate financial loss suffered by the survivor and children on bereavement.[65]

Throughout the judgment, Lady Hale also referred to Ms McLaughlin by name. In combination, this approach serves to bring the individual litigant, and the social context of the human rights provisions in question, to the fore rather than undertaking an exclusively technical or doctrinal analysis. While not delivering his own judgment in this particular case, this tool often appears as part of Lord Kerr's judgments also,[66] bringing an important human and contextualising element to judicial reasoning which demonstrates deep engagement with the litigant and their everyday life.[67]

Let us turn now to the fourth case for consideration: *RR v Secretary of State for Work and Pensions* (*RR*).[68] This case succeeded the earlier *R (Carmichael) v Secretary of State for Work and Pensions*[69] and concerned remedies for those negatively affected by the government's 'bedroom tax'. This required a deduction to eligible rent for social sector housing if it was determined that the number of bedrooms in the property exceeded the size of the household. The appellant, RR, lived with his severely disabled partner and received housing benefit for their two-bedroom social housing property. The couple lived in separate bedrooms to accommodate medical equipment and to enable effective sleep for RR as caregiver. A reduction to RR's benefit entitlement was applied. After a decision in his favour at the First-tier Tribunal, which found discrimination on the grounds of disability and applied section 3(1) of the Human Rights Act to read down the

[63] ibid [40].
[64] ibid [4]–[12].
[65] ibid [12].
[66] See, eg, Lord Kerr's judgment in *R (EM (Eritrea)) v Secretary of State for the Home Dept* [2014] UKSC 12, [2014] AC 1321.
[67] See further Lady Hale (ch 2).
[68] *RR* (n 13).
[69] *R (Carmichael) v Secretary of State for Work and Pensions* [2016] UKSC 58, [2016] 1 WLR 4550. See also *R (Rutherford) v Secretary of State for Work and Pensions* [2016] EWCA Civ 29, [2016] HLR 8.

relevant legislation, the case was appealed to the Court of Appeal but was stayed until the *Carmichael* judgment was delivered. Following the finding that Article 14 of the ECHR, read with Article 8, was violated in *Carmichael*, the Housing Benefit and Universal Credit (Size Criteria) (Miscellaneous Amendments) Regulations 2017 were introduced. *RR* went straight to the UKSC where the main issue for consideration was the effect of *Carmichael* on decision-makers in the housing benefit system regarding claims predating the 2017 amendment.[70] The appellant argued that section 6 of the Human Rights Act made it unlawful for decision-makers to apply the 'bedroom tax' in a manner that breached the ECHR. Lady Hale delivered the Court's judgment and concluded that a public authority, court or tribunal could disapply 'a provision of subordinate legislation which would otherwise result in their acting incompatibly with a Convention right, where this is necessary in order to comply with the HRA'.[71] In so far as it affirmed the power of public authorities to remedy discrimination relevant to families with relations of care that differ from the norm, *RR* can be regarded as an outcome compatible with gender equality goals.[72]

Two main tools were engaged by Lady Hale in delivering judgment for the Court. The first of these is interpretation or deployment of domestic human rights case law in a way that supports a grappling with the equality issues in the case at hand. In making his argument, the appellant relied on a domestic disability living allowance case which also engaged section 6 of the Human Rights Act: *Mathieson v Secretary of State for Work and Pensions*.[73] This case involved suspension of the allowance to a child in hospital in violation of Article 14 read alongside Article 1 of Protocol 1, which was determined to be unlawful under section 6(1) of the Human Rights Act. Lady Hale confirmed the comparison with the present case and also explored subsequent case law where *Mathieson* had been applied.[74] She rejected the respondent's argument that *Mathieson* was a 'one off', reading the jurisprudence instead to assert that 'the courts have consistently held that, where it is possible to do so, a provision of subordinate legislation which results in a breach of a Convention right must be disregarded'.[75]

Alongside this, Lady Hale also engaged in statutory interpretation of the Human Rights Act in a way that supports engagement with the central gender equality concerns arising. In *RR*, it is again possible to see how interpretation of this legislation can be a key for outcomes that support such concerns. In her conclusion on the ability of public authorities to disapply a provision of subordinate legislation which violated ECHR rights, Lady Hale stated that 'subordinate legislation is subordinate to the requirements of an Act of Parliament. The Human

[70] *RR* (n 13) at [3].
[71] ibid [27].
[72] On care and vulnerability see further Martha Albertson Fineman, 'The Vulnerable Subject: Anchoring Equality in the Human Condition' (2008) 20 *Yale Journal of Law and Feminism* 1.
[73] *Mathieson v Secretary of State for Work and Pensions* [2015] UKSC 47, [2015] 1 WLR 3250.
[74] *RR* (n 13) [18]–[23].
[75] ibid [30].

Rights Act is an Act of Parliament and its requirements are clear.'[76] She stressed that the Human Rights Act 'draws a clear and careful distinction between primary and subordinate legislation'[77] in both section 3 and section 6. The Human Rights Act was thus read, alongside relevant case law, to support disapplication of the relevant regulations in the case at hand. Taken together, these two tools led to an outcome which is capable of responding to disability and caring relationships and engaging with state obligations in such contexts.

The final case for consideration is *R (AR) v Chief Constable of Greater Manchester Police*.[78] This case pertained to an acquittal for a sexual offence which was disclosed in an Enhanced Criminal Record Certificate (ECRC), and whether this disclosure violated Articles 6 and 8 of the ECHR. The appellant had been acquitted of the rape of a 17-year-old girl who was a passenger in his taxi. In the course of a job application for a lecturing post this was disclosed in an ECRC. The issue before the UKSC focused on Article 8 and the extent to which interference with this right was justified and proportionate. The role of appellate courts in reviewing a judge's finding of proportionality was also raised. The Court dismissed the appeal, finding that the requirement to protect 'young and vulnerable persons'[79] outweighed the effect of disclosure on the appellant. In reaching this conclusion, this case took into account the importance of safeguarding against sexual abuse, and the potential for it, in relevant employment contexts. The case undoubtedly raises very difficult issues of balance between the rights of the individual appellant and the rights of wider society, in particular women and young people.[80] In *AR*, the UKSC struck this balance in a way that recognised that an interference with Article 8 is generated in the ECRC process but acknowledged the societal justification for such interference.

One overarching tool is evident in this case, which is familiar from discussion above. In delivering the Court's judgment Lord Carnwath made use of the tool of approaching proportionality in a manner that is compatible with gender equality concerns and analysis, namely the need to protect society from potential sexual offending. Rejecting the appellant's reliance on *R (RK) v Chief Constable of South Yorkshire Police*[81] to assert that the officers or judge needed to conduct a 'detailed analysis' of the evidence at trial in order to render the interference with Article 8 justified, he also noted that 'it is to be borne in mind that the information about the charge and acquittal was … a matter of public record, and might have come to a potential employer's knowledge from other sources'.[82] Taken together with the significance of the acquittal to the employment position applied for, and the seriousness of the offence engaged, the ECRC disclosure

[76] ibid [27].
[77] ibid [28].
[78] *AR* (n 13).
[79] ibid [17], citing HH Judge Raynor QC at first instance.
[80] See also, eg, Clare McGlynn, '*R v A (No 2)*' in Hunter, McGlynn and Rackley (n 2).
[81] *R (RK) v Chief Constable of South Yorkshire Police* [2013] EWHC 1555 (Admin).
[82] *AR* (n 13) [70].

was taken as proportionate on the facts. In a postscript to the judgment, Lord Carnwath made clear that the limited issues raised in the appeal facilitated this 'clear conclusion' to be reached.[83] However, he does note that the ECRC process raises wider concerns, including regarding acquittal disclosures. This suggests that, when making its decision and engaging in an analysis of proportionality, the Court in *AR* gave careful consideration to the nature of the role applied for and the particular relationships it would involve.

Further Strengthening Human Rights Judging Attentive to Gender Equality

Following this analysis of recent human rights case law, it is necessary to consider what conclusions might be drawn. Without doubt, the cases explored above demonstrate use of gender equality-attentive judging tools which are tailored to the area of human rights law. Some of these tools are used frequently: specifically, interpretative approaches to domestic and regional human rights jurisprudence, interpretation of justification and proportionality, and statutory interpretation of the Human Rights Act to support analysis of gender equality issues. Other tools appear less frequently: engagement of alternative human rights sources and approaches which foreground the human aspect of human rights are detectable, but not in every case. Sometimes these tools are intentionally drawn upon in a feminist way – for example, by Lady Hale – while at other times their use may facilitate, but not actively pursue, aims of gender justice. Nevertheless, what emerges from this study is that an approach to human rights judging that demonstrates reasoning compatible with gender equality does exist within the UKSC. Examination of this recent set of case law demonstrates that judges are making use of a human rights-focused toolbox to engage with the legal issues arising. Between 2017 and 2020 use of these tools was particularly evident in the work of some judges – Lady Hale and, significantly for the purpose of reflections in this collection, Lord Kerr again appeared at the forefront – and many elements of good practice can be identified that stand to be thought through further. In order to continue to enhance and develop this work and discussion of it in the UK system I suggest that two points in particular may be considered.

First, following from the above, judges at all levels can be encouraged to reflect on their approach to human rights judging, how they read the cases that come before them, and the extent to which they employ the judging tools identified above or, potentially, others. As the actors with leading expertise in judicial decision-making, and holding significant power to shape the law,[84] it is

[83] ibid [72].

[84] Albeit, of course, they are not the only actors who do so: Margaret Davies, 'The Law Becomes Us: Rediscovering Judgment' (2012) 20 *Feminist Legal Studies* 167.

important for judges to enter into conversations about these tools, their utility, the frequency of their use, and their future. Whether overtly committed to understandings of justice and equality that are influenced by feminist thinking, or interested in how the law can better respond to and integrate the people it acts upon more generally, there is scope for all judges engaging with human rights law to be reflexive about the tools above and how they might fit in their work. It may be that judges have not yet dedicated detailed thought to how these tools may intersect with equality issues, even as they deploy them, or considered the potential they may hold. Naturally, these conversations are particularly important at the appellate level – in particular the Court of Appeal and the UKSC – where the judges are at the forefront of shaping jurisprudence and setting key precedents which integrate best practice.

Second, in thinking about how commitment to gender equality in judging might be furthered in the area of human rights law there is also a place for increased dialogue between judges and human rights scholars working on gender equality. Many of the tools that appear to be used in the cases discussed intersect with tools that have been employed by scholarly work on human rights and gender, domestically, regionally and internationally.[85] Where scholars working in this field analyse a particular judgment or line of case law, they often engage alternative approaches to justification, interpretation of the Human Rights Act, or domestic and ECtHR case law, for example. There may be much in common, therefore, between academic legal analysis and judging in this area. It is of course important to note that judges are in a unique position that does not fully equate with the legal academic. Nevertheless, given the overlap on the means through which both groups approach law and legal reasoning, furthering discussion of the judge's toolbox may usefully involve open conversations on best practice between the bench and academia which begin with what they may have in common and the two-way learning that may emerge.

These conversations – internally within the judiciary and externally with other actors working on human rights law in broader ways – must go beyond general discussions on gender equality and judging to home in on the particular tools that are tailored to this area of law. This is essential not only to begin to move forward a human rights jurisprudence attentive to gender equality, but also to potentially move to a new stage in the feminist judging methodology both in academic thinking and in judicial practice. As scholars continue to explore

[85] eg Harriet Samuels, 'Feminizing Human Rights Adjudication: Feminist Method and the Proportionality Principle' (2013) 21 *Feminist Legal Studies* 39; Susan Easton, 'Feminist Perspectives on the Human Rights Act: Two Cheers for Incorporation' (2002) 8 *Res Publica* 21; Ivana Radacic, 'Gender Equality Jurisprudence of the European Court of Human Rights' (2008) 19 *European Journal of International Law* 841; Keina Yoshida, 'Towards Intersectionality in the European Court of Human Rights: The Case of *BS v Spain*' (2013) 21 *Feminist Legal Studies* 195; Gayle Binion, 'Human Rights: A Feminist Perspective' (1995) 17 *Human Rights Quarterly* 509; Karen Knop, *Gender and Human Rights* (Oxford, OUP, 2004).

feminist judging in the 'real world', nuances between areas of law are important and a set of additional, tailored toolboxes of use in undertaking and analysing human rights judging can begin to emerge. The analysis of this chapter has shown that in this work Lord Kerr's judicial legacy offers significant points of departure and analysis that stand to be engaged further in expanding the starting point offered in this chapter. Lord Kerr's work, accordingly, may emerge as a central part of the discussion on the judge's toolbox, its contents, and the future directions that may be pursued on equality and judicial practice.

4

Lord Kerr's Dissents: Jewels in the Crown of the Supreme Court

RACHEL CAHILL-O'CALLAGHAN*

> The opportunity to dissent may not be the ultimate jewel in the Crown of British justice but it is certainly a gem to be treasured.[1]

Introduction

The quotation from Lord Kerr introducing this chapter highlights that judicial dissent has long been an important facet of the common law tradition.[2] A published dissent in this context renders transparent the judicial independence necessary for robust and legitimate decision making. It also provides an insight into the individual Justice and the factors that impassion him or her to stand in opposition. This chapter will examine the factors that underpin Lord Kerr's decisions to dissent and the values that serve as a constant anchor in his dissenting opinions. But dissent does not simply serve as a beacon of independence, it is also evidence of the judicial difference essential to robust decision making. The UK Supreme Court (UKSC) is characterised as a collegiate court, where members of the court are prepared to engage with different views to achieve the best decision.[3] As such, a collegiate court acknowledges the important role that different perspectives and philosophies perform in refining and ensuring high

* The author would like to thank Professor Alan Paterson OBE, Pauline Roberts and Dr Bernadette Rainey for their constructive comments.

[1] Lord Kerr, 'Dissenting judgments – Self Indulgence or Self Sacrifice?', The Birkenhead Lecture, 8 October 2012, available at www.supremecourt.uk/docs/speech-121008.pdf.

[2] ibid. There are some notable exceptions to this tradition, eg, the Judicial Committee of the Privy Council. It was only in 1966 that dissenting opinions within the JCPC were allowed to be published: see the Judicial Committee (Dissenting Opinions) Order 1966 (SI 1100).

[3] Alan Paterson, *Final Judgment: The Last Law Lords and the Supreme Court* (Oxford, Hart Publishing, 2013) passim.

quality decision making.[4] A published dissent is evidence that behind closed doors those who are making the decisions in the highest courts are challenged. It is evidence of robust collegiate decision-making processes which value and retain difference, and thus serve to limit consensus and the bias that consensus perpetuates.[5]

Although this important role in the UKSC is shared by all Justices, Lord Kerr has been the most consistent voice of overt opposition. In the context of other apex courts, Lord Kerr was not a prolific dissenter – indeed, he consistently espoused a commitment to collegiate decision making – but it was Lord Kerr who was the most likely to stand alone in opposition to the majority.[6] To be effective in refining judicial decision making, a dissent must have three characteristics: it must be perceived by the majority as consistent; it must be seen as robust; and the majority must engage with the dissenting opinion.[7]

This chapter will explore the consistent positions articulated in Lord Kerr's dissents, highlighting his steadfast resolve to advocate for those rendered vulnerable by the legal system and his determination to extend the interpretation of the European Convention of Human Rights (ECHR) to protect them. Underpinning his decisions to oppose the majority are the values that Lord Kerr affirmed and it is the constant affirmation of these values that provides the consistency essential for an effective dissent.

Many judges and academics have noted significant engagement with different opinions behind closed doors, but published engagement with a dissenting opinion is something more. It is a public acknowledgment, by the majority, of the strength of the opposing argument. It is also evidence of engagement with the opposing position and the refining effect this may have. Although this form of public engagement is often evident when multiple judges oppose the majority, it is less evident when there is a single voice of dissent. But this is not true of Lord Kerr. In contrast to many of the Justices in the UKSC, a lone dissenting opinion delivered by Lord Kerr elicited significant critical engagement by his peers.

Throughout his time on the Supreme Court bench, Lord Kerr stood against the majority to robustly defend a core set of values. In doing so, his dissenting judgments bore all the characteristics of effective dissents that served to refine the decision making of the court. Given the decrease in dissenting judgments in the UKSC, it is increasingly important to treasure dissents and those who are prepared to stand alone to deliver them.

[4] Deanell Tacha, 'The C word: On Collegiality' (1995) 56 *Ohio State Law Journal* 585.

[5] Cass Sunstein, *Why Societies Need Dissent* (Boston, Harvard University Press, 2003).

[6] Personal communication from Professor Alan Paterson. Lord Kerr was one of the least likely to deliver a concurring judgment. See Rachel Cahill-O'Callaghan, *Values in the Supreme Court: Decisions, Divisions and Diversity* (Oxford, Hart Publishing, 2020) 137.

[7] There are many reasons why the majority may not openly engage with a dissent, but in the absence of public deliberations engagement in a published judgment is the only public evidence of engagement behind closed doors.

The Values of Dissent

> [Dissents] speak loudly of the independence of our judiciary and, in consequence, inspire the confidence that the public place in the administration of justice in this country. The opportunity to dissent has never been more important than it is today.[8]

Lord Kerr notes, above, the important public role of dissent. It has been argued by Adler that in many cases decided by the apex court of appeal this expression of judicial difference is a reflection of the 'competing shifting values of society'.[9] The publication of dissenting judgments draws public attention to those values and enhances judicial legitimacy.[10] Although Lord Kerr suggested that this argument is perhaps 'too high-flown',[11] the fact that a number of the cases which divided judicial opinion in the UKSC have received significant media attention would suggest that it has some traction.[12] Indeed, in many of the cases which closely divided the Supreme Court, the judgments revealed the tensions between the different value positions that exist in society.

One such example divided the court on whether the abortion legislation in Northern Ireland, at the time, was incompatible with Articles 3 and 8 of the ECHR.[13] The case dealt with a procedural and substantive issue. The procedural issue challenged the standing of the Northern Ireland Human Rights Commission (NIHRC) to bring proceedings for judicial review. On this issue the majority (Lord Mance, Lord Reed, Lord Lloyd-Jones and Lady Black) held that the NIHRC had no standing, and the Court had no jurisdiction to declare the majority's view on the substantive issue. The substantive issue considered whether the law prohibiting abortion in Northern Ireland was compatible with the ECHR, in so far as that law prohibits abortion in cases of fatal foetal abnormality, rape and incest.[14] Unusually, despite the majority position on standing, the Justices delivered a decision on this issue. The judgments reveal the opposing values that underpinned the outcome.

This case, like many heard in the UKSC, raised issues on which '[d]iametrically opposed views, and every shade of opinion in between, are held with equal sincerity and conviction. Each side of the debate appeals to moral or religious values which are held with passionate intensity'.[15] The majority (Lady Hale, Lord Mance, Lord Kerr, Lord Wilson and Lady Black) held that the legislation was incompatible with Article 8 (the right to respect for private and family life), although Lady

[8] The Birkenhead Lecture (n 1) 21–22.

[9] John Adler, 'Dissents in the Courts of Last Resort: Tragic Choices' (2000) 20 *Oxford Journal of Legal Studies* 221.

[10] ibid.

[11] The Birkenhead Lecture (n 1) 8.

[12] See, eg, *R (Nicklinson) v Ministry of Justice* [2014] UKSC 38, [2015] AC 657.

[13] *In the matter of an application by the Northern Ireland Human Rights Commission for Judicial Review* [2018] UKSC 27, [2019] 1 All ER 173. See also Lady Hale (ch 2), Kathryn McNeilly (ch 3) and Brice Dickson (ch 6).

[14] ibid [41] per Lady Hale.

[15] ibid [336] per Lord Reed.

Black provided that the incompatibility was only in the limited context of fatal foetal abnormality. But Lord Kerr, with whom Lord Wilson agreed, went further and held that the legislation was incompatible with Article 3, which provides that 'no one shall be subjected to torture or to inhuman or degrading treatment or punishment.' In doing so, Lord Kerr asserted the duty of the state to protect those who are vulnerable, drawing on the lived experience of those who were affected by the decision:

> Termination of pregnancy is one of life's most traumatic and fraught experiences. To be required to travel away from home and to undergo an abortion in unfamiliar surroundings without the normal support network that a woman would expect and hope to have is in itself deeply upsetting. A girl or woman who has become pregnant as a result of rape or incest is already in a vulnerable position and liable to suffer extreme distress. So too a mother who has been told that the child she carries will not survive. That distress can only be increased and compounded by forcing the woman to seek termination of her pregnancy in a different country, away from her family and friends and without the support of her own doctor. The fact of being required to do so is in itself sufficient to expose her to the risk of inhuman and degrading treatment.[16]

Lord Kerr not only sought to ensure that the state protected the most vulnerable in society, he also advocated for the right of women and girls to assert their autonomy:

> Binding the girls and women of Northern Ireland to that edict means that they may not assert their autonomy in their own country. They are forbidden to do to their own bodies that which they wish to do; they are prevented from arranging their lives in the way that they want; they are denied the chance to shape their future as they desire.[17]

The relationship between vulnerability and autonomy was at the centre of Lord Kerr's position that the NIHRC must have standing to effectively support vulnerable individuals in asserting their autonomy:

> Moreover, the number of women who have had to endure the trauma of a fatal foetal abnormality pregnancy or a pregnancy which is the consequence of rape or incest and who would be prepared, after the event, to assert a violation of their rights cannot be presumed to be significant. If NIHRC is unable, by reason of a lack of standing, to bring proceedings to protect such women's rights, I consider that they will be deprived of the practical and effective remedy which Article 13 guarantees.[18]

The position expressed by Lord Kerr was not shared by all in Northern Ireland nor the majority on the Court. The division was due to the nature of the questions of

[16] ibid [238].
[17] ibid [261].
[18] ibid [200].

law the Court was asked to resolve; a decision which centred on competing values, as Lord Reed recognised:

> These are highly sensitive and contentious questions of moral judgement, on which views will vary from person to person, and from judge to judge, as is illustrated by the different views expressed in the present case.[19]

At the heart of the majority decision to deny standing was the separation of powers and the role of the court in a democracy as articulated by Lord Reed:

> National courts can equally respect the judgements made by the democratic institutions of their society, applying the principle of proportionality in a manner which reflects the constitutional principle of the separation of powers.[20]

It was also Lord Reed who argued that the legislation on abortion in Northern Ireland at that time was compatible with both Article 8 and Article 3, stating that:

> Nevertheless, a society cannot be bound under the Convention to permit behaviour which it considers morally repugnant, merely because a prohibition can be obviated. On the contrary, the fact that a prohibition imposed for moral reasons can be obviated may tend to support its proportionality, since it imposes less of a restriction in reality on those who do not share the moral values which underpin it.[21]

These brief extracts from the judgments reflect the values at the heart of the decision. Values which can be organised into 10 overarching motivations.[22] The values expressed in the decision to deny standing to the NIHRC were those of *tradition and conformity*; values which affirm the subordination of self for socially imposed expectations, including those imposed by religion, legal or social norms. These values prioritise the inhibition of actions that may disrupt or undermine the functioning of social groups. In contrast, the values expressed by Lord Kerr are those encompassed in *universalism and self-direction. Universalism* is the broadest value, with the motivational goal of the understanding, appreciation, and protection of the welfare of all people and nature. *Universalism* encompasses equality, social justice and protecting the vulnerable. Lord Kerr also emphasised *self-direction*, which affirms individual autonomy and freedom. The decision in this case opposes values encompassed in *conformity* and *tradition* against *universalism* and *self-direction.* These values are at the heart of many of the decisions

[19] ibid [362].
[20] ibid [341] per Lord Reed.
[21] ibid [358].
[22] Shalom Schwartz, 'Universals in the Content and Structure of Values: Theoretical Advances and Empirical Tests in 20 Countries' (1992) 25 *Advances in Experimental Social Psychology* 1; Shalom Schwartz et al, 'Refining the Theory of Basic Individual Values (2013) 103 *Journal of Personality and Social Psychology* 663.

that closely divided the Supreme Court in which Lord Kerr opposed the majority. Although an individual can affirm every value motivation, in reaching a decision between competing values it is the prioritisation of values that is important. In many of his dissenting decisions, Lord Kerr prioritised those values encompassed in *universalism* above other values.

The majority of cases where Lord Kerr was joined in opposition were heard by expanded panels, many of which raised an important point in relation to the ECHR.[23] In all of these cases where Lord Kerr dissented, he sought to extend the protection of individual rights by finding the legislative foundation incompatible with the ECHR so as to enable those at their most vulnerable to assert their autonomy. For example, in *Nicklinson*, which raised the difficult issue of the compatibility of the legislation governing assisted suicide with the ECHR, Lord Kerr wrote:

> [T]here is 'no defensible moral principle' in denying the appellants the means of achieving what, under Article 8 and by all the requirements of compassion and humanity, they should be entitled to do. To insist that these unfortunate individuals should continue to endure the misery that is their lot is not to champion the sanctity of life; it is to coerce them to endure unspeakable suffering.[24]

This case also dealt with 'sensitive life and death questions' and for many an issue of morality.[25] In *Nicklinson*, the majority chose not to find the law incompatible with the ECHR and so avoided having to issue a declaration to that effect, holding instead that the 'determination of the criminal law on a difficult, sensitive and controversial issue is one which is very much for Parliament'.[26] This was not the position held by Lord Kerr. He argued that:

> The view that Parliament might have the means to consider the issue more fully or on a broader canvas does not impel the conclusion that the courts should shy away from addressing the question whether the provision is incompatible with a Convention right, judged on the material that has been presented. On the contrary, such is the court's duty when presented with that claim.[27]

Again, Lord Kerr rejected the traditional position and affirmed values encompassed within *universalism* and *self-direction*. Lord Kerr decided 21 cases in which he was not alone in his opposition to the majority. Eight of these cases were 'close-call' decisions in which an opinion of a single judge swayed the final outcome of the case. Each case represented a decision between opposing values,

[23] Of the 21 cases in which Lord Kerr was not alone in his opposition of the majority, 14 were heard by expanded panels and eight of these involved determinations of compatibility with the ECHR. The dominant rights were those protected by Arts 8, 3, 2 and 14.

[24] See *Nicklinson* (n 12) [358].

[25] ibid [315] per Lady Hale.

[26] ibid [99].

[27] ibid [347].

and in each case Lord Kerr affirmed the values encompassed within *universalism* and *self-direction*.[28] Although many other Justices espouse and affirm the values encompassed within *universalism*, Lord Kerr was the most consistent advocate of those values and in doing so he supported the most vulnerable in society.[29]

The consistent, robust, affirmation of these values in opposition to the majority plays an important external role. It enhances judicial legitimacy through the reflection of the competing value positions that exist in society. Publication of the dissent acknowledges judicial difference and provides overt evidence of the 'conscientious exercise of judicial power' that ensures that the voices of opposition are heard.[30] But Lord Kerr's consistent position also served an important role inside the court.

The Value of Dissent: Refining Judicial Decision Making

The dissenting judge challenges the majority and if a dissent is effective it may refine judicial decision making.[31] Indeed, Justice Scalia, a former Associate Justice of the US Supreme Court, argued that 'the most important internal effect of a system permitting dissents and concurrences is to improve the majority opinion'.[32] Justice Bader Ginsburg also noted that 'an impressive dissent can lead the author of the majority opinion to refine and clarify her initial circulation'.[33] Lord Kerr suggested that this refining effect of dissent was evident in the UK Supreme Court:

> In my firm opinion (and I would say this, of course) the existence of contrary views and their enunciation in dissenting judgments do not inevitably detract from the authority of the opinion of the majority. On the contrary, where the majority has been required to address and deal with challenges to their reasoning, their judgments should be the more cogent and compelling as a consequence.[34]

These Justices highlight the power of dissent in refining the decision of the majority. This refining effect of dissent is not limited to coherence and clarity; disagreement and dissent also play an important role in limiting cognitive bias.

[28] Lord Kerr was most often joined in opposition by Lady Hale. Lady Hale was on the bench in 17 of the cases in which Lord Kerr was not alone in his opposition of the majority decision. She joined him in opposition in 11 of these cases. This is not to suggest that the Justices agreed on the reasoning, only that they agreed on the disposition of the case.

[29] For more detailed analysis of the value position of Lord Kerr see Cahill-O'Callaghan (n 6) 137–42.

[30] Justice Michael Kirby 'Consensus and Dissent', 10th Annual Hawke Lecture, Adelaide, 10 October 2007.

[31] The refining effect of dissent on decision making is the central theme of Sunstein's book on dissent (n 5).

[32] Antonin Scalia, 'The Dissenting Opinion' (1994) 19 *Journal of Supreme Court History* 33, 33.

[33] Ruth Bader Ginsburg, 'The Role of Dissenting Opinions' (2010) 95 *Minnesota Law Review* 1.

[34] The Birkenhead Lecture (n 1) 10–11.

Sunstein demonstrated the extensive psychological, social and institutional pressures that are exerted to promote consensus.[35] Pressures which are enhanced in decisions which engage political or moral debates. This pressure perpetuates the status quo, and silences minority voices, and in doing so conformity perpetuates bias. There is no suggestion of a single position dominating the UKSC, or a pressure to consensus imposed by the leadership of the Court, but the presence of an overt effective dissent, and of individuals who are prepared to stand alone to deliver it, is evidence that the refining effect of opposition continues to be embraced in the Court.

Cognitive Bias and Effective Dissent

Bias, in this chapter, does not carry with it the negative connotations that are typically associated with bias in a legal context.[36] This chapter is not asserting that the bias in this judicial context discriminates against a class of persons who are traditionally disadvantaged.[37] Rather, bias in a judicial context is the perpetuation of modified groupthink which underpins shared positions and consensus, and in turn may result in the dominance of a particular legal position or reasoning.[38] Groupthink is most evident when there is a small group of decision makers making an important and complex decision, and the outcome of the decision is undetermined.[39] It is further enhanced with shared frames of reference including the legal, social and institutional norms within which the decision is being reached.[40]

In this context, dissent challenges existing norms and assumptions and encourages the majority to scrutinise their decision making. It can disrupt, reshape and reframe the dominant positions.[41] As such, dissent serves to limit the influence of cognitive bias and improve decision quality by encouraging decision makers to think more divergently.[42] This is true even when a single individual opposes the majority.[43] This chapter does not argue that cognitive bias underpins consensus; rather, that evidence of overt dissent suggests a robust and challenging

[35] Sunstein (n 5) 14–38.

[36] See, eg, Kate Malleson 'Judicial Bias and Disqualification after *Pinochet (No.2)*' (2000) 63 *MLR* 119.

[37] Deborah Beim and Jonathan Kastellec, 'The Interplay of Ideological Diversity, Dissents, and Discretionary Review in the Judicial Hierarchy: Evidence from Death Penalty Cases' (2014) 76 *Journal of Politics* 1074.

[38] Irving Janis, *Victims of Groupthink: A Psychological Study of Foreign-Policy Decisions and Fiascoes* (Boston, Houghton Mifflin, 1972). Although groupthink is modified by impartiality, Hinkle and Nelson have evidenced the process in judicial panel decision-making: Rachael Hinkle and Michael Nelson, 'The Intergroup Foundations of Policy Influence' (2018) 71 *Political Research Quarterly* 729.

[39] Janis (ibid).

[40] Hinkle and Nelson (n 38).

[41] eg, Charlan Nemeth et al, 'Improving Decision Making by Means of Dissent' (2001) 31 *Journal of Applied Social Psychology* 48.

[42] ibid.

[43] Jeffrey Sonnenfeld, 'What Makes Great Boards Great' (2002) 80 *Harvard Business Review* 106; Paterson (n 3).

decision-making process which limits the potential for bias. But not all disagreements achieve this moderating effect. As mentioned above, an effective dissent must reflect three characteristics. It must be sufficiently robust but not dogmatic, it must be perceived by the other decision makers as a consistent position[44] and it must be considered by the majority. These characteristics are evident in the dissents delivered by Lord Kerr.

Delivering Dissent: Robust Opposition

> So far as that view [Hutchinson's view of greatness] connects judicial greatness with a willingness to forge one's own path or resist the pull of conformity then dissent offers the clearest manifestation of this.[45]

The association between judicial greatness and dissent recognises the benefits but also the costs of dissent. Dissent in the final courts is an affirmation of a judge's decision to overtly recognise his or her difference and to stand apart from the majority. But this is not without personal costs to the judge in time, effort and potentially collegiality. The psychological pressures are enhanced when there is institutional pressure to reach consensus. Although there is no clear evidence of this pressure in the UKSC, there was a significant increase in consensus during Lord Kerr's tenure. This may, in part, be related to the leadership of the court, as strong leadership is associated with increased collaborative decision making and thus a reduction in overt opposition. It may also be due to structural changes adopted by the leadership of the court, in particular the decision not to convene expanded panels.[46]

Lord Kerr served during the tenure of four Presidents: Lord Phillips, Lord Neuberger, Lady Hale and the current President Lord Reed.[47] During Lord Kerr's

[44] Stefan Schulz-Hardt, Marc Jochims and Dieter Frey, 'Productive Conflict in Group Decision Making: Genuine and Contrived Dissent as Strategies to Counteract Biased Information Seeking' (2002) 88 *Organizational Behaviour and Human Decision Processes* 563; Tobias Greitemeyer, Stefan Schulz-Hardt and Dieter Frey, 'The Effects of Authentic and Contrived Dissent on Escalation of Commitment in Group Decision Making' (2009) 39 *European Journal of Social Psychology* 639.

[45] Andrew Lynch, 'Introduction: What Makes a Dissent "Great"?' in Andrew Lynch (ed), *Great Australian Dissents* (Cambridge, CUP, 2016) 2; Allan C Hutchinson, *Laughing at the Gods: Great Judges and How They Made the Common Law* (Cambridge, CUP, 2012) 14.

[46] Expanded panels are associated with division in the court. This may be associated with the diversity of judicial opinion which an expanded panel enables and the difficulty in achieving consensus: see Cahill-O'Callaghan (n 6). There has been a significant reduction in the use of expanded panels following Lord Phillip's tenure as President. Alan Paterson, 'Creating a Group Orientated Supreme Court – Lord Neuberger's Legacy' (2021) 28 *International Journal of the Legal Profession* 107 and Alan Paterson, 'Presidency and the UK Supreme Court: Lord Neuberger's Legacy' in Daniel Clarry (ed), *The UK Supreme Court Yearbook 2018–2019, Vol 10* (Appellate Press, 2021) 248.

[47] Lord Kerr was on the bench when the UKSC opened in October 2009 and his final decision was confirmed in *Mastercard Incorporated v Walter Hugh Merricks* [2020] UKSC 51, released on 11 December 2020, 10 days after his death. Before his retirement, the court decided 736 cases. Of those decisions, 55 (7.6%) included a single dissent and a further 91 (12%) included more than just one dissent.

time on the bench, the average rate of division was 21 per cent, but this reduced from 26 per cent during the tenure of Lord Phillips, to 20 per cent with Lord Neuberger and further reduced during the tenure of Lady Hale to 16 per cent. Although the rate of division has increased with Lord Reed (22 per cent), it has not so far attained the early rates of division.

It is notable that despite the increase in agreement on the Supreme Court, Lord Kerr remained consistent in his opposition.[48] During his time on the Court, he decided 288 cases. Of these, almost one quarter divided judicial opinion on the final disposition of the case.[49] It is in the frequency of opposition that sets Lord Kerr apart from his peers. On average a Justice will find themselves in opposition to the majority (alone or in the company of others) in 7 per cent of cases. With the exception of Lord Rodger and Lord Sales, Lord Kerr was the most likely to oppose the majority throughout his tenure, and did so in 12 per cent of cases.[50]

The nature and form of division also speaks to the pressure to consensus in the UKSC. In panel decision making, the psychological pressures to conform are less when more than one person shares the burden of opposition. Indeed, seminal work by Solomon Asch identified that 37 per cent of subjects facing a unanimous majority buckled under pressure and gave conforming incorrect answers. When he added a second dissenter, the rate of conformity reduced significantly to 5 per cent.[51] This enhanced psychological pressure to reach consensus borne by the sole dissenter may explain, in part, the low rate of individual dissent in the UKSC. During the tenure of Lord Phillips, Justices were as likely to oppose the majority alone as with another. This has fundamentally changed. The rate of single dissents significantly decreased during the tenure of Lord Neuberger (7 per cent) to 4 per cent during Lady Hale's presidency and to the current low of 2 per cent under Lord Reed.

On average an individual Justice will dissent alone in 2 per cent of the cases he or she hears. Lord Kerr doubled that number, delivering a dissenting judgment alone in 4 per cent of cases. Although the rate at which he dissented alone did decrease with each successive President, Lord Kerr was the most likely of all the Justices to dissent alone.[52] It is his commitment to stand apart from his

[48] Lord Kerr opposed the majority in 14% of the cases he heard during the tenure of Lord Phillips, 13% during Lord Neuberger's tenure. This reduced during Lady Hale's tenure to 10%.

[49] The rate of division of the UK Supreme Court varies over time, with the average rate being slightly lower at 21%. Although a case was more likely to result in division when Lord Kerr sat on the bench, this was only slightly so.

[50] Lord Rodger opposed the majority in 13% of the cases he heard. Of the most recent appointments, Lord Sales has been in opposition in six of the first 36 cases he has decided (17%).

[51] Solomon Asch, 'Studies of Independence and Conformity: A Minority of One Against the Unanimous Majority' (1956) *Psychological Monographs* 1.

[52] The pattern of Lord Kerr's lone dissents changed over time, with a reduction associated with each President. Lord Brown, who spent less time on the bench, achieved the same rate of dissent. Lord Kerr dissented alone in 8% of the cases he heard during Lord Phillip's tenure. This reduced to 4% in Lord Neuberger's tenure and to 2% in Lady Hale's. He did not dissent alone in any cases during Lord Reed's tenure.

peers – to robustly oppose the majority with others or bear the burden alone – that sets Lord Kerr apart. If a great judge is one who is prepared to bear the costs of delivering a judgment in opposition to the majority, then Lord Kerr deserves this accolade.[53]

But robust opposition is not all that is needed to ensure an effective dissent. The dissent must give voice to a consistent, 'discernible judicial attitude or a philosophy which is plaintively or persistently raised against the mainstream of the Court's opinion'.[54] It is the consistent prioritisation of *universalism* by Lord Kerr that is central to this perception of earnestness and fundamental to the refining effect of his dissent.

Values and the Consistency of the Lone Dissent

At the heart of consistency is the motivation that underpins dissent. Central to the decision to dissent alone is the concept of disagreement and the motivation to highlight that the majority are wrong. It is this simple position that was presented by Lord Kerr when he noted that 'on the whole, judges dissent for … the seemingly banal reason that they have decided that their view is right or that *the conclusions that their colleagues have reached are wrong*'.[55] This view suggests that in every case, where a judge disagrees with an outcome, the judge will be willing to incur the costs of writing a separate judgment.[56] But decision making in the UKSC is a collegiate process and Paterson[57] has highlighted the numerous occasions where difference is resolved behind closed doors: through compromise, as a response to colleagues' opposing arguments, or simply because it is what the law requires.[58] Indeed, Lord Neuberger suggests that many issues of difference are resolved at this early stage:

> Normally the meetings at least serve to identify the areas of disagreement and agreement. But they often serve to bridge gaps, to refine ideas, and to get rid of confusing material, or even to achieve compromises which is excellent, provided that they are principled and clarifying, rather than messy.[59]

[53] It is a testament to Lord Kerr that his dissents did not create any ill will in the Court (personal communication from Professor Alan Paterson).

[54] Lynch (n 45) 3.

[55] The Birkenhead Lecture (n 1) 17 (emphasis added).

[56] Jeffrey Segal and others, 'Ideological Values and the Votes of the US Supreme Court Revisited' (1995) 57 *The Journal of Politics* 812; Jeffrey Segal and Harold Spaeth, *The Supreme Court and the Attitudinal Model Revisited* (Cambridge, CUP, 2002).

[57] Paterson (n 3).

[58] Harry Edwards, 'The Effects of Collegiality on Judicial Decision Making' (2003) 151 *University of Pennsylvania Law Review* 1639.

[59] Lord Neuberger, 'Tweaking the Curial Veil', The Blackstone Lecture, 15 November 2014, available at www.supremecourt.uk/docs/speech-141115.pdf.

A published lone dissent therefore requires more than disagreement. It requires a sufficient commitment by the judge to his or her position to publicly acknowledge the difference. The decision to dissent, particularly alone, must be motivated by something deeper than simple disagreement. It requires what Justice Brennan refers to as 'passion': 'the individual emotional and intuitive response to a given set of facts or arguments that moves a judge to act to redress injustice and to alleviate suffering'.[60] This emotional and intuitive response is a response to the value decision. This instinctive response may be refined, affirmed or rejected with deliberation and reasoning. In cases where deliberation does not provide a clear outcome, the decision may remain anchored in the instinctive value response. It is the passion evoked by strongly held values that Danelski argues is at the heart of the decision to dissent alone.[61]

The recognition by the majority of the consistent passion and value positions of the dissenting judge suggests a perception of the strength of position required to effectively challenge the majority.[62] In his tribute to Lord Kerr, Lord Reed noted the role that instinct played in Lord Kerr's decision to dissent and the important role this played in moderating the decision making of the court:

> He has left a very substantial legacy notwithstanding the fact that a significant proportion of his judgments have been dissenting. Some of those may yet bear fruit and they all demonstrate that there was another way of viewing the case beyond the majority decision. They reflect a very valuable quality that Brian's strong and instinctive sense of justice has provided, a counterbalance to members of the court who instinctively take a more legalistic approach.[63]

It is this instinctive response that mediates the role of values and it is in a published lone dissent, where a judge is 'free from the deadening effects of compromise', that we gain the clearest insight into the passions and the values of the individual and those facets of the law that they hold most dear.[64]

Lord Reed noted the passions of Lord Kerr that were evident to his peers. Indeed, Lord Reed suggested that it was Lord Kerr's judicial career in Northern Ireland that set him apart and underpinned his particular 'sensitivity to the responsibility that judges have to ensure that the lawfulness of government incursions into individual freedoms is subject to careful scrutiny'.[65] Lord Kerr suggested

[60] William Brennan, 'Reason, Passion, and 'The Progress of the Law' (1988) 10 *Cardozo Law Review* 3, 9, cited in Stephen Wizner, 'Passion in Legal Argument and Judicial Decision Making: A Comment on Goldberg v. Kelly' (1988) 10 *Cardozo Law Review* 179.

[61] David Danelski, 'Values as Variables in Judicial Decision-Making: Notes toward a Theory' (1965) 19 *Vanderbilt Law Review* 721, 728.

[62] Joseph Priester and Richard Petty 'Source Attributions and Persuasion: Perceived Honesty as a Determinant of Message Scrutiny' (1995) 21 *Personality and Social Psychology Bulletin* 637.

[63] Lord Reed's tribute to Lord Kerr on his retirement from the Supreme Court, available at www.supremecourt.uk/news/tribute-for-lord-kerr.html (at 6'10").

[64] Wizner (n 60).

[65] Lord Reed (n 63) at 2'33".

that this was not simply a responsibility but a duty. It is this duty and his passion to protect fundamental rights that was evident in the reasoning of the majority of Lord Kerr's lone dissenting opinions.

Lord Kerr dissented alone in 13 cases during his tenure on the bench. Ten of these cases centred on the determination of compatibility with rights enshrined in the ECHR, and the majority concerned the criminal justice system. As Lord Reed noted, Lord Kerr's dominant concern was 'for the vulnerable and his insistence that proper care must be taken in the administration of justice especially when something as important as depriving someone of their liberty is at stake'.[66]

In the criminal context, Lord Kerr recognised the vulnerability of the individual throughout the legal process and the duty on the state and its officers to mitigate this. As he noted in his dissent in *McGowan*:

> There is no warrant for the belief that vulnerability descends at the moment that one is taken into custody and that it is absent until that vital moment. The selection of that moment as the first occasion on which legal representation becomes necessary is not only arbitrary, it is illogical.[67]

This vulnerability, Lord Kerr suggested, is a result of both the potential coercive atmosphere the power differential may create, and the instinct of the agents who exert this power. He was particularly concerned that state powers would be used in an arbitrary fashion, relying on agents of the state making decisions on a 'hunch' or 'professional intuition'.[68] This anxiety was clear in his dissent in *Beghal v Director of Public Prosecutions*,[69] where he recognised the potential inequality that such instinctive decisions could perpetuate:

> The startling reality that this legislation authorises the use of a coercive power, at least partly, on the grounds of race and religion should be starkly confronted. That not only permits direct discrimination, it is entirely at odds with the notion of an enlightened, pluralistic society all of whose members are treated equally.[70]

This position adopted by Lord Kerr alone was later endorsed by the European Court of Human Rights (ECtHR). *Beghal v DPP* concerned a Muslim woman who was stopped at an airport for questioning under paragraph 2 of Schedule 7 to the Terrorism Act 2000. Despite her request for a lawyer, she was subjected to questioning by the airport security authorities. She refused and was charged with wilfully failing to comply with the requirement to provide answers. Her counsel argued that the exercise of the statutory powers breached her rights under

[66] ibid at 5'33". Of the 13 cases in which Lord Kerr delivered a dissent alone, nine concerned aspects of the criminal law. See also John Jackson (ch 15).

[67] *McGowan v B* [2011] UKSC 54, [2011] 1 WLR 3121, [136].

[68] *Beghal v Director of Public Prosecutions* [2015] UKSC 49, [2016] AC 88, [99].

[69] ibid.

[70] ibid 104. Lord Kerr was citing elements of the argument made by Mr Squires on behalf of the Equality and Human Rights Commission, which was an intervener in *Beghal*.

Article 5 (the right to liberty), Article 6 (the right to a fair trial) and Article 8 (the right to a private life) of the ECHR. The majority of the UKSC held that the application of the legislation was compatible with the ECHR. Mrs Beghal then took her case to the ECtHR, which agreed with the position adopted by Lord Kerr and held that Schedule 7 was not in accordance with the law and was in breach of Article 8 of the ECHR.[71] Lord Kerr's dissent is one of the rare dissents that are vindicated by history.

It was the affirmation of the need to protect the most vulnerable against the arbitrary and discriminatory exercise of state power which provided a consistent thread in many of Lord Kerr's lone dissents. Lord Kerr also asserted and sought to protect the central role of lawyers in the protection of vulnerable defendants to ensure a fair trial.[72] In *Ambrose* he observed:

> There is no reason to suppose that a person questioned by police while not in detention would not experience the same need to acquiesce in the power of the police to require answers to potentially highly incriminating questions. In as much, therefore, as a coercive atmosphere is required in order to stimulate the need for the protection that a lawyer's presence brings …[73]

Indeed, in *Birnie*[74] Lord Kerr alone required that the police should ascertain the reasons why a defendant had waived his right to a solicitor. At the heart of the requirement for reasons was the understanding that the decision should be 'voluntary, informed and unequivocal'.[75] In his opposition to the majority Lord Kerr was not only advocating for the presence of a lawyer to protect the vulnerable in the face of coercive police power, he was also affirming the need to ensure the effective autonomy of the accused; both being necessary to protect against miscarriages of justice:

> It is in the interests of society as a whole that those whose guilt or innocence may be determined by reference to admissions that they have made in moments of vulnerability are sufficiently protected so as to allow confidence to be reposed in the reliability of those confessions … If it has taught us nothing else, recent experience of miscarriage of justice cases has surely alerted us to the potentially decisive importance of evidence about suspects' reactions to police questioning … and to the real risk that convictions based on admissions made without the benefit of legal advice may prove, in the final result, to be wholly unsafe. The role that a lawyer plays when the suspect is

[71] *Sylvie Beghal v UK* (2019) 69 EHRR 28. The Court also held that the application under Art 5 was admissible but that the application under Art 6 was inadmissible because it did not engage criminal law protections.

[72] See his dissenting judgments in *Ambrose v Harris* [2011] UKSC 43 [2011] 1 WLR 2435; *R (G) v Governors of the X School* [2011] UKSC 30, [2012] 1 AC 167; *McGowan v B* (n 67); *Jude v HM Advocate* [2011] UKSC 55, [2012] SC (UKSC) 222; *Beghal v DPP* (n 68).

[73] *Ambrose v Harris* (ibid) [148].

[74] *Birnie v HM Advocate*, dealt with by the UKSC alongside *Jude v HM Advocate* (n 72).

[75] *McGowan v B* (n 67).

> participating in what may be a pivotal moment in the process that ultimately determines his or her guilt is critical.[76]

Lord Kerr opposed the majority in *Hallam v Secretary of State for Justice* to correct these wrongs and compensate those who subsequently had their convictions quashed following the production of fresh evidence.[77]

It is this desire to protect the vulnerable and ensure that they can fully engage in the legal process which was also at the heart of Lord Kerr's dissents against the use of 'closed material' in criminal proceedings.[78] Central to his opposition was the need of 'equality of arms' to ensure fairness.[79] Indeed, Lord Kerr preferred that a trial would not proceed rather than proceed with an inequality of arms. A cancelled trial, Lord Kerr argued, was a 'more palatable course than to permit a proceeding in which one party knows nothing of the case made against him and which, by definition, cannot be subject to properly informed challenge'.[80]

In each of these cases, where Lord Kerr alone opposed the decision of the majority, he affirmed a constant position to protect those rendered vulnerable within the justice system. But he also sought to protect those who had been through the criminal justice system. Here again, his compassion for those rendered vulnerable and their potential for rehabilitation was clear:

> Rehabilitation is our criminal justice system's way of acknowledging and encouraging the potential for personal growth and change. If we continue to define ex-offenders throughout their lives on the basis of their offending we deprive them of reintegration into society on equal terms with their fellow citizens.[81]

In all of his dissenting judgments, whether alone or with others, Lord Kerr's instinctive sense of justice consistently sought to protect the most vulnerable in society and ensure that the rights enshrined within the ECHR were not encroached upon by the state. It was the consistency in his value positions which was the foundation of Lord Kerr's consistency in dissent. Indeed, of all the Justices in the Supreme Court Lord Kerr was the most likely to affirm the values encompassed in *universalism* and *self-direction*, whether he was in the majority or dissent.[82]

[76] *Ambrose v Harris* (n 72).

[77] *Hallam v Secretary of State for Justice* [2019] UKSC 2, [2020] AC 279. Lord Kerr was joined by Lord Reed in this minority position.

[78] *Bank Mellat v HM Treasury (Nos 1 and 2)* [2013] UKSC 38/39, [2014] AC 700. Lord Kerr was supported in opposition by Lord Hope and Lord Reed. He was alone in his opposition to the majority in *Home Office v Tariq* [2011] UKSC 35, [2012] 1 AC 452.

[79] *Home Office v Tariq* (ibid) [105].

[80] ibid [110].

[81] *Gaughran v Chief Constable of Police Service* [2015] UKSC 29, [2016] AC 345, [95]. This case was about retention of DNA by the Police Service of Northern Ireland. Lord Kerr alone held that it was incompatible with Art 8 ECHR and once again he was vindicated when the case reached the European Court of Human Rights: *Gaughran v UK* App No 45245/15, judgment of 13 February 2020. See also *In the matter of Lorraine Gallagher* [2019] UKSC 3, [2020] AC 185 and Kathryn McNeilly (ch 3).

[82] For further details on this consistent expression of values, see Cahill-O'Callaghan (n 6).

The consistent affirmation of these values and his determination to deliver a dissenting judgment in defence of these values was evidence of the strength of the position at the heart of his dissents. It was, perhaps, the acceptance of this earnestness that was the foundation of the engagement with his reasoning in dissent by his peers.

Listening to Dissent: The Importance of Engagement

The effectiveness of dissent to refine decision making is dependent on how the other Justices receive the information. Dooley and Fryxell, when studying uncertain decisions,[83] highlighted the equal importance of both the delivery and the receipt:

> Thus, rather than speak only of the variety and amount of information provided by dissent in the strategic decision process, it is equally important to consider team member attributions that might affect the way in which dissenting information is processed, interpreted, and acted on.[84]

The authors argue that to maximise the effectiveness of dissent, there must be constructive processing of the information received. There are many facets to how individuals in a group decision-making system receive and process information but central to the enhancement of decision quality is engagement.[85] Engagement in this context is the process defined by Paterson as critical engagement, not simply acknowledgement of the dissenting view but discussion of the foundation of the disagreement.[86] This critical engagement serves to encourage reflection and refine decision making in the UKSC, as Lord Phillips noted in *Edwards*:

> When initially I saw in draft the judgment of Lord Dyson, my reaction was that it was so plainly right in the result that my inclination was simply to add my agreement to it. The judgments of Lady Hale and Lord Kerr have, however, caused me to give further consideration to this difficult area of the law. While I have not changed my mind as to the result, the route by which I have reached it is not on all fours with that of Lord Dyson.[87]

[83] The authors examine strategic decision making in a hospital setting.

[84] Robert Dooley and Gerald Fryxell, 'Attaining Decision Quality and Commitment from Dissent: The Moderating Effects of Loyalty and Competence in Strategic Decision-Making Teams' (1999) 42 *Academy of Management Journal* 389, 389.

[85] See, eg, Tom Postmes, Russell Spears and Sezgin Cihangir, 'Quality of Decision Making and Group Norms' (2001) 80 *Journal of Personality and Social Psychology* 918; Lotte Scholten et al, 'Motivated Information Processing and Group Decision-Making: Effects of Process Accountability on Information Processing and Decision Quality' (2007) 43 *Journal of Experimental Social Psychology* 539.

[86] Paterson (n 3) 135.

[87] Lord Phillips in *Edwards v Chesterfield Royal Hospital NHS Foundation Trust* [2011] UKSC 58, [2012] 2 AC 22, [70].

Lord Kerr suggested in his 2012 lecture that dissenting opinions were overtly and consistently considered in the judgments of the majority:

> In contemporary experience, majority and dissenting judgments now engage directly with each other. Judgments of the Supreme Court, for instance, constantly cross refer. They examine lines of argument in each other's judgment and venture contrary views.[88]

What Lord Kerr says here may be true behind closed doors, but in published judgments the level of engagement varies based on the form of dissent, the author, and how the dissent arose. Critical engagement with the minority position by the majority is commonplace when the case closely divides judicial opinion. In contrast, there is very limited overt engagement by the majority with the reasoning of the lone dissenting judgment.[89] Indeed, in many cases, the leading and concurring judgments of the majority do not acknowledge the presence of an opposing judgment.

Although the absence of overt engagement in the reasoning of the majority judgment is not evidence that a refining of the majority decision did not happen behind closed doors, it does suggest that the engagement was not worth noting. This lack of critical engagement may be related to the perception by those supporting the majority position of the certainty of their decision, rather than the strength or weakness of the dissenting reasoning. Indeed, Supreme Court Justices who perceive no uncertainty in the decision they reach may not consider the need to critically engage with the opposing position.[90] However, it was a testament to the strength of the position of Lord Kerr that, even when he delivered a dissenting judgment alone, his judgments elicited overt critical engagement. On average in the UKSC, there was evidence of overt recognition of, and critical engagement by, the majority with the reasoning of any dissenting judgment in 30 per cent of cases, but Lord Kerr elicited detailed critical engagement at twice that rate (60 per cent).[91] This engagement was due to the importance of the arguments he presented, and the clarity and strength with which he presented them, as articulated by Lord Neuberger and Lord Dyson in the joint concurring judgment they delivered in response to Lord Kerr's dissent in *Beghal v DPP*:

> However, because we consider that there is force in the opposite view, we will briefly express our reasoning on the two main points which have caused Lord Kerr to reach the opposite conclusion in relation to Article 8.[92]

[88] The Birkenhead Lecture (n 1).

[89] It is unusual for the majority to engage with a sole dissent unless the dissent was originally the lead judgment (personal communication from Professor Alan Paterson).

[90] Robyn Dawes, David Singer and Frank Lemons, 'An Experimental Analysis of the Contrast Effect and its Implications for Intergroup Communication and the Indirect Assessment of Attitude' (1972) 21 *Journal of Personality and Social Psychology* 281.

[91] This data was estimated from a subset of cases from 2009–12. There is no evidence that the level of engagement changed.

[92] *Beghal v DPP* (n 68) [72]; Lord Hughes' lead judgment did not engage with Lord Kerr's dissent.

This was not the only case where an opinion was framed as a direct response to a dissent delivered by Lord Kerr.[93] Such was the legal strength of Lord Kerr's dissent in *R (Lord Carlile) v Secretary of State for the Home Department* that all of the majority judgments engaged with his dissenting arguments. Unusually, Lord Sumption who delivered the lead judgment in the case, dedicated a section of his judgment to 'Lord Kerr's judgment' noting:

> I have naturally reflected further on these issues in the light of the judgment of Lord Kerr, which strongly expresses the opposite view.[94]

The 'power' of Lord Kerr's dissenting judgments in criminal cases, particularly in a Scottish context, was often recognised by Lord Hope.[95] It is the strength of argument and consistency of Lord Kerr's position that led Lord Hope to question placing Lord Kerr on a panel hearing such cases.[96] But it is also these characteristics which served such an important role in refining the judgments of the UKSC bench.

Conclusion

> Great judges 'are not afraid to take a stance and will not always get it right' … Even if their views do not always prevail or carry the day entirely, they manage by dint of their example and efforts to change the legal world and the way others think about the judicial role.[97]

During his time on the Supreme Court, Lord Kerr's instinctive sense of justice underpinned robust and consistent dissents which amplified the plight of the most vulnerable in society and sought to protect them by extending the scope of the ECHR. His consistent, persistent, and erudite arguments provided an effective opposition to those in the majority. In doing so, Lord Kerr refined the judgments of others and effected change in the decisions of the bench.

In publishing a dissenting judgment, a judge amplifies the importance of judicial difference and overtly demonstrates the robust opposition which is essential to limit consensus and the bias that consensus may perpetuate. During his 11-year tenure on the Supreme Court, Lord Kerr was joined by 31 other Justices. Although many have been prepared to stand alone in opposition to the majority,

[93] See Lord Brown's judgment in *McGowan v B* (n 67) and Lord Clarke's judgment in *R (Lord Carlile of Berriew QC) v Secretary of State for the Home Dept* [2014] UKSC 60, [2015] AC 945.

[94] Lord Sumption's lead judgment in *Lord Carlile* (ibid) [48].

[95] See, eg, Lord Hope's judgment in *McGowan v B* (n 67).

[96] Lord Hope, *UK Supreme Court … and Afterwards: 2009–2015* (Edinburgh, Avizandum Publishing Ltd, 2019) 118.

[97] Hutchinson (n 45) 14. Citation omitted.

it is Lord Kerr who was the most consistent in so doing. In recent years, few Justices have delivered a dissenting judgment alone. In the context of this increasing propensity to agreement, it is perhaps time to reflect on the important role that dissent plays in the Supreme Court and consider the factors that forged this path to consensus. It is time to reignite the consistent robust opposition that Lord Kerr provided and recognise dissent as a jewel in the crown of the Supreme Court.

5

Lord Kerr and the Northern Ireland Constitution: Three Key Cases

GORDON ANTHONY

Introduction

Chapters in essay collections of this kind typically take one of two forms: they either examine some of the most recent rulings of the judge to whom the book is dedicated, or they take a topic that intersects with his or her work in some more general way and write a wider commentary on the law.[1] This chapter adopts a different approach to the work of Lord Kerr. Focusing on case law on the Northern Ireland constitution – essentially, the Belfast (Good Friday) Agreement and the Northern Ireland Act 1998 (as amended)[2] – it examines three judgments that he delivered whilst sitting in Northern Ireland's High Court and Court of Appeal in the early 2000s. The judgments in question – *Robinson*,[3] *Northern Ireland Human Rights Commission* (*NIHRC*)[4] and *De Brún*[5] – each adopted a pragmatic approach to novel questions of law and gave definition to important aspects of the Northern Ireland constitution. The rulings in that way contributed to the wider

[1] For examples of each approach see, respectively, Kathryn McNeilly (ch 3) and Claire Archbold (ch 14).

[2] On the Belfast Agreement in its original terms, see Colin Harvey (ed), *Human Rights, Equality and Democratic Renewal in Northern Ireland* (Oxford, Hart Publishing, 2001). For the text of the Agreement see www.gov.uk/government/publications/the-belfast-agreement. Note that references to the Northern Ireland constitution also include references to the range of political agreements that have been concluded since the Belfast (Good Friday) Agreement and which led to amendment of the Northern Ireland Act 1998, primarily the St Andrews Agreement (2006) and the Hillsborough Agreement (2010). See Richard Humphreys (ed), *Reconciling Ireland: Fifty Years of British-Irish Agreements* (Newbridge, Irish Academic Press, 2021).

[3] *Re Robinson's Application* [2001] NIQB 49 (subsequently heard on appeal in the Court of Appeal of Northern Ireland, *Re Robinson's Application for Judicial Review* [2002] NICA 18, and in the House of Lords, *Robinson v Secretary of State for Northern Ireland* [2002] UKHL 32, [2002] NI 390 – discussed below).

[4] *Re Northern Ireland Human Rights Commission's Application for Judicial Review* [2001] NI 271 (subsequently heard on appeal in the House of Lords, *Re Northern Ireland Human Rights Commission* [2002] UKHL 25, [2002] NI 236 – discussed below).

[5] *Re De Brún and McGuiness's Application* [2001] NIQB 3.

process of democratic renewal in Northern Ireland, even if its political institutions have had only a 'staccato' existence in the intervening years.[6]

The primary point developed in the chapter is that Lord Kerr's rulings were characteristic of a more assertive constitutional role for judicial review throughout the UK, but that that role is now coming under threat. Until recently, the idea that the courts ought to play such a role was a largely uncontroversial one, as developments in judicial review had complemented legislative initiatives in relation to human rights and the devolution of power to Northern Ireland, Scotland and Wales.[7] However, along with a fundamentally changed political context (including as a result of Brexit) has come a different narrative about the judicial role, which has centred upon criticisms of 'judicial overreach' and questions about the need for politically led reform.[8] While some preliminary work on possible reforms has doubted whether there is empirical evidence to support concerns about judicial overreach,[9] there remains a very clear political intention to rebalance the UK constitution. This, of course, raises questions about the legitimacy of any such efforts not just in the UK as a whole but also in the particular context of Northern Ireland. As will be argued below, there are compelling reasons to resist any such rebalancing: not only would it strain the idea of the separation of powers in the UK more broadly, it would undermine the role that the courts play as the guarantors of key features of the Northern Ireland constitution – a role that has much of its origins in *Robinson*, *NIHRC* and *De Brún*.[10]

The chapter begins with a section on *Robinson* that includes a discussion of the nature of the Northern Ireland constitution and some of its core aspects. It then contains two sections on *NIHRC* and *De Brún*, which develop the point about how

[6] For the term 'staccato' see *Robinson v Secretary of State for Northern Ireland* [2002] UKHL 32, [2002] NI 390, [7] per Lord Bingham. For other commentary on these and related cases see John Morison and Marie Lynch, 'Litigating the Agreement: Towards a New Constitutionalism for the UK from Northern Ireland' in John Morison, Kieran McEvoy and Gordon Anthony (eds), *Judges, Transition and Human Rights: Essays in Memory of Stephen Livingstone* (Oxford, OUP, 2007) 105.

[7] Tom Hickman, *Public Law after the Human Rights Act 1998* (Oxford, Hart Publishing, 2008); and Michael Keating, *State and Nation in the United Kingdom: The Fractured Union* (Oxford, OUP, 2021).

[8] Two reviews have been commissioned: one into the workings of administrative law, the other into aspects of the Human Rights Act 1998. See, respectively, www.gov.uk/government/groups/independent-review-of-administrative-law#terms-of-reference and www.gov.uk/guidance/independent-human-rights-act-review. For commentary on overreach see, eg, David Campbell and James Allan, 'Procedural Innovation and the Surreptitious Creation of Judicial Supremacy in the United Kingdom' (2019) 46 *Journal of Law and Society* 347. See, too, the work of the *Judicial Power Project*, at judicialpowerproject.org.uk.

[9] See the report of the *Independent Review of Administrative Law*, March 2021, available at assets.publishing.service.gov.uk/government/uploads/system/uploads/attachment_data/file/970797/IRAL-report.pdf. For the government's response and subsequent consultation paper see *Judicial Review Reform: The Government Response to the Independent Review of Administrative Law*, March 2021, available at assets.publishing.service.gov.uk/government/uploads/system/uploads/attachment_data/file/975301/judicial-review-reform-consultation-document.pdf.

[10] For a fuller argument to this effect see Gordon Anthony, 'The Quartet Plus Two: Judicial Review in Northern Ireland' in TT Arvind et al (eds), *Executive Decision-Making and the Courts: Revisiting the Origins of Modern Judicial Review* (Oxford, Hart Publishing, 2021) ch 12.

Lord Kerr's rulings helped to define the Northern Ireland constitution and make connections to some more recent case law from Northern Ireland. The conclusion returns to the wider theme about proposals for limiting the judicial role and argues that any such limitations could only create an imbalance in the constitution, at least if the rule of law is to be regarded as its 'ultimate controlling factor'.[11]

Robinson

The Northern Ireland constitution is defined by a number of values and principles that underpin a form of consociational democracy within the devolved institutions.[12] At their height, these position Northern Ireland as something of a constitutional compromise, at least in so far as its status as a part of the United Kingdom is contingent upon majority electoral support for that position, with Irish unification being expressly recognised as an alternative majority preference.[13] That foundational feature of the Belfast Agreement – known as the 'consent' principle – is complemented by a model of power-sharing that seeks to safeguard political equality between Northern Ireland's Unionist and Nationalist ethno-national groupings.[14] While this has always begged a question about the status of those who do not identify with those two main groupings – known, perhaps unfortunately, as 'Others'[15] – it was nevertheless key to the Agreement as was endorsed by parallel referenda in Northern Ireland and Ireland. Also key to its design were measures that were intended to mark a break with past legal and political difficulties: amendment of Articles in the Irish Constitution of 1937 that laid territorial claim to Northern Ireland;[16] the creation of North-South and East-West institutions;[17] the decommissioning of paramilitary weapons;[18] the early release of paramilitary prisoners;[19] the reform of policing;[20] and enhanced protections for rights (including through the creation of NIHRC and an Equality Commission for Northern Ireland).[21]

[11] *R (Jackson) v Attorney-General* [2005] UKHL 56, [2006] 1 AC 262, [107] per Lord Hope.

[12] See generally Brendan O'Leary, *A Treatise on Northern Ireland, Volume III* (Oxford, OUP, 2019).

[13] Northern Ireland Act 1998, s 1 and Sch 1.

[14] Northern Ireland Act 1998, Part III and, eg, s 42.

[15] Northern Ireland Act 1998, s 16C(3)(c), and Assembly Standing Order 3(11)-(12), available at www.niassembly.gov.uk/globalassets/documents/standing-orders/so-march2021-updates.pdf.

[16] Articles 2 and 3. For commentary see Desmond Clarke, 'Nationalism, the Irish Constitution, and Multicultural Citizenship' (2000) 51 *Northern Ireland Legal Quarterly* 100.

[17] Namely, the North-South Ministerial Council (and Implementation Bodies), the British-Irish Council and the British-Irish Intergovernmental Conference: see Belfast Agreement, Strands Two and Three, and Northern Ireland Act 1998, ss 52A–55.

[18] Belfast (Good Friday) Agreement, Part 7 (as preceded by the Northern Ireland Arms Decommissioning Act 1997).

[19] Northern Ireland (Sentences) Act 1998 and, eg, *Re McClean's Application* [2005] UKHL 46, [2005] NI 490.

[20] Police (NI) Act 1998 and Police (NI) Act 2000.

[21] See, respectively, Northern Ireland Act 1998, ss 68–71 and Sch 7, and Northern Ireland Act 1998, ss 73–76 and Schs 8 and 9.

The *Robinson* case concerned the rules that governed power-sharing within the Northern Ireland Executive Committee and, in particular, the role of the Assembly in electing the First and deputy First Ministers. Under section 16(8) of the Northern Ireland Act 1998 (as then in force) the election of the First and deputy First Ministers was to be held within six weeks of the date of the first meeting of a newly elected (or restored) Assembly, with section 32(3) requiring the Secretary of State to 'propose a date for the poll for the election of the next Assembly' in the event that the posts remained vacant. Crucially, section 16(3) required that the candidates for the posts should stand jointly and be elected with 'the [cross-community] support of a majority of the members voting in the election, a majority of the designated Nationalists voting and a majority of the designated Unionists voting'. This was one area where the Belfast Agreement's emphasis on ethno-national interests took form, as Members of the Assembly were required to designate themselves as 'Unionist', 'Nationalist' or 'Other' when signing the Roll of Membership and to vote on that basis on matters that included elections under section 16.[22] In the months preceding *Robinson*, the Assembly had been suspended because of a political dispute about aspects of sequencing in the peace process (notably as related to decommissioning of paramilitary weapons[23]) but had been restored on 23 September 2001. On 2 November 2001 – the last full day within the prescribed six-week period under section 16(8) – the Assembly failed to elect the nominated candidates for First and deputy First Minister (David Trimble and Mark Durkan) because it could not command a majority of designated Unionist members. The deputy leader of the then anti-Agreement Democratic Unionist Party, Peter Robinson, brought proceedings seeking an order to compel the Secretary of State to call fresh Assembly elections in accordance with his duty under section 32(3). The Secretary of State, whilst accepting that he had a duty to call Assembly elections, sought an extension of time from the Court to allow him to consider what might be the most appropriate date for those elections. In the event, a number of 'Other' Members of the Assembly temporarily redesignated themselves as 'Unionist' so that a further vote on David Trimble's and Mark Durkan's candidature could be carried with cross-community support on 6 November 2001. The Secretary of State thereupon decided that the most appropriate date for Assembly elections would be 1 May 2003, which was the date that had originally been set by the 1998 Act.

The case returned to court and came to focus on three main points: (1) whether the requirement that an election take place within a six-week period was mandatory; (2) whether it was open to the Assembly to elect the First and deputy First Ministers outside the period specified by section 16(8); and (3) whether the Secretary of State was obliged, when fixing a date under section 32(3), to choose a date which was constitutionally prompt and not set in the light of the

[22] See Northern Ireland Act 1998, s 4(5) and Standing Order 3(11)–(12).
[23] For some of the context see *Re De Brún and McGuinness's Application* [2001] NI 442.

'invalid' election of 6 November 2001. Dismissing the application for judicial review, Kerr J rejected the argument that the election requirement in section 16(8) should be seen as mandatory or, moreover, that the court should 'impose an inflexible time limit on one of the critical elements of the plan for government of Northern Ireland'. Finding that the legislation did not provide that an election outside the six-week period should be considered invalid, the judge drew upon academic and judicial authority to support the related finding that decisions may, where the public interest so demands, validly be taken after a statutory time limit has expired. Having concluded that 'the purpose of the Northern Ireland Act 1998 … would be frustrated if the time limit contained in section 16(8) were to be applied in a rigid, inflexible fashion … this is an example of those cases where public policy demands latitude in the application of the time limit', the judge determined that the argument in relation to section 32(3) should likewise fail:

> I consider that the Secretary of State has been given a wide discretion by section 32(3) in his choice of date to propose for the next election to the Assembly. It was submitted on his behalf that it was open to him to take into account political developments and to reflect those in the proposal that he makes under section 32. I accept that argument. Having held that the election of Mr Trimble and Mr Durkan was valid, I am satisfied that the Secretary of State was entitled to take the result of that election into account. The Secretary of State has concluded that there is a prospect of stable government for Northern Ireland and this had influenced his decision to select 1 May 2003. I consider that he was entitled to have regard to that factor … Moreover, a decision such as this is taken in a political context and the political considerations which inform it place it firmly in the category of soft-edged review where it is inappropriate for the courts to intervene.[24]

It is important to place Kerr J's findings on these points in context. In short, the application to the court would, if successful, have precipitated early elections to the Northern Ireland Assembly at the very time when there was growing Unionist opposition to the Belfast Agreement. While that opposition was ultimately to lead to suspension of the Assembly in 2002 – a period of suspension that lasted until 2007 and ended only when there was agreement on, among other things, appointing the First and deputy First Ministers on the basis of party-political strength[25] – Kerr J's ruling had sought to create space for Northern Ireland's

[24] The quotation, and the words extracted above, can be found at pp 13–17 of the judgment (*Re Robinson's Application* [2001] NIQB 49). The academic and judicial authority relied upon included, primarily, HWR Wade and CF Forsyth, *Administrative Law*, 8th edn (Oxford, OUP, 2000) 231 and *Simpson v Attorney-General* [1955] NZLR 271.

[25] Suspension was effected under the terms of the Northern Ireland Act 2000 and restoration (in 2007) was the result of the St Andrews Agreement and related legislation: see Gordon Anthony, 'The St Andrews Agreement and the Northern Ireland Assembly' (2008) 14 *European Public Law* 151. The new rules on appointment of the First and deputy First Ministers are found in Northern Ireland Act 1998, s 16A. And note that the rules on 'designation' were also amended at the time of St Andrews to prevent temporary redesignation of the kind seen during the case: Northern Ireland Act 1998, s 4(5A) and Standing Order 3(13).

institutions to work. Although he was able to do so only by departing from traditional, literal interpretive techniques, the majorities in the appellate courts held that his approach had been the correct one.[26] Nicholson LJ, in the Court of Appeal, thus stated that the Northern Ireland Act 1998 'should be construed, if possible, so as to preserve the Belfast Agreement, not to imperil it', whilst the majority in the House of Lords explicitly favoured a purposive approach to interpretation. For Lord Hoffmann, this was because the Belfast Agreement:

> was the product of multi-party negotiations to devise constitutional arrangements for a fresh start in Northern Ireland … The 1998 Act is a constitution for Northern Ireland, framed to create a continuing form of government against the history of the territory and the principles agreed in Belfast.[27]

Lord Bingham likewise said that the Act should be interpreted 'generously and purposively, bearing in mind the values which the constitutional provisions are intended to embody'.[28]

Robinson was thereafter to become synonymous with two lines of judicial reasoning. The first was case law in Northern Ireland in which the courts expressly referred to the Belfast Agreement as an interpretive aid in disputes about, among other things, the reintegration of former paramilitary prisoners and language rights.[29] While such references to the Agreement have not (of course) always been determinative of the issues before the courts, recourse to it has nevertheless given it a position of elevated importance within the legal system. The essence of Lord Kerr's legacy can thus be found here: the Northern Ireland constitution is to be read not just on the narrow terms of the Northern Ireland Act 1998 but also with reference to the political Agreement and democratic values that underlie it.

The second line of reasoning has been UK-wide and centred upon ideas of 'common law fundamental rights' and 'common law constitutional statutes'.[30]

[26] For the minority view, doubting the correctness of the interpretive approach, see eg Carswell LCJ in *Re Robinson's Application for Judicial Review* [2002] NICA 18: 'It is a difficult and invidious task for judges sitting in a court of law to adjudicate upon matters which have a highly charged political content, where the exercise of political judgment is at the centre of decision-making. That task is, however, imposed upon us by law and we have to discharge our function in the manner required of a judicial tribunal, looking only to those matters which are properly within our purview. Those matters are concerned solely with the interpretation of the governing statute, and I have sought to construe its terms in such a way as to ascertain and give effect to the intention of Parliament, eschewing all other considerations'.

[27] *Robinson v Secretary of State for Northern Ireland* [2002] UKHL 32, [2002] NI 390, 402, [25].

[28] ibid 398, [11].

[29] See, respectively, *Re McComb's Application* [2003] NIQB 47, [31] per Kerr J and *Re Coláiste Feirste's Application* [2011] NIQB 98, [22] per Treacy J. For other references to the Agreement see, eg, *R (Miller) v Secretary of State for Exiting the European Union* [2017] UKSC 5, [2018] AC 61, [128]; *Re McMahon's Application* [2019] NICA 29, [34]; *De Souza v Secretary of State for the Home Dept* [2019] UKUT 355 (IAC), [58]; and *Re JR80* [2019] NICA 58, [5].

[30] On which see John Laws, *The Common Law Constitution* (Cambridge, CUP, 2014) and *The Constitutional Balance* (Oxford, Hart Publishing, 2021).

This line of reasoning has defined the more assertive constitutional role for judicial review that was noted in the introduction, and it has seen the courts modify UK law's Diceyan narrative of sovereignty by, among other things, imposing formal limitations on the powers of the Westminster Parliament.[31] While this has since led to the criticisms of judicial overreach that were also noted in the introduction above, the case law has seen the courts address the challenge of, among other things, devolution to Northern Ireland, Scotland and Wales. At its height, that case law has seen the Supreme Court hint at a 'divided sovereignty' and federalising jurisprudence for the UK, and, even though the courts have since retrenched to a position of Diceyan orthodoxy (largely in case law on 'Brexit'), *Robinson* and the other case law continue to illuminate the creative potential of the common law.[32] *Robinson* is, in the result, a Northern Ireland case that has, somewhat exceptionally, helped to shape constitutional law in the UK more widely.

NIHRC

Turning to *NIHRC*, this case was much less politically charged than *Robinson*, albeit both cases concerned questions about how to interpret discrete provisions in the Northern Ireland Act 1998. The primary question in the case was whether NIHRC's statutory duty to keep 'under review the adequacy and effectiveness in Northern Ireland of law and practice relating to the protection of human rights' – found in section 69(1) of the Act – included the power to intervene in judicial proceedings. The issue arose when NIHRC sought a judicial review of a coroner's decision that, in the absence of an express statutory power to intervene, it did not enjoy the power to which it laid claim. Its application was heard in the High Court by Carswell LCJ, who dismissed the challenge because there was nothing in the relevant provisions of the Northern Ireland Act 1998 which either expressly or by necessary implication suggested that such a power existed. Although the wider statutory powers of the NIHRC at that time included advising the Secretary of State and Northern Ireland Assembly and, through section 69(6), promoting 'understanding and awareness of the importance of human rights', Carswell LCJ

[31] For the origins of the terms see Mark Elliott, 'Embracing "Constitutional" Legislation: Towards Fundamental Law?' (2003) 54 *Northern Ireland Legal Quarterly* 25. On the potential scope of constitutional statutes see Farrah Ahmed and Adam Perry, 'Constitutional Statutes' (2017) 37 *Oxford Journal of Legal Studies* 461. For more on parliamentary sovereignty see Aileen McHarg (ch 12).

[32] For the creative potential of the common law see, eg, *R (Miller) v Prime Minister* [2019] UKSC 41, [2020] AC 373. For 'divided sovereignty' see *Jackson* (n 11) [102] per Lord Steyn; for federalising jurisprudence see *Re Recovery of Medical Costs for Asbestos Diseases (Wales) Bill* [2015] UKSC 3, [2015] AC 1016, [118]–[120] per Lord Thomas; and for a return to orthodoxy see *Miller* (n 29) and *The UK Withdrawal from the European Union (Legal Continuity) (Scotland) Bill* [2018] UKSC 64, [2019] AC 1022.

concluded that the statute conferred only a number of specific functions rather than any overall responsibility.[33] As the judge put it:

> The Human Rights Commission has not been given any overall function such as advancing the observance of human rights. On the contrary, its functions set out in section 69 are specific and fairly precise and do not seem to me capable by reasonable implication of extending to making submissions to the coroner at an inquest.[34]

Precisely the opposite understanding was to underpin Kerr J's dissenting judgment in the Court of Appeal. Finding that it was 'unmistakable' that NIHRC had been given an overall role in advancing the observance of human rights, the judge also considered that section 69(6) of the Northern Ireland Act 1998 should be read as guaranteeing an express right to apply to intervene in proceedings. The applicant had argued that the provision should be read disjunctively and in a manner that recognises that there is a dual role in promoting awareness of the importance of human rights on the one hand and advancing understanding of human rights on the other. In accepting the argument, Kerr J considered that it would be 'incongruous' if NIHRC had the power to give advice to the Secretary of State and Northern Ireland Assembly under some provisions of section 69 while its powers under section 69(6) were to be restricted to reminding others of the importance of human rights. On this basis, he considered that, if NIHRC performs the dual function under section 69(6), there is no reason why courts should 'be excluded from the educative effect' of NIHRC's discharge of its function in relation to promoting understanding. This, the judge was careful to emphasise, did not mean that there would be a proliferation of interventions by NIHRC as he considered that the courts and practitioners would themselves become increasingly familiar with human rights principles. But what it did mean was that the courts should recognise the importance of the overall function performed by NIHRC, with the power of intervention being seen either as 'embraced by the express provisions' of section 69(6) or, if necessary, as 'incidental to or consequential upon its general duty to promote the observance of human rights'.[35]

The case was to be appealed to the House of Lords, where the majority agreed with Kerr J's approach. While the majority found that the Act did not include any express power to intervene and that statutory bodies have only the powers and duties that are given to them, it held that the power to intervene was either reasonably incidental to some of the powers in section 69 and/or incidental to or consequential upon others. At the heart of the ruling was, again, the tension between literal and purposive interpretation, where the majority preferred the more flexible approach. For instance, Lord Hutton traced NIHRC's role through

[33] The full range of powers were found in the Northern Ireland Act 1998, ss 69–71.

[34] *NIHRC* [2000] NIQB 61, [19].

[35] *Re Northern Ireland Human Rights Commission's Application for Judicial Review* [2001] NI 271, 295–96.

the Belfast Agreement and Northern Ireland Act 1998, including section 69(6), and said:

> it can be argued that the power relates to educating the public and public bodies as to the importance of human rights, particularly by research and educational activities, and that the power does not extend to making submissions to a court on a point of human rights law. But on a more liberal approach … I am of opinion that the making of legal submissions to a court can be regarded as incidental to the power of promoting understanding of human rights.[36]

Lord Woolf put the point in even more striking terms: 'I would find it extraordinary if a body having the express powers of the Commission did not have the ability to intervene'.[37]

What was the significance of *NIHRC*? At one level, it is possible to regard the case as nothing other than an application of familiar public law principles, as the House of Lords followed long-standing authorities on the powers of statutory bodies.[38] However, to the extent that this suggests that the case had no added constitutional importance, that is to overlook the nature of the wider function that NIHRC was arguing it should perform. NIHRC was, in short, one of a number of new institutions that were intended to mainstream rights into Northern Ireland society more generally, and it sought, through its case, the power to place human rights law at the centre of legal proceedings.[39] By holding that NIHRC had that very role to play, Kerr J and the majority in the House of Lords thus accepted that the institutional architecture of the Belfast Agreement was novel and that the powers of (in this instance) NIHRC should not be narrowly construed. Seen in that way, the case was less about familiar public law principles and more about new understandings of the role of rights in post-conflict Northern Ireland.

In the years since the House of Lords ruling, NIHRC's powers under the Northern Ireland Act 1998 have been significantly expanded and in 2018 they included the power to bring human rights proceedings in its own name where 'there is or would be one or more victims' of an unlawful act within the meaning of sections 6 and 7 of the Human Rights Act 1998.[40] In an interesting footnote to the original case, Lord Kerr sat in the Supreme Court when it was required to rule on the nature of that power in the context of a challenge that NIHRC brought to the law on abortion in Northern Ireland.[41] (The law in question was

[36] *Re Northern Ireland Human Rights Commission* [2002] NI 236, 257, [60].

[37] ibid 247, [33]. The only dissent came from Lord Hobhouse.

[38] See, eg, *Attorney-General v Great Eastern Railway Co* (1880) 5 App Cas 473, cited at [2002] NI 236, 254, [53] per Lord Hutton.

[39] On NIHRC's role, as originally conceived, see Stephen Livingstone, 'The Northern Ireland Human Rights Commission' (1999) 22 *Fordham International Law Journal* 1465.

[40] Northern Ireland Act 1998, s 71(2A)–(2C), inserted by the Justice and Security (NI) Act 2007, s 14(2).

[41] *Re Northern Ireland Human Rights Commission's Application for Judicial Review (reference by the Court of Appeal (Northern Ireland))* [2018] UKSC 27, [2018] NI 228. See too Lady Hale (ch 2) 42–4 and Brice Dickson (ch 6) 109–11.

found in sections 58 and 59 of the Offences Against the Person Act 1861 and section 25(1) of the Criminal Justice Act (NI) 1945; NIHRC challenged it as incompatible with Articles 3, 8 and 14 of the ECHR.) A majority of the Supreme Court here held that NIHRC did not have standing to bring the challenge because it had not been joined in the proceedings by a victim for the purposes of the law on abortion. While the minority (including Lord Kerr) considered that this was an 'arid question' because, among other things, NIHRC could have found and supported women who would have been victims of an unlawful act, the difference between the majority and minority ultimately fell away.[42] This was because the Court went on to consider the issue of compatibility notwithstanding the absence of standing, for the reason that the compatibility challenge had 'been fully argued' and it would 'be unrealistic and unhelpful to refuse to express' conclusions on it.[43] In the event, those (*obiter*) conclusions pointed towards an incompatibility: a differently constituted majority thus stated that there was an incompatibility with Article 8 of the ECHR, whilst Lords Kerr and Wilson (in that majority) stated that the law was also incompatible with Article 3 of the ECHR.

The Supreme Court's ruling in this case has been noted because it has been central to some academic commentary about judicial overreach in the UK. In an article that was highly critical of the Court, David Campbell and James Allan have described the ruling as 'a procedural innovation which was … extraordinary' because it amounted to abstract review even though the majority had ruled that such review was not possible on the facts. Noting that '[o]ne cannot really say that [the Court] found the legislation to be incompatible because their descriptions were categorically and deliberately *obiter*', Campbell and Allan state that there is 'no point speaking of possible legal limits because the example set … is to ignore legal limits even when acknowledged'.[44] Criticising the Court for having 'told parties *in advance* what is very likely to be the result of future litigation of matters never properly brought before the court' they add that, even though their critique was not 'focused on the desirability or otherwise of the courts actively seeking to involve themselves in undeniably "political" cases', they 'would not wish to dissimulate over [their] intense opposition' to such involvement.[45] The significance of their comments in this regard is returned to in the conclusion below.

[42] ibid 237–39, [11]–[18] per Lady Hale and 294–304, [168]–[213] per Lord Kerr (with whom Lord Wilson agreed). Note that s 71(2B) and (2C) of the Northern Ireland Act 1998 have since been amended to accord with the minority view in *NIHRC*: see European Union (Withdrawal Agreement) Act 2020, Sch 3, para 5.

[43] ibid 246, [42](c) per Lord Mance.

[44] See Campbell and Allan (n 8) 361 and 362.

[45] See Campbell and Allan (n 8) 364. For subsequent case law brought in the light of the ruling see *Re Ewart's Application* [2019] NIQB 88 and [2020] NIQB 33 (referenced in Campbell and Allan (n 8) at n 43).

De Brún

The final case to be discussed is *De Brún*,[46] which concerned the lawfulness of an exercise of Ministerial power under the Northern Ireland Act 1998. The particular issue in the case was the lawfulness of a decision of the then First Minister David Trimble to refuse to nominate Sinn Féin Ministers to meetings of the North-South Ministerial Council in accordance with section 52 of the Act. The North-South Ministerial Council brings together Ministers from Northern Ireland and Ireland to co-operate in areas of mutual interest, and its work was paralleled, in broad terms, by a British-Irish Council that attracted Unionist support. By section 52 of the Act, as was then in force, the First Minister and deputy First Minister had a duty jointly to:

> make such nominations of Ministers and junior Ministers … as they consider necessary to ensure (a) such cross-community participation in the North-South Ministerial Council as is required by the Belfast Agreement; and (b) such cross-community participation in the British-Irish Council as is so required.

On the facts, the First Minister had refused to nominate Sinn Féin Ministers because the IRA had not yet engaged in a process of decommissioning its weapons in accordance with Belfast Agreement. His evidence to the Court was that his refusal was intended to persuade Sinn Féin to use any influence it may have had to secure decommissioning.

The case centred on the law on discretionary powers, where the applicant's primary submission was that the First Minister had no discretion because section 52 was in the form of a mandatory duty. In making this point, the applicant referred the court to a number of passages of the Belfast Agreement and the Ministerial Code of Conduct, and submitted that these, and the wording of section 52 itself, all indicated that the First Minister had an obligation to appoint the Minister with executive responsibility for the relevant policy area.[47] Dismissing this argument, Kerr J accepted that, while such Ministers should normally be nominated, the First Minister nevertheless had discretion in the matter. His reasoning here was essentially that, so long as Ministers were nominated jointly and they satisfied the requirement of cross-community participation, the First Minister had scope to choose between prospective nominees. This, the court said, would allow the First

[46] *De Brún and McGuiness* (n 5).

[47] The passages of the Agreement to which the Court was referred were in Strand Two; the reference to the Ministerial Code was to para 5.1, which read: 'In accordance with section 52(1) of the Northern Ireland Act 1998 (the Act), the First Minister and the deputy First Minister acting jointly must make such nominations … For each meeting, the First Minister and the deputy First Minister will normally nominate each Minister or junior Minister with executive responsibility in the areas to be considered at the meeting'.

Minister to refuse to nominate a Minister whom he regarded as unsuitable in the sense that:

> that Minister was working against the implementation of the Agreement … The subjective nature of the decision and the political considerations which inform it [would] place it firmly in the category of soft-edged review where it would be inappropriate for the courts to intervene … [T]he First Minister would be exercising his discretion in assessing the suitability of the prospective nominee to contribute to the work of the [NSMC].[48]

However, where the First Minister refused 'to nominate a Minister who was in every way suitable to attend the meeting simply because he wished to induce that Minister – or the political party to which he belonged – to act in a particular way', this would go beyond the limits of the discretion: 'a decision not to nominate in order to bring pressure on a political opponent does not involve any assessment of his suitability for the nomination nor does it seek to fulfil the purpose of section 52'.[49]

The applicant's secondary argument – which was successful – was that the First Minister had exercised his power under section 52 for a collateral purpose. Counsel for the First Minister had argued that the court should read section 52 in the light of the wider objectives of the Agreement, including the commitment to achieve the decommissioning of terrorist arms. Although the court recognised that the Northern Ireland Act 1998 is '[a]n Act to make new provision for the government of Northern Ireland for the purpose of implementing the Agreement', it nevertheless concluded that the First Minister was bound, when exercising his power under section 52, to do so in a manner consistent with the section's emphasis on the work of the NSMC:

> In the present case, however, the implementation has a number of aspects and no single theme emerges either from the Agreement or the Act itself. Indeed, in order to promote the objective espoused by Mr Trimble (decommissioning of weapons), he has adopted a strategy that will at least inhibit – if not frustrate – another objective (effective North/South Council meetings). I have concluded, therefore, that the decision of the First Minister to refuse to nominate Ms De Brún and Mr McGuinness is for a purpose that is collateral to the purpose of section 52 and that it cannot be rescued by recourse to a separate objective of the Agreement.[50]

At one level, *De Brún* may seem like an unremarkable case to discuss in addition to those that have been considered above: Kerr J here too referred to the Belfast Agreement when setting the parameters for his ruling; a subsequent appeal to the Court of Appeal was dismissed; and the matter did not progress further.[51] The case does, however, merit attention in so far as it gives an insight into the relationship

[48] *De Brún and McGuiness* (n 5) 16.
[49] ibid 16–17.
[50] ibid 9.
[51] The Court of Appeal's judgment is reported at [2001] NI 442.

between law and politics under the Northern Ireland constitution and the role of the courts in policing that relationship. *De Brún* was, in short, one of a large number of politically charged Agreement-related cases that came before the courts in the early 2000s, and these foreshadowed a pronounced form of legal constitutionalism in Northern Ireland.[52] In hearing some of those early cases, Kerr J was plainly aware of the need to identify limits to the judicial role, where the standard of 'soft-edged review' that he noted in passing in *De Brún* (and in *Robinson*) became a synonym for judicial self-restraint.[53] However, to the extent that Kerr J thereby accepted that some decisions will be 'the stuff of politics',[54] he equally accepted that political decision-makers should not escape judicial control simply by reason of their status. It was an understanding that was to place the courts at the very heart of the Northern Ireland constitution.

Conclusion

This chapter began with three observations about Kerr J's rulings in *Robinson*, *NIHRC* and *De Brún*: that they gave early shape to important aspects to the Northern Ireland constitution; that they were characteristic of a more assertive constitutional role for the courts in the UK more widely; and that that role is now threatened by a political intention to rebalance the UK constitution. In noting the third point, mention was made of concerns about so-called 'judicial overreach', where a narrative has been developed not just in political despatches but also in academic work. Reference was later made to Campbell and Allan's article on the Supreme Court's ruling in the recent abortion case – they expressed their concerns about the Court's lack of adherence to procedural law and its willingness to proclaim upon substantive issues, and said that the case was 'not adjudication as adjudication has previously been understood in constitutional theory and practice … It [was] adjudication in advance; that is, it [was] not adjudication at all'.[55]

How, then, to conclude? Certainly, Campbell and Allan's comments deserve close consideration, as there are legitimate concerns about the undue extension

[52] For the other cases see Morison and Lynch (n 6). For subsequent cases see, among others, *Re Turley's Application* [2021] NICA 10; *Re Buick's Application* [2018] NICA 26; *Re Minister of Enterprise, Trade and Investment's Application* [2017] NICA 28; *Re Conradh Na Gaeilge's Application* [2017] NIQB 27; and *Re CAJ's Application* [2015] NIQB 59. On legal (and political) constitutionalism see Paul Craig, *UK, EU and Global Administrative Law: Foundations and Challenges* (Cambridge, CUP, 2015) 166–99.

[53] The standard was also referenced by the Court of Appeal: see, eg, *Re Williamson's Application* [2000] NI 281, 303–04, per Carswell LCJ. It might be noted that Lord Kerr's approach in 'political' cases did not always meet with approval on appeal: see, eg, his approach in *In Re Duffy* [2006] NICA 28, which was overturned by the House of Lords at *Re Duffy* [2008] UKHL 4, [2008] NI 152; see also Brice Dickson and Conor McCormick (ch 1) 10.

[54] *Re Murphy's Application* [2001] NI 425, 434.

[55] See Campbell and Allan (n 8) 364.

of the powers of any of the branches of the State, in any democratic system.[56] That said, their comments rest upon normative preferences about the nature of public law, where other commentators regard active judicial invigilation of decision-making as an important means of bringing balance to inter-institutional relations.[57] Work of the latter kind typically focuses on the creative potential of the common law, where the rule of law doctrine has been described as the 'ultimate controlling factor' on which constitutional law is based.[58] Political proposals to rebalance the UK constitution could, of course, only challenge that idea, and they would, if acted upon, strain the separation of powers through a misunderstanding of the judicial role. As *Robinson*, *NIHRC* and *De Brún* made clear within the particular setting of Northern Ireland, the judicial role is about a dynamic conception of the rule of law that can take form in the purposive interpretation of statute, judicial control of government decision-making, and, where appropriate, judicial self-restraint. Those features of the rule of law have equally defined its workings in the UK more widely, where the corpus of contemporary law has been shaped, in more recent years, by Lord Kerr's contribution from the Supreme Court. It is to be hoped that that contribution – and that which helped to create constitutional continuity in Northern Ireland – is not undermined by what would ultimately be 'political overreach'.

[56] See Harry Woolf, 'The tensions between the executive and the judiciary' (1998) 114 *LQR* 579. For some comparative common law perspectives see Dean Knight, *Vigilance and Restraint in the Common Law of Judicial Review* (Cambridge, CUP, 2018).

[57] See, eg, Trevor Allan, *The Sovereignty of Law: Freedom, Constitution and Common Law* (Oxford, OUP, 2013). For a summary of some of the competing perspectives on public law see Paul Craig, 'Public Law and Public Laws' in Mark Elliott and David Feldman (eds), *The Cambridge Companion to Public Law* (Cambridge, CUP, 2015) 153.

[58] *Jackson* (n 11) [107] per Lord Hope. See also Tom Bingham, *The Rule of Law* (London, Penguin, 2010).

6

Lord Kerr and Articles 2 and 3 of the ECHR

BRICE DICKSON*

Introduction

This chapter focuses on the contribution made by Lord Kerr to the protection of two crucial human rights – the right to life and the right not to be ill-treated. It seeks to convey the degree to which he was prepared to stick his neck out in support of those rights. At times he went beyond what was required by the jurisprudence of the European Court of Human Rights (ECtHR) in Strasbourg, and he did not blanch at differing from his colleagues. The cases referred to are mostly decisions of the Supreme Court, but some are cases in which he sat while serving in Northern Ireland. His Privy Council judgments did not directly deal with either of the two rights, but he did have occasion to hear cases concerning application of the death penalty.[1] The death penalty also featured in one of the last major judgments he wrote for the Supreme Court – *Elgizouli v Secretary of State for the Home Department*[2] – where, alone among his six colleagues in the case, he held that the common law had now reached the point where it recognised the principle that it is unlawful to facilitate the trial of any individual in a foreign country where doing so would put that person in danger of being executed. Although that judgment does not relate directly to Articles 2 or 3 of the European Convention on Human Rights (ECHR), it provides powerful support for the view that Lord Kerr's commitment to the values embedded in those provisions ran very deep. It also speaks to an exceptional willingness on his part to enable the common law to move with the times.

* I am grateful to Dr Conor McCormick for his very helpful comments on a draft of this chapter. Remaining defects are entirely my own responsibility.

[1] He overturned, or at least delayed, three death sentences: *Tido v The Queen* [2011] UKPC 16; *Lockhart v The Queen* [2011] UKPC 33; *Lovelace v The Queen* [2017] UKPC 18. See too Derek O'Brien (ch 9) 162–166.

[2] *Elgizouli v Secretary of State for the Home Dept* [2020] UKSC 10, [2020] 2 WLR 857, [102]–[147], esp [141].

Article 2 of the ECHR – The Right to Life

Decisions in Northern Ireland

The applicability of Article 2 arose in several cases coming before Sir Brian in Northern Ireland. Although it would be ridiculous to suggest that he should have accepted a pro-human rights argument on every occasion it was made to him, it remains fair to say that *overall* he initially displayed a relatively cautious approach to the development of Article 2 jurisprudence. As will be seen, a prominent exception was his judgment in *Officer L's Application*.[3]

As regards the substantive right to be protected from being killed, in *R v Clinton* he agreed, as a member of the Court of Appeal, that, if a person wanted to defend him- or herself against a threat of death by acquiring a firearm, the state could nevertheless impose on that person, without breaching Article 2, a requirement to obtain a firearm certificate.[4] Such a restriction on the right was within the state's margin of appreciation. Later, Sir Brian granted leave to apply for judicial review to an applicant who wanted a government Minister to confirm that the applicant was not, as alleged, an agent of the state, as these allegations placed him at risk of being murdered by the paramilitary group he had apparently betrayed;[5] but when the merits of the application came to be dealt with, by Carswell LCJ, it was held that the applicant's right to life had to be balanced against competing interests, including the risk that, if the government departed from its 'neither confirm nor deny' policy in such cases, the lives of many other agents could be put at risk.[6] The application was therefore rejected.

In *Officer L's Application*, also decided by the Court of Appeal, Kerr LCJ ruled that where a public inquiry is deciding whether Article 2 is engaged when witnesses ask to be anonymised and screened from the public, the inquiry panel should address a straightforward question: 'will there be a real risk to their lives if they are required to give evidence under their own names and unscreened'?[7] This endorsed the decision of the first instance judge (Morgan J, as he then was) but it was overturned by the House of Lords, where the Court's judgment was again given by Lord Carswell, Sir Brian's immediate predecessor as Lord Chief Justice.[8] The Law Lords held that Article 2 is engaged only if, viewed objectively, a risk to the witness's life would be *created or materially increased* if the witness gave evidence without anonymity. That meant that the criterion preferred by Kerr LCJ, which was easier for a witness to meet and made the scope of Article 2 broader, was replaced by one which narrowed its scope.

[3] *Officer L's Application* [2007] NICA 8.
[4] *R v Clinton* [2001] NICA 207.
[5] *Scappaticci's Application for Leave to Apply for Judicial Review* [2003] NIQB 40.
[6] *Re Scappaticci's Application for Judicial Review* [2003] NIQB 56.
[7] *Officer L's Application* (n 3).
[8] *In re Officer L* [2007] UKHL 36, [2007] 1 WLR 2135.

As regards the procedural dimension of Article 2 – the right to a thorough investigation into a suspicious death – reference has been made earlier in this book to Kerr J's involvement in several judicial review applications relating to the killing of Pearse Jordan in 1992.[9] In a case comparable to one of those applications in 2000, he ruled in *David Wright's Application* that Article 2 did not give the father of a murder victim the right to see the police's file on the investigation into the murder[10] and in *The Committee on the Administration of Justice's Application* he rejected a request from a non-governmental organisation that it should be granted access to material held by the police and the Police Ombudsman concerning the murder of solicitor Rosemary Nelson in 1999; this was on the basis that Article 2 could be relied upon only by victims, as stipulated by both the ECHR and the Human Rights Act 1998.[11] Neither of these decisions was challenged on appeal or through an application to the ECtHR.

More controversially, in *Teresa Kelly's Application*, as Chief Justice, Brian Kerr rejected the argument that the Police Service of Northern Ireland (PSNI) could not independently investigate a killing if there was an allegation of state collusion in the matter. He pointed out that:

> In a series of cases the European Court of Human Rights has recognised that the independence of the police force investigating the death may be a critical element of Article 2 compliance but it has not suggested that in every case where collusion is alleged an independent police force must be engaged.[12]

Likewise, he was a member of the Court of Appeal which held in *PSNI v McCaughey and Grew* that there was no obligation to conduct an Article 2-compliant inquest into a death occurring before the Human Rights Act came into force.[13] That decision, however, was overruled by the House of Lords[14] and when, as Lord Kerr, he had occasion to reconsider the same point in the Supreme Court, he faithfully applied the House's position.[15]

Kerr LCJ also held in the Divisional Court that Article 2 came into play when decisions are being made about whether someone should be prosecuted in relation to a death. This was in *Lawrence Kincaid's Application*, where the precise issue was whether Article 2 obliged the Public Prosecution Service (PPS) to give reasons for not prosecuting a man who had shot and injured the applicant.[16] But the Court

[9] See Brice Dickson and Conor McCormick (ch 1) 5–6.

[10] *David Wright's Application* [2000] NIQB 17.

[11] *The Committee on the Administration of Justice's Application* [2005] NIQB 25.

[12] *Teresa Kelly's Application* [2004] NIQB 72, [28]. The validity of the position under domestic law may be affected by the appeal to the UKSC in *McQuillan's Application for Judicial Review* [2019] NICA 13. This was heard in June 2021 and judgment is pending at the time of writing.

[13] *PSNI v McCaughey and Grew* [2005] NICA 1.

[14] See *McCaughey v Chief Constable of the PSNI* [2007] UKHL 14, [2007] 2 AC 226. See also Brice Dickson and Conor McCormick (ch 1) 9.

[15] *In re an application by Brigid McCaughey for Judicial Review* [2011] UKSC 20, [2012] 1 AC 725.

[16] *Lawrence Kincaid's Application* [2007] NIQB 26.

then held that, while Article 2 was certainly engaged in such instances, it had not been violated because the ECHR does not require such reasons to be provided in every case. The applicant had already been informed that the PPS felt it could not refute clear evidence that the man who had shot him was acting in self-defence. Kerr LCJ stressed that the duty to investigate a killing thoroughly applies even if the alleged perpetrator is not an agent of the state,[17] and he urged the PPS to consider every request for reasons on its individual merits,[18] but on this occasion he chose not to go beyond the European Court's stance by ordering reasons for non-prosecutions to be given in every case.[19]

In the earlier case of *Colette Hemsworth's Application* Kerr J did not think that Article 2 required an extra-statutory scheme for funding participants at an inquest to be as extensive as the statutory scheme in place: he intimated that the boundaries of the right to an effective investigation have to be drawn somewhere.[20] This decision was upheld by the Court of Appeal,[21] but the applicant eventually obtained legal aid after a second application for judicial review.[22]

Decisions in the Supreme Court

Less than a year after his promotion to the top court in 2009 Lord Kerr was confronted with the difficult case relating to the death of Private Jason Smith, a member of the Territorial Army who was called up for service in Iraq a few months after the invasion of that country by 'the coalition of the willing' in 2003. A few months later, while on active service, he died of heatstroke. The two questions for the Supreme Court were: was Private Smith 'within the jurisdiction' of the UK when he died, and did the inquest into his death have to comply with the procedural requirements derived from Article 2?[23] Lord Kerr reached two bold conclusions on the first question, but on the second he reaffirmed a limitation to the right to life.

The first bold conclusion was that members of the armed forces *are* entitled to the protection of the ECHR when they are serving abroad. On that issue

[17] ibid [13]–[15], citing, amongst other cases, *Menson v UK* (2003) 37 EHRR CD220.

[18] ibid [20]. In 2003, in *Hugh Jordan's Application* [2003] NIQB 1, Kerr J held that even if Art 2 requires prosecuting authorities to give reasons for a non-prosecution, this cannot apply to decisions taken before the Human Rights Act 1998 came into force. He felt bound by *Adams' Application* [2001] NI 1.

[19] ibid [16]–[18], citing two cases from Northern Ireland in Strasbourg: *McShane v UK* (2002) 35 EHRR 23 and *Jordan v UK* (2003) 37 EHRR 2.

[20] *Colette Hemsworth's Application* [2003] NIQB 5.

[21] *In re an application by Colette Hemsworth for Judicial Review* [2005] NICA 12.

[22] *In re an application by Colette Hemsworth for Judicial Review (No 2)* [2004] NIQB 26 (Weatherup J). The applicant later obtained a unanimous judgment from the ECtHR that the UK had breached Art 2 by allowing the investigation into her husband's death in 1997 to be excessively delayed: *Hemsworth v UK* App No 58559/09, judgment of 16 July 2013.

[23] *R (Smith) v Oxfordshire Assistant Deputy Coroner* [2010] UKSC 29, [2011] 1 AC 1.

he was one of three dissenters, the others being Lady Hale and Lord Mance.[24] A further six judges held that the ECHR does *not* travel with the armed forces. In justifying his position Lord Kerr explained why he thought that Lord Bingham – a stalwart of liberalism and himself the son of an Ulsterman – was wrong to say in *R (Gentle) v Prime Minister* that British soldiers in Iraq, while subject to the UK government's authority, were 'clearly not within the jurisdiction of the UK'.[25] In adopting his stance Lord Kerr relied on logic and principle. He distinguished *Gentle*, which was solely about whether resort to the use of lethal force in Iraq was justifiable, and he observed that Lord Bingham's remark was *obiter dictum*.[26] As far as Lord Kerr was concerned, '[t]o suggest … that soldiers are within the jurisdiction of the United Kingdom for every conceivable legal purpose other than Article 1 seems to me to involve the acceptance of one anomaly too many',[27] and he posed the brilliantly simple question: 'if [the soldiers] were not within the jurisdiction of the UK, in whose jurisdiction were they?'[28] Without expressly mentioning the 'mirror principle',[29] he was prepared to go beyond the ECtHR on the jurisdictional issue, partly because he detected that that Court had already enunciated principles allowing exceptions to be made to the 'territorial' approach to the issue.[30]

Lord Kerr's second bold conclusion was that an individual can fall within a state's jurisdiction even though the state is in no position to ensure that each and every one of that person's Convention rights can be guaranteed – again, a minority view in the Supreme Court. He relied on two ECtHR judgments, including one by the Grand Chamber, to support the proposition that the 'whole package of rights principle' is not an indispensable requirement for a finding that jurisdiction exists[31] and he distinguished the *Banković* case, about the NATO bombing of broadcasting stations in Belgrade, where the Grand Chamber of the ECtHR had seemed to support the opposite view, since that was a case on whether there was control over territory, not over individuals.[32]

However, in response to the argument that treating serving soldiers as falling under the UK's jurisdiction would inevitably require courts to scrutinise the implications of the military's policies, the planning and control of its operations, and its tactical decisions during those operations, Lord Kerr simply said that he

[24] ibid [311].

[25] *R (Gentle) v Prime Minister* [2008] UKHL 20; [2008] AC 1356, [8(3)].

[26] *Smith* (n 23) [320].

[27] Art 1 of the ECHR reads: 'The High Contracting Parties shall secure to everyone within their jurisdiction the rights and freedoms defined in Section I [i.e. Arts 2 to 18] of this Convention'.

[28] *Smith* (n 23) [317].

[29] ibid [330]. This is the principle derived from *R (Ullah) v Special Adjudicator* [2004] UKHL 26, [2004] 2 AC 323, whereby English courts are to protect human rights to the same extent as the ECtHR does – 'no more and no less'. See also Brice Dickson and Conor McCormick (ch 1) 25–27.

[30] ibid [312] and [331]–[333].

[31] ibid [326]–[328]; the judgments were in *Drozd and Janousek v France and Spain* (1992) 14 EHRR 745 and *Carson v UK* (2010) 51 EHHR 13 (GC).

[32] *Banković v Belgium et al* (2007) 44 EHRR SE5. The application was declared inadmissible.

did not fear those consequences, implying either that they would not occur or that the scrutiny involved would make allowances for the risks and inherent dangers of war. Maybe that was a slightly disingenuous position because, even if it is true that the ECtHR's remarks in this context have to date focused on the necessity for careful planning and control in order to avoid *civilian* casualties, the state's Article 2 duty to protect the lives of its armed forces does mean that awkward questions may need to be asked at a subsequent inquest or trial if, unfortunately, there is a higher than expected casualty rate amongst the armed forces during a military operation. The truth is, though, that even if such detailed scrutiny ensues – as it can, for example, under Israeli law[33] – this would not necessarily impede the effectiveness of the armed forces. Courts would be bound to take account of the dilemmas faced by commanders when considering whether to send soldiers into danger in order to prevent even greater danger arising elsewhere. As we shall see, Lord Kerr had already accepted that point in a policing case in Northern Ireland.[34] He would also soon have a chance to clarify his position.

It is remarkable that, within only a few years, Lord Kerr and his fellow dissenters in *Smith* were doubly vindicated. This first occurred when a unanimous Grand Chamber of the ECtHR reviewed the House of Lords' decision in the *Al-Skeini* case[35] and found that all six of the Iraqi victims in that case – not just one of them as the House of Lords had held – were within the jurisdiction of the UK when they were killed.[36] The Supreme Court had decided the *Smith* case in the period between the House of Lords' decision in *Al-Skeini* and the ECtHR's decision, but the latter made no reference to what Lord Kerr and others had said in *Smith*. In its interpretation of 'jurisdiction', however, the Grand Chamber was much closer to Lord Kerr's views than to those of the majority in *Smith*.[37]

Then, in 2013, in a second vindication of the minority in *Smith*, the Supreme Court effectively overruled its own decision of just three years earlier. Confusingly, the litigant whose name is used in the title of the later case – the mother of a soldier killed in Iraq – was again Smith.[38] Seven Supreme Court Justices unanimously held that, at the time when the soldiers travelling in a Snatch Land Rover were killed by an improvised explosive device, they *were* within the UK's jurisdiction for the purposes of the ECHR.[39] The Justices applied

[33] Eli Salzberger, 'Judicial Activism in Israel' in Brice Dickson (ed), *Judicial Activism in Common Law Supreme Courts* (Oxford, OUP, 2007) 250–57.

[34] *E v Chief Constable of the Royal Ulster Constabulary* [2008] UKHL 66, [2009] AC 536: see the text at n 98 below.

[35] *R (Al-Skeini) v Secretary of State for Defence* [2007] UKHL 26, [2008] 1 AC 153.

[36] *Al-Skeini v UK* (2011) 53 EHRR 589.

[37] Several of the judges in the Grand Chamber sat with Lord Kerr when he was an ad hoc judge in *Hatton v UK* (2003) 37 EHRR 28. They would therefore have been familiar with his approach to the ECHR.

[38] *Smith v Ministry of Defence* [2013] UKSC 41, [2014] AC 52. The High Court and Court of Appeal felt bound by the earlier *Smith* decision: [2011] EWHC 1676 (QB), [2011] HRLR 795; [2012] EWCA Civ 1365, [2014] AC 52.

[39] ibid [17]–[55] per Lord Hope, with whom Lord Walker, Lady Hale and Lord Kerr agreed; [102] per Lord Mance, with whom Lord Wilson agreed; [153] per Lord Carnwath.

the ruling by the ECtHR in *Al-Skeini*. As explained by Lord Hope, with whom Lord Kerr agreed, the ECtHR effectively revised what it had previously said in *Banković* about the 'whole package principle': it suggested that the duty under Article 1 of the ECHR – to secure the rights and freedoms defined in Articles 2 to 18 of the Convention – *could* be 'divided and tailored' in accordance with what is relevant to the situation of the individuals concerned.[40]

It is interesting that Lord Kerr chose not to deliver a separate judgment in the second *Smith* case, even though the Court was endorsing his earlier dissenting remarks. He maintained this silence even though his colleague Lord Mance, whose leading dissenting judgment Lord Kerr had endorsed in the first *Smith* case, decided to differ from the majority (including Lord Kerr) in the second *Smith* case as regards whether the Snatch Land Rover claims should be struck out on the basis that, even though the soldiers were within the UK's jurisdiction, the claims were not 'within the scope' of Article 2 of the ECHR. The majority's view was that it would be premature to strike out the claims as it was not yet clear to what extent they would be challenging high-level policy decisions, operational planning or control decisions, or decisions made in the heat of battle. If they fell into the first or last of those categories they would be outside the scope of Article 2. Lord Mance (with whom Lord Wilson agreed) took a more absolutist approach, holding that judges should never be asked to conduct a retrospective review of the UK's policies, strategy and tactics relating to the use of its armed forces in combat.[41]

In the interval between the two *Smith* cases Lord Kerr had the opportunity to express further views about the right to life in an appeal from Northern Ireland, *In re McCaughey*.[42] The central issue was whether an inquest into two deaths resulting from actions of British soldiers in Northern Ireland in 1990, almost 10 years before the Human Rights Act 1998 came into force, nevertheless had to comply with the investigative requirements of Article 2. The lower courts had held[43] that they were bound by the House of Lords' earlier decision in *In re McKerr*,[44] which appeared to rule out applying Article 2 to any death occurring before the entry into force of the 1998 Act. This was notwithstanding a later decision to the contrary by the Grand Chamber of the ECtHR in *Šilih v Slovenia*.[45] The Supreme Court, by six to one (Lord Rodger dissenting[46]) held that the Grand Chamber's decision did mean that the inquest had to comply with Article 2. Interestingly, in

[40] *Banković* (n 32) para 317.

[41] *Smith* (n 38) [146] and [150].

[42] *McCaughey* (n 15).

[43] *Re McCaughey and Quinn's Application for Judicial Review* [2009] NIQB 77; [2010] NICA 13.

[44] *In re McKerr* [2004] UKHL 12, [2004] 1 WLR 807.

[45] *Šilih v Slovenia* (2009) 49 EHRR 37.

[46] The Attorney General for Northern Ireland intervened in *McCaughey* (n 15) to provide what Lord Kerr described at [107] as 'trenchant criticism' of the judgment in *Šilih*. Lord Rodger used the same description at [151] when citing the joint dissenting judgment of Judges Bratza and Türmen in *Šilih*.

an earlier decision of the Court of Appeal connected to the inquest into the death of Martin McCaughey, Kerr LCJ, as he then was, had ruled that the *McKerr* judgment meant that the inquest was not governed by Article 2 and so the police were not under a duty to disclose certain documents to the coroner as the relevant statutory provision did not have to be interpreted in line with the Human Rights Act 1998.[47] But that decision was unanimously reversed by the House of Lords, on the basis that, regardless of the human rights position, ordinary principles of statutory interpretation required section 8 of the Coroners' Act (NI) 1959 to be construed as requiring the police to disclose information to the coroner both during and before an inquest.[48]

In the 2011 *McCaughey* case Lord Kerr valiantly attempted to deduce from the majority's judgment in *Šilih* some principles by which to determine whether enough of a connection existed between the death and the critical date (here the entry into force of the 1998 Act) to require the application of the procedural right in Article 2. He then held that in the case before him a sufficient connection had been established because, even if the investigation had begun before the critical date, a significant part of it was occurring after the date.[49]

This 'significant connection' issue also arose in Lord Kerr's next venture into Article 2 territory, in *R (Keyu) v Secretary of State for Foreign Affairs*, a case about killings perpetrated by British soldiers while serving in Malaya in 1948.[50] Lords Neuberger and Mance each delivered lengthy judgments holding that the Article 2 duty to investigate the deaths did not apply, because they had occurred more than 10 years before the critical date (here the day on which the UK had become bound by the ECHR). In *Šilih v Slovenia*[51] the Grand Chamber of the ECtHR had chosen that time period as an appropriate one for the retroactive application of the duty to investigate. Lord Kerr expressed agreement with Lord Mance on whether the deaths took place within the jurisdiction of the UK, but because he differed from both Lord Neuberger and Lord Mance on how to determine the critical date, and on two other key issues, he delivered his own lengthy judgment.

For Lord Kerr the day on which the UK had become bound by the ECHR was not the date on which the UK accepted the right of individuals to lodge an application in Strasbourg (1966) but the date on which the ECHR came into force for the UK after it had ratified the ECHR (1953). He closely examined the Strasbourg jurisprudence on the point and maintained that, in the absence of clear guidance from the ECtHR, the Supreme Court should not be deterred from forming its own judgment on the matter, but he also accepted that there was 'a need for caution'.[52]

[47] *PSNI v McCaughey and Grew* (n 13).

[48] *Jordan v Lord Chancellor and another* [2007] UKHL 14, [2007] 2 AC 226.

[49] *McCaughey* (n 15) [119]–[120]. Lord Kerr derived his principles not just from the majority judgment in *Šilih* but from Judge Lorenzen's concurring judgment, which found the majority's position hard to understand in places.

[50] *R (Keyu) v Secretary of State for Foreign Affairs* [2015] UKSC 69, [2016] AC 1355.

[51] *Šilih* (n 45).

[52] *Keyu* (n 50) [235].

What saved him from having to be more definite on the point was that the deaths in this case had occurred even before the ECHR was adopted in 1950 and no-one was arguing that the 10-year rule should go back as far as that. One can also detect in his judgment a desire for a more nuanced approach to Article 2. He said that Article 2 rights, like other Convention rights, 'do not generally lend themselves to the application of inflexibly prescriptive rules'.[53] On the other hand, Lord Neuberger (with whom Lord Hughes agreed) thought that Lord Kerr's approach would leave the law in 'a somewhat unpredictable state'.[54]

Lord Kerr also differed from Lord Neuberger and Lord Mance on the potential role of customary international law in this context. Lord Neuberger had said that, even if it could be shown that there was a rule of customary international law requiring deaths as long ago as 1948 to be investigated, it would be inappropriate for it to be incorporated into the common law because Parliament had already legislated in the area, including through the Human Rights Act 1998, a position he thought was supported by four of the judges in the earlier case of *McKerr*.[55] While Lord Kerr accepted that it would be 'inapt' to construct a common law duty paralleling a statutory duty, he saw 'a strong argument' for allowing such a duty to find expression in the common law if there were no legislative duty.[56] This is another example of his firm commitment to enhancing the common law's approach to human rights.

The *Keyu* case prompted a more general question about what role 'proportionality' should play in the law on judicial review. Lord Kerr thought that a 'more loosely structured' approach should be adopted if a fundamental right is not involved in the case, one which tests the decision in terms of its 'suitability or appropriateness, necessity and the balance or imbalance of benefits and disadvantages'.[57] This again is a test which in some judges' eyes might lead to unpredictability, but no more so perhaps than the conventional approach based on *Wednesbury* unreasonableness.

Lord Kerr's final tussle with Article 2 was in the *Finucane* case, where he delivered one of the longest judgments of his career.[58] At issue was whether the widow of Patrick Finucane, a Belfast solicitor who was murdered in 1989, was entitled to have a public inquiry into her husband's death, either because she had a legitimate expectation of such an inquiry in view of an assurance to that effect given by Prime Minister Tony Blair in 2004 or because not holding such an inquiry would violate her rights under Article 2. The five-judge Supreme Court held that, while a legitimate expectation that a public inquiry would be held had indeed been created, it was acceptable for an inquiry not to be held if for political reasons

[53] ibid [209].
[54] ibid [90].
[55] ibid [117], citing *In re McKerr* (n 44) (per Lords Nicholls, Rodger, Hoffmann and Brown).
[56] *Keyu* (n 50) above at [270].
[57] ibid [282], citing Lord Mance in *Kennedy v Charity Commission* [2014] UKSC 20, [2015] AC 455, [54].
[58] *In re Geraldine Finucane* [2019] UKSC 7, [2019] 3 All ER 191.

the government took a decision in good faith and on genuine policy grounds not to hold one. Yet the Court went on to conclude, even though Mrs Finucane's legal team was not calling for this, that there still had not been an Article 2-compliant investigation into this murder.

Was Lord Kerr correct to hold that the government could resile from a Prime Minister's undertaking to hold a public inquiry? At first glance it seems unreasonable, but there are two strong reasons in favour of his position. First, the ECtHR's case law on Article 2 requires an effective investigation of a suspicious killing but does not specify that in certain cases a public inquiry must be conducted instead of a normal investigation, so long as the latter meets the requirements of expedition, effectiveness, transparency and involvement of the deceased's family. Second, in a democracy it must be possible for governments to resile from an undertaking if they can articulate serious policy reasons for doing so. If one was to find fault with the Supreme Court's ruling it would lie in the fact that Lord Kerr's judgment does not directly unpack the 'political issues' and 'contemporary considerations' which meant that a public inquiry no longer had to be held in the *Finucane* case. What exactly had changed since Tony Blair gave his assurance? Intriguingly his Lordship referred to earlier paragraphs in his judgment describing the circumstances of the government's change of heart, but he was not specific as to which of those circumstances were crucial.[59] There had been an independent review of the investigation into Mr Finucane's murder by Desmond da Silva QC, but his conclusions seemed only to bolster the case for an inquiry rather than reduce it. It seems that Lord Kerr (and his colleagues) determined that the change of heart was the result of the political judgment of the Prime Minister and that such judgments should not be second-guessed by the judiciary. This, with respect, displayed an unusual timidity. Is it reconcilable with the stance taken by Lord Kerr and 10 of his colleagues later the same year when they were assessing the legality of Prime Minister Boris Johnson's prorogation advice to the Queen in *R (Miller) v Prime Minister*?[60]

Article 3 of the ECHR – The Right not to be Ill-Treated

Many of the issues arising in relation to Article 2, especially the duty to investigate thoroughly, also arise in relation to Article 3. In addition, there is the issue of whether poor treatment reaches the threshold of inhuman or degrading treatment. Lord Kerr was more willing than most judges to keep that threshold relatively low.

[59] ibid [71], cross-referring to [41]–[43].
[60] *R (Miller) v Prime Minister* [2019] UKSC 41, [2020] AC 373.

The clearest indication of this attitude is apparent from his judgment in *In the matter of an application by the Northern Ireland Human Rights Commission for Judicial Review* in 2018 (the *NIHRC* case).[61] That was where the extensive criminalisation of abortion in Northern Ireland was challenged as being incompatible with the ECHR. By a majority of four to three (Lord Kerr being one of the three) the Supreme Court held that the Commission did not have standing to bring the case, because there was no specified victim involved. But all seven Justices went on to consider whether, if the Commission did have standing, the ECHR was violated. Interestingly, that was not the approach which Kerr LCJ and his colleagues in the Court of Appeal had taken in 2009 when, having held that the Northern Ireland Commissioner for Children and Young People had no standing to challenge the lawfulness of the defence of reasonable parental punishment to a charge of assaulting a child, they did not proceed to consider the issue by way of *obiter dicta*.[62] And in 2003 Kerr J rejected a judicial review application lodged by the Family Planning Association in Northern Ireland challenging the failure of the Minister for Health and Social Services to issue guidance on when an abortion could be obtained and to investigate the difficulties in accessing termination of pregnancy services.[63] The Court of Appeal, however, reversed that decision the following year.[64]

By a majority of five to two the Justices in the *NIHRC* case said that a mother's right to a private life under Article 8 of the ECHR *would be* violated if she was unable to obtain an abortion in instances where a foetus suffers from fatal foetal abnormality syndrome, meaning that the baby will die before or in the process of being born or very shortly thereafter. By a majority of four to three they also said that Article 8 would be violated in instances where the mother had been raped or was the victim of incest. Lord Kerr was a member of both majorities. But only he and Lord Wilson – not even Lady Hale[65] – were prepared to find that the treatment which such women experience when required to continue with childbirth against their will was a violation of Article 3.

The fact that Lord Kerr began his lengthy judgment with five paragraphs depicting the plight of three women who had suffered the trauma of bearing foetuses suffering from fatal foetal abnormality left his readers in no doubt as to where his sympathies lay in this case and was a clear pointer – although he stressed that he would be deciding the case dispassionately[66] – to what his conclusions were

[61] *In the matter of an application by the Northern Ireland Human Rights Commission for Judicial Review* [2018] UKSC 27, [2019] 1 All ER 173. See also Lady Hale (ch 2) and Kathryn McNeilly (ch 3).

[62] *Northern Ireland Commissioner for Children and Young People's Application* [2009] NICA 10.

[63] *In re an application by the Family Planning Association of Northern Ireland for Judicial Review* [2003] NIQB 48. See also Brice Dickson and Conor McCormick (ch 1) 6. See too Lady Hale (ch 2) 40.

[64] *Family Planning Association of Northern Ireland v Minister for Health, Social Services and Public Safety* [2004] NICA 39.

[65] She said (*NIHRC* (n 61) [34]) that it was unnecessary to decide the Art 3 point because of her conclusion that Art 8 was clearly breached.

[66] ibid [141].

likely to be. He described in impressively simple terms the absolute character of the right conferred by Article 3:

> If the treatment to which an individual is subjected can properly be regarded as torture or inhuman or degrading, it does not matter a whit what the person or agency which is responsible for the perpetration of that treatment considers to be the justification for it. Nor does it matter that it is believed to be necessary to inflict the treatment to protect the interests of others. Torture and inhuman or degrading treatment are forbidden. That is an end of it.[67]

Nor, he said, could treatment that contravenes Article 3 be excused because it occurred out of good motives.[68] In Lord Kerr's view it was 'beyond question that many women in Northern Ireland who have had to continue with a pregnancy against their will, or who have had to travel to England to obtain an abortion, have had to undergo treatment forbidden by Article 3'.[69] Moreover he was quite clear that what such women suffer is a result of 'treatment'. This applied not just to the carrying to term of a foetus who is doomed to die or is the consequence of rape or incest, but also, it seems, to the liability to prosecution if the woman were to proceed to have an abortion in Northern Ireland.[70] The implications of that conclusion are significant. Might it mean, for example, that the severe anxiety experienced by a spouse, who cannot assist his or her disabled and desperately ill but perfectly lucid partner to commit suicide, amounts to a breach of Article 3? Does the discretion which prosecutors have to decide whether to prosecute someone for assisting a suicide make the spouse's 'treatment' inhuman or degrading in the way that Lord Kerr suggested was the case for women who cannot get clear advice on whether an abortion will be legal?[71]

A lot depends, as the learned judge made clear, on whether there is a risk of inhuman or degrading ill-treatment occurring as a result of the state of the law. But it is difficult to be more precise as to the size of the risk required. In the *NIHRC* case figures were not presented, presumably because they do not exist, as to what percentage of women who are pregnant with a fatally ill child, or as a result of rape or incest, do actually suffer (at the least) degrading treatment, defined as treatment 'such as to arouse in victims feelings of fear, anguish and inferiority capable of humiliating and debasing them'.[72] Lord Kerr simply stated that it was undeniable that some girls or women who are told that the baby they are carrying has a fatal abnormality or who become pregnant as a result of rape or incest will suffer

[67] ibid [215]. For a powerful defence of the absolute character of Art 3 see Natasa Mavronicola, *Torture, Inhumanity and Degradation under Article 3 of the ECHR* (Oxford, Hart Publishing, 2021).

[68] ibid [216]–[219].

[69] ibid [223].

[70] ibid [231].

[71] ibid [232]–[234]. In *Gäfgen v Germany* (2010) 52 EHRR 1 the ECtHR's Grand Chamber said, at para 107: 'Torture, inhuman or degrading treatment cannot be inflicted even in circumstances where the life of an individual is at risk. No derogation is allowed even in the event of a public emergency threatening the life of a nation'.

[72] *RR v Poland*, App No 27617/04, judgment of 26 May 2011, para 150.

profound psychological trauma: '[t]hat circumstance is sufficient to give rise to a violation of Article 3 where proper safeguards to mitigate the risk of such trauma are not put in place'.[73] In effect, he took judicial notice of the fact that profound psychological trauma is common enough to merit a finding that the current law violated Article 3.[74]

The Risk of Ill-treatment Occurring Abroad

That is also the calculus which has had to be made in other settings in which Article 3 arises, especially in immigration and deportation cases. Here too Lord Kerr was centrally engaged. In *W (Algeria) v Secretary of State for the Home Department* he agreed with his four colleagues that a court (including the Special Immigration Appeals Commission) did have the power to make *ex parte* an *irrevocable* order requiring non-disclosure of a witness's identity in a situation where a person is appealing against deportation on the basis that they might suffer ill-treatment contrary to Article 3 in the country to which they are to be returned.[75] The court would need to decide what weight to give to the witness's evidence (which could be challenged by the Home Secretary) before deciding whether to risk a breach of Article 3 by ordering deportation. The Supreme Court said the same attitude would be taken to risks that Article 2 might be breached, but in relation to potential breaches of other ECHR Articles a non-disclosure order would almost certainly never be issued.[76]

Whether or not there was a real risk of ill-treatment in a foreign country was also the question in *R (EM (Eritrea)) v Secretary of State for the Home Department*, where Lord Kerr gave a judgment with which all of his colleagues in the case agreed.[77] He held that, although there was a presumption that all EU Member States (including, here, Italy) would comply with their international obligations regarding the processing of asylum claims, this did not mean that the need to examine evidence on whether in fact those obligations would be fulfilled could be dispensed with. Contrary to what the Court of Appeal had held,[78] basing itself

[73] *NIHRC* (n 61) [235].

[74] One can contrast this conclusion with that in *Re Fulton's Application* [2000] NI 447, where a prisoner argued that his segregation from other prisoners violated Art 3. Considering all of the circumstances, Kerr J ruled that the prisoner's anxiety disorder was not caused only by his segregation, and that transferring him to a different prison, which was what he was demanding, would put him at serious risk of harm from certain other prisoners and be contrary to government policy following the Belfast (Good Friday) Agreement in 1998.

[75] *W (Algeria) v Secretary of State for the Home Dept* [2012] UKSC 8, [2012] 2 AC 115. The suggestion was that the witness knew that assurances given by the Algerian government – that deportees would not be ill-treated if returned – would be broken.

[76] ibid [38] per Lord Dyson.

[77] *R (EM (Eritrea)) v Secretary of State for the Home Dept* [2014] UKSC 12, [2014] AC 1321.

[78] *R (EM (Eritrea)) v Secretary of State for the Home Dept* [2012] EWCA Civ 1336, [2013] 1 WLR 576.

on its interpretation of a decision by the Court of Justice of the European Union (CJEU) in an earlier case against the UK,[79] Lord Kerr ruled that the existence of the presumption did not automatically mean that claims not to be removed to EU countries were 'clearly unfounded';[80] rather, the presumption could be rebutted even if there did not appear to be a *systemic* problem in Italy's asylum processes. Pre-empting what he was later to stress in the *NIHRC* case about the absolute character of Article 3, he said: '[i]t is self-evident that a violation of Article 3 rights is not intrinsically dependent on the failure of a system'.[81] The four appeals in this case were therefore remitted to the High Court for a full examination of the evidence as to whether, if returned to Italy, the appellants would be at real risk of being subjected to inhuman or degrading treatment.[82]

In passing, it is worth noting that in *EM (Eritrea)* Lord Kerr went out of his way to fully endorse the view expressed in the Court of Appeal by Sir Stephen Sedley concerning the authoritativeness of the UN High Commissioner for Refugees (UNHCR) in this context. Sir Stephen said that in *MSS v Belgium* the ECtHR had treated the UNHCR's judgment as 'pre-eminent and possibly decisive' and he added:

> The High Commissioner for Refugees … is today the holder of an internationally respected office with an expert staff …, able to assemble and monitor information from year to year and to apply to it standards of knowledge and judgment which are ordinarily beyond the reach of a court. In doing this, and in reaching his conclusions, he has the authority of the General Assembly of the United Nations, by whom he is appointed and to whom he reports. It is intelligible in this situation that a supranational court should pay special regard both to the facts which the High Commissioner reports and to the value judgments he arrives at within his remit.[83]

Those comments echo what Lord Kerr had said in a Supreme Court judgment issued three weeks earlier.[84] Lord Kerr went on to stress that he was not suggesting that the UNHCR's views should always be determinative in a UK court ('[t]he UNHCR material should form part of the overall examination of the particular circumstances of each of the appellant's cases, no more and no less'[85]) but it is implied that he thought a domestic court would have to have good reasons for deciding not to follow the UNHCR's lead. Within a year Lord Kerr's judgment

[79] Cases C-411/10 and C-493/10 *NS (Afghanistan) v Secretary of State for the Home Dept* [2013] QB 102. The Court of Appeal felt bound by that judgment, which it said had modified the test set out in *MSS v Belgium* (2011) 53 EHRR 28 (GC).

[80] This was the test required by the Nationality, Immigration and Asylum Act 2002, s 92(4)(a) and the Asylum and Immigration (Treatment of Claimants, etc) Act 2004, Sch 3, para 5(4).

[81] *EM (Eritrea)* (UKSC) (n 77) [42].

[82] Here the Supreme Court expressly applied the ECtHR's approach in *Soering v UK* (1989) 11 EHRR 439.

[83] *EM (Eritrea)* (CA) (n 78) [41], cited by Lord Kerr, *EM (Eritrea)* (UKSC) (n 77) [72].

[84] *IA (Iran) v Secretary of State for the Home Dept* [2014] UKSC 6, [2014] 1 WLR 384. There the Supreme Court differed from the UNHCR's position, but on the basis of new evidence.

[85] *EM (Eritrea)* (UKSC) (n 77) [74].

in *EM (Eritrea)* was cited by the Grand Chamber of the ECtHR with apparent approval in *Tarakhel v Switzerland*.[86] The ECtHR held (by 14 to 3) that Switzerland could not return a married couple and their five children to Italy, from where they had travelled a few months earlier having previously left their home in Iran, without first obtaining specific guarantees from the Italian authorities that the family would be taken care of in a manner appropriate to the age of the children and the family's unity.

Lord Kerr was also party to a Supreme Court hearing in *MP (Sri Lanka) v Secretary of State for the Home Department*, where a question was referred for a preliminary ruling by the CJEU: did EU law require Member States to provide protection to a third country national who was in danger of being returned to Sri Lanka, where he had previously been tortured but where that risk no longer existed.[87] The CJEU's Grand Chamber ruled that EU law does require such protection if the person is still suffering physical or psychological problems resulting from the torture and may not receive adequate treatment for those problems in Sri Lanka.[88]

The Duty of the Police not to Cause Ill-Treatment

On three occasions in the Supreme Court Lord Kerr had to consider the applicability of Article 3 in a policing context, including in an appeal from Northern Ireland. It also arose in another case concerning public order policing in Northern Ireland, which he dealt with while serving as Lord Chief Justice in a way that was endorsed by both the House of Lords and the ECtHR.

The first of the Supreme Court cases was *Ruddy v Chief Constable of Strathclyde Police*,[89] where a man who had been arrested in Scotland was suing the police for alleged ill-treatment suffered while in their custody. Lord Kerr and his colleagues fully agreed with the judgment of Lord Hope and added nothing to it. The case was partly about how civil claims should be processed under Scottish law but it was also about whether claims against officials relating to alleged violations of Article 3 had to be brought by way of judicial review. Lord Hope held that they did not, thereby largely aligning Scottish law with what already appeared to be the law in England and Wales.[90] He stressed that Mr Ruddy was not asking for any decision of the Chief Constable or the Lord Advocate to be reviewed or set aside: he was seeking compensation for the fact that he had been ill-treated.[91]

[86] *Tarakhel v Switzerland* App No 29217/12, judgment of 4 November 2014.
[87] *MP (Sri Lanka) v Secretary of State for the Home Dept* [2016] UKSC 32.
[88] Case C-353/16 *MP*, judgment of 24 April 2018.
[89] *Ruddy v Chief Constable of Strathclyde Police* [2012] UKSC 57, 2013 SC (UKSC) 126.
[90] ibid [17], citing *Wandsworth London Borough Council v Winder* [1985] AC 461 and *Roy v Kensington and Chelsea and Westminster Family Practitioner Committee* [1992] 1 AC 624.
[91] ibid [15] and [19].

One of the subsequent Supreme Court cases was much more significant on this point. In *Commissioner of Police of the Metropolis v DSD* two female victims of a serial sex offender, a black cab driver in London, were suing the police service for its failure to properly investigate the sexual offences he committed against them.[92] Until then the general principle had been that police services did not owe a duty of care towards victims of crimes but this case was examined in light of the investigative duty imposed by Article 3 of the ECHR. The High Court, the Court of Appeal and the Supreme Court all held in the women's favour, but in the Supreme Court Lord Kerr went further than at least two of his colleagues in the justification he gave for his decision.[93] First, he ruled that there could be non-compliance with Article 3 not only when there had been a systemic failure in policing operations but also when there had been a serious but non-systemic failure, a point he had previously made in *EM (Eritrea)*.[94] Second, he held that the duty to thoroughly investigate applies to all cases of ill-treatment, not just to those involving ill-treatment by agents of the state. Third, he found that just because the police may not owe a common law duty of care when conducting their operations, this does not prevent them from being liable for a breach of the Human Rights Act 1998: a duty of care exists only if it is fair, just or reasonable to impose one, but the duty to investigate is mandatory. On all of these points Lord Kerr supported his position by referring to jurisprudence of the ECtHR. In answer to the argument that the Supreme Court should not go further than the ECtHR in its interpretation of Article 3 he maintained that he was not doing so; even if he was doing so in relation to the third of the points, he was then interpreting the Human Rights Act in its context within UK domestic law, not the ECHR. Lord Neuberger and Lady Hale agreed with Lord Kerr's reasoning, but while Lord Hughes and Lord Mance agreed with his conclusions they would not go as far as Lord Kerr in the steps he took to get there. Lord Mance, in particular, was rather critical of the way the ECtHR sometimes goes about its business, accusing it of:

> start[ing] from a solidly rationalised principle, but then extend[ing] it to situations to which the rationale does not apply, without overt recognition of the extension, without formulating any fresh rationale and relying on supposed authority which does not actually support the extension.[95]

This case is a good illustration of how focused Lord Kerr could be not just on how best to interpret the case law of the ECtHR but also on how to reconcile it convincingly with his preferred position in domestic law.

Lord Kerr's approach attracted support within the ECtHR itself. In a 2016 case about the right of expectant mothers to have a home-birth, which was lost

[92] *Commissioner of Police of the Metropolis v DSD* [2018] UKSC 11, [2019] AC 196.
[93] ibid [29], [59] and [66]–[72].
[94] See the text at nn 77–82 above.
[95] *Commissioner of Police* (n 92) [142].

by the applicants,[96] a group of five dissenting judges in the Grand Chamber alluded to what Lord Kerr and Lord Reed had jointly said in the important case of *Montgomery v Lanarkshire Health Board* about the need for the law to recognise that health systems are moving away from a paternalistic approach to the doctor-patient relationship.[97]

Of the policing cases arising from Northern Ireland, the first involved the plight of schoolgirls who were obstructed from going to school by extreme 'loyalist' protestors nearby: the *E* case. This was a case taken against the police by one of the mothers of the children, alleging that the police had failed to implement the criminal law effectively to ensure safe passage to the school for her and her daughter. The implication was that, if the police had adopted different tactics, they could have better protected the schoolchildren from being inhumanly and degradingly treated (or worse). But the claim was unsuccessful at every level – the High Court and Court of Appeal of Northern Ireland,[98] the House of Lords[99] and the ECtHR (where the application was declared inadmissible because it was manifestly unfounded).[100] It was in the High Court that Kerr J dealt with the claim. Having taken stock of the fact that under the ECHR, as interpreted by the ECtHR, authorities must take reasonable measures to prevent ill-treatment of which they have or ought to have knowledge,[101] he said:

> The immediate reaction of right-thinking people is that those who intimidated, threatened and attacked those children and parents … should have been prevented from doing so; they should have been arrested and prosecuted. Sadly, policing options and decisions do not readily permit such uncomplicated solutions, particularly in such a uniquely fraught situation. Those who had to decide how to deal with this protest were obliged to have regard to the effect that their decisions might have in the wider community. It is not difficult to understand that an aggressive, uncompromising approach to the protest might have been the catalyst for widespread unrest elsewhere. It is precisely because the Police Service is better equipped to appreciate and evaluate the dangers of such secondary protests and disturbances that an area of discretionary judgment must be allowed them, particularly in the realm of operational decisions.[102]

This decision was controversial, but of course it by no means gave the police *carte blanche* in respect of all future operational decisions. That was made abundantly clear in the second appeal from Northern Ireland in the Supreme Court.

In *DB v Chief Constable of the PSNI* the issue was whether the PSNI had properly understood their powers to terminate a parade that was illegal because it had not

[96] *Dubská and Krejzová v Czech Republic*, App Nos 28859/11 and 28473/12, judgment of 15 November 2016, dissenting opinion of Judges Sajó, Karakaş Nicolaou, Laffranque and Keller, para 15.

[97] *Montgomery v Lanarkshire Health Board* [2015] UKSC 11, [2015] AC 1430, [81]. See too Lady Hale (ch 2) 40–41.

[98] *In re E's Application* [2004] NIQB 35; [2006] NICA 37.

[99] *E v Chief Constable* (n 34).

[100] *PF and EF v UK* App No 28326/09, decision of 23 November 2010.

[101] *Osman v UK* (2000) 29 EHRR 245, para 116.

[102] *E's Application* (n 98), [45]–[46].

been officially notified in advance.[103] Writing for the Court, Lord Kerr pointed out that the police have a duty, under the general law, to prevent the commission of offences, including participation in unlawful parades. Here the PSNI had wrongly believed that they had only a power to prevent the commission of general public order offences. He therefore reversed the decision of the Court of Appeal[104] and restored the judgment of Treacy J in the High Court.[105] Lord Kerr seemed to approve of how Treacy J had distinguished the case of *E v Chief Constable of the RUC*.[106] There, the claimant had to show that there was a positive obligation to prevent breaches of Articles 2 and 3 and that it had been violated. She failed because 'there was a substantial body of evidence … that policing the operation in that case differently might have led to an extension of the protest to other locations and resulted in a risk to lives of other civilians'.[107] In the *DB* case it was not necessary to decide whether any Articles of the ECHR had been breached (including the right to freedom of assembly under Article 11) because the police had simply misunderstood their powers. For the same reason it was unnecessary to decide whether a proportionality test should be applied when assessing the legality of the policing operation.[108]

Lord Kerr's decisions on Article 3 in a policing context seem to display an eminently pragmatic but also principled approach. In each of them he expertly steered a consistent path through the thicket of conflicting arguments.

Conclusion

Senior judges, however long they are in office, do not often get an opportunity to issue several judgments dealing with the same discrete area of law. Happily, Lord Kerr was able to contribute significantly to the evolution of both Articles 2 and 3 within UK law. He was prepared to go beyond the ECtHR when he deemed it appropriate, but he also had his views endorsed by that Court. He also sought to protect the right to life under the common law, basing himself in part on the requirements of the ECHR and its Protocols 6 and 13.[109] His commitment to human rights is perhaps best illustrated by the statements he made in 2015 advocating the abandonment of the dualist approach to human rights treaties: he suggested they should be considered part of our domestic law as soon as they have

[103] *DB v Chief Constable of Police of Northern Ireland* [2017] UKSC 7, [2017] NI 301.
[104] *In re an application by DB for Judicial Review* [2014] NICA 56.
[105] *DB's Application* [2014] NIQB 55.
[106] *E v Chief Constable* (n 34).
[107] ibid [6], cited by Lord Kerr in *DB v Chief Constable* (n 103) [33].
[108] In *E v Chief Constable* (n 34) Lord Carswell categorically stated that the proportionality test *should* be applied in these situations: [54].
[109] See his impressive judgment in *Elgizouli* (n 2).

been ratified.[110] No-one could surely argue that such a change to UK law would be a difficult step, especially as the UK government now delays its ratification of such treaties until it is sure that domestic law is compliant with them.[111] It would be a fitting tribute to Lord Kerr's memory if Parliament were to enact a statute to bring about that change in the near future.

[110] *R (SG) v Secretary of State for Work and Pensions* [2015] UKSC 16, [2015] 1 WLR 1449, [247]–[257]. Lord Kerr defended this position in his contribution to an online event run by Garden Court Chambers on 2 November 2020 commemorating the 70th anniversary of the ECHR, available at: https://www.gardencourtchambers.co.uk/events/echr-70-lord-kerr-of-tonaghmore-in-conversation-with-nuala-mole-founder-of-the-aire-centre-hosted-by-garden-court-chambers (at 37'10").

[111] See, eg, Preventing and Combating Violence Against Women and Domestic Violence (Ratification of Convention) Act 2017, s 1.

7

Scrutinising Social Security Law and Protecting Social Rights: Lord Kerr and the Benefit Cap

GRÁINNE McKEEVER*

Introduction

Lord Kerr's work as a member of the Supreme Court has generated a substantial contribution to many areas of law, showcasing a breadth and depth of expertise that merits examination. This chapter offers a chance to reflect on his contribution to social security law, a complex area bedevilled by detail wrapped around politics and ideology. Lord Kerr's legacy of social security judgments covers discrimination in benefit entitlement;[1] recovery of overpayments and loan deductions from social security benefits;[2] the status of a pregnant woman as a 'worker' for the purpose of benefits;[3] as well as the duties owed to those with disabilities and care needs.[4] While each of these deserves discussion in their own right, this chapter's contribution to reviewing Kerr's legacy is to provide a context in which two of his most significant judgments on social security can be considered. These judgments highlight the critical issues underpinning how social security law is made.

The chapter begins with an overview of how social security in the UK has developed, from the begrudging acknowledgment of the state under the Poor Laws

* My thanks to Ciara Fitzpatrick, Charles O'Sullivan and Mark Simpson, Ulster University, for their generous and helpful comments on earlier drafts of this chapter and to Claire McVicker for her research assistance.

[1] *In the matter of an application by Siobhan McLaughlin for Judicial Review* [2018] UKSC 48, [2018] 1 WLR 4250.

[2] *The Child Poverty Action Group v Secretary of State for Work and Pensions* [2010] UKSC 54, [2011] 2 AC 15; *R (Cooper) v Secretary of State for Work and Pensions* [2011] UKSC 60, [2012] 2 AC 1.

[3] *Jessy Saint-Prix v Secretary of State for Work and Pensions* [2012] UKSC 49, [2013] 1 All ER 752.

[4] *R (McDonald) v Royal Borough of Kensington & Chelsea* [2011] UKSC 33, [2011] 4 All ER 881; *R (KM) v Cambridgeshire County Council* [2012] UKSC 23, [2012] 3 All ER 1218; *R (L) v Westminster City Council* [2013] UKSC 27, [2013] 1 WLR 1445; *Secretary of State for Work and Pensions v MM* [2019] UKSC 34, [2020] 1 All ER 829.

that some duty was owed to the poor and destitute, to the relatively enlightened approach of the post Second World War welfare state with a Keynesian model of providing a modicum of economic welfare through social security, through to today's work-first model of state support for the poor underlined by conditionality that, in some instances, brings to life the historical principle of 'less eligibility' re-purposed as 'fairness' to the taxpayer. Translating such policy into practice is the job of social security law, which must balance the need for clarity and efficiency within the hugely bureaucratic social security system with the principle of legality.[5] Sitting within this transition are political considerations of finance and expenditure, the need to prioritise the democratic mandate of government over the personal preferences of judges, and the need to ensure that judicial review does not become judicial overreach. That judges have to be alive to these considerations is common ground in any discussion of their work, but the balancing of rights in an environment as costly and contentious as social security entitlement means that judging social security is difficult.

The last decade has produced some highly controversial social security policy, including the social sector size criteria (colloquially known as the 'bedroom tax'), which restricts housing benefit to the number of bedrooms that claimants are deemed to need. Extensive litigation before the Supreme Court[6] and the European Court of Human Rights[7] has been required to establish that 'necessary' includes bedrooms for disabled spouses and grandchildren and housing adaptations for victims of domestic violence. More controversial has been the two-child limit under universal credit and tax credits, which are both means-tested benefits that support parents who are unemployed or on low incomes.[8] This limit restricts child-related entitlements to the first two children of the family born on or after 6 April 2017. The administrative easement for this policy – the so-called 'rape clause' that creates an exemption for children born from non-consensual intercourse – does little to reduce the controversy. What it does provide, however, is some shape to the notion of 'fairness to taxpayers' that twenty-first century social security policy encapsulates, where social security entitlement is not based on objective need but on society's tolerance to support particular circumstances. A similarly shaped policy – the benefit cap – offers the same notional protection for taxpayers, capping the amount of income an out-of-work household can receive from social security benefits, regardless of need.

[5] See Lon Fuller, *The Morality of Law* (New Haven, Yale UP, 1964).

[6] *R (MA) v Secretary of State for Work and Pensions* [2016] UKSC 58, [2016] 1 WLR 4550.

[7] *JD and A v UK* (2019) Apps Nos 32949/17 and 34614/17.

[8] The controversy has been highlighted in the Supreme Court's decision in *R (SC, CB and 8 children) v Secretary of State for Work and Pensions* [2021] UKSC 26, which both acknowledges the controversy and itself generates further controversy: see Charlotte O'Brien, 'Inevitability as the New Discrimination Defence: UK Supreme Court Mangles Indirect Discrimination Analysis while Finding the Two-Child Limit Lawful' (2021) Oxford Human Rights Hub, available at ohrh.law.ox.ac.uk/inevitability-as-the-new-discrimination-defence-uk-supreme-court-mangles-indirect-discrimination-analysis-while-finding-the-two-child-limit-lawful.

It is this legal measure that provides this chapter's focus: analysing Lord Kerr's contribution to social security law in the cases of *R (SG) v Secretary of State for Work and Pensions*[9] and *R (DA) v Secretary of State for Work and Pensions*.[10]

The Development of Social Security

It is disquieting to look back at the 'Old' Poor Law of the seventeenth century as the starting point to explain twenty-first century welfare provision, but the cultural hold of this legislation,[11] and the successor 'New' Poor Law Acts of the nineteenth century,[12] has been virtually unshakable. The Poor Laws prioritised controlling taxpayer expenditure and managing erroneous expectations of generosity through the principle of less eligibility: 'The first and most essential of all conditions is that [the pauper's] situation on the whole shall not be made really or apparently so eligible as that of the independent labourer of the lowest class'.[13] In reality, less eligibility was only meaningful in psychological rather than economic terms, through the stigmatisation of the pauper whose poverty – regarded as a consequence of their individual failings – was a direct affront to hard working citizens whose taxes were being taken to fund relief.[14] Beyond the workhouse, relief was dependent on individuals proselytising their deservingness before the authorities, generating an unpredictable policy outcome while denying agency for the poor. The out-workings of the legislation inevitably defied most definitions of fairness.

This system prevailed through to the early twentieth century, by which point the consequences of poverty had become as much of a problem for the state as it was for the poor. At the same time, there was a shift in public attitudes towards the poor who, while still stigmatised, were not seen as solely responsible for their dire economic circumstances. Both elements, combined with the aftermath of the First and Second World Wars, drove public demand for new solutions to poverty. The welfare settlement that was implemented after the Second World War was based on a blueprint created by William Beveridge that centred social security in a welfare state.[15] This encapsulated state responsibility to insure its citizens against major economic shocks in the life course, providing 'cradle-to-grave' protection in return for worker contributions to an existing national insurance fund, combined with national assistance benefits for those (assumed to be a minority) who were not covered either as workers or their dependants. Benefits were set at subsistence level in what was a more benevolent form of

[9] *R (SG) v Secretary of State for Work and Pensions* [2015] UKSC 16, [2015] 1 WLR 1449.
[10] *R (DA) v Secretary of State for Work and Pensions* [2019] UKSC 21, [2019] 1 WLR 3289.
[11] Act for the Relief of the Poor 1601.
[12] Poor Law Amendment Act 1834.
[13] *Report of Royal Commission on Poor Law* (1834), para 228.
[14] Anne Digby, *British Welfare Policy* (London, Faber and Faber, 1989).
[15] Beveridge Report, *Social Insurance and Allied Services* (Cmd 6404, 1942).

'less eligibility', but children were protected through a universal child benefit, unrelated to the income of parents.[16] The assumptions on which much of Beveridge's model depended, however, were not sustainable, particularly in relation to children who were being parented outside a 'traditional' family unit, creating difficulty for those without the means to support themselves.

While the nomenclature of 'a new Beveridge' for subsequent reforms has largely been unmerited, there have been significant social security changes throughout the twentieth and twenty-first centuries.[17] This trajectory, however, was largely retrogressive, so that 'the image of welfare as a public burden has taken root, its recipients viewed as separate from "society" which foots the bill'.[18] The insurance principle has been eroded alongside an increased reliance on means-tested benefits distributed through the 'targeting' of claimants under the objectives of fairness and efficiency but with a stigmatising effect. The universality of coverage has been abandoned – the last bulwark being child benefit, which is now means tested through the tax system. The complexities of the social security system have grown considerably, vying between the need to maintain 'bright line' rules to enable efficient decision making[19] and the recognition of multitudes of varying circumstances which may require state support.[20]

The efforts to simplify the social security system reached their zenith under universal credit (UC), introduced by the Welfare Reform Act 2012, implemented alongside extensive social security cuts under the umbrella of austerity. This included a previously politically toxic benefit cap that sets a statutory cap on the maximum amount of income that an out-of-work household can receive from social security benefits, including child benefit and housing support.[21] The prism of 'fairness' – a concept asserted rather than explored – continued to be used to reflect the re-engineered attitudes towards the poor as a 'moral underclass', once again portraying their behavioural deficiencies as the cause of their poverty.[22] The solution that inevitably comes with framing the problem this way is for the poor to take responsibility for their own circumstances, making whatever life adjustments are required to keep them out of poverty – from limiting the size of their family, to moving to cheaper accommodation, to increasing their income from work.

[16] Family Allowance Act 1945.

[17] Nicholas Timmins, *The Five Giants: A Biography of the Welfare State* (Glasgow, Harper Collins, 2017).

[18] John Mesher, 'The 1980 Social Security Legislation: The Great Welfare State Chainsaw Massacre' (1981) 8 *British Journal of Law and Society* 119, 120.

[19] Emma Laurie, 'Judicial Responses to Bright Line Rules in Social Security: In Search of Principle' (2009) 72 *MLR* 384.

[20] Neville Harris, *Law in a Complex State: Complexity in the Law and Structure of Welfare* (Oxford, Hart Publishing, 2013).

[21] Chris Grover, 'The Household Benefit Cap: Understanding the restriction of benefit income in Britain' (2020) *Journal of Social Policy* 1.

[22] Anne Daguerre, 'Policy styles and welfare reform in Britain and the USA: The Conservative-Led Coalition Government and the Obama Administration Compared' (2020) 27 *Journal of Social Security Law* 130.

Making Social Security Law

There was a large degree of political and public consensus that facilitated this social policy trajectory, but the dominance of the executive in rule-making within the UK suggests that parliamentary opposition to the implementing legislation would be unlikely to change the outcome.[23] Reflecting on the Social Security Acts of 1980, Mesher concluded that the long-standing legal vulnerability of social security entitlement was now matched by its political vulnerability, so that 'the emptiness of the right to benefit has been exposed'.[24] If political scrutiny of social security rights has been weakened, the question remains whether, or to what extent, parliamentary or judicial scrutiny can compensate.

Social security law relies heavily on secondary legislation, leaving it open to criticism that the implementing detail behind the primary legislation does not receive effective parliamentary scrutiny. The argument runs that scrutiny of the primary legislation is a review of the general principles, with insufficient legislative detail to understand who will be impacted and how, with this assessment then relegated to regulations where parliamentary control is considerably reduced, as regards both the time allocated for scrutiny and the options available for amending the legislation.[25] The absence of effective scrutiny of the compatibility of legislation with human rights obligations heightens the risk that such rights will be breached[26] and increases the prospect of 'kicking human rights scrutiny up to the judiciary'.[27]

Further criticism is that even the regulations now provide insufficient detail on how policy will be operationalised,[28] kicking this function downwards to the discretion of 'street level bureaucrats'.[29] Rather than an agreed minimum floor of benefit, social security has instituted a maximum ceiling that claimants may be entitled to. Legal arguments that this ceiling is too low have been offset by political statements on discretionary allowances which – in theory – raise the ceiling sufficiently to avoid any detrimental impact.[30] Meers highlights the dangers of such

[23] Meg Russell and Daniel Gover, *Taking Back Control: Why the House of Commons Should Govern Its Own Time* (London, University College London, 2021) available at www.ucl.ac.uk/constitution-unit/taking-back-control-why-house-commons-should-govern-its-own-time.

[24] Mesher (n 18) 125.

[25] Gráinne McKeever, 'Legislative scrutiny, co-ordination and the Social Security Advisory Committee: From system coherence to Scottish devolution' (2016) 23 *Journal of Social Security Law* 126.

[26] House of Lords and House of Commons, Joint Committee on Human Rights, *Twenty-First Report – Legislative Scrutiny: Welfare Reform Bill* HL 233, HC 1704 (2011).

[27] Charlotte O'Brien, '"Done Because We Are Too Menny": The Two-Child Rule Promotes Poverty, Invokes a Narrative of Welfare Decadence, and Abandons Children's Rights' (2018) 26 *International Journal of Children's Rights* 700, 723.

[28] McKeever (n 25).

[29] Michael Lipsky, *Street-level Bureaucracy: Dilemmas of the Individual in Public Services* (New York, Russell Sage Foundation, 1980); Jed Meers, 'Forms of fettering: Application forms and the exercise of discretion in the welfare state' (2020) 42 *Journal of Social Welfare and Family Law* 221.

[30] Jed Meers, 'Panacean payments: The role of discretionary housing payments in the welfare reform agenda' (2015) 22 *Journal of Social Security Law* 115.

discretionary support as a fix for disproportionately harsh policy which blurs the boundaries of responsibility, allowing for 'conflicts at the heart of policy formation to be deliberately fudged; decisions to be shielded from the gaze of the public and the courts; and responsibility for the impact of budget reductions to be externalised'.[31] Discretionary support has played a key role in justifying the harshness of some bright line rules, most notably discretionary housing payments (DHPs), awarded by local authorities on a discretionary basis to meet shortfalls in rent.[32] DHPs have been identified by government as suitable candidates for mitigating the impact of policies, including the benefit cap, but they exist as a time-limited discretion, not as a statutory right 'and give those affected no peace of mind'.[33] Whether this legal ensemble of bright line rules and administrative discretion 'curtails judicial control of government' is worth considering.[34]

Judicial Review

Feldman has argued that there has been an overall increase in the 'reach and grounds for judicial review of administrative and executive action' in part because of the Human Rights Act 1998 (HRA), which places justiciable obligations on public authorities.[35] While the high profile nature of several Supreme Court cases on social security suggests increased legal activism in relation to the government's social security policies, Daguerre notes that '[j]udicial reviews remain underused in social security contrary to other policy areas such as immigration and asylum'.[36] Judicial review is an appropriate means of challenging government decision-making and contributes to democratic accountability,[37] although Cotterrell suggests that judicial review as a form of democracy may be more aspirational than real.[38] *The Independent Review of Administrative Law* confirms that judicial review is an essential ingredient of the rule of law and of access to justice – a constitutional right that is also protected by the European Convention on Human Rights (ECHR).[39] It acknowledges that the HRA makes reviewable that which would not have been reviewable under common law but, as Lord Kerr

[31] Jed Meers, 'Discretion as blame avoidance: Passing the buck to local authorities in "welfare reform"' (2019) 27 *Journal of Poverty and Social Justice* 41, 41.

[32] Child Support, Pensions and Social Security Act 2000, ss 69 and 70.

[33] *R (DA) v Secretary of State for Work and Pensions* [2017] EWHC 1446 (Admin), [28].

[34] Robert Thomas and Joe Tomlinson, 'A different tale of judicial power: Administrative review as a problematic response to the judicialisation of tribunals' [2019] *Public Law* 537, 561.

[35] David Feldman, *Law in Politics, Politics in Law* (Oxford, Hart Publishing, 2013) 9.

[36] Daguerre (n 22).

[37] Edward Faulks et al, *The Independent Review of Administrative Law* (*IRAL*), CP 407 (2021).

[38] Roger Cotterrell, 'Judicial Review and Legal Theory' in Genevra Richardson and Hazel Genn (eds), *Administrative Law and Government Action: The Courts and Alternative Mechanisms of Review* (Oxford, Clarendon Press, 1994) 18–19.

[39] Faulks, *IRAL* (n 37) para 1.43.

has explained, this is merely a consequence of parliamentary sovereignty: 'It's parliament … which has said to the judges, "Please look at this legislation and tell us whether it's compatible with the [ECHR]".'[40] The overall success rate of HRA challenges is low, indicating both judicial conservatism and robust respect for executive powers that the HRA does not dislodge.[41]

The prospect of a successful judicial review of social security legislation is further limited by the need to squeeze social rights within the predominantly civil and political rights protected under the ECHR.[42] As Daguerre argues, '[t]he softness of social security rights in the Convention means that it is relatively easy for a government to explain why they are eroding these rights if there is significant cost to the public purse'.[43] Other international treaties that more obviously protect social security rights, including the United Nations Convention of the Rights of the Child (UNCRC), which have been ratified but not incorporated into domestic law, have weaker constitutional status, reducing the extent to which they can be relied upon.[44] Despite this, challenges to the dilution or removal of social rights continue to be made, requiring judges to balance legitimate political choices on resource priorities and government policies with the rule of law as a legal principle.

The Benefit Cap Legislation

The government legislated for the benefit cap under the Welfare Reform Act 2012, stipulating that the limit on household income from social security benefits (excluding disability benefits) would be set at 'estimated average earnings'.[45] This was then implemented in regulations, which set the limit at £18,000 per year for a single claimant without dependent children and £26,000 per year for all other claimants.[46] As the purpose of the cap was to encourage people to change their circumstances and, above all, to work, households that had sufficient income from work were exempt.[47]

The 2012 Act was debated in both Houses of Parliament, including at parliamentary committees, where several objections and opposition amendments relating to the benefit cap were put forward. The first objection was that the

[40] Lord Kerr, cited in Owen Bowcott, 'UK needs judges to limit government power, says Lord Kerr', *The Guardian*, 19 October 2020. See also Faulks, *IRAL* (n 37) para 26.

[41] Joe Tomlinson, Lewis Graham and Alexandra Sinclair, 'Does judicial review of delegated legislation under the Human Rights Act 1998 unduly interfere with executive law-making?', *UK Constitutional Law Blog* (22 February 2021) at https://ukconstitutionallaw.org/.

[42] Philip Larkin, 'Delineating the gulf between human rights jurisprudence and legislative austerity: The judicial entrenchment of "less-eligibility"' (2016) 23 *Journal of Social Security Law* 42.

[43] Daguerre (n 22) 144.

[44] O'Brien (n 27) 723, see too the *SC* case (n 8) [74]–[86].

[45] Welfare Reform Act 2012, s 96(6).

[46] Benefit Cap (Housing Benefit) Regulations 2012, SI 2012/2994.

[47] ibid, reg 2(1), (5).

comparators of income from out-of-work benefits and net median weekly earnings were false, since households receiving net average income might also be receiving benefits. This reality was acknowledged by the government but the rule was maintained on the basis that it was simple and clear, and therefore better able to influence behaviour.[48] The second objection was that the cap would disproportionately impact large families and so it should be adjusted for household type. Again, the government acknowledged that families with several children would be impacted but that this still maintained fairness, since families who were in work had to live within their means and adjust their circumstances in the way that workless households would now be required to do. Finally, and perhaps most significantly, an amendment that child benefit should be excluded from the cap was accepted in the House of Lords since this was (at the time) a universal benefit intended to support and protect children, regardless of the working status of their parents. When the amended legislation returned to the House of Commons, the government controversially invoked 'financial privilege' to remove the amendment, arguing that the cost implications were too significant to accept.[49] Child benefit was therefore included within the income limit for the benefit cap.

The government's first year review of the cap did not address the range of issues that its advisory body, the Social Security Advisory Committee (SSAC), had recommended for effective evaluation,[50] focusing instead on the policy objectives of fairness and behavioural change. The conclusion of the Department for Work and Pensions was that both objectives were met: the policy enjoyed popular public support,[51] and there was evidence of employment-focused behavioural change.[52] The review confirmed that 61 per cent of capped households constituted a single parent with child dependents and one third of capped claimants were judged to be in poverty.[53]

Under the Welfare Reform and Work Act 2015, the benefit cap was revised downwards to a fixed annual limit,[54] not linked to earnings, and exempting carer's allowance and guardian's allowance, the latter being paid to the guardian of a child whose parents are deceased. Sixty-one per cent of households expected to be affected by the new cap were female lone parents.[55] The rationale for the reduced

[48] *Hansard*, HC vol 528, cols 54, 952 and 975 (17 May 2011).

[49] Daniel Gover and Meg Russell, 'The House of Commons' "Financial Privilege" on Lords Amendments: Perceived Problems and Possible Solutions' [2015] *Public Law* 12.

[50] SSAC, *Report by the Social Security Advisory Committee on: The draft Universal Credit Regulations 2013; The Benefit Cap (Housing Benefit) Regulations 2012 (S.I.2012 No. 2994); The draft Universal Credit, Personal Independence Payment, Jobseeker's Allowance and Employment and Support Allowance (Claims and Payments) Regulations 2013* (2012) 85–90.

[51] Department for Work and Pensions, *The benefit cap: A review of the first year* (Cm 8985, 2014) 13.

[52] ibid 18.

[53] ibid 22.

[54] Welfare Reform and Work Act 2015, s 8(2), implemented by the Benefit Cap (Housing Benefit and Universal Credit) (Amendment) Regulations 2016, SI 2016/909.

[55] Department for Work and Pensions, *Equality Analysis for The Benefit Cap (Housing Benefit and Universal Credit) (Amendment) Regulations 2016* (2016) available at www.legislation.gov.uk/uksi/2016/909/pdfs/uksiod_20160909_en.pdf.

cap was that the original cap was successful in changing behaviours and encouraging claimants into work, and so a lower cap would build on this to encourage more people into work.[56] As Simpson notes, however, such 'claims of "success" … have been heavily criticised by both the UK Statistics Authority and a Parliamentary committee'.[57] Fairness continued to be a policy objective, as was reducing benefit expenditure. The impact analysis stated that the UNCRC was taken into consideration, including Article 3 (the duty to treat the best interests of the child as a primary consideration), and, while there was no indication of the cap's potential impact on children, it was stated that it was not in the best interests of a child to live in a workless household.[58]

Overall, the passage of both the 2012 and 2015 Acts and the benefit cap regulations that flowed from them cannot be said to have happened without any scrutiny. Very little changed, however, and whether such scrutiny was effective ultimately became a matter for judicial review.

The Benefit Cap Cases

The application of the benefit cap provides no right of appeal and so the only mechanism to challenge it is through judicial review.[59] Two such judicial reviews made their way to the Supreme Court, the first in 2015 against the original benefit cap and the second in 2019 against the revised cap.

The *SG* Case (2015)

The first case, *SG*, concerned the – unsuccessful – argument that the cap contravened Article 14 of the ECHR,[60] in conjunction with Article 1 of Protocol 1 (A1P1),[61] indirectly discriminating against women, who are statistically more likely to be affected by the cap than men, both as single parents and as victims of domestic violence.[62] The case involved two lone parent mothers, both of whom had experienced domestic violence and whose circumstances meant they were

[56] Department for Work and Pensions, *Welfare Reform and Work Act: Impact assessment for the benefit cap* (2016) at assets.publishing.service.gov.uk/government/uploads/system/uploads/attachment_data/file/548741/welfare-reform-and-work-act-impact-assessment-for-the-benefit-cap.pdf.

[57] Mark Simpson, 'Case analysis: *R (DA) v Secretary of State for Work and Pensions* [2017] EWHC 1466 (Admin)' (2017) 24 *Journal of Social Security Law* 149, 153.

[58] DWP, *Equality Analysis* (n 55).

[59] See also Lady Hale (ch 2) and Kathryn McNeilly (ch 3).

[60] Art 14 of the ECHR provides for the enjoyment of ECHR rights and freedoms without discrimination – in this case on grounds of sex. See also Rory O'Connell (ch 16).

[61] Protocol 1, Art 1 to the ECHR provides for the right to peaceful enjoyment of possessions.

[62] The 3:2 majority decision comprised Lords Reed, Hughes and Carnwath in the majority, with Lord Kerr and Lady Hale dissenting.

detrimentally affected by the cap. Neither the reliance on A1P1 nor the differential impact of the cap on men and women were contested. The legitimacy of the aims of the benefit cap policy (securing the economic well-being of the country, incentivising work, and having a reasonable limit on household income from benefits) were also accepted by the five-judge panel; however the proportionality issue divided them, as did the potential application of the UNCRC in interpreting the issue of discrimination and its enforceability in UK law.

Lord Reed, in the lead majority judgment, pointed to the need to keep a respectful distance between judicial opinion and economic and social policy. He reviewed in some detail the different stages of parliamentary scrutiny of the legislation, including the government's decision to include child benefit within the cap so as to not compromise the policy objective. The level of benefits that someone might receive under or but for the cap was defined as a political question, with Lord Reed noting that '[i]t is not the function of the courts to determine how much public expenditure should be devoted to welfare benefits'.[63] Lord Reed endorsed the Court of Appeal's determination that the level of the cap did not reduce claimants to a state of destitution, with the further qualification that, in any event, the local authority's duty towards the children would be triggered if the family were homeless.[64] The arguments of interest (for this chapter) concerned the relationship between the rights of the mother and the child, and thus the relationship between the ECHR and the UNCRC, and whether the cap could be justified as a proportionate measure. It was agreed that the test for whether the cap was disproportionate was for it to be 'manifestly without reasonable foundation' (MWRF) – a bar sufficiently high for Meers to argue that claimants will inevitably fail to clear it.[65] The extensive review of this test by Lord Reed in the later case of *SC* does little to displace Meer's argument, even with Lord Reed's acknowledgment that 'a stricter standard of review than might otherwise be necessary' might be applied in some cases, 'such as the impact of a measure on the best interests of children'.[66]

The majority concluded that the case was grounded in Article 14 of the ECHR, along with A1P1, and not in Article 3 of the UNCRC, either as an interpretative tool for Article 14 ECHR or as a substitution for arguments on discrimination. In Lord Carnwath's view:

> even if Article 3(1) had a role to play in illuminating Article 14, this could only be where the alleged indirect discrimination, or differential treatment, was in respect of children. In the present case, by contrast, the allegation is of discrimination, not against children, but against their mothers.[67]

[63] *SG* (n 9) [72].

[64] ibid [73]. See Mark Simpson, Gráinne McKeever and Ciara Fitzpatrick, 'Destitution in the UK: Bridging the gap in human rights protection' (forthcoming, 2022).

[65] Jed Meers, 'Problems with the "manifestly without reasonable foundation" test' (2020) 27 *Journal of Social Security Law* 12. On MWRF see Rory O'Connell (ch 16).

[66] *SC* (n 8) [158].

[67] *SG* (n 9) [129].

Lord Hughes agreed, although he suggested the case might be different under Article 8 of the ECHR, regarding the right to private and family life.[68] Despite this, Lord Carnwath, Lady Hale and Lord Kerr all found that the cap breached Article 3 of the UNCRC. For Lord Carnwath, this was not fatal to the government's case. For Lady Hale and Lord Kerr, however, this highlighted the deadly flaws in the government's arguments on justification and mitigation, and therefore of proportionality.

In Lady Hale's judgment the government needed to offer a legitimate reason why it was acceptable to have a discriminatory impact, and why depriving individuals (including children) of subsistence benefits was proportionate to the policy aim. In her analysis, the Secretary of State had misdirected himself in offering only a generalised defence of it being better for children to live in 'working' households. Ultimately, Lady Hale's conclusion was that the policy could not be in the child's best interests and that the government therefore had not given effect to its duty to give primacy to those best interests. In finding for the appellants, Lady Hale relied on the UNCRC as an interpretative principle.

For Lord Kerr, who agreed with Lady Hale's assessment, ultimately the issue was more straightforward, albeit more radical: the UNCRC was directly enforceable in UK domestic law.[69] This was not a position endorsed by any other member of the Court and currently remains an outlier in domestic jurisprudence.[70] Lord Kerr's judgment, however, identifies three ways in which the UNCRC could be used: as an aid to statutory interpretation; as an aid to the development of the common law; and as a basis for legitimate expectation.[71] This was in line with the well-established presumption of compatibility of domestic legislation with international law, which itself established that the government's commitment to a human rights standard meant it should be held to account in court for compliance with that standard.[72]

Lord Kerr also offered an alternative to the direct enforcement of the UNCRC. Where the UNCRC right is directly relevant to the domestic issue to be decided:

> then recourse to the standards that the international instrument exemplifies is not only legitimate, it is required … This … is merely allowing directly relevant standards to infuse our thinking about what the content of the domestic right should be.[73]

[68] ibid [146].

[69] ibid [257].

[70] A Westlaw search of UK cases either relying on the UNCRC or citing *SG* reveals only one that raises the prospect of potentially relying on Lord Kerr's statement that the UNCRC is directly enforceable; in other cases the UNCRC arguments are dealt with as having the potential to lend interpretative value to ECHR provisions. Lord Reed's unequivocal conclusion in *SC* that UK courts should not invoke unincorporated international treaties in interpreting domestic law, on the basis that to do otherwise contradicts a fundamental principle of constitutional law, suggests a definitive attempt to close down Lord Kerr's argument to the contrary: *SC* (n 8) [91].

[71] *SG* (n 9) [238].

[72] Mel Cousins, 'The European Convention on Human Rights, the UN Convention on the Rights of the Child and the "benefit cap": *R (SG (previously JS)) v Secretary of State for Work and Pensions*' [2015] *European Human Rights Law Review* 298; Peter Laverack, 'International human rights law in judicial review: *Moohan v Lord Advocate* and *R (JS) v Secretary of State for Work and Pensions* as guides to the present and the post-Human Rights Act legal landscapes' [2016] *European Human Rights Law Review* 73.

[73] *SG* (n 9) [261].

In Lord Kerr's analysis, depriving children of basic necessities was 'antithetical' to the idea that their interests had been the government's primary consideration.[74] His judgment focuses on the need to scrutinise rigorously not just the mother's rights but those of the children, disagreeing with Lord Carnwath that these rights could be dissociated from each other, stating: 'No hermetically sealed compartmentalisation of their interests is possible'.[75] The 'yardstick' of proportionality was accepted as being that set out by the European Court of Human Rights in *Stec v UK*,[76] so that the question was whether the cap was MWRF.[77] On this basis, Lord Kerr also found for the appellants.

The *DA and DS* Case (2019)

It was perhaps evident from the discussion in *SG* that a challenge to the reduced benefit cap might lie under the UNCRC, together with Article 8 of the ECHR, not least because of the extraordinary pronouncement by Lord Kerr that it was directly enforceable. The *DA and DS* case therefore looked not just at the rights of the parent, but at those rights as parasitic on the rights of the child. As with *SG*, the two central issues were based on the UNCRC and the issue of proportionality.

The – equally unsuccessful – argument was that the cap indirectly discriminated against lone parent mothers and their children, contrary to Article 14 of the ECHR, taken with A1P1 and Article 8 of the ECHR, together with Article 3 UNCRC.[78] The appellants were lone parent mothers and their children. There was agreement across the bench that social policy and discrimination were always suitable for judicial scrutiny and that it was the government's responsibility to justify why lone parents were not exempted from the cap, as claimants of guardian's allowance had been. The disagreement lay, once again, in whether the cap was proportionate to the policy objective – particularly in relation to whether the test was that it needed to be MWRF – and the weight that the UNCRC brought to those conclusions.

Lord Wilson's judgment (with which Lord Hodge agreed) looked at the practicability of lone parents with young children being able to escape the benefit cap, noting the limited data on the extent to which DHPs can 'rescue' capped households.[79] Poverty was seen as being 'hotly contested', but there was a recognition that removing benefits designed to address need set at below subsistence level would push people below the poverty line.[80] There was also an acceptance

[74] ibid [269].

[75] ibid [265]. As Simpson (n 57) points out, Lord Carnwath's view also goes against that set out in a previous Supreme Court decision: see *McLaughlin* (n 1).

[76] *Stec v UK* (2006) 43 EHRR 1017. See also Rory O'Connell (ch 16).

[77] ibid [268].

[78] The 5:2 majority decision comprised Lords Hughes, Carnwath, Reed, Wilson and Hodge in the majority, with Lord Kerr and Lady Hale dissenting.

[79] *DA* (n 10) [31].

[80] ibid [33].

that the UNCRC could inform the interpretation of Article 8 and Article 14 of the ECHR,[81] although Lord Wilson countered the 'move afoot, exemplified by Lord Kerr's judgment in [*SG*] … for UK courts to treat the UNCRC … as … part of our domestic law' by stating categorically that it was not to be treated as such.[82] Noting the parliamentary scrutiny of the 2015 Act, Lord Wilson concluded 'by a narrow margin' that the government was not in breach of Article 3 of the UNCRC.[83] The government also succeeded in persuading the five judges in the majority that the cap, while discriminatory, was not MWRF and that there was therefore no breach of Convention-related rights.

Lords Carnwath, Reed and Hughes, who formed the majority in *SG*, concurred in their conclusions in *DA and DS*. Lords Carnwath and Hughes addressed the argument that the standard to be applied in assessing the proportionality of the cap was that of MWRF rather than the broader standard of 'fair balance',[84] leading Lord Carnwath to state that this 'should be regarded as beyond "future doubt"'.[85] Lord Hughes took Lord Kerr's position as his starting point – that the MWRF test was rooted in the case law of the European Court of Human Rights – and from there concluded that it was open to a domestic court to apply this test to the government's socio-economic policy decisions, as the Supreme Court had done in other cases.[86] The effect, in Lord Wilson's view, was that the state was required to provide a justification for any discrimination, and the claimant must then show that the justification is MWRF.[87]

The idea that the burden would be on the claimant to prove the government's position was MWRF was rejected outright by Lord Kerr, mainly on the basis that the evidence required to establish this 'will customarily be in the hands of the decision-maker and not readily accessible to the person who seeks to challenge the proportionality of the measure'.[88] His judgment disregards Lord Carnwath's declaration that the applicability of the MWRF test was beyond doubt,[89] and Kerr's position was supported by Lady Hale.[90] For Lord Kerr, the case was a chance to revisit his judgment in *SG* and to state that he had been wrong to apply the MWRF test to the final stage in the proportionality analysis,[91] because doing so 'imperils the proper discharge of [the domestic court's] duty'.[92] Accordingly, Lord Kerr concluded the proper test is 'whether the government has established that there is a reasonable foundation for its conclusion that a fair balance has been struck'.[93]

[81] ibid [76] and [72].
[82] ibid [67].
[83] ibid [87].
[84] ibid [98]. See also Meers (n 65).
[85] ibid [110].
[86] ibid [125].
[87] ibid [66].
[88] ibid [177].
[89] ibid [110].
[90] ibid [147].
[91] ibid [174].
[92] ibid [169].
[93] ibid [177].

Lord Kerr also stated that he was not intending to rely on his statement in *SG* that the UNCRC should be directly enforceable, nor to reopen the debate, noting that it was not an issue that had been taken up by other courts. Nonetheless, Article 3 of the UNCRC was still relevant.[94] The government's duty was to keep faith with the spirit of the UNCRC, which was an issue that could not be determined on a mechanistic approach to consideration of whether there had been technical compliance.[95] As in *SG*, Kerr concluded that in giving primacy to the best interests of the child it was not sufficient merely to acknowledge the UNCRC-based issues. The government had not addressed the criticisms of the policy and on this basis its argument failed:

> There is simply no warrant for the claim that refusal to extend exemption from the cap to the DA and DS cohorts will improve the fairness of the social security system or increase public confidence in its fairness. That sweeping statement partakes of a declamation for which no tangible evidence is proffered. To the contrary, a proper understanding of the impact on those whom the appellants represent, so far from increasing public confidence in the social security system, is likely to lead any right-thinking person to the opposite conclusion.[96]

Once again, Lord Kerr highlighted that the court's duty in scrutinising legislation was to consider the impact of the underpinning policy over and above the government's justification for it. His conclusion was that the government had not discharged its obligations under the UNCRC, and so, with Lady Hale, he found for the appellants.

Adding Value(s) to Social Security Law

The Supreme Court's decisions on the benefit cap have demonstrated that the cap is legal, but the clarity of outcome is offset by the significant divergence of judicial opinion. As Larkin has said, the judgments by Lord Reed and Lady Hale (and, by association, Lord Kerr) in *SG* provide 'almost textbook examples of different approaches to linking established human rights jurisprudence to social security provision'.[97]

Lord Hope's statement that UK Supreme Court Justices are 'strong-minded people … with views ranging from most conservative to most liberal' is borne out by the benefit cap cases.[98] Having such diversity of perspectives is, undoubtedly, a healthy feature of executive oversight through judicial review. Cahill-O'Callaghan

[94] ibid [182].
[95] ibid [187].
[96] ibid [189].
[97] Larkin (n 42) 61.
[98] Cited in Rachel Cahill-O'Callaghan, 'The influence of personal values on legal judgments' (2013) 40 *Journal of Law and Society* 596. See also Rachel Cahill-O'Callaghan, *Values in the Supreme Court: Decisions, Division and Diversity* (Oxford, Hart Publishing, 2020).

shows us that Lord Kerr associated judicial dissent with 'independence and the right to reach a different decision, stating that "the great dissents in British legal history speak loudly of the independence of our judiciary"'.[99] Independence within a collaborative and collegiate court indicates a robustness of process and outcome that enables a range of judicial values being brought to bear on Supreme Court decisions. In Cahill-O'Callaghan's seminal analysis of the values of the Supreme Court justices, Kerr's judgments are strongly associated with the values of universalism and benevolence, both of which point to the goal of enhancing and protecting the welfare of others, encompassing protection of the vulnerable, equality and social justice, tolerance and respect for human rights. Her analysis does not include any of Lord Kerr's social security judgments but the values evident in the benefit cap cases seem unlikely to change the characterisation of his judicial approach. Lord Kerr's judgments are less reflective of the values of conformity, tradition, conservation or security, which are more likely to be exhibited by other judges including fellow judges in the benefit cap cases, characterised by Dickson as restrained,[100] or hesitant to extend the law.[101] Value diversity therefore becomes balance.

In his lecture to mark the tenth anniversary of the Supreme Court, Lord Kerr argued that 'it is important that the courts of this country remain alive to changes in social values, standards and the expectations of the society we serve'.[102] The challenge of holding to this standard in social security law is that political values may conflict with the core purpose of social security: the right to live free from poverty and the security of protection when illness, bereavement, disability, parenthood or unemployment occur, raising legitimate questions over what the social values, standards and expectations of society are. The political narrative on social security has seen the pendulum swing from the undeserving beneficiaries of the Poor Laws, to the social insurance of the welfare state, to the presumption that fairness is measured against society's tolerance to support particular circumstances. But what is missing is a discussion of what fairness is, and how public tolerance, supported by political and parliamentary structures that prioritise an ideological version of fairness, may not be the best benchmark. Lord Kerr's judicial values suggest that other considerations are necessary, not least the human rights standards that the government agreed to abide by, and then failed to do so, according to the UK Parliament's Joint Committee on Human Rights.[103] Dickson noted in 2015 that 'Lord Kerr has emerged as

[99] Rachel Cahill-O'Callaghan, *Values in the Supreme Court* (n 98) 98. This is echoed in Faulks, *IRAL* (n 37) para 23: 'Disagreement is, however, hardwired into our culture. Our adversarial system of justice is premised on disagreement; our judicial system, unlike many continental systems, allows for dissent at every level'.

[100] Referring to Lords Hughes, Reed and Hodge: Brice Dickson, 'Activism and Restraint within the UK Supreme Court' (2015) 21(1) *European Journal of Current Legal Issues*.

[101] ibid, referring to Lords Carnwath and Wilson.

[102] Lord Kerr, *The impact of the Supreme Court on the law of Northern Ireland* (4 December 2019), Ten-year anniversary lecture series, available at www.supremecourt.uk/docs/ten-year-anniversary-lecture-lord-kerr.pdf.

[103] *Twenty-First Report* (n 26) para 1.35.

perhaps the strongest advocate for an approach to developing the common law in a way which gives great weight to human rights considerations, expects high standards of all public authorities and takes full account of people's varied vulnerabilities'.[104] Lord Kerr's subsequent judgment in *DA and DS* confirms this, not just in his continued engagement with the ECHR and UNCRC but also in his overall attitude to what is possible, pushing the limits of judicial power beyond narrow 'mechanistic' issues of legality in difficult cases that divide judicial opinion.

Lord Kerr's judgments have demonstrated his ability to use human rights instruments in an innovative way,[105] independently of the approach of the lower courts but also inviting them to do so, as indicated by his observation in *DA and DS* that no other courts had yet taken up his 'constitutionally radical' statement that the UNCRC was directly enforceable.[106] His observation remains accurate: the only substantive reference to his position in *SG* (bar those side-stepped by the lower courts in *DA and DS*),[107] was through the Children's Commissioner's intervention in *R (Public Law Project) v Lord Chancellor*, where she reserved the right to submit elsewhere that the UNCRC should be held to be binding in domestic law without the need for legislative incorporation, as per Lord Kerr's dictum.[108] The Court of Appeal's response was to say:

> with great respect, that I think it of the first importance to give full weight to the constitutional principle that the Executive, which enters into Treaty obligations, is not (save under powers delegated by Parliament, and subject to certain irrelevant exceptions) a source of law in the United Kingdom.[109]

Lord Reed's judgment in *SC* confirms the Court of Appeal's position.[110]

Lord Kerr's dictum brings him into the territory of judicial activism that could 'entirely transform our dualist system by which international law is separated from domestic law enacted by Parliament',[111] particularly since he did

[104] Dickson (n 100).

[105] Tom Royston and Charlotte O'Brien, 'Exclusion of unmarried partners from parental bereavement benefit is unlawfully discriminatory' (2018) 25 *Journal of Social Security Law* D77–D78.

[106] Claire Fenton-Glynn, 'Austerity and the benefit cap: In whose best interests?' (2015) 37 *Journal of Social Welfare and Family Law* 467.

[107] The High Court was satisfied that the UNCRC could be taken into account without needing to be directly applied: *DA* (n 33). The Court of Appeal stated that there was no need to explore the 'further issues' of direct applicability of the UNCRC for the purposes of the appeal: *R (DA) v Secretary of State for Work and Pensions* [2018] EWCA Civ 504, [145].

[108] *R (Public Law Project) v Lord Chancellor* [2015] EWCA Civ 1193. This case went on to the Supreme Court, where the Children's Commissioner again intervened and where the issue of discrimination was one of the grounds of appeal. Ultimately, however, the case succeeded on the ground that the regulations being challenged were ultra vires and the Court stated that it would not deal with the discrimination issue, so no further exploration of the direct applicability of the UNCRC was required: *R (Public Law Project) v Lord Chancellor* [2016] UKSC 39, [2016] AC 1531.

[109] *Public Law Project* (CA) [27] per Laws LJ.

[110] *SC* (n 8) [90]–[91].

[111] Dominic Grieve, 'Can a Bill of Rights do better than the Human Rights Act?' [2016] *Public Law* 223, 232. See also Mario Mendez, 'Neglecting the treaty-making power in the UK: The case for change' (2020) 136 *LQR* 630.

not need to make this finding in order to reach the outcome he wanted.[112] But it was not a maverick position: it was founded on legal argument foreshadowed by Lord Slynn in *Lewis*,[113] and rather more firmly expressed by Lord Steyn in *In re McKerr*,[114] which now demanded 'an exception to the dualist theory' for human rights treaties.[115] The building blocks of common law have often opened up human rights in the UK and law (and progress) thrives on dissent.[116] In 2003 Lord Nicholls was a dissenting voice in the House of Lords in arguing that Article 8 of the ECHR encompassed the child's 'basic need' for 'accommodation with his parent'.[117] The Court of Appeal subsequently adopted Lord Nicholls' approach that the state's duty under Article 8 included addressing the child's poverty, or potential street homelessness,[118] to the extent that was 'necessary to allow family life to continue'.[119] This interpretation appears to be more readily accepted by the courts today,[120] just as Lord Kerr's statement is likely to speak more clearly to a future age.

His statement is, nonetheless, radical in relative terms. More generally, his liberal approach to the development of rights under the ECHR contrasts with the conservative views of his colleagues and predecessors. Lord Bingham saw the ECHR's potential for law making as small, confined to what the European Court had already ruled, with 'no licence to freewheel'.[121] This stands in stark contrast to Lord Kerr's statement that:

> it is not open to courts of this country to adopt an attitude of agnosticism and refrain from recognising such a right simply because Strasbourg has not spoken … [N]ot only is it open to this court to address and deal with those arguments on their merits, it is our duty to do so.[122]

Paterson highlights that while Lord Kerr's views are stark, they are not extreme, citing support for some of them from his Supreme Court colleagues Lady Hale and Lord Brown.[123] From a Court of Appeal perspective, Laws LJ makes a persuasive argument for domestic courts to 'have full regard not only to local conditions but also to the imperative of the constitutional balance', avoiding an approach that would 'confine the law in a Strasbourg straightjacket' which undermines

[112] Kathryn Hollingsworth, 'Judging Children's Rights and the Benefit Cap: *R (SG and Others) v Secretary of State for Work and Pensions*' (2015) 27 *Child and Family Law Quarterly* 445.

[113] *Lewis v AG of Jamaica* [2001] 2 AC 50 (JCPC).

[114] *In re McKerr* [2004] 1 WLR 807.

[115] *SG* (n 9) [254].

[116] Cass Sunstein, *Why Societies Need Dissent* (Cambridge, Harvard UP, 2003).

[117] *R (G) v Barnet LBC* [2003] UKHL 57, [55].

[118] *R (N) v Greenwich LBC* [2016] EWHC 2559 (Admin).

[119] *Anufrijeva v Southwark LBC* [2003] EWCA Civ 1406.

[120] *R (PK) v Harrow LBC* [2014] EWHC 584 (Admin).

[121] Feldman (n 35) 37.

[122] *Ambrose v Harris* [2011] UKSC 43, [2011] 1 WLR 2435, [128]–[130].

[123] Alan Paterson, *Final Judgment: The Last Law Lords and the Supreme Court* (Oxford, Hart Publishing, 2013) 230. See also Colm O'Cinneide, 'Rights under Pressure' [2017] *European Human Rights Law Review* 43.

'the autonomous development of human rights law'.[124] Judicial propriety, judicial values and judicial activism exist on a continuum: there is not a single threshold point for any of them, or a set of scales that allows us to declare one judgment right and another wrong. Once again, the issue is about balance. To have a Supreme Court composed only of conservative or liberal judges would impoverish the scrutiny of government actions and parliamentary process, as well as imperilling the value of dissent in a legal system based on judicial precedent.

Lord Kerr's views on social security were vital. Lord Reed's reliance in *SG* on the local authority's duty to claimants at risk of homelessness reflects something that may be true in law but is not reflected in the reality for those whose path to destitution has been via the social security system.[125] Their reality is reflected more accurately in Lord Kerr's perspective that a social security measure which reduced a claimant to reliance on this duty is one that would erode the confidence of 'any right-thinking person' in the social security system.[126] At the very least, this evidences an urgent debate over what the social values in relation to the social security system should be, or indeed the values of a system of human rights protection. Lord Reed's judgment in *SC* acknowledges the intense controversy over the fairness of measures like the two-child limit, but concludes that such controversial questions cannot be answered by any process of legal reasoning, having already ruled out the use of international treaties as a framework to address the legitimacy – and fairness – of controversial policies and their impacts.[127] In the absence of political or parliamentary champions who can challenge the narrative, however, where else can social rights be championed? 'Kicking this up' to the judiciary is not just a form of democratic accountability but a means of rectifying the democratic deficit for those who have not benefited from the 'rights revolution' that was anticipated by the HRA,[128] and for whom policy validated by parliamentary scrutiny results in '[r]eal misery … being caused to no good purpose'.[129] Robust challenges to government choices are necessary and robust defences must go beyond acknowledging that there is an issue. O'Brien's analysis of the parliamentary scrutiny of the two-child limit – directly concerned with the rights protected under the UNCRC – finds no evidence that the best interests of the child were a primary consideration in the scrutiny by the House of Commons, the House of Lords, the Public Bill Committee and the published associated materials, including the Impact Assessment.[130] Her question is, where will the UNCRC have an impact if not on this directly harmful measure? Lord Kerr's question

[124] John Laws, *The Constitutional Balance* (Oxford, Hart Publishing, 2021) 126. See also Colm O'Cinneide, *Human Rights and the UK Constitution* (London, British Academy, 2012).

[125] Gráinne McKeever, Mark Simpson and Ciara Fitzpatrick, *Destitution and Paths to Justice* (London and York, Legal Education Foundation and Joseph Rowntree Foundation, 2018).

[126] *DA* (n 10) [189].

[127] *SC* (n 8) [208].

[128] Larkin (n 42); Faulks, *IRAL* (n 37) para 34.

[129] *DA* (n 33) [43] per Collins J.

[130] O'Brien (n 27).

is why bother signing the UNCRC if its existence makes no real difference? His judgments, exemplified in the benefit cap cases, bring credibility to both judicial review and human rights and in doing so evidence the value of meaningful scrutiny in the making of social security law.

Conclusion

The benefit cap continues to bite, with the number of capped households more than doubling in 2020 during the Covid-19 outbreak.[131] One of its features is to provide a 'grace period' for those who were in work prior to becoming unemployed – a mitigation that will have proved valuable for those who lost their jobs at the start of the Covid-19 pandemic – but that grace period has now expired. In November 2020, the SSAC advised government that the cap should be removed, increased or eased by extending the grace period, noting that the opportunities to avoid the cap – increasing work or moving to cheaper accommodation – were not realistic at that time.[132] The government stated that it had no plans to extend the grace period, reiterating that the cap restores fairness between workless households and 'taxpayers in employment'.[133] A policy that speaks to fairness will struggle to be heard over the increasing volume of people, including children, living in poverty and destitution. The increased generosity of universal credit during the pandemic has been a central feature of public understanding of what the system provides, but the £20 weekly uplift is, in many cases, cancelled out by the benefit cap threshold. Public confidence in the social security system will be sorely tested as these time-limited and inadequate protections come to be experienced by more and more people.

Social rights and social security entitlement are part of the journey towards social change. The current destination will be a difficult place for many to survive but we can see from Lord Kerr's judgment that other directions of travel are possible. He may have foreshadowed another pendulum swing, from austerity to post-pandemic security, when the cry for a new Beveridge has potential to be heard. The political perspective at Westminster may be slower to change, but devolutionary developments including the incorporation of the UNCRC into Scots law,[134] along with the alignment of 'fairness' with statutory principles of

[131] Department for Work and Pensions, *Benefit cap: Number of households capped to November 2020* (2021).

[132] SSAC, *A review of the Covid-19 temporary measures: Occasional Paper No 24* (2020).

[133] Letter from the Secretary of State for Work and Pensions, Therese Coffey, to Chair of the Work and Pensions Committee, Stephen Timms, 10 December 2020, at committees.parliament.uk/publications/4028/documents/40255/default.

[134] UNCRC (Incorporation) Scotland Bill 2020–21. The Scottish government's competence to implement this legislation is currently the subject of litigation before the Supreme Court.

dignity and respect that protect social security as a human right,[135] and the implementation of the socio-economic rights duty under the Equality Act in Wales,[136] are catching up with Lord Kerr. The combined statutory and common law effect could be transformative.

The loss of Lord Kerr from the Supreme Court is our loss in being able to anticipate his judgments: potentially radical, compassionate, broad-minded and able 'to mould the common law to the realities of changing social conditions and to address issues of public policy'.[137] His contribution has been evident not just in his majority views but in the counter-balance that his dissenting judgments brought to the Supreme Court's perspective, keeping alive the importance of framing the government's duty to meet the basic needs of its citizens. His legacy would be well served if policy makers, advocates and judges had to ask themselves 'could we get this past Lord Kerr'? Opening minds to this theoretical challenge would make for a much more robust assessment of the weaknesses of social security law and the potential for protecting the social rights of claimants. The 'Kerr test' will undoubtedly be used by those who continue to challenge social security law and policy and to scrutinise government decisions that impact on those most in need of the state's support.

[135] Social Security (Scotland) Act 2018, s 1.

[136] Equality Act 2010 (Authorities subject to a duty regarding Socio-economic Inequalities) (Wales) Regulations 2021, SI 2021/295 and Equality Act 2010 (Commencement No 15) (Wales) Order 2021, SI 2021/298.

[137] Feldman (n 35), referring to the qualities of Lord Simon of Glaisdale.

8

Two Journeys Intertwined: Lord Kerr and EU Law

IMELDA MAHER*

The career of Lord Kerr as a lawyer coincides with United Kingdom (UK) membership of the European Union (EU).[1] He was called to the Northern Ireland Bar in 1970, becoming a member of the Bar of England and Wales in 1974, a year after accession[2] and his retirement occurred a few months before the UK left the EU. Lord Kerr was appointed to the High Court of Northern Ireland[3] a few years after the seminal *Factortame II* case, where the House of Lords accepted the principle of supremacy/primacy of EU law over domestic law, noting that the principle had been well-established by the time the UK had joined the EU in 1973.[4] This was also the first time that the House of Lords had referred a case to the Court of Justice of the European Union (CJEU)[5] for consideration.[6] The primacy principle, alongside the doctrine of direct effect under which EU law rights and obligations for individuals are enforced by national courts,[7] and the obligation on Member States

* With thanks to Margaret Gallagher and Rónán Riordan for research assistance.

[1] The European Union was preceded by the European Communities and the European Economic Community. For ease of reference, EU will be used throughout.

[2] European Communities Act 1972, repealed by the European Union (Withdrawal) Act 2018, s 1. It ceased to have effect at the end of the Brexit transition period (31 December 2020). See the European Union (Withdrawal Agreement) Act 2020, s 39(1).

[3] See www.supremecourt.uk/about/former-justices.html#01.

[4] *Factortame Ltd v Secretary of State for Transport (No 2)* [1991] 1 AC 603; see Lord Bridge at 658. The Court awarded interim relief to protect EU law rights even though this meant setting aside provisions in an Act of Parliament. Paul Craig, 'Britain in the European Union' in Jeffrey Jowell, Dawn Oliver and Colm O'Cinnéide (eds), *The Changing Constitution*, 8th edn (Oxford, OUP, 2015) ch 4; Josef Drexl, 'Was Sir Francis Drake a Dutchman – British Supremacy of Parliament after Factortame' (1993) 41 *American Journal of Comparative Law* 551.

[5] Prior to the Lisbon Treaty the Court was the European Court of Justice (ECJ) but for ease of reference CJEU will be used throughout.

[6] Case C-213/89 *The Queen v Secretary of State for Transport, ex parte Factortame* EU:C:1990:257, [1991] 1 All ER 70. On senior courts and the preliminary reference procedure, now Art 267 of the Treaty on the Functioning of the EU (TFEU), see Monica Claes, 'Luxembourg, Here We Come? Constitutional Courts and the Preliminary Reference Procedure' (2015) 16 *German Law Journal* 1331.

[7] Case 26/62 *Van Gend en Loos* [1963] ECR 1. The scope of this doctrine has been developed over the years: see Damian Chalmers and Luis Barroso, 'What *Van Gend en Loos* Stands For' (2014) 12

to ensure effective legal protection for EU law through provision of remedies,[8] meant that EU law was considered and enforced by courts in the UK.

This chapter is at the intersection of EU law and judicial studies, where scholars from law and politics explore the relationships and interactions between national courts and EU law, adopting both doctrinal and quantitative analysis. Alter, a political scientist, showed how the responses of higher and especially constitutional courts, differed from lower courts in their embrace of EU law. For the latter it marked an expansion rather than a reduction in jurisdiction.[9] Chalmers, in his study of EU law in UK courts, and Rodger, in a similar study of Scotland, showed that even though EU law was constitutionally significant and had significant regulatory impact, it arose relatively infrequently in UK courts.[10] The chapter is also located in the literature on the UK Supreme Court, including Cahill-O'Callaghan,[11] Paterson,[12] Hunter and Rackley,[13] Dickson's study of judicial activism in the Supreme Court,[14] and the Dickson and McCormick[15] analysis of the connections between the Supreme Court and Northern Ireland in its first decade – an analysis where Lord Kerr is central. This chapter offers a different perspective by focusing on the career of one senior judge and where, when and how he encountered EU law.[16] It reflects on one judge's experience of EU law – a single (and singular) judicial journey in the complex environment of the relationship between domestic and EU Law in the UK.

International Journal of Constitutional Law 105; Morten Rasmussen, 'Revolutionizing European Law: A History of the Van Gend en Loos Judgment' (2014) 12 *International Journal of Constitutional Law* 136.

[8] Art 19(1) of the Treaty on European Union (TEU) and Art 47 of the EU Charter of Fundamental Rights (CFR). This obligation is supported by the principle of equivalence, tempered by the procedural autonomy of national courts: see Case C-14/83 *Von Colson v Land Nordrhein-Westfalen* [1984] ECR 1891. Anthony Arnull, 'The Principle of Effective Judicial Protection in EU Law: An Unruly Horse?' (2011) 36 *European Law Review* 51. National courts can also award damages for breach of EU law: see Case C-6/90 *Francovich v Italy* [1993] 2 CMLR 66.

[9] Karen Alter, *Establishing the Supremacy of European Law* (New York, OUP, 2001).

[10] Damian Chalmers, 'The Positioning of EU Judicial Politics within the United Kingdom' (2000) 23 *West European Politics* 169; Damian Chalmers, 'Judicial Preferences and the Community Legal Order' (1997) 60 *MLR* 164; Barry Rodger, 'The Application of EU Law by the Scottish Courts: An Analysis of Case-Law Trends Over Forty Years' (2017) *Juridical Review* 59; Barry Rodger, Imelda Maher and Rónán Riordan, 'A Decade of EU Law in the Courts of Scotland and Ireland: National Legal Systems Compared' (2021) 41 *Legal Studies* 311.

[11] Rachel Cahill-O'Callaghan, *Values in the Supreme Court: Decisions, Division and Diversity* (Oxford, Hart Publishing, 2020).

[12] Alan Paterson, *Final Judgment: The Last Law Lords and the Supreme Court* (Oxford, Hart Publishing, 2014).

[13] Rosemary Hunter and Erika Rackley, 'Judicial Leadership on the UK Supreme Court' (2018) 38 *Legal Studies* 191.

[14] Brice Dickson, 'Activism and Restraint within the UK Supreme Court' (2015) 21(1) *European Journal of Current Legal Issues*.

[15] Brice Dickson and Conor McCormick, 'Northern Ireland Dimensions to the First Decade of the United Kingdom Supreme Court' (2020) 83 *MLR* 1133.

[16] The study only looks to case law. To locate cases, Westlaw and Lexis were searched, with Westlaw UK the focus. Having identified the cases where Lord Kerr was a judge (in either jurisdiction), regard was then had to substance. In Westlaw, the advanced search function was used (dates range: after 1 January 1993 and before 6 September 2020), with a search in the judge section using Kerr/Lord Kerr and then those searches being alternated with keywords: EU/ European/ European Union.

Regard is first had to the EU law cases in which Lord Kerr sat in Northern Ireland, his judicial career there being significant although EU law was not an important part of it. The chapter then turns to a brief overview of EU law cases which Lord Kerr heard when on the Supreme Court, before analysing the six judgments he gave concerning EU law and those cases where a reference was made to the CJEU, before concluding. The chapter shows how EU law was part of the warp and weft woven into the career of a judge of the Supreme Court when the UK was a member of the EU.

Lord Kerr, EU Law and Northern Ireland

The constitutional and regulatory impact of EU membership on the English legal order emerged gradually in the courts of the UK.[17] Despite the potential scope of EU law and the constitutional challenges posed, Chalmers' study of EU law in UK courts between 1971 and 1998 showed that the bulk of EU law arose in relatively narrow and highly concentrated areas of law, suggesting limited impact outside those fields but major constitutional questions being raised, for example in *Factortame*.[18] There were 1,088 EU law cases over this 28-year period, of which only 17 cases arose in Northern Ireland. Thus, it is not surprising that only two cases regarding EU law came before Lord Kerr in Northern Ireland; both in the High Court and both concerning competition law.

In his first reported EU law case in 1995, Kerr J (as he was then) found against a harbour authority, quashing its refusal to allow the applicants to operate as general stevedores at the harbour, on the grounds that it should have sought further information and allowed representations.[19] The argument based on abuse of market dominance under EU competition law failed:[20] the harbour did not constitute a geographic market in its own right as it did not provide a unique service[21] and, even if the authority was dominant, it was not in a substantial part of the EU and it was unlikely there was abuse affecting trade between Member States. Three years later, Kerr J once again considered competition law, this time dismissing the application for judicial review of a decision granting state aid to a developer of a shopping centre on the basis that no economic advantage was conferred on the developer or its tenants, as the grants ensured development that would not otherwise have taken place.[22]

[17] Craig (n 4); Tony Prosser, *The Economic Constitution* (Oxford, OUP, 2014) ch 3.

[18] eg, despite the availability of remedies for breach of EU law, few cases have been brought in the UK or Germany: see Tobias Lock, 'Is Private Enforcement of EU Law Through State Liability a Myth? An Assessment 20 Years after Francovich' (2012) 49 *Common Market Law Review* 1675.

[19] *Re Anley Maritime Agencies Ltd* [1999] EuLR 97, decided 18 October 1995 (Queen's Bench Division, NI).

[20] Art 102 TFEU. The case pre-dated the Competition Act 1998.

[21] Thereby distinguishing the main authority, *B&I Line plc v Sealink Harbours Ltd* [1992] 5 CMLR 255.

[22] *Re Peninsula Securities Ltd* [1998] EuLR 699 (Queen's Bench Division, NI); see now Arts 107(1) and 108(3) TFEU.

In his six years as Lord Chief Justice of Northern Ireland he did not address any substantive EU law issues. This, of course, would change when he was appointed to the House of Lords and soon afterwards to the newly established Supreme Court in 2009.

Lord Kerr, EU Law and the Supreme Court

Over his 11-year career as a member of the Supreme Court Lord Kerr was a judge in 43 cases in which EU law was raised.[23] Of these, one was a Privy Council case.[24] The first EU law case in the Supreme Court in which Lord Kerr sat concerned a European Arrest Warrant (EAW). In *Louca v Germany* the Court dismissed an appeal where the appellant had argued that the warrant under which he was to be extradited to Germany was invalid without reference to previous EAWs issued against him that had previously been (correctly) withdrawn.[25] The last Supreme Court case concerning EU law on which Lord Kerr sat was *Villiers*,[26] where he agreed with the majority judgment of Lord Sales.[27] The majority held that the Maintenance Regulations (based on EU law) did apply to intra-UK cross-border proceedings, even though the regulations on divorce jurisdiction, also based on EU law, did not.[28]

Of the 43 cases concerning EU law that Lord Kerr heard in the Supreme Court, he gave the lead judgment in six instances. In 35 cases he was in the majority or there was a unanimous judgment from the Court; he dissented in two cases. In her study of Supreme Court decisions Cahill-O'Callaghan noted that Lord Kerr was the Supreme Court judge most likely to dissent (6 per cent of cases).[29] This figure is a little less for cases involving EU law, where he dissented in only two out of the 43 cases (4.65 per cent).

Chalmers, in his study of EU law in all British higher courts, found a surprisingly narrow focus of litigation, with 25 per cent of the 1,088 cases relating to

[23] Lord Kerr also sat in *Schütz (UK) Ltd v Werit* [2013] UKSC 16, [2013] 2 All ER 177, which concerned the interpretation of the 'making' of a patented item under the Patents Act 1977. Lord Neuberger gave the judgment of the Court, noting that the legislation was intended to conform with the European Patent Convention and discussing German case law. As the EPC is not an EU instrument the case does not, strictly speaking, concern EU law.

[24] *French v Portugal* [2013] UKPC 16, [2014] AC 40 (an appeal from Gibraltar). The Board dismissed an appeal against the surrender of the defendant on the basis of a European Arrest Warrant. The procedural argument was not accepted by the Court as the delay in question was not deemed excessive.

[25] *Louca v Germany* [2009] UKSC 4, [2009] 1 WLR 2550.

[26] *Villiers v Villiers* [2020] UKSC 30, [2020] 3 WLR 171.

[27] Lady Black gave a separate judgment in the majority. Lord Wilson gave a dissenting judgment, with which Lady Hale agreed.

[28] Civil Jurisdiction and Judgments (Maintenance) Regulations 2011, SI 2011/1484, Sch 6, based on Council Regulation (EC) No 4/2009, [2009] OJ L7/1. The majority held that the European Communities Act 1972 allowed for the extension of the EU rules to intra-state disputes.

[29] See Cahill-O'Callaghan (n 11). The study is based on the first nine years of the Supreme Court.

taxation.[30] Sex discrimination litigation was next, accounting for 15.7 per cent of cases, with the remainder of cases concerning free movement of goods, free movement of persons (excluding issues of service provision and establishment), and intellectual property. For Lord Kerr, immigration and asylum cases were the most common,[31] constituting 20.9 per cent (nine) of the EU law cases he heard in the Supreme Court;[32] employment law[33] and extradition law[34] were next at 16.2 per cent and 13.9 per cent (seven cases and six cases respectively); four cases each on conflicts of law[35] and environmental law;[36] three cases concerning each of consumer law/free movement of goods,[37] public law[38] and social security law;[39] with the four remaining cases covering a range of issues.[40] The preponderance of immigration and asylum cases mirrors the change found by Rodger in his study of EU law in the Scottish Courts and also reflects the experience of the higher

[30] See Chalmers, 'The Positioning of EU Judicial Politics' (n 10).

[31] Categorisation of case law is not an exact science, eg a case may raise employment, equality and pension issues (*O'Brien v Ministry of Justice* [2017] UKSC 46, [2017] 4 All ER 997) but each case is counted only once.

[32] *R (ZO (Somalia)) v Secretary of State for the Home Dept* [2010] UKSC 36, [2010] 1 WLR 1948; *FA (Iraq) v Secretary of State for the Home Dept* [2011] UKSC 22, [2011] 4 All ER 503; *R (EM (Eritrea)) v Secretary of State for the Home Dept* [2014] UKSC 12, [2014] AC 1321; *R v McGeough* [2015] UKSC 62, [2015] 1 WLR 4612; *MP (Sri Lanka) v Secretary of State for the Home Dept* [2016] UKSC 32, [2017] 2 All ER 155; *R (Agyarko) v Secretary of State for the Home Dept* [2017] UKSC 11, [2017] 1 WLR 823; *VS (Lithuania) v Secretary of State for the Home Dept* [2017] UKSC 54, [2017] 1 WLR 2926; *SM (Algeria) v Entry Clearance Officer, UK Visa Section* [2018] UKSC 9, [2018] 1 WLR 1035; *Secretary of State for Work and Pensions v Gubeladze* [2019] UKSC 31, [2019] AC 885.

[33] *Parkwood Leisure Ltd v Alemo-Herron* [2011] UKSC 26, [2011] ICR 920; *Russell v Transocean International Resources Ltd* [2011] UKSC 57, [2012] 2 All ER 166; *O'Brien* (n 31); *Walker v Innospec Ltd* [2017] UKSC 47, [2017] 4 All ER 1004; *R (Unison) v Lord Chancellor* [2017] UKSC 51, [2020] AC 869; *P v Commissioner of Police of the Metropolis* [2017] UKSC 65, [2018] 1 All ER 1011; *Gilham v Ministry for Justice* [2019] UKSC 44, [2019] 1 WLR 5905.

[34] *Louca* (n 25); *Assange v Sweden* and *Assange v Sweden (Application to Re-Open Appeal)* [2012] UKSC 22, [2012] 2 AC 471; *R (HH) v Westminster City Magistrates Court* [2012] UKSC 25, [2013] 1 AC 338; *Zakrzewski v Poland* [2013] UKSC 2, [2013] 1 WLR 324; *Lithuania v Bucnys* [2013] UKSC 71, [2014] AC 480; *Konecny v Czech Republic* [2019] UKSC 8, [2019] 1 WLR 1586.

[35] *Joint Administrators of Heritable Bank plc v Winding Up Board of Landsbanki Islands HF* [2013] UKSC 13, [2013] 1 WLR 725; *Re N (Children)* [2016] UKSC 15, [2017] AC 167; *Aspen Underwriting Ltd v Credit Europe Bank NV* [2020] UKSC 11, [2021] AC 493; *Villiers* (n 26).

[36] *R (Morge) v Hampshire County Council* [2011] UKSC 2, [2011] 1 WLR 268; *Walton v Scottish Ministers* [2012] UKSC 44, 2013 SC (UKSC) 67; *R (Buckinghamshire County Council) v Secretary of State for Transport* [2014] UKSC 3, [2014] 1 WLR 324; *R (Evans) v Attorney General* [2015] UKSC 21, [2015] AC 1787.

[37] *Robertson v Swift* [2014] UKSC 50, [2014] 1 WLR 3438; *Scotch Whisky Association v Lord Advocate* [2017] UKSC 76, 2018 SC (UKSC) 94; *X v Kuoni Travel Ltd* [2019] UKSC 37 and [2021] UKSC 34.

[38] *R (Chester) v Secretary of State for Justice* [2013] UKSC 63, [2014] AC 271; *R (Miller) v Secretary of State for Exiting the EU* [2017] UKSC 5, [2018] AC 61; *UK Withdrawal from the European Union (Legal Continuity) (Scotland) Bill* [2018] UKSC 64, [2019] AC 1022.

[39] *St Prix v Secretary of State for Work and Pensions* [2012] UKSC 49, [2013] 1 All ER 752; *Mirga v Secretary of State for Work and Pensions* [2016] UKSC 1, [2016] 1 WLR 481.

[40] Copyright: *Public Relations Consultants Association Ltd v Newspaper Licensing Agency Ltd* [2013] UKSC 18, [2013] 2 All ER 852; public procurement: *Healthcare at Home Ltd v Common Services Agency* [2014] UKSC 49, [2014] 4 All ER 210; tax: *Volkswagen Financial Services (UK) Ltd v Revenue and Customs Commissioners* [2017] UKSC 26, [2017] STC 824; data protection: *Elgizouli v Secretary of State for the Home Dept* [2020] UKSC 10, [2020] 2 WLR 857.

courts in Ireland.[41] Lord Kerr also sat on the two *Miller* cases, the first of which, relating to whether or not the triggering of Article 50 TEU required legislation, is included in the figures, given the discussion of that provision. The second *Miller* case on the prorogation of Parliament is not included, as it was a constitutional law case that arose out of Brexit but did not raise any EU law questions.[42]

Lord Kerr on EU Law

As already stated, Lord Kerr gave judgment in six cases concerning EU law. Four of the cases concerned immigration and asylum law and one concerned availability of a spouse's pension to a gay couple, reflecting Lord Kerr's interest and reputation in human rights law,[43] with one case on consumer law. In *ZO (Somalia)*[44] Lord Kerr gave the judgment of the Court, holding that an asylum seeker who makes a second asylum application after the first application is rejected, is entitled to work, under the Reception Directive,[45] while awaiting the outcome of the second application. Lord Kerr started his judgment by referring to the EU Charter and the Geneva Convention as he quoted from the recitals of the Directive, setting the tone for the judgment. He rejected the argument that the Directive should be read in isolation. The Treaty[46] envisaged a comprehensive charter on asylum; the legislative history of the Directive suggested it included repeat applications, especially drawing on the more inclusive language of the Procedures Directive.[47] He saw it as 'anomalous and untoward that an applicant who makes a subsequent application after his first application has been finally disposed of should be denied access to standards that are no more than the minimum to permit him to live with some measure of dignity'.[48] Given the clarity of the Directive, the Court would

[41] Rodger (n 10); Jo Shaw, 'Scotland: 40 years of EU Membership' (2012) 8 *Journal of Contemporary European Research* 547. For EU law in Irish courts see Imelda Maher, 'EU Law and the Courts: The Mundane and the Exceptional' in Eoin Carolan (ed), *Judicial Power in Ireland* (Dublin, Institute of Public Administration, Ireland, 2018).

[42] *R (Miller) v Prime Minister* [2019] UKSC 41, [2020] AC 373.

[43] Lord Kerr saw his most important case as the legal challenge which led to reform of abortion laws in Northern Ireland: *In the matter of an application by the Northern Ireland Human Rights Commission for Judicial Review* [2018] UKSC 27, [2019] 1 All ER 173: Owen Bowcott, 'Lord Kerr: "respectable arguments" for both jury and non-jury trials', *The Guardian*, 19 October 2020. For the role of Lord Kerr in the trend towards a more human rights-based approach in Northern Irish cases, see Dickson and McCormick (n 15).

[44] *ZO (Somalia)* (n 32).

[45] Council Directive 2003/9/EC on minimum standards for the reception of asylum seekers, [2003] OJ L31/18, Art 11. The Immigration Rules implemented the Reception Directive, Rule 360 dealing with work.

[46] Now Art 78 TFEU.

[47] Council Directive 2005/85/EC, [2005] OJ L326/13 now replaced by Directive 2013/32/EU of the European Parliament and of the Council of 26 June 2013 on common procedures for granting and withdrawing international protection, [2013] OJ L180/60.

[48] *ZO (Somalia)* (n 32), [31].

not adopt an interpretation inconsistent with that purpose even though it raised administrative difficulties for the authorities. Finally, the Court refused to make a preliminary reference to the CJEU, seeing the interpretation as meeting the standard of being equally obvious to other national courts in the EU.[49] The test applied by the Court was that if, on a careful examination of the reasoning underlying any contrary argument against the view it had formed, it could not be accepted on any conventional basis of reasoning, then the reference should not be made. This suggests that the Court did not see the argument of the state as having much merit. There were tens of thousands of asylum seekers in the system affected by this judgment who could thus work while the large backlog in the asylum system was cleared.[50]

The *FA* case, decided in the same year,[51] concerned the differences in rights of appeal from decisions of the Secretary of State in relation to claims for asylum and for humanitarian protection. The EU principle of equivalence of remedy requires remedies in EU law to be no less favourable than those in domestic law[52] but it was not clear whether the procedures for asylum could be deemed a comparator for those under humanitarian protection given it combined EU and domestic law; hence, the Court referred that case to the CJEU.

In *EM (Eritrea)* the issue was whether proof of systemic failure in the asylum system of an EU Member State was necessary before the asylum seeker would have substantial grounds for a claim of a real risk of inhuman or degrading treatment to avoid being returned there.[53] The Dublin Regulation which created the first country of arrival presumption for those claiming asylum was in issue (as well as breach of Article 3 of the ECHR).[54] The Court of Appeal saw the *NS* case, a decision of the CJEU,[55] as requiring it to set a very high threshold for an applicant by requiring the applicant to prove systemic failure, irrespective of evidence of personal experience and circumstances suggesting a serious risk of inhuman or degrading treatment. Lord Kerr thought it would be remarkable for the law to ignore the risk of degrading or inhuman treatment unless there was proof of systemic failure. Hence, working from first principles, he read the *NS* case as being wide enough to include operational failure for the individual. There was no discussion of making a preliminary reference even though the Supreme Court was overruling the Court of Appeal on the interpretation of a judgment of the

[49] Case 283/81 *CILFIT Srl v Ministro della Sanita* EU:C:1982:335, [1982] ECR 3415, para 16.

[50] Adam Wagner, 'Minimum standards of dignity must be upheld for asylum seekers' (29 July 2010, *UK Human Rights Blog*), available at ukhumanrightsblog.com/2010/07/29/minimum-standards-of-dignity-must-be-upheld-for-asylum-seekers.

[51] *FA (Iraq)* (n 32).

[52] The key case on equivalence is Case C-33/76 *Rewe-Zentralfinanz eG and Rewe-Zentral AG v Landwirtschaftskammer für das Saarland* EU:C:1976:188. Paul Craig and Gráinne de Búrca, *EU Law: Text, Cases, and Materials*, 7th edn (Oxford, OUP, 2020) 222 et seq.

[53] *EM (Eritrea)* (n 32). See too Brice Dickson (ch 6) 111.

[54] Council Regulation 343/2003 (Dublin Regulation), [2003] OJ L50/1. Lord Kerr calls it a presumption rather than a rule.

[55] Joined Cases C-411/10 and C-493/10 *R (NS) (Afghanistan) v Secretary of State for the Home Dept* EU:C:2011:865, [2013] QB 102.

CJEU central to deciding the case. Lord Kerr instead interpreted the EU case in a manner which reconciled it and the decision of the European Court of Human Rights on a similar issue in the *MSS* case.[56]

McGeough considered whether information given in an asylum application could be used in a criminal prosecution in the UK.[57] The defendant was convicted of IRA membership in part based on information he had revealed to Swedish authorities when he unsuccessfully applied for asylum there in the 1980s. He unsuccessfully challenged the disclosure of this information based on the Procedures Directive.[58] The general scheme of the EU asylum regime does not require blanket confidentiality in all circumstances and there was no specific requirement for it in this instance. The information was legally obtained from Sweden, which had a culture of legal disclosure, and an analogy with UK law that might not have allowed disclosure was not deemed apposite.

The question of equal treatment of a gay couple in relation to pension rights for surviving spouses arose in the *Walker* case, where Lord Kerr gave a robust and expansive majority judgment, in favour of the claimant.[59] There was an exception included in the equality legislation that restricted its retrospective application to occupational pensions.[60] The Court held this provision was at odds with the non-discrimination principle enshrined in the relevant Directive. The CJEU drew a distinction between the retroactive application of legislation to past situations (which, like many jurisdictions, is prohibited unless expressly provided for) and its immediate application to continuing situations (which is generally allowed). The Court of Appeal had found against the claimant based on the *Barber* case, which allowed for prospective application of a judgment on equal treatment on pensions. Lord Kerr rejected this approach, narrowing the scope of the *Barber* case so that it applies only where the outcome would otherwise be catastrophic.[61] Once the Directive was transposed into UK law, the rate of pension was based on all the claimant's years of service and his partner qualified for a spousal pension the day they married, as would be the case for a heterosexual couple. Lord Kerr held that non-discrimination based on sexual orientation was now a principle of EU law. This meant that, in so far as the implementing statutory instrument contradicted that principle in relation to occupational pensions, it had to be disapplied.

[56] *MSS v Belgium and Greece* (2011) 53 EHRR 2. See Cathryn Costello, 'Dublin-case NS/ME: Finally, an End to Blind Trust across the EU?' (2012) 2 *Asiel & Migrantenrecht* 83.

[57] *McGeough* (n 32).

[58] Specifically, Art 22 of the Procedures Directive (n 47).

[59] *Walker* (n 33). Lady Hale and Lord Reed agreed with the judgment. The relevant EU law is Council Directive 2000/78/EC of 27 November 2000 establishing a general framework for equal treatment in employment and occupation (Employment Equality), [2000] OJ L303/16.

[60] Equality Act 2010, Sch 9, para 18.

[61] Case C-262/88 *Barber v Guardian Royal Exchange Assurance Group* [1990] ECR I-1889, [1991] 1 QB 344. Lord Carnwath and Lord Hughes disagreed with this expansive reading of the *Barber* case, saying they would await further case law from the CJEU on the matter, but they also found for the appellant.

Robertson is a rare example of a small claims case being considered by the Supreme Court. Lord Kerr addressed the issue of the return of a deposit for cancellation of a furniture removal contract.[62] Allowing the appeal, the Court held that notice of the right to cancel a consumer contract was not a prerequisite for that right. On that basis, the consumer could secure the return of the deposit. Lord Kerr notes that national implementing measures must be interpreted as far as possible in light of the purpose and wording of the Consumer Protection Directive,[63] referring to both CJEU case law[64] and English case law.[65] On this basis the Regulations were given a purposive interpretation, with Lord Kerr quoting copiously from CJEU cases.

Lord Kerr in Dissent in EU Law Cases

Lord Kerr gave the lead judgment in *Elgizouli* but he was in a minority of one in his view that there was now a common law principle prohibiting assistance to another government if it might result in the death penalty.[66] The appellant was challenging the decision of the Secretary of State to provide mutual legal assistance (MLA) to the US government in the prosecution of the appellant's son on terrorist charges, where the death penalty could be imposed, despite the longstanding practice of the UK government not to provide such assistance where there was such a penalty. The majority of the Court held that the common law did not prevent the assistance but that under the Data Protection Act 2018 the information could not be provided. Part 3 of the Act implemented the Enforcement Directive, the recitals of which expressly mention that data is not to be used in the context of the death penalty.[67] In this instance the transfer of the data could be only for special circumstances if it was necessary and if the fundamental rights of the subject did not override the public interest. Direct, personal evaluation is required and had not taken place. Lord Kerr saw EU law (specifically the prohibition on the death penalty in Article 2(2) of the CFR) as having settled opposition to the death penalty in every circumstance. In doing so, he did not regard it

[62] *Robertson* (n 37).

[63] The Consumer Protection (Cancellation of Contracts Concluded away from Business Premises) Regulations 1987, SI 1987/2117 implemented Council Directive 85/577/EEC of 20 December 1985 to protect the consumer in respect of contracts negotiated away from business premises (Consumer Contracts Directive), [1985] OJ L372/31.

[64] Case C-350/03 *Schulte v Deutsche Bausparkasse Badenia AG* EU:C:2005:637, para 71.

[65] In particular *Vodafone 2 v Commissioners for Her Majesty's Revenue and Customs* [2009] EWCA Civ 446, [2010] Ch 77.

[66] *Elgizouli* (n 40). Here we are concerned only with the EU law discussion. Lord Carnwath, at [171], explained that what Lord Kerr was suggesting for the common law was not incremental development.

[67] EU Directive 2016/680 of the European Parliament and of the Council of 27 April 2016 on the protection of natural persons with regard to the processing of personal data by competent authorities for the purposes of the prevention, investigation, detection or prosecution of criminal offences or the execution of criminal penalties, and on the free movement of such data, [2016] OJ L119/89.

necessary to decide whether the discretion left to Member States to provide assistance to Japan in cases of the death penalty, subject to conditions in the EU-Japan Agreement, suggested that there was no such settled opposition.[68] He emphasised the influence of EU law on the common law:

> It cannot be irrelevant to the development of our common law that the UK was a member of the EU for more than 40 years. The influence that EU law in general and its hostility to the death penalty in particular has on a decision as to the current state of the common law is undeniable.[69]

On this basis, he argued that the common law could adopt a principle against assistance where there is a death penalty. His reliance on EU law was significant for his argument, as the case law of the European Court of Human Rights did not address such assistance. EU law provided the influence he needed to extend the common law, but his colleagues did not go so far, all instead relying only on the Data Protection Act 2018.

Lord Kerr also dissented in part in the *Morge* case.[70] The Court dismissed an appeal in a judicial review of a planning authority's decision to allow a bus route along a disused railway line. The applicant was concerned about the impact of the development on several legally protected bat species. The Court held that the authority could rely on the opinion of Nature England, which advises on nature conservation, in deciding to grant planning as it polices compliance with the relevant conservation legislation (based in turn on the Habitats Directive).[71] In this instance, Nature England had removed its objections to the development following a comprehensive bat survey undertaken by the authority. Lord Brown gave the leading judgment,[72] with which Lord Walker, Lady Hale and Lord Mance agreed, while also explaining why they disagreed with Lord Kerr. Lord Kerr did not agree with the majority that the planning authority could rely on the opinion of Nature England to show that it had met its obligations under the Habitat Directive. Nature England had not expressly referred to the Directive in its report and perhaps, if it had, the authority could have relied on it. Hence Lord Kerr saw a greater responsibility for the planning authority under the Directive than the majority did.

[68] Art 11(1)(b) of the EU-Japan Agreement on Mutual Legal Assistance in Criminal Matters [2010] OJ L 39, 20.

[69] *Elgizouli* (n 40) [134].

[70] *Morge* (n 36).

[71] Art 12(1)(b) of Council Directive 92/43/EEC of 21 May 1992 on the conservation of natural habitats and of wild fauna and flora, [1992] OJ L206/7, implemented by the Conservation (Natural Habitats &c.) Regulations 1994, SI 1994/2716 (as amended).

[72] In one paragraph he mentioned that a preliminary reference to the CJEU could be made. He did not analyse the test for making such a reference, instead simply concluding that he did not think that Court would do a better job than the Supreme Court. This perhaps eclipses the role of the CJEU as the only body capable of providing an authoritative interpretation of EU law.

The Preliminary Reference Cases

There were nine cases where Lord Kerr sat and the Supreme Court referred questions of interpretation on EU law to the CJEU, each of which is discussed sequentially below.[73] This is the procedure that marks the highest level of engagement between any national court and the CJEU, and which is of greater significance when the question is referred by the most senior domestic court.[74] Nine references over 11 years amounts to just under one reference a year, which shows a marked change from the first 15 years of EU membership, when no reference was made by the House of Lords.[75] The process requires the Court to frame questions relating to interpretation or validity of EU law, which the CJEU then answers usually within 12 to 18 months. The UK Supreme Court, as a court of last resort, has to make a reference where this is necessary to decide a case.[76] The nine cases in which Lord Kerr sat concerned tax, consumer law, copyright law, refugee law, free movement rules and workers' rights. No major constitutional issue arose. In general, these are relatively short single judgments indicating the opinion of the Supreme Court on the point of law being referred. In two instances, the CJEU position differed from the opinion offered by the Supreme Court as to how the law could be interpreted: in relation to collective bargaining rights on the transfer of undertakings and to the recognition of traditional Islamic adoption for the purposes of free movement of citizens.[77]

In the first case where Lord Kerr was on the panel and a reference was to be made (*FA*), it was in fact not progressed.[78] Three weeks later, the Supreme Court made another reference in the *Parkwood Leisure* case.[79] This is one of the cases where the CJEU came to a different view from the Supreme Court, when it sought clarification as to whether national law could go further than the Transfer of Undertakings Directive to protect dynamic contractual rights so as to

[73] This study did not extend to an analysis of all cases to see if there were any where a reference should have been made and was not. However, see *ZO (Somalia)*, discussed in the text at n 44 above, where Lord Kerr expressly declined to make a reference.

[74] Art 267 TFEU. The CJEU is the sole authoritative interpreter of EU law: see Arts 17 and 19(3) TEU; Claes (n 6). On the procedure in Ireland see Elaine Fahey, *Practice and Procedure in Preliminary References to Europe: 30 Years of Article 234 EC Case Law from the Irish Courts* (Dublin, First Law, 2007).

[75] The *Factortame* case was the first reference made: see n 4 above. On national courts and preliminary references see Jos Hoevenaars and Jasper Krommendijk, 'Black Box in Luxembourg: the bewildering experience of national judges and lawyers in the context of the preliminary reference procedure' (2021) 46 *European Law Review* 61.

[76] However, if the matter has previously been decided by the CJEU or is very clear, then a reference is not necessary. The Supreme Court frequently refers to this *acte clair* doctrine before deciding to make a reference.

[77] *Parkwood Leisure* (n 33), and *SM (Algeria)* (n 32).

[78] *FA (Iraq)* (n 32). The Court invited the parties to make submissions in writing within 28 days on the questions to be referred to the CJEU, but the matter was not progressed: see *R (The United Road Transport Union) v Secretary of State for Transport* [2012] EWHC 1909, [42].

[79] *Parkwood Leisure* (n 33). The judgment was given by Lord Hope.

bind subsequent transferees to collective bargaining arrangements in relation to employee pay.[80] The Supreme Court saw some scope for such an interpretation in national law consistent with well-established interpretive principles of EU law[81] and hence the reference was made. However, the CJEU held that a dynamic interpretation was not possible under the Directive if the subsequent employer did not have the possibility of participating in the collective bargaining negotiations.[82] The Supreme Court's judgment is notable for its considered analysis of its interpretative obligations under EU law and the scope for discretion. The CJEU judgment, on the other hand, consistently with its earlier case law,[83] takes a much narrower interpretation of the specific provision.

Over a year later, in *St Prix*, Lady Hale gave the judgment of the Court, referring a case to the CJEU as to whether a woman who stops work in late pregnancy is deemed a worker for the purposes of claiming income support. The CJEU agreed that she was a worker under the EU treaties, despite temporary cessation due to pregnancy.[84] The question of whether the temporary storage of copyrighted material on computers incidentally, as part of the use of those computers, necessitated a copyright licence under the Copyright Directive was referred to the CJEU in the following year.[85] Lord Sumption indicated that the Court was of the view that a licence was not required but, given the important transnational nature of the issue and the need for a definitive answer to the question, the case was referred and the CJEU provided an interpretation in line with that suggested by the Court.[86] There was then a three-year gap before the next reference in the *MP* case, where the Supreme Court referred the question whether the appellant was entitled to subsidiary protection under the Qualifications Directive[87] if there was no risk of ill treatment but a real risk of serious harm to his psychological health if he were to be returned to his country of origin, due to his having been tortured there in

[80] The Transfer of Undertakings (Protection of Employment) Regulations 1981, SI 1981/1794 were the relevant regulations at the time, implementing Council Directive 77/187/EEC of 14 February 1977 on the approximation of the laws of the Member States relating to the safeguarding of employees' rights in the event of transfers of undertakings, businesses or parts of businesses (Transfers of Undertakings), [1977] OJ L61/26.

[81] Under Case 14/83 *Von Colson and Kamann v Land Nordrhein-Westfalen* [1984] ECR 1891 national courts are required to interpret implementing legislation in a manner consistent with relevant EU law: see *Pickstone v Freemans plc* [1989] AC 66; *Litster v Forth Dry Dock & Engineering Co Ltd* [1990] 1 AC 546.

[82] Case C-426/11 *Alemo-Herron v Parkwood Leisure Ltd* EU:C:2013:521.

[83] Case C-499/04 *Werhof v Freeway Traffic Systems GmbH & Co KG* EU:C:2006:168, [2006] ECR I-2397.

[84] *St Prix* (n 39), and Case C-507/12 *Saint Prix v Secretary of State for Work and Pensions* [2015] 1 CMLR 5. Art 45 TFEU was the relevant provision. The Supreme Court judgment is notable for the comment, at [19], that pregnancy is not a lifestyle choice.

[85] *Public Relations Consultants Association* (n 40).

[86] Case C-360/13 *Public Relations Consultants Association Ltd v Newspaper Licensing Agency Ltd* EU:C:2014:1195, [2014] AC 1438.

[87] Council Directive 2004/83/EC of 29 April 2004 on minimum standards for the qualification and status of third country nationals or stateless persons as refugees or as persons who otherwise need international protection and the content of the protection granted, [2004] OJ L304/12.

the past.[88] The CJEU decided that the Directive could cover such circumstances, provided there was a real risk of being intentionally deprived, in the country of origin, of appropriate care for the physical and mental after-effects of torture (a question of fact for the national court to determine and clearly established in this instance).[89]

There were two references in 2017. *Volkswagen* concerned the deduction of general overhead costs where part of a transaction, in this instance the hire purchase element of a car purchase, is not subject to VAT.[90] Almost in passing, the Court noted it was making a reference, a definitive interpretation of the EU rules being necessary.[91] In *O'Brien*,[92] lengthy litigation concerning the right of part-time judges (Recorders) paid on a per diem rate to pensions led to a reference to determine whether the calculation of pension was only from the date when the UK implemented the Part Time Work Directive.[93] The Supreme Court was of the view that the Directive applied from the date the pension fell due, so the full period of service had to be considered – an interpretation also adopted by the CJEU.[94]

In *SM*,[95] the only reference in 2018, Lady Hale gave the judgment of the Court regarding the right of family reunification for a child under the legal guardianship of a French national in the Islamic kefalah system, which is not recognised in the UK as a legal form of adoption. The Court held that the child clearly fell within Article 3(3) of the Directive as a dependent member of the EU citizen's household and referred to obligations to protect the welfare of children under UK Law, the UN Convention on the Rights of the Child, the ECHR and the EU Charter of Fundamental Rights. Even though the child fell within this provision, the Court still made a reference to the CJEU as to the meaning of 'family member' under Article 2(2) of the Directive, as that status would confer

[88] *MP (Sri Lanka)* (n 32). Lord Toulson gave the brief judgment. It had already been decided that MP was entitled to discretionary leave to remain under Art 3 ECHR. However, humanitarian protection under the Directive would give him much more extensive rights, including family reunification and the right of settlement after five years' residency: see Ayesha Christie, Matrix Case Comments, 20 December 2016.

[89] Case C-353/16 *MP v Secretary of State for the Home Dept* EU:C:2018:276, [2018] 1 WLR 5585.

[90] *Volkswagen Financial Services* (n 40).

[91] Lord Carnwath gave the judgment of the Supreme Court. In Case C-153/17 *Volkswagen Financial Services (UK) Ltd v Revenue and Customs Comrs* [2019] 4 WLR 32 the CJEU decided that it is for the national court to determine whether the method used by HMRC for calculating the deductible proportion of VAT took account of the actual and non-negligible allocation of a share of the general costs for the purposes of the transaction giving rise to a right to deduct under Arts 168 and 173(2)(c) of the VAT Directive (Council Directive 2006/112/EC of 28 November 2006 on the common system of value added tax, [2006] OJ L347/1).

[92] *O'Brien* (n 31).

[93] Council Directive 97/81/EC of 15 December 1997 concerning the Framework Agreement on part-time work concluded by UNICE, CEEP and the ETUC (Part Time Work), [1998] OJ L14/9, extended to the UK by Council Directive 98/23/EC of 7 April 1998, [1998] OJ L131/10 and implemented by the Part Time Workers (Prevention of Less Favourable Treatment) Regulations 2000, SI 2000/1551.

[94] *O'Brien v Ministry for Justice* [2019] 1 CMLR 40.

[95] *SM (Algeria)* (n 32).

an automatic right of reunification. Lady Hale made it clear in her judgment that there was scope for the provision to be read to include circumstances such as this. Nonetheless, in its decision on the point the CJEU gave the provision a narrower interpretation, emphasising the responsibility of the national authorities under Article 3(2) to take account of the best interests of the child.[96]

The last preliminary reference on which Lord Kerr sat was *Kuoni*,[97] where the Supreme Court referred questions on the Package Tours Directive[98] as to whether a victim of a rape conducted by a maintenance staff member who offered to conduct her to the reception of her hotel constituted a breach of contract by the tour operator. The Court set out the views of the parties of the case and made the reference. The CJEU held that the unforeseeable event defence was not available to the tour operator where loss is caused by the deliberate act of the supplier's employee, it being for the national court to determine the scope of the service provider's obligations considering the employee's conduct. By the time the case came back to the Supreme Court Lord Kerr had died, but his four colleagues went on to take a broad view of the obligations owed by tour operators to consumers under package holiday contracts, thereby denying the tour operator in this case a contractual defence.[99]

Lord Kerr gave the judgment of the Court in one reference case only and the reference ultimately did not materialise. The Supreme Court judgments provide a sophisticated analysis of EU law and all cases give expression to the idea of a judicial dialogue between two apex courts, with the Supreme Court often indicating its own view on how the EU law could be interpreted.[100]

Conclusion

Lord Kerr, as a member of the Supreme Court, sat on cases concerning EU law each year, on average just under four EU law cases a year. He was adept at working across and negotiating the relationship between the two legal orders, readily engaging with EU law as part of the judicial dialogue between the apex courts of

[96] *SM v Entry Clearance Officer, UK Visa Section* [2019] 1 WLR 5505; unusually, 13 judges sat in this case.

[97] *X v Kuoni Travel Ltd* (n 37); Case C-578-19 *X v Kuoni Travel Ltd* EU:C:2021:213. For a note on this case see Tom Collins, 'No "unforeseeable event" defence for deliberate acts of hotel employees: CJEU gives judgment in *X v Kuoni*', at www.lexology.com/library/detail.aspx?g=3f4e0efd-daeb-40ce-89fc-5383da038ce1.

[98] Council Directive 90/314/EEC of 13 June 1990 on package travel, package holidays and package tours, [1990] OJ L158/59, implemented by the Package Travel, Package Holidays and Package Tours Regulations 1992, SI 1992/3288.

[99] *X v Kuoni Travel Ltd* [2021] UKSC 34.

[100] See, eg, Francis Jacobs, 'Judicial Dialogue and the Cross-Fertilization of Legal Systems: The European Court of Justice' (2003) 38 *Texas International Law Journal* 547; Matteo Bonelli, 'The Taricco saga and the consolidation of judicial dialogue in the European Union' (2018) 25 *Maastricht Journal of European and Comparative Law* 357.

the Supreme Court and the CJEU. Brexit has fundamentally changed the relationship between the EU and UK legal orders, and it will be for those now in the Supreme Court to tease out the nuances and complexities of that relationship. For Lord Kerr, while the EU law cases ranged across a limited number of fields, he gave principled and significant judgments on the status of the death penalty in EU law and in the common law; the importance of public authorities complying with the rule of law; and the existence of an EU law principle of non-discrimination on grounds of sexual orientation. These showed him to be a progressive judge championing the rights of the individual in relation to the exercise of public authority.

9

Lord Kerr and the Judicial Committee of the Privy Council

DEREK O'BRIEN

Introduction

Upon his appointment as a Lord of Appeal in Ordinary in June 2009, and four months thereafter as one of the original 12 Justices of the United Kingdom Supreme Court (UKSC), Lord Kerr became eligible to sit as a member of the Judicial Committee of the Privy Council (JCPC). The JCPC currently serves as the final court of appeal for all of the independent countries of the Commonwealth Caribbean (with the exception of Guyana, Barbados, Belize and Dominica);[1] a small number of other independent states (Gambia, Mauritius and Tuvalu); all of the British Overseas Territories; and the Crown Dependencies of Jersey, Guernsey and the Isle of Man. When hearing these appeals the JCPC sits as the highest appellate court in the jurisdiction from which the appeal in question is being brought.[2]

While the JCPC's overseas jurisdiction may be declining, it remains, in the words of Lord Neuberger, 'a fully-fledged appellate court with a unique international character'.[3] Lord Neuberger, whose tenure on the JCPC overlapped with that of Lord Kerr, has also described the experience of the JCPC's Justices trying cases from jurisdictions other than their own as 'very enriching … both personally and legally'.[4] Though we do not know whether Lord Kerr concurred with this view, as

[1] All of these countries send their appeals to the Caribbean Court of Justice, which was established in 2006.

[2] In addition to its overseas jurisdiction, the JCPC was chosen, in 1998, to serve as the court of final appeal in devolution issue cases, a role it discharged until 2009 when devolution cases were brought under the Supreme Court's jurisdiction by the Constitutional Reform Act 2005. It has been argued that one of the reasons why this role was originally assigned to the JCPC was because of its experience in determining constitutional issues arising from its overseas jurisdictions: see, eg, Roger Masterman, 'The constitutional influence of the Judicial Committee of the Privy Council on the UK apex court: institutional proximity and jurisprudential divergence?' (2020) 71 *NILQ* 285.

[3] Lord Neuberger, 'The Judicial Committee of the Privy Council in the 21st Century' (2014) 3 *Cambridge Journal of International and Comparative Law* 30, 44.

[4] Lord Neuberger (ibid) 31. Lady Hale has also said that their experience in dealing with Commonwealth Constitutions as members of the JCPC has benefited Supreme Court Justices when

he never made his feelings about his role as a member of the JCPC known publicly,[5] we do know that a large amount of his time during his tenure as a Justice of the UKSC would have been consumed in JCPC work. According to a study conducted by Rosemary Hunter and Ericka Radley conducted between 2009 and 2015, UKSC Justices sat on an average of 39 per cent of the JCPC cases decided during their tenure.[6] The same study notes that the number of JCPC cases on which Lord Kerr sat fluctuated from year to year, but a trawl through the decided cases on the JCPC's website reveals that during his time as a UKSC Justice Lord Kerr heard no fewer than 192 cases in the JCPC.[7]

The large volume of appeals which Lord Kerr heard as a member of the JCPC makes it impossible to examine each of these cases individually within the space of this chapter. Furthermore, the wide variety of issues that form the subject matter of appeals to the JCPC and the diverse range of jurisdictions from which appeals to the JCPC emanate make a thematic or comparative approach problematic. I therefore propose for the purposes of this chapter to consider only those appeals which arose from the independent countries of the Commonwealth Caribbean and, within this group, to focus on those that touched upon public law issues. This approach has two advantages. Firstly, public law was one of Lord Kerr's areas of specialisation and it is therefore reasonable to presume that he would have made an important contribution to the resolution of these appeals. Secondly, the constitutions of Commonwealth Caribbean countries are all members of the same family, being based on the Westminster model of democracy, and each contain a Bill of Rights based on the European Convention of Human Rights,[8] so that the problems usually associated with comparative constitutional law,[9] if not entirely avoided, are at least minimised.

Having decided to focus my attention on appeals that touch upon public law issues, I have identified five broad categories of cases in which Lord Kerr was involved: firstly, those that concern the operation of Public Service Commissions within the region; secondly, those that are concerned with the appointment, dismissal and terms of service of the region's judges; thirdly, those that concern the operation of the death penalty in the region; fourthly, those that are concerned with the constitutional protection against discrimination; fifthly, and finally, those that raise administrative law issues. For reasons of space I will limit myself to examining one significant judgment within each of these categories, significance being

dealing with devolution cases: see Lady Hale, 'Devolution and the Supreme Court – 20 years on' (Speech to the Scottish Public Law Group, 14 June 2018, 18, available at www.supremecourt.uk/docs/speech-180614.pdf). Roger Masterman has, however, questioned this assertion: see (n 2) 3.

[5] At least to this author's knowledge.

[6] Rosemary Hunter and Erika Rackley, 'Judicial Leadership on the UK Supreme Court' (2018) 38 *Legal Studies* 191, 201.

[7] In addition, it may be noted that Lord Kerr chaired the Joint UKSC and JCPC User Group.

[8] With the exception of Trinidad and Tobago, which modelled its Bill of Rights on the Canadian Bill of Rights 1960.

[9] See, eg, Antonia Barragia, 'Challenges in Comparative Constitutional Law Studies: Between Globalization and Constitutional Tradition' *Law and Method, Special Issue, Comparative Law*, October 2017, available at https://ssrn.com/abstract=3081474.

loosely defined here as encompassing those cases which raise issues of particular jurisprudential, social or political interest.

I should say from the outset that, being based on my own subjective evaluation of whether a judgment is significant, my approach makes no claim to being scientific. However, I hope that such an approach may be permitted within the pages of a volume intended to honour the memory of Lord Kerr. It is also important to mention at the outset that, with one or two notable exceptions which I highlight below, all of the judgments which I examine are single judgments and only three of them are cases in which Lord Kerr was responsible for delivering the judgment. It is difficult, therefore, always to draw definitive conclusions from these judgments about Lord Kerr's personal judicial philosophy. I am confident, however, that the judgments I have selected for analysis are consistent with that distinctively 'liberal' approach to constitutional adjudication, with its focus on the rights of citizens against the state, for which Lord Kerr was best known.[10]

Public Service Commissions

All of the Commonwealth Caribbean's independence constitutions provided for the creation of a variety of Public Service Commissions (PSCs). As Lord Diplock observed in *Thomas v Attorney General of Trinidad and Tobago*, the rationale for creating these PSCs was:

> [T]o insulate members of the Civil Service, the Teaching Service and the Police Service … from political influence exercised directly upon them by the Government of the day. The means adopted for doing this was to vest in autonomous commissions, to the exclusion of any other person or authority, power to make appointments to the relevant service, promotions and transfers within the service and power to remove and exercise disciplinary control over members of the service.[11]

Since independence the JCPC has regularly entertained appeals from public servants and others within the region disappointed with the decisions of their respective PSCs. Indeed, during Lord Kerr's tenure the JCPC heard no less than seven appeals regarding decisions of PSCs in which Lord Kerr was involved as a member of the panel.[12] Usually, in the case of such appeals the JCPC has adopted a very hands-off approach, preferring to defer to the local knowledge of the PSC concerned regarding the matters in issue.[13] However, in the case which I wish to

[10] Brice Dickson, 'Activism and Restraint Within the UK Supreme Court' (2015) 21(1) *European Journal of Current Legal Issues*.

[11] *Thomas v Attorney General of Trinidad and Tobago* [1982] AC 113.

[12] *Public Service Appeal Board v Maraj* [2010] UKPC 29; *Prime Minister Patrick Manning, Ganga and Others v Commissioner of Police/Police Service Commission* [2011] UKPC 28; *Sankar v Public Service Commission* [2011] UKPC 27; *The Public Service Commission v Ganga Persad Kissoon* [2011] UKPC 20; *Attorney General of Trinidad and Tobago v Dumas* [2017] UKPC 12; *Mohammad v Public Service Commission* [2017] UKPC 31 and *Jamaicans for Justice v Police Service Commission* [2019] UKPC 12.

[13] See, eg, *Sankar* (n 12).

consider under this heading, *Jamaicans for Justice v Police Service Commission*,[14] the JCPC's approach was markedly less deferential. Though this is significant in its own right, the broader significance of the case lies in the Board's determination to play its part in responding to the appalling record of extra-judicial killings in Jamaica and '[the] long-standing status quo of ineffective investigation into questionable shootings and allegations of excesses by agents of the state'.[15]

The appellants, a non-governmental human rights organisation, originally sought to challenge a decision of the Police Service Commission of Jamaica (the Commission) to promote a Police Superintendent. Prior to initiating proceedings, the appellants had informed the Commission that it had received 13 complaints of unprofessional conduct against the Superintendent concerned, including 10 complaints of fatal shootings by officers under his command. The Commission's response was to consult with the Commissioner of Police (the Commissioner), who provided the Commission with a one page report prepared by the Jamaican Constabulary Force's Bureau of Special Investigation (BSI) which was mildly critical, but broadly supportive, of the Superintendent. This report was not sent to the appellants, who wrote again to the Commission, this time referring to a report prepared by the UN Special Rapporteur on Torture who had complained about the Superintendent's 'very obstructive, uncooperative and openly threatening conduct when they visited his police station'.[16] Though the appellants' letter was forwarded to the Commissioner, he continued to support the Superintendent's promotion, describing him as 'fearless and prepared to tackle the criminal elements in the society'.

Notwithstanding the Commissioner's defence of the Superintendent, the Commission requested and received a report from the BSI relating to a number of fatal shootings in which the Superintendent had been involved. In five of these there had been verdicts of justifiable homicide and in the remainder the investigation was either incomplete or a ruling was awaited from the Director of Public Prosecution. In addition the Commission interviewed the Superintendent himself, as a result of which the Commission formed the view that he was a 'fearless and effective police officer who was placed repeatedly in policing divisions accounting for the highest incidents of crime, particularly murder'. He was, accordingly, appointed to act as a Senior Superintendent for three months during which time the Commission would request further information. Alarmed by reports in the media about the possible promotion of the Superintendent, the appellants provided the Commission with a list of 28 complaints against the Superintendent and officers under his command. However, the DPP having reported that it had completed its investigation and that there would be no criminal charges brought against the Superintendent, the Commission recommended to the Governor General that

[14] *Jamaicans for Justice* (n 12).

[15] *Gerville Williams v Commissioner of the Independent Commission of Investigations* [2012] JMFC Full 1, cited by the JCPC at *Jamaicans for Justice* (n 12) [12].

[16] Cited ibid [5].

the Superintendent be appointed to the role of Senior Superintendent, and duly advised the appellants of the appointment.

Initially, the appellants filed a claim for judicial review before the Jamaican Supreme Court seeking to quash the Commission's decision and an order of mandamus directing the Commission to conduct 'an effective, thorough and impartial investigation' into the 28 complaints of misconduct that the appellants had drawn to the Commission's attention. Having failed at first instance, the appellants appealed to the Jamaican Court of Appeal. By this point their focus had shifted from requiring the Commission to conduct an investigation to requiring it to cause such an investigation to be undertaken by the Independent Commission of Investigations (INDECOM). This is a statutory body, independent of the Jamaican Constabulary Force and Security Services, which was established by the Jamaican Parliament 'to undertake investigations concerning actions by members of the Security Forces and other agents of the state that result in death or injury to persons'.[17] The Court of Appeal, however, rejected the appellants' application, holding that while the Commission undoubtedly had the power, pursuant to regulation 15(1) of the Police Service Regulations 1961, to ask INDECOM for a report, it was a matter for the Commission whether or not it chose to do so.

In a unanimous judgment delivered by Lady Hale, the Board declared that the Court of Appeal of Jamaica had been wrong to conclude that, while the Commission had the *power*[18] to call for a report from INDECOM, it was not under a *duty* to do so. In the Board's view the Court of Appeal had been preoccupied with the wrong question, namely whether there was an express statutory duty on the Commission to call for a report from INDECOM. The Board preferred to approach the question from the perspective of the Constitution, which requires every public body, including the Commission, to exercise its functions in a manner which is compatible with the rights guaranteed by the Constitution, including the rights to life, to due process of law and to equality before the law. The last of these rights, in the Board's view, afforded protection against irrationality, unreasonableness, fundamental unfairness or the arbitrary exercise of power. In any event, these were 'fundamental common law principles governing the exercise of public functions'.[19] Regardless of whether the Commission had a statutory duty to call for a report from INDECOM, it had a common law duty to do so, since there was a reasonable prospect that a properly informed Commission, furnished with a report from INDECOM, might have made a different decision with regard to the police officer's promotion.[20]

By any measure the Board's decision represents a remarkable intrusion into the autonomy of the Commission, which had consulted with the Commissioner, called for and received a report from the BSI, and interviewed the Superintendent

[17] The Independent Commission of Investigations Act 2010.
[18] Pursuant to reg 15(1) of the Police Service Regulations 1961.
[19] *Jamaicans for Justice* (n 12) [24].
[20] ibid [28].

in person. The Board's decision went much further than the Jamaican Court of Appeal, which had concluded that the Commission had only to 'give proper consideration to the Commissioner's recommendation for the promotion of the Superintendent'. In the Board's view such intrusion into the autonomy of the Commission was, however, justified by:

> [T]he grave concern, both nationally and internationally, that police, or some members of the [Jamaican Constabulary Force], were overly inclined to take the law into their own hands in dealing with it, thus risking violations of the right to life, to due process of the law and to equality before the law of the people involved.[21]

Judges

It goes without saying that judges in the Commonwealth Caribbean have a vital role to play in holding their executives and legislatures to account, but it is worth emphasising the importance in such small, closely-knit jurisdictions of adequate institutional safeguards to protect the independence of judges in order to ensure that they are able effectively to discharge this responsibility. In particular, it is important to guard against political interference in the appointment and removal of judges and in their terms and conditions of service.

During his time on the JCPC Lord Kerr was involved in four appeals from the Commonwealth Caribbean which touched upon these issues[22] but for the purposes of this chapter I wish to focus on one particular case, *Archie v Law Association of Trinidad and Tobago.*[23] I have chosen this case because it throws into dramatic relief the sheer intensity of the disagreements that can arise in the context of these small closely-knit Commonwealth Caribbean societies that have, for historical and deeply rooted societal reasons, diminishing levels of trust in public institutions. In the context of a multicultural society such as Trinidad and Tobago, the level of intensity is made all the greater by the racial and political cleavages between the Afro-Caribbean and Indo-Caribbean communities.

The appeal in this case was brought by the Chief Justice of Trinidad and Tobago, Ivor Archie, who objected to an investigation of his conduct by a committee of the Law Association of Trinidad and Tobago (the LATT). The investigation had been prompted following newspaper reports that the Chief Justice had tried to influence Supreme Court Justices to change their state-provided personal security in favour of a private company with which his close friend, Dillan Johnson (DJ), a convicted felon, was associated; that DJ was among 12 people whom the Chief Justice had recommended to a senior Housing Development Corporation (HDC) should be

[21] ibid.

[22] The others were *Maharaj v Prime Minister Trinidad and Tobago* [2016] UKPC 37, *Barrow v Attorney General of St Lucia* [2016] UKPC 38 and *Attorney General of Trinidad and Tobago v Maharaj* [2019] UKPC 6.

[23] *Archie v Law Association of Trinidad and Tobago* [2018] UKPC 23.

provided with a HDC unit; and that DJ had joined the Chief Justice while on official business abroad.

The Chief Justice's appeal raised five questions for the Board to consider. Firstly, whether section 137 of the Constitution, which sets out the procedure that has to be followed in order to remove a senior judge from office, prevented the LATT from conducting its own investigation into a senior judge's conduct. Secondly, whether the LATT had the power under the Legal Profession Act 1986 (LPA) to conduct such an investigation. Thirdly, whether the rules of natural justice applied to such an investigation. Fourthly, if they did, whether there was an appearance of bias on the part of the LATT. Fifthly, again if the rules of natural justice did apply, whether the investigation had treated the Chief Justice unfairly and/or in breach of one of the other principles of natural justice.

In the Board's view the answer to the first question was that the LATT was not prevented by section 137 from conducting its investigation, since the LATT was in no position to make findings of fact which were in any way binding upon the Chief Justice or upon any tribunal which might be established under that section.[24] Having regard to the relevant provisions of the LPA, which empower the LATT to 'promote, maintain and support the administration of justice and the rule of law' and 'to do such other things as are incidental or conducive to the achievement of [that purpose]',[25] the Board was also satisfied that the LATT had power both to conduct its investigation and to make a complaint about the Chief Justice.[26] In answer to the third and fourth questions the Board accepted that the rules of natural justice applied but deferred to the judgment of the Court of Appeal, which had concluded that the test for apparent bias (as laid down in *Porter v Magill*[27]) had not been met in this case. As the Board observed:

> The local courts in Trinidad and Tobago are far better placed than is this Board to consider what the fair-minded and informed observer in Trinidad and Tobago would make of the matters complained of. It is not for this Board to disagree.[28]

Finally, in answer to the fifth question the Board also agreed with the Court of Appeal of Trinidad and Tobago that the LATT had done all that could reasonably be required of it in terms of procedural fairness in responding to the Chief Justice's request for information and materials.[29] All of the Chief Justice's grounds of appeal having been rejected by the JCPC, the LATT was free to pursue its investigation.

By way of postscript, and as an illustration of the turbulence of the political waters which the Board had to navigate in adjudicating the dispute between LATT and the Chief Justice, it is worth noting that at the conclusion of LATT's investigation it made a formal request to the Prime Minister to recommend to the President

[24] ibid [24].
[25] ibid [27].
[26] ibid [31].
[27] *Porter v Magill* [2002] 2 AC 357.
[28] *Archie* (n 23) [37].
[29] ibid [40].

that the question of removing the Chief Justice should be investigated in accordance with section 137 of the Constitution. This recommendation was rejected by the Prime Minister, which prompted the LATT to bring proceedings for judicial review against the Prime Minister. This resulted in a finding by the High Court of Trinidad and Tobago that the Prime Minister, in rejecting the LATT's recommendation, had improperly taken into account an irrelevant consideration, namely his belief that the LATT was being used as 'a tool by his political enemies' and that their recommendation to appoint a tribunal to investigate the Chief Justice's conduct was 'a bold political trap'.[30] The Prime Minister was, accordingly, ordered to reconsider his decision. As at the time of writing this chapter, however, the Chief Justice remains in situ and the Prime Minister has yet to appoint a tribunal to investigate his conduct.

Death Penalty

One of the issues that has proved most consistently problematic for the JCPC over the last half century when hearing appeals from the Commonwealth Caribbean has been how to respond to the inclusion in the region's constitutions of saving clauses which preserve the constitutionality of the death penalty. Such clauses are of two kinds. The first, which I will call a *partial* savings clause, preserves all forms of punishment that were lawful prior to independence.[31] The second, which I will call a *general* savings clause, is even more extensive, affording immunity to all laws that were in force at the time of independence; such laws cannot be held to be inconsistent with any of the rights and freedoms guaranteed by the constitution.[32]

The problematic nature of these saving laws clauses and their immunising effect on the constitutionality of the death penalty has caused the JCPC to overrule itself on no less than three occasions: in *Lewis v Attorney General of Jamaica*,[33] in *Boyce and Joseph v The Queen*[34] and, most recently, in *Hunte v Trinidad and Tobago*.[35] It is the third of these occasions with which I am principally concerned here because

[30] *LATT v Prime Minister of Trinidad and Tobago* Claim No CU 2019–03989, unreported but available at webopac.ttlawcourts.org/LibraryJud/Judgments/HC/kokaram/2019/cv_19_03989DD19feb2020.pdf.

[31] A typical example is s 17(2) of the Jamaican Constitution. While s 17(1) prohibits torture and inhuman or degrading treatment or punishment, s 17(2) provides that 'Nothing contained in or done under the authority of any law shall be held to be inconsistent with or in contravention of this section to the extent that the law in question authorises the infliction of any description of punishment which was lawful in Jamaica immediately before the appointed day'.

[32] See, eg, s 28 of the Jamaican Constitution: 'Nothing contained in any law in force immediately before the appointed day shall be held to be inconsistent with any of the provisions of this Chapter, and nothing done under the authority of any such law shall be held to be done in contravention of any of these provisions'.

[33] *Lewis v Attorney General of Jamaica* [2000] UKPC 35, [2001] 2 AC 50.

[34] *Boyce and Joseph v The Queen* [2004] UKPC 32, [2005] 1 AC 400.

[35] *Hunte v Trinidad and Tobago* [2015] UKPC 33.

it involved the Board overruling its decision in *Ramdeen v The State*,[36] a case in which Lord Kerr was among the majority. However, to understand the background to the Board's decisions in *Ramdeen* and *Hunte* it is necessary first to say something about how the JCPC's approach to the constitutionality of the death penalty has evolved over the last two decades or so.

The starting point for this discussion is the Board's seminal decision in *Pratt and Morgan v Attorney General of Jamaica*.[37] In this case the Board declared that, even if the death penalty *per se* was immunised from constitutional review by the existence of section 17(2) of the Constitution of Jamaica, to execute a man who had been in prison awaiting execution for more than five years was, nevertheless, *presumptively* unconstitutional. As a result, the appellants, who had been on death row far in excess of five years, had their death sentences commuted to life imprisonment.

Encouraged by this development, lawyers for condemned prisoners continued to press the JCPC to impose even more restrictions on the operation of the death penalty and even to reconsider the constitutionality of the death penalty itself. Their efforts were rewarded in a trilogy of cases in 2002. In the first of these cases, *Reyes v The Queen*,[38] on appeal from Belize, the Board was persuaded – the partial savings clause in Belize's Constitution having expired by this point – to declare that a mandatory death penalty was a cruel and inhuman punishment. This opened the door in the second and third cases of the trilogy, *Hughes v The Queen*[39] and *Fox v The Queen*,[40] to a declaration by the JCPC that in those countries with constitutions that contained only a partial savings clause, the clause should be interpreted as saving only laws which *authorise* the death penalty, not laws which *require* the infliction of the death penalty, such as a law imposing a mandatory death penalty.

Hughes and *Fox* had been concerned with the immunising effect of a *partial* savings clause, but, a year later, in the case of *Roodal v The State*,[41] the JCPC was persuaded to go one step further and remove the immunity afforded to a law prescribing a mandatory death penalty by a *general* savings clause contained in the Constitution of Trinidad and Tobago. Deploying the modifying power contained in section 5(1) of the Constitution Act of Trinidad and Tobago 1976, the JCPC construed a law prescribing a mandatory death penalty as providing instead for a discretionary death penalty so as to bring it into conformity with the constitutional prohibition against inhuman and degrading treatment or punishment.

Within a matter of months, however, in *Boyce and Joseph v The Queen*,[42] a case in which the constitutional matrix was virtually identical to that of *Roodal*, a nine-member panel of the Board overruled its decision in *Roodal*.

[36] *Ramdeen v The State* [2014] UKPC 7, [2015] AC 562.
[37] *Pratt and Morgan v Attorney General of Jamaica* [1994] 2 AC 1.
[38] *Reyes v The Queen* [2002] UKPC 11, [2002] 2 AC 235.
[39] *Hughes v The Queen* [2002] UKPC 12, [2002] 2 AC 259.
[40] *Fox v The Queen* [2002] UKPC 13.
[41] *Roodal v The State* [2003] UKPC 78, [2005] 1 AC 328.
[42] *Boyce and Joseph v The Queen* [2004] UKPC 32, [2005] 1 AC 400.

Delivering judgment for the majority, Lord Hoffmann declared that deploying the modifications clause as the Board had done in *Roodal* was irrational. Because the mandatory death penalty was preserved from constitutional inconsistency by the general savings clause, there was no possible lack of conformity between an existing law prescribing a mandatory death penalty and the fundamental rights and freedoms guaranteed by the Constitution. There was, therefore, no need to trigger the modifications clause to read down the law prescribing the mandatory death penalty to bring it into conformity with the Constitution.

Immediately after handing down its judgment in *Boyce* the same panel of justices handed down their judgment in *Matthew v The State*,[43] on appeal from Trinidad and Tobago. The appellant in the latter had been sentenced to death under Trinidad and Tobago's mandatory death penalty law, but was hoping, on the basis of the judgment in *Roodal*, to have his sentence overturned. Unfortunately for the appellant, his hopes were dashed by the Board's decision in *Boyce*. All was not lost, however, because the Board accepted that even if *Roodal* had been wrongly decided it would be an inhuman punishment for the appellant now to be executed rather than having his sentence determined by a judge exercising a discretion. In order to avoid such a cruel fate, the Board resolved to exercise the power conferred by section 14(2) of the Constitution of Trinidad and Tobago to set aside the sentence of death and, instead, to impose a sentence of life imprisonment.

With the scene thus set it is now possible to examine the Board's decision in *Ramdeen*, in which Lord Kerr concurred with the majority judgment delivered by Lord Toulson. In this case the appellant's appeal against conviction had been dismissed, but while her appeal was pending before the Board she had added an appeal against sentence on the ground that her execution more than five years after conviction would constitute inhuman punishment. On its face this should have involved a straightforward application of the presumption laid down in *Pratt and Morgan* two decades earlier. The issues that the appeal raised were, however, anything but straightforward because of the route by which the appeal had reached the JCPC.

Lawyers for the government argued that the JCPC was bound by its judgment in *Walker v The Queen*,[44] which had been handed down immediately after the Board's decision in *Pratt and Morgan*. In *Walker* the Board, cognisant of the very large number of prisoners on death row in Jamaica, had given special leave to the appellants to appeal against their sentences to enable the Board to examine whether it had jurisdiction to deal directly with these cases by way of an appeal against sentence. The Board, however, concluded that its jurisdiction was controlled by the Judicial Committee Acts of 1833 and 1844. The JCPC could act only as an appellate court and since the proceedings were not appeals against a judgment of the Court of Appeal of Jamaica and the lawfulness of the *original* conviction

[43] *Matthew v The State* [2004] UKPC 33.
[44] *Walker v The Queen* [1994] 2 AC 36.

and sentence could not be disputed, the JCPC could not decide as a court of first instance whether the appellants' execution would now infringe their constitutional rights. In other words, the JCPC had no jurisdiction to deal directly with their case by way of an appeal against sentence.

Lawyers for the appellants, however, relied on the Board's more recent judgment in *Matthew.* They argued that, as in *Matthew*, the Board was here seized of an appeal. While it was true that there could, strictly speaking, be no appeal against sentence since the mandatory death penalty had already been declared by the Board to be lawful, it was submitted that this should not deter the Board from following *Matthew* and commuting the death sentence. The majority were persuaded by this argument. In the majority's view, no matter how anomalous it might seem for the Board to exercise a jurisdiction which properly belonged to the High Court of Trinidad and Tobago, which enjoys an exclusive original jurisdiction to provide a remedy for violation of a constitutional right,[45] the combination of the time which had elapsed during the course of the judicial process and the fact that the Board was seized of the case justified the Board in commuting the death sentence.

A little over a year later, however, in *Hunte*, a panel of seven Justices of the JCPC, which included all of the Justices who had heard the appeal in *Ramdeen*, with the exception of Lord Kerr, overruled its decision in *Ramdeen.* Ironically, the majority judgment was once again delivered by Lord Toulson. Like *Ramdeen*, *Hunte* also involved an appeal against conviction, but here the appellants had from the outset taken the precaution, in the event that their appeals against conviction were unsuccessful, of also appealing against sentence on the grounds that it would now be unconstitutional to execute them (applying the principles in *Pratt and Morgan*). In doing so the appellants relied on the ruling in *Ramdeen* that once the Board was seized of an appeal against conviction it also had jurisdiction to deal with an appeal against sentence.

On behalf of the majority Lord Toulson stated at the outset that he had been wrong to assume that the Board had jurisdiction in *Ramdeen* to hear the appeal against sentence and to commute the death penalty. Acknowledging that the Court of Appeal of Trinidad and Tobago would have had no jurisdiction to entertain an appeal against sentence, since there was no dispute that a mandatory death sentence was lawful, for the Board to grant leave to appeal against sentence and to order commutation of the sentence 'would be equivalent to granting an appeal where there was no decision of the Court of Appeal to appeal against and making an order which the Court of Appeal would have no decision to make'.

Having decided that there was 'no satisfactory logical way of reconciling what was done in *Matthew* and *Ramdeen* with the reasoning in *Walker*', Lord Toulson proceeded to overrule both the decision in *Ramdeen* and also the decision in *Matthew.* While Lord Toulson accepted that the need for legal certainty meant

[45] Constitution of Trinidad and Tobago 2010, s 14.

that the Board should be reluctant to depart from recent fully reasoned decisions unless there were strong grounds to do so,[46] he considered that there were at least three factors that justified the Board doing so in this case. Firstly, *Matthew* was not fully reasoned. Secondly, it would be damaging to the rule of law to exercise a purported judicial power contrary to the provisions of the Constitution. And, thirdly, to allow *Matthew* and *Ramdeen* to stand as an exception to the principle in *Walker* would lead to uncertainty as to the extent of the exception and to anomalies wherever the line was drawn.

Lady Hale was not, however, persuaded by this reasoning. In her view the key question for the Board was whether it was obliged to prolong their 'death row' experience by refusing relief to the appellants and insisting they bring separate proceedings in the High Court of Trinidad and Tobago. Even if *Walker* had been rightly decided, she argued, it was authority only for the proposition that leave to appeal against sentence cannot be given for the sole purpose of arguing that a sentence which was lawful when imposed had become unlawful to carry out. Where an appeal is before the Board for some other reasons, the Board should not close its ears to the argument that it would be unconstitutional to carry out the sentence and prevent a very serious violation of the appellant's constitutional rights.

We will, of course, never know whether Lord Kerr, had he been a member of the panel which heard the appeal in *Hunte*, would have joined Lady Hale in dissenting. However, based on his record as a Justice of the Supreme Court, which included many famous dissents[47] in which he either joined, or was joined by, Lady Hale,[48] and the weight that Lord Kerr was accustomed to give to human rights considerations, there must be, at the very least, a strong likelihood that he would not have wanted to prolong the appellant's ordeal on death row and would, therefore, have agreed with Lady Hale in allowing the appeal.

Discrimination

The cognitive dissonance experienced by Justices of the JCPC, obliged because of the existence of savings clauses to uphold laws which would otherwise violate the rights and freedoms guaranteed by the region's constitutions, has not been limited to death penalty cases. As we will see in the case which we are about to examine in this section, *Johnson and Balwant v Attorney General of Trinidad and Tobago*,[49] Lord Kerr and his fellow Justices, which included Lady Hale, must also have felt

[46] See Lord Slynn in *Lewis* (n 33) [46].

[47] eg, *Sharif v Camden London Borough Council* [2013] UKSC 10, cited by Dickson (n 10). See also Rachel Cahill-O'Callaghan (ch 5).

[48] eg, *R (Nicklinson) v Ministry of Justice* [2014] UKSC 38, [2015] AC 657.

[49] *Johnson and Balwant v Attorney General of Trinidad and Tobago* [2009] UKPC 53.

a keen sense of mental discomfort in being required, by reason of the inclusion of a savings clause in Trinidad and Tobago's 1976 Constitution, to uphold public service regulations that were palpably discriminatory.

The appellants in this case were both females. The first appellant was a divorced female police officer. The second appellant was an unmarried civil servant. Both women submitted that they wished to marry but were prevented from doing so because of the effect of the Police Service Commission Regulations (PSCR) and the Statutory Authorities Service Commission Regulations (SASCR), respectively. These provided that married women could be dismissed on the grounds that their family obligations were affecting the efficient performance of their duties. Unsurprisingly, the JCPC had no hesitation in finding that both the PSCR and the SASCR violated the right not to be discriminated against on the ground of sex together with the right to equality before the law, pursuant to section 4 of the Constitution. It was no matter that the appellants were not actually married. It was sufficient that the regulations affected the appellants as female officers when deciding whether or not to marry. Male officers were not similarly affected when deciding whether to marry.

Ordinarily, this would have rendered the regulations void pursuant to section 2 of the Constitution.[50] However, because the PSCR and SASCR pre-dated the Constitution they were preserved by the general savings clause for existing laws contained in section 6 of the Constitution. Though invited to do so by the appellants' counsel, the Board was not prepared to use the modification clause contained in section 5(1) of the Constitution Act to read down the PSCR and SASCR to bring them into conformity with section 4 of the Constitution. This was exactly the argument that the appellants had relied upon in *Boyce* and *Matthew*, and while the Board did not expressly endorse the majority judgments in those cases it is perhaps, unsurprising that the Board was not inclined to reopen 'those hard-fought decisions'.[51] Being unable to strike down laws which were clearly discriminatory, the Board had instead to content itself with describing the PSCR and SASCR as 'the relics of a bygone age' and expressing the hope that steps would soon be taken to remove them.[52]

Administrative Law

The final case in which Lord Kerr was involved which I wish to examine in this chapter, *Belize Bank Ltd v Attorney General of Belize*,[53] is of significance for at least

[50] s 2 provides that: 'This Constitution is the supreme law of Trinidad and Tobago, and any other law that is inconsistent with this Constitution is void to the extent of the inconsistency'.

[51] *Johnson* (n 49) [19].

[52] ibid [25].

[53] *Belize Bank Ltd v Attorney General of Belize* [2011] UKPC 36.

three reasons. The first is that it was the last appeal to come before the JCPC from Belize.[54] Secondly, it highlights a striking difference in approach by some of the JCPC Justices with regard to the deference owed to the decisions of local courts. The third reason is that it is surely among the most politically sensitive cases that Lord Kerr encountered during his time on the JCPC. To make good on this third point I will briefly describe the political background to this appeal before examining the judgment itself.

The appellant in this case, Belize Bank Ltd (BBL), was owned by Lord Ashcroft, a British-Belizean businessman.[55] According to newspaper reports, Lord Ashcroft had made 'significant contributions' to the Peoples United Party (PUP), led by Said Musa, and had helped the PUP to sweep the United Democratic Party (UDP) from office in 1998, by enabling it to outspend its rivals by as much as 10 to one.[56] As well as BBL, Lord Ashcroft, owned numerous other business interests in Belize, including a telephone company, a shipping registry and a TV company. It is a measure of the importance of Lord Ashcroft and his businesses to the Belizean economy that, in 2007, when BBL faced 80 separate charges of failing to comply with anti-money-laundering laws, the case was withdrawn for fear that the damage to BBL that would ensue from conviction would trigger the collapse of the national economy.[57] According to Dean Barrow, the leader of the UDP, Lord Ashcroft was: '[A]n extremely powerful man. His net worth may well be equal to Belize's entire GDP. He is nobody to cross'.[58]

After 10 years in office, the PUP and its leader, Said Musa, were widely seen as 'corrupt, incompetent and ineffectual'.[59] In part, this perception was based on the PUP's relationship with Lord Ashcroft and the belief that the PUP was 'at his service'.[60] Understandably, the UDP made this one of the central planks of its election campaign, focusing in particular on an undertaking given by Musa's government to BBL guaranteeing a debt owed to BBL by United Health Services Company Ltd (UHS), a private company operating a hospital in Belize. The suspicion was that BBL had received a sum of US$10m from Venezuela Development Bank (VDB) payable to the Government of Belize to be used for housing and a sporting complex but had instead diverted the funds to meet the undertaking by Musa's government to repay the debt owed by UHS to BBL.

Having won a sweeping victory in the 2008 elections,[61] the UDP wasted no time in investigating the circumstances of the transfer of the US$10m from VDB

[54] By the time that the case came before the JCPC, Belize had ratified the appellate jurisdiction of the Caribbean Court of Justice and terminated the right of appeal to the JCPC.

[55] Lord Ashcroft is perhaps better known in the UK as a major donor to, and a former deputy chairman of, the Conservative Party.

[56] Jamie Doward and Ian Cobain, '"Lord Ashcroft of Belize" facing eviction as country turns upon him', *The Guardian*, 1 November 2009.

[57] ibid.

[58] ibid.

[59] ibid.

[60] ibid.

[61] Winning 25 of the 31 available seats.

to the Government of Belize. Just days after the election, the new Prime Minister, Dean Barrow, declared that he would:

> [C]ontinue to pursue justice on behalf of the Belizean people and will leave no stone unturned to bring to account those who have robbed the people of this country.[62]

Following an investigation of BBL by the Central Bank of Belize, on 14 March 2008, the Central Bank issued a directive under section 36(5) of the Banks and Financial Institutions Act 2000 (BFIA) requiring BBL, forthwith, to credit the government's account with the Central Bank with the US$10m which had allegedly been wrongly diverted to BBL. On the same day, at a press conference, the Prime Minister described the behaviour of the former Prime Minister and a number of his ministers as 'absolutely reprehensible' and 'highly immoral'.[63] Five days later, at a further press conference, the Prime Minister declared that he was putting BBL on notice that his government would be taking legal advice as to whether BBL were obliged to return the money that they had received from VDB to the government 'for the people of this country'.[64]

In the meantime, BBL having given notice that it intended to appeal against the directive issued by the Central Bank pursuant to section 36, it fell to the Minister for Finance (a portfolio held by the Prime Minister) to arrange for the appointment of a BFIA Appeal Board (the Appeal Board) to deal with BBL's appeal. In accordance with the usual practice in Belize, the Minister of Finance accepted the recommendation of the Financial Secretary in appointing two members of the Appeal Board. The third member of the Appeal Board was an *ex officio* member, a nominee of the Chief Justice pursuant to section 70(2) BFIA. It was the procedure by which the Appeal Board had been appointed that was the central issue before the JCPC.

On behalf of BBL it was argued that the involvement of the Prime Minister (in his role as Minister of Finance) in appointing two members of the Appeal Board meant that it could not be regarded as an independent and impartial tribunal as required by section 6(7) of the Constitution. Since the appellants did not seek to argue that the Appeal Board was actually biased, the Board was invited instead to apply the test of apparent bias as formulated by the House of Lords in *Porter v Magill*, namely 'whether the fair minded and informed observer, having considered the facts, would conclude that there was a real possibility that the tribunal would be biased'.[65] The appellants submitted that the Appeal Board failed this test for a variety of reasons. Firstly, the Prime Minister had previously stated in very strong language that the US$10m from Venezuela should have gone to the government, not to BBL; secondly, the government itself, of which Dean Barrow was Prime Minister as well as Finance Minister, had a direct interest in the outcome

[62] Quoted by the JCPC at *Belize Bank* (n 53) [4].
[63] ibid [11].
[64] ibid [12].
[65] *Porter v Magill* [2001] UKHL 67, [103].

of the appeal to the Appeal Board; thirdly, the possibility of bias was not eliminated by the fact that the two lay members were recommended by the Financial Secretary, since he was an *ex officio* director of the Central Bank whose directive was the subject of the appeal; and, fourthly, the two lay members had previously worked at the Central Bank.

The majority judgment was delivered by Lord Kerr, who dismissed the appeal. In Lord Kerr's view, in determining whether there was a real possibility that the Appeal Board could be biased there were a variety of factors that a fair minded and informed observer would need to take into account. Firstly, the small size of the population of Belize, which meant the pool of available appointees was not large, especially since there were only five commercial banks operating in Belize at the time and knowledge of banking, finance or a related discipline was one of the prerequisites for appointment as a member of the Appeal Board.[66] Secondly, the appointment was made on the recommendation of the Financial Secretary, a career civil servant, who was 'duty bound to serve whatever government was in power and bound also not to allow party political allegiance to dictate advice to ministers or the central discharge of his duties'.[67] There was nothing in the material before the Board which suggested that the Financial Secretary or the Governor of the Central Bank had any particular agenda to promote in the review of BBL's conduct in relation to the transfer of the US$10m. Thirdly, consideration needed to be given to the dual role of the Prime Minister, who had a responsibility to recover money that he believed had been wrongly diverted from public resources, while at the same time as Minister of Finance being obliged to make appointments to the Appeal Board. Though the Prime Minister had been, in Lord Kerr's words, 'robust' in his criticism of the former Prime Minister and clearly would be able to extract political capital from the conduct of the former Prime Minister, this would not in Lord Kerr's view lead a fair minded and informed observer to conclude that this gave rise to the risk that the two independent members of the Appeal Board whom he had appointed 'would behave other than in a perfectly proper fashion'.[68]

Lord Brown, by contrast, in a solitary dissenting judgment, considered that in the light of the appointment procedure adopted, the fair minded and informed observer would very much regard the 'objective impartiality of the Appeal Board as constituted … to be open to doubt'.[69] In Lord Brown's view it was inevitable that a fair minded and informed observer would have been struck by the thought that the Finance Secretary may have chosen the two lay members of the Board, and the Prime Minister may so readily have accepted his recommendation, because they felt that the two lay members would 'instinctively be more sympathetic, i.e. predisposed to the Central Bank's and government's cause than BBL'.[70]

[66] ibid [31].
[67] ibid [42].
[68] ibid [57].
[69] ibid [98].
[70] ibid [112].

It is impossible to know whether the disagreement between Lord Kerr and Lord Brown, though couched in terms of the application of the apparent bias test, had more to do with the former's instinctive sympathy for the underdog in a contest between the Belizean government and a financial Goliath, like BBL. The disagreement between Lord Kerr and Lord Brown was not, however, the only point of disagreement between the Justices who heard this case. Lord Dyson, while concurring with the majority, nevertheless considered that both Lord Kerr and Lord Brown had been wrong to approach the question of apparent bias as if they were deciding the issue as a first instance tribunal. According to Lord Dyson, both Justices had tacitly assumed that:

> [T]here is single universal answer to this question, whether it is being determined in an English court or any other court and regardless of where that other court might be and regardless of the traditions and cultures of the country in which the court operates, I do not think that is a correct assumption to make.[71]

Lord Dyson added that if he had been sitting as a first instance judge in England, he would have reached the same conclusion as Lord Kerr. However, Lord Dyson was of the opinion that the Board should recognise that it was not sitting as a first instance tribunal in England, but rather it was hearing an appeal from the Court of Appeal of Belize which was itself hearing an appeal on a point of law from the Chief Justice of Belize. This required the Board to recognise that the judges of Belize were better equipped than the Board to assess how the fair minded and informed observer would assess matters, particularly bearing in mind that Belize was a small country, with a small pool of persons likely to satisfy the statutory criteria for appointment as lay members of the Appeal Board. The Chief Justice for Belize, whose judgment had been upheld by the Court of Appeal, had decided that the apparent bias test had not been satisfied. In Lord Dyson's view, the Chief Justice's decision should be upheld: the assessment of the possibility of bias 'fell to be made by a Belizean court by reference to the perception of the possibility of bias by a fair minded and informed Belizean' and the JCPC should only interfere with that decision if satisfied that it was clearly wrong, which was not the case here.[72]

Presumably because Lord Dyson agreed with Lord Kerr's conclusion that the apparent bias test had not been met, Lord Kerr did not respond to Lord Dyson's criticism that he had approached the question as if he were deciding the issue as a first instance tribunal. In Lord Kerr's defence it could be said that in *Archie v LATT* Lord Kerr had adopted exactly the approach that Lord Dyson was recommending by deferring to the Court of Appeal of Trinidad and Tobago on whether the apparent bias test had been satisfied in that case. This should not be taken to mean that Lord Kerr had formed a definitive view on the extent of deference to be afforded by the JCPC to local courts. It may well be that in different circumstances he would have been sympathetic to Lord Brown's view that Lord Dyson's

[71] ibid [65].
[72] ibid [82].

was entirely the wrong approach and came close to abnegating the Board's proper role in a politically fraught case. The JCPC's responsibility was to ensure 'to the benefit of Belizean themselves and of their standing in the wider international community, that the highest international standards of justice are maintained in that country'.[73] The Board owed no more deference to the Belizean judges on this issue of apparent bias than the European Court of Human Rights would afford UK judges on the same issue.[74]

Conclusion

Though I have selected only public law cases from the Commonwealth Caribbean, and though I have selected only those cases which I regard as significant, I hope that I have been able to give an insight into the complexity, as well as the variety, of issues that confronted Lord Kerr during his tenure as a Justice of the JCPC. Save where his hands were tied by the region's infamous savings clauses, as in *Johnson and Balwant*, the cases I have examined confirm, I believe, Lord Kerr's record of upholding the rights of the individual against the state and its institutions, whether they be a PSC as in *Jamaicans for Justice*, or even the Chief Justice as in *Archie v LATT*. While recognising that the judgment in *Belize Bank* may not immediately fit into this category, I would argue that it is not too difficult to reconceptualise that judgment as one of the people versus the state, given the economic might of the appellant bank and the hold it had over the government of the day when it received the transfer of funds from VDB. And while the majority in *Hunte* may have concluded that Lord Kerr had erred in his eagerness to uphold the rights of the individual against the state in *Ramdeen*, we know from Lady Hale's dissenting judgment in *Hunte* that in doing so Lord Kerr was in very good company.

[73] ibid [113].
[74] ibid.

10

Lord Kerr and the New Judiciary in Northern Ireland

JOHN MORISON

Introduction: The Changing Legal World in Northern Ireland

Other contributions to this book, and indeed the whole volume itself, pay well-deserved tribute to Lord Kerr's immense contributions to the law in general, and particularly during his final judicial role in the UK's highest court. This chapter is a short reflection on some aspects of the changing legal world in Northern Ireland that provided the background to much of Lord Kerr's career, and, in particular, one specific area – that relating to the changing face of the judiciary in Northern Ireland – where Lord Kerr's contribution can be seen within a context of a rapidly changing, and indeed currently still on-going transformation of the legal environment in that part of the world that he held most dear.

While the idea of there being a Chinese curse relating to 'living in interesting times' may be something of a myth, Brian Kerr undoubtedly lived his legal life in what was incontrovertibly a period that saw Northern Ireland move from relative tranquility through enormous stress and conflict, and ultimately to a new dispensation. As a student in what was then the Faculty of Law at Queen's University of Belfast from 1965–69 the young Brian Kerr would have experienced Belfast in a 'pre-troubles' context and, of course, the emergence of the civil rights movement and active student politics. Lord Kerr has spoken warmly of his time as a student at Queen's.[1] The Law Faculty was then based in a number of terraced houses in University Square in South Belfast. The few dozen students were offered what was undoubtedly a smaller scale, more personalised experience than that afforded to the almost 1,000 undergraduate and postgraduate students who are now based in

[1] See his interview with JUSTICE, 11 December 2014, available at justice.org.uk/lord-kerr-tonaghmore. For the post-troubles context see Brice Dickson and Conor McCormick (ch 1).

a £20 million pound conversion of the building that was in the 1960s the (then newly built) Main Library Tower. Following a degree programme lasting four years, rather than the current three-year duration, Brian Kerr's transition to legal practice in 1970 was made in the absence of the training provided by Queen's at the Institute of Professional Legal Studies, which came into existence only in 1977.

The world of practice at the Bar Library in Belfast in 1970 was also on a smaller scale and qualitatively different to what it is now, as indeed was the wider society. The 1971 census reports a population figure of some 1.5 million (in contrast to 1.8 million currently) but also, perhaps more revealingly, presents figures relating to those employed in a number of categories of occupations – from textile workers, through to furnace, forge and factory workers, engineering and allied trade, to paper and printing workers – that are redolent of a world that has largely disappeared.[2] The decline of traditional industry and agriculture, and its replacement as a source of employment by a large public sector and the highest level of benefits per capita in the UK, which was to reach its height in the late 1980s, was just getting underway in the early 1970s, with consequent changes to the nature of society and legal practice about to come.[3] Indeed the same census reports that there were 727 people employed in the category of 'Judges, barristers, advocates and solicitors' (of whom only 26 were women). Most solicitors operated in one person practices with only very limited specialisation, and the Bar Library attached to the High Court in Belfast was populated by only a few dozen barristers. The population that these lawyers served had the lowest average income per individual in the UK. Although legal aid had been introduced in 1965 (16 years later than in England and Wales), it was initially administered by the Law Society of Northern Ireland, and, despite the numbers of those qualifying for legal aid being higher, awards were generally significantly lower than elsewhere in the UK. Rates of divorce in Northern Ireland were traditionally lower than in Great Britain with fewer than 500 divorces per annum between 1971 and 1975,[4] large scale commercial work was limited, and arguably the crime rate too was lower.[5]

Meanwhile the emergence of the 'security state' was only beginning as the legal system in general and lawyers in particular responded to what McEvoy has characterised as a series of 'critical junctures'[6] by introducing, variously, internment

[2] See Northern Ireland General Register Office, *Census of Population 1971 Economic Activity Tables, Northern Ireland* (HMSO, 1972), available at www.nisra.gov.uk/sites/nisra.gov.uk/files/publications/1971-census-economic-activity-tables-part-1.PDF.

[3] For discussion of these trends see Robert Osborne and Robert Cormack, *Religion, Occupations and Employment 1971–1981* (Belfast, Fair Employment Agency, 1987); Frank Gaffikin and Mike Morrissey, *Northern Ireland: The Thatcher Years* (London, Zed Books, 1990); and Marie Fox and John Morison, 'Lawyers in a Divided Society: Legal Culture and Legal Services in Northern Ireland' (1992) 19(1) *Journal of Law and Society* ('*Tomorrow's Lawyers*') 124.

[4] See the Northern Ireland Statistics and Research Agency (NISRA), 'Divorces 1971–2018' at www.nisra.gov.uk/publications/divorce-statistics.

[5] See, further, John Morison and Ray Geary, 'Crime, Conflict and Counting: Another Commentary on Northern Ireland Crime Statistics' (1989) 28 *Howard Journal of Criminal Justice* 9.

[6] Kieran McEvoy, 'What Did the Lawyers Do During the "War"? Neutrality, Conflict and the Culture of Quietism' (2011) 74 *MLR* 350.

without trial in 1971;[7] a juryless criminal trial process with slimmed down rules of evidence via the 'Diplock Courts';[8] and a series of supergrass trials.[9] Those involved in the conflict engaged with the legal process in a range of ways too, varying from complete disengagement, through a refusal to recognise the authority of the courts, to a tactic of challenging as much as possible in the courts.[10] By the time Brian Kerr was Junior Crown Counsel (from 1978–83) and then Senior Crown Counsel (from 1988–93) the state was extensively involved in a series of important cases relating to the policing of the security situation. This was accompanied often not only by a range of appeals to the Northern Ireland Court of Appeal and the House of Lords[11] but by increased disputation in Strasbourg via a series of challenges to aspects of the state's handling of the security situation under the European Convention of Human Rights.[12] At the constitutional level, Northern Ireland was undergoing major disruption as direct rule, introduced in 1972, was augmented by a series of initiatives designed to provide a constitutional solution to the wider problems in society.[13]

All of this provided a most interesting and dynamic background for practice at the bar and, from 1993, the discharge of the duties of a High Court Judge. It may be said that in contrast to Britain, where political dispute generally is mediated by rules and institutions commanding widespread consensus, in Northern Ireland the conflict very often is rooted in the legal rules and institutions themselves. In his practice and during his time on the bench Brian Kerr undoubtedly developed a keen sense of the political context of his work, and some of the contributions to this volume discuss this more fully. Here the focus will be on a less well-known, but perhaps no less political role played by Brian Kerr while Lord Chief Justice of Northern Ireland from 2004 to 2009. It was during this time, as Chair of the new Northern Ireland Judicial Appointments Commission, that he played a vital part in the re-engineering of the judiciary in that jurisdiction.

[7] See, generally, Kevin Boyle, Tom Hadden and Paddy Hillyard, *The Law and State: The Case of Northern Ireland* (London, Martin Robertson, 1973) and Laura Donohue, *Counter-Terrorist Law and Emergency Powers in the United Kingdom 1922–2000* (Dublin, Irish Academic Press, 2001).

[8] John Jackson and Sean Doran, *Judge Without Jury: Diplock Trials in the Adversary System* (Oxford, Clarendon Press, 1995).

[9] Steven Greer, *Supergrasses: A Study in Anti-terrorist Law Enforcement in Northern Ireland* (Oxford, Clarendon Press, 1995).

[10] See Kieran McEvoy, 'Law, Struggle, and Political Transformation in Northern Ireland' (2000) 27 *Journal of Law and Society* 542.

[11] See, further, Stephen Livingstone, 'The House of Lords and the Northern Ireland Conflict' (1994) 57 *MLR* 333 and Brice Dickson, 'The House of Lords and the Northern Ireland Conflict – A Sequel' (2006) 69 *MLR* 383.

[12] See further Brice Dickson, *The European Convention on Human Rights and the Northern Ireland Conflict* (Oxford, OUP, 2010); Colin Warbrick, 'The European Convention and the Prevention of Terrorism' (1983) 32 *International and Comparative Law Quarterly* 82; Stephen Livingstone, 'A week is a long time in detention: *Brogan and Others v the UK*' (1989) 40 *NILQ* 280.

[13] See further Brigid Hadfield, *The Constitution of Northern Ireland* (Belfast, SLS Ltd, 1992) and John Morison and Stephen Livingstone, *Reshaping Public Power: Northern Ireland and the British Constitutional Crisis* (London, Sweet and Maxwell, 1995).

The Legal Context in Post-Agreement Northern Ireland

This author has argued previously that the wider constitutional changes consequent on the Belfast Agreement have produced such significant changes and opened up such possibilities in the legal system generally that it is possible to consider the jurisdiction as a new legal space.[14] Some of this is a result of working through aspects of the peace process which has introduced an opportunity for something like the 'new beginning' here too – as was described more generally in relation to the governance of Northern Ireland.[15] In another sense it is more directly a result of various formal changes around the fulfilment of the devolutionary direction set in the Agreement and the Northern Ireland Act 1998 (and its various amendments and additions) which have charted the way towards a fuller version of devolution, including the continuation of Northern Ireland as a separate jurisdiction with a degree of apartness from the rest of the UK. The fact that the developments in the justice system from 1998 onwards can be interpreted simultaneously as both a chance to remake a new legal order, *and* an evolution of the former dispensation is perhaps further indicative of the nature of the Belfast Agreement as an exercise in beneficial ambiguity. This new legal space was in part a result of the opportunity that the wider peace process brought for a new start, and as an outworking of a number of formal changes around devolution, and in particular the further devolution of justice functions. Together these operate to provide not only the continuation of the separate formal jurisdiction but also a degree of 'apartness' and exceptionality that contribute to what may be seen as a unique legal context. Both aspects of this must be considered in turn.

Since the inception of the jurisdiction in its present format one hundred years ago the judiciary in Northern Ireland has operated with a strong degree of independence. This was true for the 50 year period of devolution and during the time of direct rule. In one sense it has remained the case even following the peace process, and the various subsequent developments. The Northern Ireland Courts Service existed as a local branch of the Lord Chancellor's Department, and although the Lord Chancellor was the formal head of the judiciary in Northern Ireland, a concordat negotiated in 1979 gave the Lord Chief Justice of Northern Ireland and his extensive office operational control over the court system locally.

[14] See John Morison, '"A Sort of Farewell": Sovereignty, Transition, and Devolution in the UK' in Richard Rawlings, Peter Leyland and Alison Young (eds), *Sovereignty and the Law: Domestic, European and International Perspectives* (Oxford, OUP, 2013) and John Morison, 'Finding Merit in Judicial Appointments: NIJAC and the Search for a New Judiciary in Northern Ireland' in Anne-Marie McAlinden and Clare Dwyer (eds), *Criminal Justice in Transition: The Northern Ireland Context* (Oxford, Hart Publishing, 2015) 131–56.

[15] See para 1 of the ANNEX: Agreement between the Government of the United Kingdom of Great Britain and Northern Ireland and the Government of Ireland, Declaration of Support, within the Belfast/Good Friday Agreement, Cm 3883 (1998).

The Constitutional Reform Act 2005 formally made the Lord Chief Justice head of the judiciary in Northern Ireland and settled the idea of the Northern Ireland jurisdiction being not only formally separate but also a place apart in the sense that it is organised and controlled locally.[16] The devolution of justice, made by the Department of Justice Act (NI) 2010 and the Northern Ireland Act 1998 (Devolution of Policing and Justice Functions) Order 2010,[17] led to the establishment of the Northern Ireland Courts and Tribunals Service as an agency of the new Department of Justice within the Northern Ireland Executive.[18] This devolution of the machinery of justice into the care of the local political structures was not only the last piece in the puzzle of the peace process, and the final stage in the formal process of devolution, but a further recognition perhaps of a new chapter in the story of the legal system.[19] Although the framework has changed, arguably the separateness and independence continues – although now in very different circumstances of post-ceasefire politics.

Other changes to the court system and the judiciary are perhaps more intangible, relating less to formal system-level change and more to an evolution of a political or cultural nature. Some of this is captured by developments whereby an oath of allegiance to the Queen is no longer a requirement of appointment as QC; there is a new law officer in the shape of the Attorney General (as well as an Advocate General); and, more generally, many of the existing senior appointments are distributed more widely across the political/ethnic spectrum than in the past. Although, in keeping with the ambiguity that characterises other aspects of the peace process, this can be interpreted simultaneously as continuity – a modification of the legal system that has pertained since 1921 – and as change that is appropriate for the new political beginning.

Whatever interpretation is chosen, the origins of much of this change lie with the provision within the Belfast (Good Friday) Agreement for a 'wide-ranging review of criminal justice (other than policing and those aspects of the system relating to the emergency legislation) to be carried out by the British government through a mechanism with an independent element, in consultation with the political parties and others'.[20] The Criminal Justice Review (CJR) was the formal

[16] See Graham Gee, Robert Hazell and Kate Malleson, *The Politics of Judicial Independence in the UK's Changing Constitution* (Cambridge, CUP, 2015) 234 et seq; and Brice Dickson, *Law in Northern Ireland*, 3rd edn (Oxford, Hart Publishing, 2018) ch 4.

[17] Northern Ireland Act 1998 (Devolution of Policing and Justice Functions) Order 2010, SI 2010/976.

[18] See further the Northern Ireland Courts Service website available at www.justice-ni.gov.uk/topics/courts-and-tribunals.

[19] See David Torrance, 'Devolution in Northern Ireland, 1998–2020' (*House of Commons Briefing Paper*, 3 February 2020); and Gordon Anthony, 'The Devolution of Policing and Criminal Justice' (2011) 17 *European Public Law* 197.

[20] Belfast Agreement, Cm 3883, reached on 10 April 1998, available at assets.publishing.service.gov.uk/government/uploads/system/uploads/attachment_data/file/136652/agreement.pdf, Annex B and *The Criminal Justice System Review Report*, 30 March 2000, available at cain.ulster.ac.uk/issues/law/cjr/report30300.htm. The ambiguity mentioned above is illustrated well in the Foreword to the earlier *Review of Criminal Justice System in Northern Ireland, Consultation Paper* 1988 (available at cain.ulster.

body established to undertake this. As has been recognised for some time, within the context of politics in Northern Ireland there is a capacity for almost any issue to be interpreted as a political or even constitutional matter.[21] The administration of justice in particular is subject to political interpretation and as such it was recognised as a vital element in the new Northern Ireland. The CJR put considerable emphasis on judges. Indeed, the final report devoted some 40 pages to the issues there, recognising that 'an effective and impartial judiciary is crucial to the well-being of any society, especially one where there have been divisions and conflict such as have been experienced in Northern Ireland'.[22]

The CJR acknowledged the need for manifest openness and fairness at every level if the court system was not to be seen as 'owned' and staffed by one community rather than the other. For those who saw the judges and the court system as inherently unionist, and therefore exclusionary, it was vital that it should be de-politicised. For those who did not accept this characterisation it was equally important that the new regime continued to adhere to the principles of merit-based appointment and impartiality that (from that perspective) had served the system well. The CJR anticipated also that judges in Northern Ireland would increasingly be called upon to interact with executive and legislative decisions. The Review predicted that in the new rights regime of the Agreement and the Human Rights Act 1998 judges would be not only weighing the merits of competing rights but also considering arguments about their economic and social impact.[23] Although the language did not refer to the courts as having a new constitutional role as such, the Review Group did acknowledge a new constitutional reality whereby judges are:

> empowered to declare primary Westminster legislation incompatible … [and] set aside lesser legislation, including Acts of a Northern Ireland Assembly … [as well as] determin[ing] whether individuals have been treated in accordance with Convention rights and whether acts of public authorities are in contravention of such rights.[24]

Part of this was a result of the wider devolution process across the UK, which (at least at that time, far from Brexit considerations) seemed to presage new, forward-looking understandings of traditional ideas of Westminster sovereignty. There were a number of significant cases across the devolved jurisdictions that

ac.uk/issues/law/cjr/review98.pdf) by then Secretary of State, Marjorie Mowlam, who writes, at 5, of how although '[t]he criminal justice system has served Northern Ireland well over the last 30 years, often in the face of considerable difficulties' there is now 'an historic opportunity for a new beginning in Northern Ireland' and this is both 'an opportunity for change, but also an opportunity to build on what has been shown to work in Northern Ireland and elsewhere'.

[21] As Vivien Hart has argued, it is characteristic of transitional forms of constitutionalism that a range of issues can come to be considered 'constitutional': see 'Constitution-Making and the Transformation of Conflict' (2001) 26 *Peace and Change* 153. In the Northern Ireland context these have been seen to range across issues of personal morality, the flying of flags and the supply of cakes.

[22] *Criminal Justice System Review Report* (n 20) para 6.3.

[23] ibid paras 6.3–6.5.

[24] ibid para 6.6.

suggested that new judicial understandings of the constitution were emerging.[25] Northern Ireland was very much involved in this development as a series of challenges to the new dispensation came about.[26] This led many to believe that this entailed a different appreciation of the constitutional role of judges, perhaps recognising their role as political actors within wider constitutional processes.[27] While this constitutional role would not necessarily fall to all judges at every level, it is perhaps suggestive of something that was new and important. Indeed, it may be argued that these understandings of the Northern Ireland constitution, and the new society it was still in the process of creating, urge a new and very particular view of what it is that judges should be doing, and who they should be. The rights basis of what is fundamentally an agonistic settlement does undoubtedly create a new sort of legal space where decisions that are fundamentally *constitutive* of the post-Agreement society are possible at any time and from almost any source.[28]

The Development of the Northern Ireland Judicial Appointments Commission

At the same time as these particularly Northern Ireland changes were occurring there were developments in Great Britain which, although coming to fruition slightly later there than in Northern Ireland, nevertheless did provide an additional impetus towards change in judicial politics. In June 2003 the UK Prime Minister, Tony Blair, announced a plan to establish a new Supreme Court, to abolish the office of Lord Chancellor, and to reform the judicial appointments process

[25] See eg *Imperial Tobacco v Lord Advocate* [2012] UKSC 61, 2013 SC (UKSC) 153, [15]; *AXA General Insurance v Lord Advocate* [2011] UKSC 46, [2012] 1 AC 868; and *Attorney General v National Assembly for Wales Commission* [2012] UKSC 53, [2013] 1 AC 792, [80], suggesting the possibility of fundamentally new understandings of the sovereignty of Parliament in relation to devolution and, arguably, indicating the prescience of the CJR's view.

[26] See further the report of an ESCR-funded study exploring the development of 'constitutional litigation' in the early days of the settlement through nine cases from Northern Ireland, and how this measured up to developing conceptions of constitutional practice and theory internationally and, particularly, in relation to ideas of transitional constitutionalism in John Morison and Marie Lynch, 'Litigating the Agreement: Towards a New Judicial Constitutionalism for the UK from Northern Ireland?' in John Morison, Kieran McEvoy and Gordon Anthony (eds), *Judges, Transitions and Human Rights* (Oxford, OUP, 2007). See also Gordon Anthony, 'Public Law Litigation and the Belfast Agreement' (2001) 8 *European Public Law* 401 and Gordon Anthony (ch 5).

[27] See also Murray Hunt, 'Reshaping Constitutionalism' in Morison, McEvoy and Anthony (n 26) 467 for a discussion of some of this literature and, more generally, Martin Shapiro and Alec Stone Sweet, *On Law, Politics and Judicialization* (Oxford, OUP, 2002).

[28] These ideas relate to wider debates about the changing nature of the judicial role generally in the context of a changing and globalising society; see Elaine Mak, *Judicial Decision-Making in a Globalised World: A Comparative Analysis of the Changing Practices of Western Highest Courts* (Oxford, Hart Publishing, 2013) and David Robertson, *The Judge as Political Theorist: Contemporary Judicial Review* (Princeton, Princeton UP, 2010).

in England and Wales. Lord Falconer replaced Lord Irvine as a new style of Lord Chancellor, and the office of Secretary of State for Constitutional Affairs was created. In July 2003 the Department for Constitutional Affairs (DCA) published a series of consultation papers[29] and, following negotiations between the Lord Chancellor and the Lord Chief Justice of England and Wales about the transfer of functions following the abolition of office of Lord Chancellor, a *Concordat*[30] agreement was reached in January 2004. This settled many of the issues relating to the appointment of judges and the independence of the judiciary in England and Wales, effectively modernising the process, making it compliant with the ECHR's separation of powers requirements, and bringing in ideas about new appointment processes. The Constitutional Reform Act 2005 brought these changes into being and, *inter alia*, created the Judicial Appointments Commission (JAC) for England and Wales in April 2006, with a statutory duty to select candidates for the judicial offices listed in Schedule 14 to the Act solely on merit; to select only people of good character; and to have regard to the need to encourage diversity in the range of persons available for judicial selection.[31]

In Northern Ireland proposals about a new appointment process for the judiciary shared some similar issues as well as having their own particular context. Changes in Northern Ireland were, however, enacted rather earlier.[32] The Northern Ireland Judicial Appointments Commission (NIJAC) was established on 15 June 2005 as an independent public body under the Justice (NI) Acts 2002 and 2004 (the 2002 and 2004 Acts).[33] NIJAC was established as the appointing body, selecting and appointing to non-Crown judicial offices in various Courts and Tribunals throughout Northern Ireland, with NIJAC able to select and make recommendations for Crown appointments up to and including High Court Judge. In total this amounts to more than 600 judicial offices. In terms of composition of

[29] See Constitutional Reform: A Supreme Court for the United Kingdom, DCA, Consultation Paper, CP 11/03; Constitutional Reform: A New Way of Appointing Judges, DCA, Consultation Paper, CP 10/03; and Constitutional Reform: Reforming the Office of the Lord Chancellor, DCA, Consultation Paper, CP 13/03.

[30] This is officially known as 'The Lord Chancellor's Judiciary-Related Functions: Proposal', and is published at House of Lords, Report of the Select Committee on the Constitutional Reform Bill [HL], Session 2003–04, HL Paper 125, 202–24 (Appendix 6).

[31] See further Kate Malleson, 'The New Judicial Appointments Commission in England and Wales: New Wine in New Bottles?' in Kate Malleson and Peter Russell (eds), *Appointing Judges in an Age of Judicial Power: Critical Perspectives from Around the World* (Toronto, University of Toronto Press, 2016) and Graham Gee and Erika Rackley (eds), *Debating Judicial Appointments in an Age of Diversity* (London, Routledge, 2017).

[32] Rather earlier again, in 2002, the Judicial Appointments Board for Scotland (JAB) was established on an administrative basis by the Scottish Ministers, with a remit to provide to the First Minister recommendations for appointment to judicial office based on merit, to consider ways of recruiting a judiciary representative of the communities served, and to undertake the recruitment processes in an efficient and effective manner. The Judiciary and Courts (Scotland) Act 2008 established the Board on a statutory basis (before it was then constituted as a statutory advisory Non-Departmental Public Body in June 2009).

[33] On the devolution of justice on 12 April 2010 the Northern Ireland Act 2009 extended NIJAC's statutory duties.

the Commission, section 3 of and Schedule 2 to the Justice (NI) Act 2002 provide for a chairman and 12 others. Five of these are to be nominated by the Lord Chief Justice and are designated as the 'judicial members'.[34] There are also 'legal profession members', comprising a barrister nominated by the General Council of the Bar of Northern Ireland and a solicitor nominated by the Law Society of Northern Ireland. Additionally, there are five 'lay members' who are not, nor ever have been, barristers or solicitors or holders of a protected judicial office.[35] This composition is broadly similar to that of the JAC in England and Wales, and indeed the Scottish Judicial Appointments Board (JAB) – although there is one significant difference in so far as the Chair of both the JAC and the JAB is required by statute to be a layperson.[36]

In contrast, it is clearly stipulated in the main body of the legislation that the Chair of NIJAC should be the Lord Chief Justice of Northern Ireland.[37] This was considered to be an important element in the composition of the appointment bodies in Great Britain, and it may be thought that the exclusion of such a requirement for NIJAC undermined attempts to move on from what was seen generally as a more judicially oriented, 'tap on the shoulder' approach to judicial succession. However this author, acknowledging his own involvement with the NIJAC referenced above but drawing also upon some evidence from the NIJAC-commissioned research study discussed below, would suggest a contrary view. The Chairmanship of Sir Brian Kerr in his role as Lord Chief Justice was an important, and indeed perhaps essential, element in ensuring the cooperation of the judiciary and wider legal profession. While there are many forward-looking practitioners and judicial office holders in Northern Ireland, the legal profession there (as perhaps elsewhere) is not invariably enthusiastic about moving on from time-honoured practices. Furthermore, as the research commissioned by NIJAC (discussed below) revealed, there was resistance among many in the pool of eligible applicants about being required to be subject to a formal interview process for what many perceived as undertaking public service – not least because it would involve evaluation by lay Commissioners from outside the world of legal practice. Perhaps it required the authority of someone with the stature of Sir Brian Kerr to advocate for the worth of the new system to the existing judiciary and the wider professions. Certainly, there was to be no dilution of the full involvement of lay Commissioners in every aspect of the selection process, including the legal aspects, and this was in contrast to the practice within the JAB where lay members

[34] According to Sch 2 to the 2002 Act, the judicial members are to be a Lord Justice of Appeal, a judge of the High Court, a County Court judge, a Resident Magistrate and a lay Magistrate.

[35] It is at this point that this author should disclose that he was appointed to NIJAC from June 2005 and served until June 2012 as a lay Commissioner. It should be made clear that any views expressed here are made in a personal capacity.

[36] See Constitution Reform Act 2005, Sch 12, Pt 1, para 2(1) and the Judiciary and Courts (Scotland) Act 2008, Sch 1, para 9(1).

[37] See Justice (NI) Act 2002, s 3(4).

were excluded from consideration of legal competencies,[38] and in the JAC where generally Commissioners did not involve themselves directly with individual selection processes.

There were also some important differences between the various appointment bodies in terms of how they went about their role of making appointments. Their shared aim was to not only provide the best possible judges but also to address the increasingly pressing concern about diversity on the bench and the need for modern judges to be drawn from as wide a background as possible. Arguments here encompass, broadly, equal opportunities, including accessing all available talent; democratic legitimacy; and the potential benefits of including different perspectives in the process of judging.[39] However the specific contexts, and the mechanisms for addressing diversity differ somewhat. In England and Wales the JAC was given an imperative that appointment should be 'solely on merit' through section 63(2) of the Constitutional Reform Act 2005, but section 64(1) referred to 'the need to encourage diversity in the range of persons available for selection for appointments'. The JAB too was to appoint 'solely on merit' but the Board was required to 'have regard to the need to encourage diversity in the range of individuals available for selection to be recommended for appointment to a judicial office'.[40] NIJAC's statutory duty also involves a requirement that appointments, or recommendations for appointment, to any of the listed judicial offices must be made 'solely on the basis of merit'.[41] However, the relevant paragraph continues by requiring the Commission to at all times engage in a programme of action that is 'designed to secure, so far as it is reasonably practicable to do so, that appointments to listed judicial offices are such that those holding such offices are reflective of the community in Northern Ireland'.[42] Furthermore, it requires the Commission, 'so far as it is reasonably practicable to do so, to secure that a range of persons reflective of the community in Northern Ireland is available for consideration by the Commission whenever it is selecting a person to be appointed, or recommended for appointment, to a listed judicial office'.[43] This is similar in some respects to that relating to the other appointing bodies but, it may be suggested, it is perhaps a more demanding formal standard.

[38] See Judiciary and Courts (Scotland) Act 2008, s 13(1).

[39] For contemporaneous accounts of this pressure see Brenda Hale, 'Equality in the Judiciary: Why Should We Want More Women Judges' [2001] *Public Law* 489 and her Kuttan Menon Memorial Lecture, 'Equality in the Judiciary' (21 February 2013), available at www.supremecourt.uk/docs/speech-130221.pdf; and Erika Rackley, 'Rethinking Judicial Diversity' in Ulrike Schultz and Gisela Shaw (eds), *Gender and Judging* (Oxford, Hart Publishing, 2013) 501. The arguments for a diverse judiciary, including more women, are insightfully discussed, and put in a Northern Ireland context, by Dermot Feenan who concludes that 'seeing the issue only in terms of equality denies a much more complex field that requires understanding of the social construction of the judge, judging, and judicial authority, and the associated exclusion of outsider groups': see 'Women Judges: Gendering Judges, Justifying Diversity' (2008) 35 *Journal of Law and Society* 490.

[40] See Judiciary and Courts (Scotland) Act 2008, s 12(2)–(3).

[41] See Justice (NI) Act 2002, Sch 3, para 6(1).

[42] ibid para 6(3)(a).

[43] ibid para 6(3)(b).

The Task for NIJAC

The statutory frameworks gave each appointment body discretion over the Committee structures it wished to develop to pursue its work generally and the imperatives placed upon it to enhance diversity in particular. In Northern Ireland, along with an Audit and Risk Committee and an Appointments Committee, NIJAC established an Equality and Diversity Committee, with administrative support from a dedicated Head of Diversity and Communication. With the support of the wider Commission this body was charged with developing policy to enable NIJAC to discharge its statutory responsibilities, particularly around developing the applicant pool for appointment. It is to the credit of NIJAC, and of course its Chairman, that right from the very beginning there was a commitment to developing policy from a firm evidence base.

Relatively little was known in detail about the composition of the judiciary across Northern Ireland. Initial thoughts may have centred around a belief that the nationalist community was underrepresented in ranks of the judiciary, and it was certainly apparent that women did not seem to be well-represented.[44] However, figures about the composition of the existing judiciary were not collected at the time of NIJAC's formation. Initial Equity Monitoring research by the Northern Ireland Statistics and Research Agency (NISRA) was able to provide a factual basis. In terms of community background, over half of judicial office holders in the Courts were Protestant (54.9 per cent). This was higher than in the legal professions generally (44.4 per cent). However, when adjustment is made for the age profile of judicial office holders in the Courts, Protestant representation would be expected to be 52.7 per cent, broadly in line with the actual representation at 54.9 per cent. Catholic representation among judicial office holders in tribunals (40.2 per cent) was lower than in the legal profession generally (53.0 per cent), and also lower than the representation which might be expected having taken account of the age profile (46.7 per cent). Perhaps more striking, however, was the confirmation from NISRA's figures that women were significantly underrepresented on the bench beyond tribunals. Only 11 out of 52 (21.2 per cent) appointments in Group 2 (comprising County Court judges; deputy County Court judges; Chief

[44] It should be noted that in contrast to Great Britain, where the issue of race soon emerged as a central one, the numbers of those from a minority ethnic background or declaring a disability within the applicant pool in Northern Ireland are very small indeed. Figures on disability among the applicant pool are not available, although around the time of NIJAC's formation the proportion of judicial office holders who had declared a disability ranged from 2.4% among lay magistrates to 6.6% among tribunal members. See the Northern Ireland Statistics and Research Agency (NISRA), *The Judiciary in Northern Ireland 2007: Equality Monitoring Report* (2007) available at www.nijac.gov.uk/sites/nijac/files/media-files/equality_report_2007.pdf. Female representation among judicial office holders in tribunals was much higher (at 45.8%) than might be expected (24%), given the age profile of judicial office holders in tribunals.

Social Security Commissioner; Social Security Commissioner and deputies) were women.[45] In Group 1 (comprising the Court of Judicature – Lord Chief Justice, Lord Justices of Appeal, High Court Judges and temporary Judges of the High Court) there were 16 appointments, but none were female.[46]

NIJAC's response to this was to commission a major piece of research from a project team drawn from the School of Law at Queen's University.[47] This drew together and built upon earlier work carried out for NIJAC and its predecessor.[48] It also preceded similar work carried out for the other appointing bodies in Great Britain. Essentially this study mapped issues of diversity and scoped the challenges facing the development of policy to ensure a reflective judiciary, particularly increasing the representation of women, which was confirmed by the research as the major challenge. This research, involving questionnaires and a series of interviews with key informants, provided a rich empirical basis to understand the challenges facing NIJAC in discharge of its statutory functions.

The research found that religion was largely perceived as an irrelevant factor in applying for judicial posts. It also uncovered the view that, while the new appointments system had done much to make judicial office more appealing to a wider group, there were some who resented the idea of submitting to a formal, competency-based system. This was found to be linked to some degree to a wider finding that there was felt to be a strong orientation towards the Bar as the natural group from which to recruit to the judiciary, particularly at the higher level. Also, it was felt strongly that the formal requirements for a post – for example, the need for a number of years' standing – were inaccurate, and indeed hiding an informal set of conditions around age, experience and background which made appointment much more likely. This was thought to be particularly true for High Court appointments, where many respondents felt that even 20 years' standing was too little for a person to be a serious candidate. The research also found a particular concern from female barristers that, should they wish a judicial career, they were being hampered by the difficulty in getting work in areas which were given higher status and by being excluded from informal connections and networks. Also, while

[45] See NISRA, *Equality Monitoring Report* (ibid) 18. This was markedly lower than in the legal profession generally (33.8%).

[46] ibid.

[47] School of Law, Queen's University Belfast, *Propensity to Apply for Judicial Office under the new Northern Ireland Judicial Appointments System: A Qualitative Study for the Northern Ireland Judicial Appointments Commission* (October 2008), available at www.nijac.gov.uk/sites/nijac/files/media-files/QUB%20Propensity%20to%20Apply%20for%20Judicial%20Office%20under%20the%20New%20Northern%20Ireland%20Judicial%20Appointments%20System.pdf.

[48] See the work commissioned in April 2004 before NIJAC was formally established by the Commissioner for Judicial Appointments for Northern Ireland, and co-funded between the Commissioner and the Northern Ireland Courts Service: Dermot Feenan, *Applications by Women for Silk and Judicial Office in Northern Ireland: A Report Commissioned by the Commissioner for Judicial Appointments for Northern Ireland*, University of Ulster Centre for the Study of Conflict (2005) and NISRA, *Survey of views about Judicial Appointments* (2007), available at www.nijac.gov.uk/sites/nijac/files/media-files/NISRA%20Survey%20of%20Views.pdf.

many solicitors thought they were capable of doing the work, they felt that they may not be recognised as such, although some early successes with appointments which would not have been expected under previous appointment regimes were providing encouragement. Overall, NIJAC was welcomed and was thought to be operating reasonably successfully in opening up this stream to non-traditional candidates in relation to the county court, magistrates' court, coroner posts and tribunal chairs. However, with regard to the High Court, there was a strong perception that NIJAC was being much less successful in overcoming traditional barriers and encouraging non-traditional candidates. In particular, the absence of female judges in the High Court was seen to reflect poorly upon the notion of a representative judiciary.

NIJAC's response to the 2008 research report, and the range of concerns that it revealed, was to put in place a *Research Informed Programme of Action*: a wide-ranging strategy designed to ensure that the research findings were addressed in a comprehensive fashion across the organisation. This resulted in numerous developments in both the outreach processes and the selection mechanisms. Perhaps most importantly, it reinforced NIJAC's commitment to a properly evidence-based approach process, with the result that a series of other research projects were undertaken to guide the development of the Commission. These related to the potentially gendered understanding of 'merit' within the process[49] and, most recently, to the difficulties of recruiting to the High Court.[50] The story of these initiatives is told elsewhere[51] but the end result at the time of writing can be seen clearly in the changed face of the judiciary in Northern Ireland today. Judicial office is now spread more evenly among those of different genders and varying professional backgrounds. It is now possible to consider a 'judicial career' involving advancement from one tier to another, and shadowing and part-time appointments are available at an increasing number of levels. Indeed, the most recent figures from NISRA[52] show that almost 50 per cent of the legal members in tribunals are female. Female representation in the Courts (at 28 per cent) is at a higher level than would be expected. At county court level and above there are 15 females and 48 males. As well as two female judges in the High Court there are

[49] Philip Leith and John Morison, *Rewarding Merit in Judicial Appointments? A research project undertaken by the School of Law, Queen's University Belfast for the Northern Ireland Judicial Appointments Commission* (2013), available at www.nijac.gov.uk/sites/nijac/files/media-files/QUB%20Rewarding%20Merit%20in%20Judicial%20Appointments.pdf.

[50] John Morison and Brice Dickson, *Barriers to High Court Appointments in Northern Ireland: A Report for the Northern Ireland Judicial Appointments Commission* (2019), available at pureadmin.qub.ac.uk/ws/portalfiles/portal/192730958/ReportFINAL.pdf.

[51] See further Morison, 'Finding Merit in Judicial Appointments' (n 14) 131; John Morison, 'Beyond Merit: The New Challenge for Judicial Appointments' in Gee and Rackley (eds) (n 31) 223–39; and John Morison, Brice Dickson and Andrew Godden, 'Barriers to High Court Appointments in Northern Ireland' (2019) 70 *NILQ* 479.

[52] NISRA, *Equity Monitoring Report 2019*, available at www.nijac.gov.uk/publication/equality-monitoring-report-2019.

now two former solicitors (one of whom was previously a county court judge) and a judge under 45 years of age. Additionally, as of September 2021 there is a new Lady Chief Justice, namely the Honourable Dame Siobhan Keegan. All of this is a considerable departure from the situation before the advent of NIJAC. Transforming the face of the judiciary in Northern Ireland is difficult in terms of both the small and the big political contexts but the origin, and indeed the continuing success of NIJAC's work can be traced clearly to the commitment of the original Commission, under the chairmanship of Brian Kerr, to drive real change as evidenced firmly through an established research basis.

PART II

Judicial Minds More Generally

11

The Life and Career of Denis Henry (1864–1925): Barrister, Ulster Unionist Politician and First Lord Chief Justice of Northern Ireland

ÉAMON PHOENIX

In the quiet Catholic churchyard at Straw, near Draperstown, County Londonderry, a plain rectangular stone marks the grave of the Right Honourable Sir Denis Henry, Bt, the only Roman Catholic ever to have become an Ulster Unionist MP and the first Lord Chief Justice of Northern Ireland.

Denis Stanislaus Henry was born on 7 March 1864, in the townland of Cahore, Draperstown, County Londonderry, the sixth son of James Henry, a prosperous Catholic merchant and landowner, and his second wife, Ellen (née Kelly). Of his 11 siblings from the two marriages (five brothers and six sisters) two brothers and two sisters were to enter religious life; one brother was a Marist priest while another, Rev William Henry SJ, became rector of the Jesuit Novitiate at Tullamore in King's County (now County Offaly). Two other brothers became solicitors.[1]

The Henrys were a well-established, wealthy family in a largely Catholic farming district which had been planted by the Drapers' Company of London during the seventeenth century Plantation. The village in the foothills of the Sperrins had been laid out in 1845 by the Drapers' Company. The district suffered considerably during the Great Famine but, thanks to the establishment of a railway connection in the 1850s, Draperstown was a flourishing market town by the time of Denis's birth. In 1862 a deputation from the Drapers' Company recorded that the village was 'flourishing'. Henry's father, James, is not mentioned by name but he was undoubtedly the unnamed 'owner of the townland of Cahore' who, the report noted, 'had rebuilt … his part of the town … giving it a most respectable appearance'. The Henrys lived in a substantial Georgian villa known as 'The Rath' with a

[1] AD McDonnell, *The Life of Sir Denis Henry: Catholic Unionist* (Belfast, Ulster Historical Foundation, 2000) 1–2; *Belfast Telegraph*, 2 October 1925.

coach-house and servants' quarters attached. In a memoir his Jesuit older brother, William, recalled that their father was 'a landlord'.[2]

The young Denis Henry received his early education at the local Boys National School where he was enrolled as a Catholic pupil in a school which had some Protestant boys as well. He proceeded to the Marist College in Dundalk, transferring in 1878, along with his brother, Patrick, to the Jesuit college of Mount St Mary's in Chesterfield. The choice of an English, rather than an Irish, Catholic public school was probably due to the fact that Denis's late uncle, Father William Henry SJ, had been a pupil there – further evidence of the family's status. Denis would appear to have been an average student. Interestingly, his period at Chesterfield overlapped with the teaching career there of the poet, Gerard Manley Hopkins.

Henry proceeded to Queen's College, Belfast, where he read law. This was an unusual choice for an Ulster Catholic in the 1880s, when the hierarchy was railing against the so-called 'Godless colleges'. After a glittering academic career, in which he achieved the distinction of winning every available law scholarship possible, he was called to the Irish Bar in 1885 at the early age of 21.[3]

A keen legal mind – attested to by his contemporaries – together with a 'captivating appearance' and 'a fine musical voice' assisted his rapid progress at the late Victorian Bar. Henry quickly established himself on the North-West Circuit, extending from Westmeath to Derry, Tyrone and Donegal, eventually taking silk in 1896 at the early age of 32. Two years later he was elected a Bencher of King's Inns. Thereafter he was much in demand as a prosecutor and in 1898 he appeared for the Crown in three murder cases in Belfast, securing convictions in each case.

It was not until he had already established himself as a successful advocate that Henry began to consider the attractions of a career in politics. However, when he finally entered political life he aligned himself not with the Irish Home Rule Party – soon to be reunited under John Redmond after the bitterness of the Parnell split – but with the Conservative and Unionist Party. Indeed, his family background, though intensely Catholic, was strongly conservative and pro-Union. As his political adversary, TP O'Connor, the celebrated Home Rule MP for Liverpool, later observed:

> He was of a somewhat unique type in Irish life, Catholic by descent and personally … yet he was entirely at variance with the politics of his co-religionists. His family had always belonged to the prosperous middle classes of Ulster. They shared none of the enthusiasms of his co-religionists and it was in this realistic atmosphere that he was brought up.[4]

The Henry family, as landlords in mid-Ulster, were remembered as opponents of the Land League in the 1880s. Like many middle-class Ulster Catholics and

[2] McDonnell (ibid) 3–4; memo by Rev W Henry, SJ (Jesuit Archives, Dublin).

[3] ibid; *Londonderry Sentinel*, 3 October 1925; *Irish News* report on sale of the former Henry residence, 26 February 2010.

[4] *Belfast Telegraph*, 2 October 1925.

Presbyterians they had been Liberals but, according to Denis Henry in a 1906 speech, had shown 'a reluctance to go with Mr Gladstone when he took up Home Rule'. Thus, while the bulk of Catholics in the north of Ireland rallied to the revitalised Home Rule Party under Parnell in the so-called 'invasion of Ulster' of 1885, the Henrys gravitated to Liberal Unionism, placing themselves in the same camp as the great mass of former Presbyterian Liberals.[5]

As early as the 1895 general election Henry publicly endorsed the Unionist nominee in South Derry. In the 1895 election the rising advocate spoke on Unionist platforms in East Donegal on behalf of the local landed magnate, ET Herdman, earning him a scornful rebuke from the nationalist *Derry Journal*. It noted with some disdain how:

> A star of North-West circuit magnitude … has appeared over the hills of Dark Donegal. Mr Denis S Henry, Barrister, has found time in the midst of his brief … to rush from the Derry Assizes to East Donegal to save his country.[6]

Speaking to an exclusively Protestant audience, Henry dealt frankly with the issue of his religion:

> While a member of another Church, he was not afraid to stand there and say that he was not ashamed of his religion – (applause) – and that he felt, as an Irishman who had the welfare of his country at heart, he could sink religious differences and support the candidature of Mr Herdman.[7]

Henry's remarks show that at this early stage in his career he subscribed to the broader, more inclusive Irish Unionism of the Anglo-Irish Southern Unionists rather than the narrower sectarian-based Unionism of the north.

Significantly, Henry attended the inaugural meeting of the Ulster Unionist Council on 3 March 1905 as a Unionist delegate, one of the very few Catholics to identify with the Orange-dominated movement. Apart from his family background it would seem that Henry's educational experience had played a role in shaping his political outlook. Unlike most Nationalists and the future Ulster Unionist leader, Sir Edward Carson, Henry rejected his Church's demand for a Catholic denominational university, declaring: 'Mixing was good for everyone as it broadened their views and let them see that other people held as honest opinions as themselves'.[8]

Henry's first attempt to enter Parliament came in the 1906 general election, when he was selected as the Unionist candidate for the highly marginal seat of North Tyrone. The 1906 contest, and the by-election which arose there the following year, provide useful insight not only into Henry's personality and outlook, but also into the manner with which Ulster politics was conducted at a local level.

[5] *Londonderry Sentinel*, 6 January 1906.
[6] *Derry Journal*, 29 July 1895.
[7] ibid.
[8] John Biggs-Davison and George Chowdharay-Best, *The Cross of St Patrick: The Catholic Unionist Tradition in Ireland* (Bourne End, Kendal Press, 1984) 290.

The Catholic Unionist's nomination for North Tyrone was significant. The constituency was one of the most peculiar in Ireland at the time. Despite a slender Catholic majority in population terms, the Nationalist strength on the register was several hundred votes below that of the Unionists. The fate of the seat turned on the votes of some 200 Presbyterian farmers who adhered to the old Liberal faith: they would support a Liberal Home Ruler but could not be relied upon to vote for a full-blooded Irish Nationalist. As a result the Nationalists had tended to allow the diminutive Liberal party a clear run and in 1906 William Dodd KC, a lawyer and Protestant Home Ruler, was the outgoing member and candidate. Thus Henry, the Catholic Unionist lawyer, was pitted against Dodd, the Protestant Home Ruler. In an exciting contest Dodd managed to hold the seat by the narrow margin of just nine votes.

The nationalist press showed little sympathy for the Catholic lawyer. The *Irish News* described Henry as 'one of that weird class of creatures known as an Irish Catholic Unionist' whose stance would be anathema to Catholics and whose religion would arouse the worst sectarian feeling among Protestants. Orangeism remained the bedrock of Ulster Unionism and Henry's meetings in Orange halls riled the Nationalists while the unionist *Londonderry Sentinel* riposted that Henry's attitude reflected his belief that 'the Orangemen of Ireland are a highly constant factor in defending the Union'.[9]

Henry deftly ignored the sectarian issue but reiterated his belief in a pluralist, non-sectarian Unionism:

> I am opposed to the establishment of any separate legislature for this country or to any legislature which may in any way tend to weaken the Union between this country and the rest of the United Kingdom. Whether this change is sought to be effected by a Home Rule Bill or under the guise of devolution, it shall have my strongest opposition.[10]

During the 1906 campaign the rising senior counsel elaborated on his views on the Union. At Strabane he stated that it was the finality of Home Rule which made the measure particularly dangerous and warned that a Home Rule Act could not be repealed or amended. At Castlederg in County Tyrone he declared that Ireland was already free enough, with full religious equality. At Plumbridge he stressed that a Dublin government would have little sympathy for Ulster or its industries.

The Dublin-based lawyer added that he could see little in common between the north and the rest of Ireland, saying that the south represented 'quite a different community altogether'. This speech marks a clear hardening of Henry's Unionism and an overt partitionism, reflecting the more 'Ulstercentric' outlook of James Craig and the Ulster Unionist Council. In 1895 Henry had addressed Donegal Unionists as an 'Irishman', yet now he seemed keen to emphasis 'the distinctiveness of Ulster'.[11]

[9] McDonnell (n 1) 11–16.

[10] *Londonderry Sentinel*, 2 January 1906.

[11] McDonnell (n 1) 14; Alvin Jackson, 'Irish Unionism' in Peter Collins (ed), *Nationalism and Unionism: Conflict in Ireland 1885–1921* (Belfast, 1994) 40–41.

The election result showed that while Henry attracted few Catholic votes, he enjoyed the overwhelming endorsement of the Conservative leadership, including Joseph Chamberlain and the Irish Chief Secretary, Walter Long, as well as local Orangemen. Henry's reliance on the Orange Order aroused a mixture of anger and bewilderment among his co-religionists. One leading nationalist cleric, Rev Philip O'Doherty PP, referred to the 'incredible state of affairs' in North Tyrone, commenting that while Judge William Kenny, a former Dublin MP, had merely been a Catholic Unionist, Henry had embraced the Orange faction too. In the annals of Irish elections, he added, 'it was a thing unknown to have a Catholic supported by the Orange lodges'. In the nationalist *Irish News*, a correspondent poked fun at 'Brother Dinish [Denis]' in doggerel verse:

> A Papist beating the Orange drum!
> Surely no slavery could be 'maner'?
> To what base uses you have come
> In the hope of a North Tyrone retainer![12]

In an election generally devoid of rancour, 5,954 voted out of a total electorate of 6,174, a remarkable testament to the organisational flair and perhaps the personating ability of both parties. When the result was announced, Henry rejected the advice of his agent to demand a recount. He congratulated the victorious Home Ruler and promised to continue their amicable relationship. The election, he observed, had shown that the north of Ireland was as tolerant as anywhere else in the United Kingdom although he had been 'technically beaten for the time being'.

Henry again fought North Tyrone in 1907, when a by-election arose following Dodd's elevation to the Bench. Unionist suspicions of the new Liberal government were stoked by the introduction of the (ill-fated) Irish Council Bill, which promised a measure of devolution. This time Henry lost to another Liberal Home Ruler, the Catholic Redmond Barry, by seven votes.

As in the previous year, over 90 per cent of votes were cast as the opposing sides spared no effort to maximise their respective turn-outs. One man died in the arms of friends while being lifted out of bed, while a Catholic student for the priesthood made a 400-mile round trip from Maynooth seminary to register his vote against Henry. One voter arrived from Buenos Aires, while brandy was administered to another man, who managed to vote for Henry before expiring.

The defeated Unionist once more suppressed his disappointment, enjoining his supporters to desist from violence: 'if you keep the peace you will please me as much as if you had returned me'. Henry could return to the Four Courts in Dublin secure in the knowledge that his Unionist credentials had been firmly established for the future.[13]

[12] McDonnell (ibid) 15–16; *Irish News*, 2 January 1906.

[13] McDonnell (ibid) 20–26; Rev W Devine (Naval Chaplain) to Judge ES Murphy, 13 March 1944 (in possession of author). In 1944 an Irish Catholic chaplain attached to British forces in Italy ministered to Captain James (later Sir) Henry, a wounded officer in the Royal Navy and the eldest

The Catholic Unionist's political ambitions were destined to remain in abeyance for the next decade as he concentrated on his legal career. He declined a nomination in North Tyrone in the 1910 general elections 'owing to increasing professional duties'[14] and took little public part in the anti-Home Rule struggle of 1912–14. His Unionism remained solid, however, despite the apparent inevitability of Home Rule, speaking on anti-Home Rule platforms in England and Scotland – 'with great effect' according to the London *Times* – to refute the impression that Unionism was a sectarian cause.[15]

Henry did not sign the Ulster Covenant (1912), which was not merely a self-consciously 'Protestant' protest against the Third Home Rule Bill, but invoked the right of Ulster Unionism to resort to violence to thwart Irish self-government. However, speaking in Dublin in November 1912, he argued that an Irish Parliament would do little to protect the rights of minorities and that 'in the thirty years since he had come to Dublin, no Unionist had held public office under the Corporation'. This was a bad augury for a future Home Rule Parliament. If Home Rule were passed, he said, displaying his characteristic courtroom wit, the loyal minority would be at the mercy of 'metropolitan misfits and provincial pirates'. In a speech which echoed the Tory rhetoric of the 1880s, Henry expressed the hope that the British public 'would decline to hand them over to a party of disorder and … disloyalists'.[16]

Henry's legal and establishment connections were strengthened in October 1910 by his marriage to Violet Holmes, the daughter of Hugh Holmes, an Irish Lord Justice of Appeal from County Tyrone. Despite the fact that his bride was a member of the Church of Ireland, the couple were married quietly according to the rites of the Catholic Church at St Ethelbert's Catholic Church, Leominster. The decision to marry outside Ireland may have been politic at a time when the implications of the 'Ne Temere' decree and the acrimonious McCann mixed marriage case (1910) was exercising Ulster Unionism. The marriage was solemnised by Denis's older brother, Rev William Henry SJ, who was then working among the Dublin poor at the Jesuit mission in Gardiner Street.

Denis was now 46, his wife 31. They would have five children: James, born in 1911, Denise, Alice, Denis and Lorna. They were brought up as Catholics while Violet adhered to her Protestant faith.[17]

son of Denis Henry. At James Henry's request the priest wrote to the officer's 'black Protestant uncle', ES Murphy, a Belfast judge and former Ulster Unionist MP, informing the family that James Henry was wounded but alive. The priest added humorously: 'He was very grateful that I should go so far to see him but I explained that I had once gone much further (from Maynooth as a student) to vote against his father in North Tyrone … Young Henry … is such a decent fellow that I was almost sorry I voted against his father'. Murphy, a prominent Orangeman, had married a sister of Denis Henry's widow and had been a close friend of the Catholic Unionist.

[14] *Northern Whig*, 20 December 1909.

[15] *The Times*, 2 October 1925.

[16] *Northern Whig*, 20 December 1909; Biggs-Davison and Chowdharay-Best (n 8) 292.

[17] Certificate of Henry's marriage, 1 October 1910 (General Register Office, London); obituary of Rev W Henry, *Province News* (Irish Jesuits), June 1928, 73–75.

Henry was now at the top of his profession, with a Georgian town-house in Dublin's fashionable Fitzwilliam Square. In a will dated November 1910 he was able to bequeath to his wife the substantial sum of £16,000. WE Wylie, a later Law Adviser to the British government in Ireland, recalled him as 'the quickest thinker and most brilliant advocate' he ever knew, a view which was shared by AM Sullivan, who defended Roger Casement in 1916. Sullivan felt that Henry was 'the best man the Irish bar produced' in his time. He had 'a clear deep mind comparable with the Lord Chief Baron [Christopher] Palles'. His features were 'handsome, his carriage dignified and he was meant … to be the leader of his profession.'[18]

Henry remained on cordial terms with political opponents such as Tim Healy KC, the maverick Nationalist MP, and TP O'Connor. One Nationalist legal colleague recalled the lack of rancour at the pre-partition Irish Bar: 'To listen to the circle often formed around Tim Healy or Denis Henry … was to enjoy a feast of reason … The [Law] Library was a microcosm of the life of Ireland … political foes sat cheek by jowl … good companions all'.[19]

Henry's legal standing was recognised in January 1914 when he was one of two counsel appointed to head an inquiry into the famous Dublin lock-out of 1913 when a clash between police and strikers resulted in two deaths. His final report exonerated the police though some 20 members were found to have committed unjustifiable assaults.

An unexpected opportunity for Henry to redress his earlier political disappointments came in April 1916 when the South Londonderry seat became vacant. With a wartime political truce in force, Henry's selection and return for his native constituency seemed a foregone conclusion. This was not the case, however. He won the nomination only after a third ballot against Colonel Chichester, the local squire, and DD Reid, a fellow barrister, and had to face a contest against a maverick independent candidate from Scotland, Dr Arthur Turnball, a critic of the government's handling of the war.

While Henry once more enjoyed the support of the Orange Order, the brief campaign which followed suggested a softening of nationalist asperities towards him. In the absence of a Nationalist contender due to the 'party truce', a local Catholic curate, Father P McGeown of Kilrea, went so far as to welcome Henry's likely election:

> At present it matters not whether a man is a Nationalist, a Unionist, or a Liberal, but to us it does matter very much that he should be a Catholic. And Mr Denis Henry KC, is a Catholic. We feel that when our interests, or the interests of our religion are at stake we shall have a supporter in our future MP.[20]

[18] Alexander Sullivan, *Old Ireland: Reminiscences of an Irish KC* (London, T Butterworth Ltd, 1927) 283.

[19] McDonnell (n 1) 30–31; TJ Campbell, *Fifty Years of Ulster 1890–1940* (Belfast, The Irish News, 1941) 136.

[20] McDonnell (ibid) 37.

Interestingly, this was the first by-election in Ireland following the Easter Rising, with the poll coming a mere 11 days after the final executions and in an atmosphere of martial law.[21] The Catholic Unionist had an easy victory, winning his native constituency by a margin of 3,395 votes.[22] Henry's early parliamentary career was low-key, though he served on the Royal Commission into the deaths of three innocent civilians including the pacifist, Francis Sheehy-Skeffington, during the Rebellion. In November 1918 he was appointed Solicitor General for Ireland in the Lloyd George coalition.

In the run-up to the post-War general election – the first test of public opinion to be held since 1910 – Henry appeared for the Unionists at the Tyrone revision sessions, held to update the electoral register, in Omagh in November 1918. When his nationalist opponent, the local Sinn Féin leader and solicitor, George Murnaghan, claimed that the 'greater part of the Unionist objections dealt with religion' – a question the court was not competent to deal with – the Catholic Unionist MP was quick to emphasise the overlap of religious and political allegiances in Ulster: 'They all knew that in Northern counties religious and political fears coincided … The Unionist population of Tyrone was 45 per cent and the Nationalists 55 per cent and, on those grounds, they [the Unionist minority] were at least entitled to some consideration'. His efforts ensured that one of the county's three designated seats, South Tyrone, would return a Unionist candidate in the subsequent general election.[23]

In the subsequent general election in December 1918, which saw Sinn Féin sweep the polls in nationalist Ireland, he successfully defended his South Derry seat against Louis J Walsh of Sinn Féin (who was, ironically, a distant cousin) and a Home Rule candidate. Selected in Kilrea Orange Hall, Henry was publicly endorsed by Carson as 'a most loyal and devoted colleague'[24] while the Orange Grandmaster in the constituency called on every member of the order to support him.

Henry warned his supporters that his Sinn Féin opponent represented 'everything that was abominable to their loyalty and allegiance'. With Sinn Féin and the Nationalists focusing on the growing threat of partition, Henry showed no enthusiasm for it. He told a meeting in Magherafelt that he felt deeply for his fellow Unionists in the south and west and stated that he would prefer to see the present constitutional arrangements unchanged so that both Unionists and Nationalists could 'enjoy the blessings and benefits of … the Union'. Unionists, he declared, would never submit to a Dublin legislature. A young Nationalist who heard Henry

[21] ibid 36–42.
[22] *Londonderry Sentinel*, 25 May 1916.
[23] *Irish News*, 22 November 1917.
[24] McDonnell (n 1) 47.

speak recalled him as 'an accomplished and convincing orator' who spoke with 'a refined, cultured Dublin accent'.[25]

The fatal split in the Catholic vote combined to give Henry a comfortable majority of nearly 5,000 votes over his nearest opponent, the constitutional Nationalist, Professor John Conway. Yet the South Derry election of December 1918 would represent the last occasion on which a Catholic won a Unionist seat in Ulster.

The return of the Tory-dominated Lloyd George coalition in 1919, with its explicit commitment to partition, enabled James Craig and the Ulster Unionists to accept four junior ministries. These included Henry, now promoted to the post of Attorney General for Ireland, a position he held throughout the violence of the Irish War of Independence. The first meeting of Dáil Eireann in January 1919 coincided with the opening shots in the independence struggle. In the House of Commons, Henry, the superb advocate whose mastery of his brief had been his hallmark, now found himself in the invidious position of having to defend the British government's controversial policy in Ireland against a background of mounting insurgency, increasing militarism and organised 'reprisals' by Crown forces.

Henry served two Irish Chief Secretaries: Ian Macpherson and, following the latter's resignation in April 1920, Sir Hamar Greenwood. Throughout this tempestuous period, Henry had to respond to persistent allegations of misconduct by Crown forces; evidence of orchestrated British reprisals for IRA attacks; the introduction of coercive legislation; and the activities of new irregular forces. These irregular forces were the Black and Tans, the Auxiliaries and the Ulster Special Constabulary – all introduced in 1920 to strengthen the collapsing Royal Irish Constabulary (RIC). His discomfiture was not eased by Greenwood's frequent absences from the Commons and the mounting indictment of the government by the British press, the Labour party, the former Prime Minister, Herbert Asquith, and the rump of the Nationalists under their formidable leader, 'Wee Joe' Devlin.[26]

One of Henry's first major challenges was a hunger-strike by Sinn Féin prisoners in Mountjoy Jail in April 1920. The Attorney General's palpable lack of reliable information on the condition of the hunger-strikers left him struggling at the despatch box. With the *Times* calling for decisive action (the prisoners were eventually released) Henry admitted in cabinet that the whole affair had been 'badly managed'.[27]

In his sensitive position as chief Irish law officer at this critical juncture Henry was closely involved in the formulation of the British government's controversial

[25] ibid 45–50; Eoin Walsh, letter in *Irish News*, 13 July 1984.

[26] McDonnell (ibid) 53–60.

[27] Keith Middlemas, *Thomas Jones, Whitehall Diary, vol 3, Ireland 1918–1925* (Oxford, OUP, 1971) 15.

Irish strategy spanning partition and the ending of the Anglo-Irish War. As the IRA campaign escalated and a system of republican courts displaced the Crown courts, he remained unrepentant in his vindication of government policy, telling the Commons in February 1920 that Ireland was virtually in a state of war:

> It is not an attack on one party, it is not an attack on the Coalition government, it is an attack on your nation. It is an attempt to drive your nation out of Ireland.[28]

Henry was responsible for introducing the draconian Restoration of Order in Ireland (ROIA) legislation, which became law in August 1920 and enabled legalised internment and the suppression of inquests. The *Irish News* condemned the proposal to establish military courts-martial with the power to impose the death penalty, while Devlin's bitter attack on the measure resulted in his suspension from the House.

In a heated exchange with TP O'Connor, Henry denied any ill-treatment of prisoners by military authorities. The government, said Henry, had striven 'for a better state of affairs' and the ROIA was a last resort. He regarded those engaged in violence as 'rebels' and 'traitors' and declared that the government was entitled to deal with them on that basis.[29]

Such stridency, however, could not conceal the fact that Henry's parliamentary responses to mounting evidence of atrocities by Crown forces were unconvincing and 'perhaps the least satisfying aspect of [his] term of office'.[30] Badly briefed and evasive, he was forced to rely on RIC and military reports on incidents involving alleged reprisals and unwarranted shootings by Crown forces. As the conflict escalated in the early months of 1921 the political and personal pressures on Henry were intense. When he refused to discuss the alleged murder of men under army escort, his silence provoked vigorous protests by Liberal and Nationalist MPs. Henry was also criticised by an official in Dublin Castle, Mark Sturgis, who alleged that he 'sat in London, afraid to set a foot in Ireland' at the height of the IRA campaign.[31] However, Henry's characteristic willingness to stand against the tide of Irish opinion and his later state-building role in Northern Ireland suggest that he did not lack personal courage.

There is no doubt that his performance as Attorney General was more impressive when explaining complex legislative matters such as the conditions of service of the RIC in Ireland, education and land purchase.

With Craig and his Ulster Unionist colleagues Henry pointedly abstained on the second reading of the Government of Ireland Act 1920, which provided for partition and separate home rule Parliaments, north and south. In the spring

[28] HC Deb, vol 125 (19 February 1920) 1170.

[29] HC Deb, vol 127 (12 April 1920) 1487; vol 125 (19 February 1920) 1171; vol 127 (25 April 1920) 2046–47.

[30] McDonnell (n 1) 71; Michael Hopkinson (ed), *The Last Days of Dublin Castle: The Diaries of Mark Sturgis* (Dublin, Irish Academic Press, 1999) 48.

[31] Hopkinson (ibid) 72.

of 1921, as the government and Sinn Féin 'skirmished on the extreme edge of negotiation',[32] he was among those in the cabinet in May 1921 who opposed a truce until the IRA had been defeated militarily. In the event of Sinn Féin refusing to operate the proposed Southern Irish Parliament – a racing certainty – he was prepared to contemplate drastic action in the form of Crown Colony government.[33]

TP O'Connor, who knew Henry well at Westminster during this period, remembered him as

> a tall, stout, red-faced man with a mane of hair rising high above his head and, in later years, very white. He had a strong face with a large nose and a very powerful jowl. If you did not know he was a distinguished lawyer you might take him for a squire of County Galway who had stood as a model to [the novelist] Charles Lever. The face indicated the nature, for though he was good-natured, he was also keenly alive to the good things of life, especially high position in his profession. These things he attained, but he had to go almost through blood and tears to reach them for he lived through a very stormy time in the history of his country.[34]

O'Connor added that, although Henry was often the subject of invective from Nationalist MPs, he and they remained on friendly terms: 'they hated his politics but they did not – nobody could – hate the man'.[35]

Any expectations of a respite from the pressures of public life were dispelled when, in August 1921, Henry was Craig's first choice for the position of Lord Chief Justice of Northern Ireland. He was sworn in before the Lord Chancellor for Ireland, Sir John Ross, at a ceremony in Portrush Town Hall on 15 August 1921. Among the audience were James Craig, now Prime Minister of Northern Ireland, and Henry's brother, Alexander Patterson Henry (known as 'Attorney' Henry), a local solicitor in Maghera. Denis was created a baronet in the same year.[36]

Henry's appointment came against the background of the July 1921 truce between the IRA and the British government, the Treaty negotiations and the transfer of law and order to the Belfast authorities in November 1921. Northern Nationalists continued to hope that the London negotiations would produce a united Irish state and showed little interest in the appointment of a Catholic as head of the new judiciary. Dismissing Henry's appointment to 'the absurd northern judiciary' the *Irish News* commented caustically in August 1921: 'Sir James Craig's government cannot undertake any work with the degree of permanency attaching to it because they know that there can be no permanency in this partition'.[37]

To the deepening political uncertainty and politico-sectarian violence, which saw 450 people killed in Belfast during 1920–22, was added the urgent task of

[32] Cecil Street, *Ireland in 1921* (London, Philip Allan & Co, 1922) 123.
[33] Middlemas (n 27) 59, 71; McDonnell (n 1) 66–67.
[34] *Belfast Telegraph*, 2 October 1925.
[35] ibid.
[36] McDonnell (n 1) 90–91.
[37] Biggs-Davison and Chowdharay-Best (n 8) 355; *Irish News*, 6 August 1921.

establishing new legal structures. The gargantuan task of creating the machinery of a new court system fell to Henry, now aged 57. He was active in the recruitment of officials to staff the new Northern judiciary, liaising with Dublin Castle and James Craig for whom he had 'a profound admiration' according to Lady Henry.[38] One of Henry's first challenges was to ensure that the Northern Ireland Supreme Court, established under the Government of Ireland Act 1920, opened on 1 October 1921, the 'appointed day' laid down by Order in Council on which the separate Northern court system would come into existence.[39]

Henry's colleagues on the new northern Court of Appeal were William Moore and James Andrews. Moore, a former Ulster Unionist MP and Carson's ally in the campaign against the Third Home Rule Bill, had been a Judge of the King's Bench Division in Dublin. Andrews was a brother of Craig's Minister of Labour, JM Andrews, and had served as standing counsel to numerous railway companies and corporations in Ulster. Sir Denis was well acquainted with his two High Court judges in the northern judiciary as both had served with him as Ulster Unionist politicians and law officers: DM Wilson had served as Solicitor General for Ireland while TW Brown had succeeded Sir Denis as Attorney General.

While Henry was personally engaged in interviewing and appointing judges and court officials, he also took steps to secure appropriate premises for the Supreme Court of Northern Ireland. As the erection of a suitable court building would take time, he secured the use of the County Courthouse on Belfast's Crumlin Road from its owners, Antrim County Council. Henry would not live to see the opening of purpose-built Law Courts in Chichester Street in 1933.

The frenetic amount of work involved in creating a new system of courts from scratch took its toll on the middle-aged jurist, already exhausted by the pressures of the Anglo-Irish conflict. As his colleague, William Moore, has recorded:

> Henry did not spare himself in constant anxious work in setting up the courts and their administration, involving him in endless discussion and negotiation with the governments in Belfast and London, with the Bar and the Law Society, council officials and many others. Added to his judicial work this made up a formidable workload.[40]

In the event, the courts which comprised the new Supreme Court of Judicature of Northern Ireland were not formally opened until 24 October 1921. The new Lord Chief Justice led his brother judges, the Attorney General and senior and junior counsel, garbed in full costume, into the County Court House in Belfast. In the course of his remarks, Henry noted that the Bar had entered 'a new era … [given that] the old Circuits of the North East and North West have disappeared – to be

[38] St John Ervine, *Craigavon, Ulsterman* (London, George Allen & Unwin Ltd, 1949) 498.

[39] For further information on the early years of the legal establishment, see Anthony Hart, *A History of the Bar and Inn of Court of Northern Ireland* (Belfast, The General Council of the Bar of Northern Ireland, 2013) ch 7.

[40] Lord Justice Moore, *Memorandum on Supreme Court of Judicature, 1 October 1921–31 July 1922*: PRONI, CAB/6/57.

merged in a new one.' He looked forward to a high standard of advocacy at the new Bar of Northern Ireland.[41]

As Lord Chief Justice, Henry was involved in several highly controversial cases which reflected the turbulent birth-pangs of the new state. In July 1922 he ruled against the plaintiff in a landmark case (*Belfast Prison, Governors of v O'Hanlon*[42]) challenging the legality of the Unionist government's Civil Authorities (Special Powers Act) 1922. The case concerned John O'Hanlon, a Portadown hotelier and former director of the Portadown Gas Company, who challenged his internment under the Act before the Northern Ireland High Court on two grounds: he contested the factual basis of any allegation against him by submitting an affidavit in which he denied involvement in any unlawful association or conspiracy and he submitted that the introduction of internment under the Special Powers Act 1922 amounted to a suspension of habeas corpus, contrary to the terms of the Government of Ireland Act 1920. O'Hanlon's counsel, Thomas J Campbell KC (later a Nationalist MP at Stormont), argued that the draconian legislation under which his client was detained left captivity to the uncontrolled will of the Attorney General, which was 'a sweeping inroad on the old established guarantees for the liberty of the subject'. Henry's judgment was a predicable defence of the emergency law. Dismissing the factual basis of the plaintiff's claim, he ruled that: 'The only question the court has to decide … is whether … O'Hanlon is legally held. We have nothing to do with the consideration of whether there is any evidence against him'.

Accordingly, Lord Chief Justice Henry ruled that O'Hanlon might be held so long as the Executive desired. Rejecting defence counsel's argument that the Special Powers Act breached the liberty of the individual, Henry held that the internment order was a 'modification of orders made in England almost every day by the Home Secretary there during the duration of the [First World] war dealing with persons of hostile origin or hostile association'. Consequently, the regulations were not ultra vires. The judgment prompted a blistering attack on Henry's judgment by the *Irish News*, which described O'Hanlon as a respectable citizen who had been 'kidnapped in the name of the law'. It declared sarcastically that the Lord Chief Justice had been too 'careful of the feelings … of Sir James Craig's "fair administration"'.[43]

In November 1923 Henry rejected claims for compensation for the victims arising over a notorious incident in Cushendall, County Antrim on 23 June 1922 when three Catholic youths were shot dead by members of the 'A' Special Constabulary within hours of the IRA assassination of Sir Henry Wilson in London. While the police claimed that the men had been engaged in a paramilitary ambush, witnesses alleged they had been innocent, while a private investigation by an English judge, Barrington-Ward KC, rejected the Specials'

[41] Hart (n 39) 173.
[42] *Belfast Prison, Governors of v O'Hanlon* (1922) 56 *Irish Times Law Reports* 170.
[43] McDonnell (n 1) 107–10.

version: 'My conclusion is that no one except the police and military even fired at all … I am unable to accept the evidence of the Special Constabulary'.[44] The Unionist government, however, suppressed the report and ordered a fresh inquiry which vindicated the Specials.

In his judgment Henry referred to the 'extraordinary conflict of testimony' between the police and the nationalist witnesses but he rejected the claim for compensation on the grounds that the deaths arose out of an unlawful assembly.[45] Such adjudications reflected Henry's earlier defence of emergency legislation during the War of Independence and his instinctive support for the forces of law and order in their defence of the new sub-state.

The stresses and strains of the Irish Revolution years had taken their toll on Henry. He died, following a seizure, on 1 October 1925, at his home, 'Lisvarna', on Windsor Avenue, Belfast. He was 61. In his final illness he received the last rites of the Catholic Church from the local parish priest and the Rector of Ardoyne Passionist Monastery in Belfast. Tim Healy claimed that the dying judge 'had a priest after sixty years', suggesting that he had long abandoned his religious practice.[46]

After a private Mass in the family home celebrated by his Jesuit brother, William, Denis Henry was buried in his native place at Straw in the rolling Sperrins. In a tribute Sir James Craig described him as 'one of Ulster's most distinguished sons'. His political opponents paid tribute to his personal qualities, his legal acumen and his compassion as a judge but, as O'Connor observed in an obituary, 'there remained some resentment among his co-religionists – and among nationalists generally – that this man of Celtic blood and of the Catholic creed should range himself in the ranks of the Orangemen'.[47]

The career of Sir Denis Henry remains unique in an island where religious and political allegiances are often synonymous. Previous Catholic Unionists like William Kenny and Father John Healy of Little Bray had come from the south of Ireland. Catholic Unionists were always in short supply in the north. Henry's name was largely forgotten until the late 1960s when, in response to civil rights claims of anti-Catholic discrimination, Unionist politicians trumpeted that the first Lord Chief Justice of Northern Ireland had been a Catholic. Yet attempts to broaden Unionism beyond its traditional Protestant base had little success in the divided state after his death and it was not until 1998 that another Catholic Unionist was elected to the Northern Ireland Assembly.[48]

[44] Michael Farrell, *Arming the Protestants: The Formation of the Ulster Special Constabulary and the Royal Ulster Constabulary, 1920–27* (London, Pluto Press, 1983) 163–65.

[45] McDonnell (n 1) 110–14; Barrington-Ward's report indicting the Ulster Special Constabulary at Cushendall was not released until the late 1970s.

[46] Frank, Callanan, *TM Healy* (Cork, Cork University Press, 1996) 627.

[47] *Belfast Telegraph*, 2 October 1925.

[48] Sir John Gorman, a former senior Royal Ulster Constabulary officer was elected in North Down as an Ulster Unionist, supportive of the Belfast (Good Friday) Agreement in 1998.

12

Giving Substance to Sovereignty: Parliamentary Sovereignty and Parliamentary Effectiveness

AILEEN McHARG

Introduction

In September 2019, an 11-member Supreme Court bench (including Lord Kerr) handed down its remarkable and unprecedented decision that the attempted prorogation of Parliament for five weeks (in the run up to the intended date of the United Kingdom's withdrawal from the European Union, on 31 October) was unlawful, and therefore null and of no effect.[1] Several aspects of the judgment were novel and controversial,[2] but the focus in this chapter is on the Supreme Court's ruling that the prorogation was unlawful because it was incompatible with the legal principle of parliamentary sovereignty. According to the Court:

> The sovereignty of Parliament would … be undermined as the foundational principle of our constitution if the executive could, through the use of the prerogative, prevent Parliament from exercising its legislative authority for as long as it pleased.[3]

The court recognised that Parliament does not remain permanently in session, and hence prorogation for short periods was undoubtedly lawful.[4] However, the Court held that:

> a decision to prorogue Parliament … will be unlawful if the prorogation has the effect of frustrating or preventing, without reasonable justification, the ability of Parliament to carry out its constitutional functions as a legislature.[5]

[1] *R (Miller) v The Prime Minister/Cherry v The Advocate General for Scotland* [2019] UKSC 41, [2020] AC 373 (hereafter *Miller 2/Cherry*).

[2] See Aileen McHarg, 'The Supreme Court's Prorogation Judgment: Guardians of the Constitution or Architect of the Constitution' (2020) 24 *Edin LR* 88.

[3] *Miller 2/Cherry* (n 1) [42].

[4] ibid [45].

[5] ibid [50].

Since the Court considered that Parliament clearly had been prevented from carrying out its constitutional role – at a time when parliamentary scrutiny of the executive was particularly important – and that no reasons for the exceptional length of the prorogation had been offered, it followed that the decision was unlawful.[6]

The Divisional Court in *Miller 2* had rejected the expanded reading of parliamentary sovereignty advanced by Lord Pannick on behalf of the claimant – as extending beyond the supremacy of statute to include the ability of Parliament to conduct its business unimpeded – as lacking in authority, indeterminate in scope, and offending against the separation of powers.[7] According to that court, '[t]he expanded concept has been fashioned to invite the judicial arm of the State to exercise hitherto unidentified power over the Executive branch of the State in its dealings with Parliament'.[8] Critics of the Supreme Court agree. By conflating the constitutional functions of the Houses of Parliament with the constitutional authority of the Crown-in-Parliament, Martin Loughlin claims that the decision 'attempts to transform a formal principle into a functional principle' which 'converts orthodoxy into heterodoxy and is … misconceived'.[9]

By contrast, defenders of the Supreme Court's decision agree with its ruling that 'the effect that the courts have given to parliamentary sovereignty is not confined to recognising the status of the legislation enacted by the Crown in Parliament as our highest form of law'.[10] Thus, while recognising the novelty of the inference drawn from parliamentary sovereignty, they regard it as compatible with the normative underpinning of the doctrine. For Mark Elliott, for example, sovereignty should not be understood 'as a merely technical rule about the hierarchical legal status of legislation enacted by Parliament' but rather as 'a fundamental principle that determines and reflects the nature of constitutional democracy in the UK'.[11]

[6] ibid [55]–[61].

[7] *R (Miller) v The Prime Minister* [2019] EWHC 2381 (QB), [58]–[64].

[8] ibid [63].

[9] Martin Loughlin, *The Case of Prorogation: the UK Constitutional Council's Ruling on Appeal from the Judgment of the Supreme Court* (London, Policy Exchange, 2019) 16, available at policyexchange.org.uk/wp-content/uploads/2019/10/The-Case-of-Prorogation.pdf. See also Richard Ekins, *Parliamentary Sovereignty and the Politics of Prorogation* (London, Policy Exchange, 2019) 14, available at policyexchange.org.uk/wp-content/uploads/2019/10/The-unconstitutionality-of-the-Supreme-Courts-prorogation-judgment.pdf; Timothy Endicott, 'Making Constitutional Principles into Laws' (2020) 136 *LQR* 175, 178; John Finnis, *The Unconstitutionality of the Supreme Court's Prorogation Judgment* (London, Policy Exchange, 2019) 5, 8, available at policyexchange.org.uk/wp-content/uploads/2019/10/The-unconstitutionality-of-the-Supreme-Courts-prorogation-judgment.pdf; Steven Spadijer, 'The Royal Prerogative Revisited: Some Reflections on the Proposed Repeal of the Fixed Term Parliaments Act and a (Lengthy) Critique of Miller No 2' (SSRN, 2021) [130]–[139], available at papers.ssrn.com/sol3/papers.cfm?abstract_id=3788525&download=yes; Stephen Tierney, 'Turning Political Principles into Legal Rules: the Unconvincing Alchemy of the *Miller/Cherry* Decision' (*Judicial Power Project*, 30 September 2019), available at judicialpowerproject.org.uk/stephen-tierney-turning-political-principles-into-legal-rules-the-unconvincing-alchemy-of-the-millercherry-decision/.

[10] *Miller 2/Cherry* (n 1) [41].

[11] Mark Elliott, 'Constitutional Adjudication and Constitutional Politics in the United Kingdom: The *Miller II* Case in Legal and Political Context' (2020) 16 *European Constitutional Law Review* 625, 631.

Similarly, Paul Craig argues that '[t]he proposition that statutes are invested with supremacy over all else has never represented the totality of the principle of parliamentary sovereignty', and '[t]he very idea that legal norms include protection for the conditions of their exercise is … standard fare within legal reasoning'.[12]

Mike Gordon notes that parliamentary sovereignty was used largely superficially by the Supreme Court to provide a legal gloss for a decision primarily about executive *accountability* to Parliament.[13] The Court itself regarded the case as a 'one off'[14] – a view shared in the report of the Independent Review of Administrative Law.[15] In this chapter, however, I seek to demonstrate that the prorogation decision forms part of a developing line of Supreme Court authority (in which Lord Kerr was centrally involved) which treats parliamentary sovereignty as a substantive rather than purely formal principle, concerned, in various ways, with the effectiveness, and not merely the authority, of Parliament's legislative function.

I begin by outlining the differing implications that have been drawn from the idea of making parliamentary sovereignty fully effective, arguing that these represent a clear departure from constitutional orthodoxy,[16] and that – paradoxically – they have the potential both to enhance and limit Parliament's legislative authority. I then explore the broader question whether parliamentary sovereignty, as traditionally understood, is a purely formal principle concerned with legal hierarchy, or rather one with wider substantive implications for the allocation and regulation of constitutional power. To the extent that the latter is true, I will argue that its substantive implications have traditionally been very different from the use now being made of parliamentary sovereignty; essentially acting as a brake upon, rather than a justification for, judicial activism in the constitutional arena. Finally, I will consider how this developing doctrine of parliamentary effectiveness relates to the substantive turn in constitutional adjudication more generally, how the doctrine might develop in future, and the appropriateness of the constitutional vision it embodies.

[12] Paul Craig, 'The Supreme Court, Prorogation and Constitutional Principle' [2020] *Public Law* 248, 254, 255. See also Nicholas Barber, 'Constitutional Hardball and Justified Development of the Law' (*Judicial Power Project*, 29 September 2019), available at judicialpowerproject.org.uk/nick-barber-constitutional-hardball-and-justified-development-of-the-law; Hasan Dindjer, 'Prorogation as a Breach of Parliamentary Sovereignty' (*UK Const Law Blog*, 16 September 2019), available at ukconstitutionallaw.org/2019/09/16/hasan-dindjer-prorogation-as-a-breach-of-parliamentary-sovereignty; Alison Young, 'Deftly Guarding the Constitution' (*Judicial Power Project*, 29 September 2019), available at judicialpowerproject.org.uk/alison-young-deftly-guarding-the-constitution.

[13] Mike Gordon, 'The Prorogation Case and the Political Constitution' (*UK Const Law Blog*, 30 September 2019), available at ukconstitutionallaw.org/2019/09/30/mike-gordon-the-prorogation-case-and-the-political-constitution.

[14] *Miller 2/Cherry* (n 1) [1].

[15] Edward Faulks et al, *The Independent Review of Administrative Law* (*IRAL*), CP 407 (2021), para 2.37.

[16] By contrast, effectiveness *is* recognised as a core condition of state sovereignty; see Nicholas Barber, *The Principles of Constitutionalism* (Oxford, OUP, 2018) 25, 29–32.

The Dimensions of Parliamentary Effectiveness

Three distinct, though related, dimensions of parliamentary effectiveness, apparently derived from the principle of parliamentary sovereignty, can be identified in the case law.

Parliament Must have the Opportunity to Legislate

The idea that underpins *Miller 2/Cherry* is that 'Parliament is sovereign only if it has meaningful opportunities to exercise its legislative powers'.[17] A similar idea – that Parliament's opportunity to legislate must not be circumvented by executive action – also appears in the majority judgment in the first *Miller* case.[18] There, the Supreme Court majority held that:

> We cannot accept that a major change to UK constitutional arrangements [in this case, withdrawal from the EU] can be achieved by ministers alone. It must be effected in the only way that the UK constitution recognises, namely by parliamentary legislation. This conclusion appears to us to follow from the ordinary application of basic concepts of constitutional law.[19]

Although the court did not explain which 'basic concepts of constitutional law' were in play, Alison Young argues that the clear implication – given its importance in the judgment more generally – is that this conclusion derives from parliamentary sovereignty.[20]

Of course, the idea that Parliament has a monopoly over legislation forms no part of the orthodox understanding of parliamentary sovereignty,[21] still less that it has a *right* to legislate. Parliament is not continuously in session,[22] and the *initiation* of legislation is primarily an executive function in Westminster systems, with opportunities for backbench MPs to legislate in the UK Parliament being heavily curtailed and dependent on government co-operation or – exceptionally, as seen during the Brexit process – the ability to wrest control of the parliamentary timetable from Ministers. In fact, in neither case did the Supreme Court regard the idea that Parliament should have the right to legislate as an absolute one: it was

[17] Dindjer (n 12).

[18] *R (Miller) v Secretary of State for Exiting the European Union* [2017] UKSC 5, [2018] AC 61 (hereafter *Miller 1*).

[19] ibid [82].

[20] Alison Young, '*Miller* and the Future of Constitutional Adjudication' in Mark Elliott, Jack Williams and Alison Young (eds), *The UK Constitution after* Miller: *Brexit and Beyond* (Oxford, Hart Publishing, 2018) 290.

[21] Mark Elliott, 'The Supreme Court's Judgment in *Miller*: in Search of Constitutional Principle' (2017) 76 *CLJ* 257, 267.

[22] The Bill of Rights 1688/Claim of Right 1689 require that Parliaments be held 'frequently', but the Inner House in *Cherry* (2019) CSIH 49 rejected reliance on this provision, and it formed no part of the Supreme Court's decision.

subject to the idea of constitutional importance in *Miller 1* and (in effect) to a proportionality test in *Miller 2/Cherry*. But, as Jason Varuhas points out, this appears to involve a further departure from orthodoxy, in treating Parliament's sovereignty, hitherto understood as an absolute rule, as a principle which could be qualified.[23]

Attempts to justify the idea that parliamentary sovereignty includes the right of Parliament to legislate variously involve unconvincing analogies, appeals to principle or the introduction of yet further departures from constitutional orthodoxy.

For example, in relation to *Miller 1*, both Craig and Young draw an analogy with the idea that constitutional statutes cannot be impliedly repealed, in order that Parliament must squarely confront the political costs of its proposed actions, to argue that it would be inconsistent if such statutes could be deprived of effect through ministerial action under prerogative powers, unless specifically authorised by Parliament.[24] Of course, this is an unrealistic depiction of the factual scenario in the case itself – there is no question that the political costs of a decision to leave the EU had not been squarely (albeit imperfectly) confronted. But more generally, this analogy turns a *limit* on Parliament's legislative freedom into a broader principle of constitutional regulation with the aim of *empowering* Parliament *vis-à-vis* the executive.

Elsewhere, Young acknowledges that the Supreme Court majority in *Miller 1* was reasoning in a deductive manner from the premise that Parliament is the most important institution in the UK constitution to the conclusion that major legal constitutional change should be enacted by Parliament and not by the executive acting alone.[25] As she acknowledges, however, this involves 'a looser chain of causation'.[26] And her qualification that this novel principle applies only to 'legal' constitutional change[27] recognises the limits of any supposed parliamentary monopoly over constitutional change in a constitutional order only partially regulated by law.

Most startlingly of all, Tom Poole defends the decision by reference to a distinction between constituent authority and (constituted) legislative capacity – that is, certain constitutional changes are of such significance as to engage Parliament's role as a constituent assembly.[28] But again, it is axiomatic that the doctrine of parliamentary sovereignty, in its orthodox incarnation, is antithetical to any such distinction.

[23] Jason Varuhas, 'The Principle of Legality' (2020) 79 *CLJ* 578, 588.

[24] Paul Craig, '*Miller*, Structural Review and the Limits of Prerogative Power' [2017] *Public Law* 48, 70; Young (n 20) 295.

[25] Young (ibid) 290.

[26] ibid, 291.

[27] ibid, at n 54. See also Gavin Phillipson, 'EU Law as an Agent of National Constitutional Change: *Miller v Secretary of State for Exiting the European Union*' (2017) 36 *Yearbook of European Law* 46, 77–78.

[28] Tom Poole, 'Devotion to Legalism' (2017) 80 *MLR* 696. Phillipson makes a similar argument (ibid) 81–84.

Similarly, in relation to *Miller 2/Cherry*, Craig draws an analogy with the continuing nature of parliamentary sovereignty:

> the precept that there can be no procedural and substantive limits to sovereignty attests to the fact that each Parliament in turn exercises the authority vested in it through representative democracy. The precept that Parliament should not be unduly foreclosed from exercising its legislative and scrutiny function is grounded in the principle that each Parliament should be able to exercise its representative authority for the period for which it has been duly elected.[29]

Once more, there is some logical distance between the idea that the latest expression of Parliamentary will prevails over earlier democratic choices and the assertion that Parliament *must in fact have the opportunity* to revisit its earlier choices.

Elliott appeals directly to arguments of principle:

> To cling to the notion of a sovereign Parliament with wholly unalloyed law-making competence that was vulnerable to legally uncontrollable powers of executive neutralisation would be absurd, since it would preserve those aspects of the sovereignty principle that go to the legal status of parliamentary sovereignty whilst dismantling the democratic scaffolding that supplies the normative support for the existence of such expansive powers in the first place.[30]

But no matter how attractive this argument may be, it again does not follow that it is either necessary or appropriate to develop a new constitutional rule to enforce it.

Parliament Must be Able to Legislate Free from Impediments

A second element of the developing doctrine of parliamentary effectiveness is that, when legislating, Parliament must be able to do so free from impediments. This idea is most clearly seen in the *Scottish Continuity Bill Reference*,[31] in respect of the Supreme Court's decision that section 17 of the UK Withdrawal from the European Union (Legal Continuity) Scotland Bill was beyond the competence of the Scottish Parliament because it amounted to an unlawful modification of section 28(7) of the Scotland Act 1998. Section 17 purported to make the exercise of future powers conferred on UK Ministers by UK legislation to make delegated legislation modifying retained EU law in devolved areas conditional upon the consent of the Scottish Ministers. The Court held that this amounted to an attempt to condition the future exercise of the Westminster Parliament's power to legislate for Scotland, which section 28(7) sought to preserve intact.

[29] Craig (n 12) 255.
[30] Elliott (n 11) 632.
[31] *Reference re the UK Withdrawal from the European Union (Legal Continuity) (Scotland) Bill* [2018] UKSC 64, [2019] AC 1022.

This aspect of the Supreme Court's decision is somewhat confusing in that the Court simultaneously rejected the argument that section 17 impinged upon the sovereignty of Parliament, since Westminster was free to amend, disapply or repeal the provision whenever it chose.[32] Given that section 28(7) was intended as a statutory affirmation of parliamentary sovereignty,[33] it is difficult to understand why an attempt to condition the exercise of future UK legislation in devolved areas could be incompatible with the statutory provision, yet compatible with the principle it embodied.[34] But whether the decision makes sense or not, it seems to evince a desire to protect Parliament's legislative freedom of action from constraints imposed by subordinate legislatures.

A similar idea may explain the decision in *Miller 1* in respect of the argument that legislation authorising the UK's withdrawal from the EU would be subject to the Sewel convention. Not only was the Court not prepared to rule on the meaning and application of the convention, *qua* convention,[35] it also held that the statutory recognition (in section 28(8) of the Scotland Act) of the requirement to seek devolved consent had not converted the convention into an enforceable legal rule. This followed, the court said, from both the content of the rule and the wording used.[36] The nature of its content appears to be a reference to the fact that the Sewel convention constrains the Westminster Parliament in the exercise of its legislative authority in relation to devolved matters. However, as I have argued elsewhere, it would have been possible to give legal effect to section 28(8) without necessarily impinging on Parliament's sovereignty.[37]

Again, therefore, the Supreme Court appeared to be giving effect to an extended understanding of parliamentary sovereignty, as requiring that Westminster's legislative capacity be kept free from legal impediments, even ones that it is free to disregard. In other words, this appears to entail a move from the rule that Parliament *cannot* be prevented from legislating as it thinks fit, to a rule that there *must be no attempt* to impose such conditions, at least on the part of the devolved legislatures. However, this is no part of the orthodox understanding of parliamentary sovereignty, which has always recognised a distinction between Parliament's unlimited legislative authority, and the existence of a range of *de facto* constraints on its legislative capacity.[38] It is also inconsistent with rules of interpretation – whether statutory or common law – which require Parliament to go to particular

[32] ibid [63].

[33] See Christopher McCorkindale, 'Devolution: A New Fundamental Principle of the UK Constitution' forthcoming in Michael Gordon and Adam Tucker (eds), *The New Labour Constitution: Twenty Years On* (Oxford, Hart Publishing, 2022).

[34] For an attempt at reconciliation, see Mark Elliott, 'The Supreme Court's Judgment in the Scottish Continuity Bill Case' (*Public Law for Everyone*, 14 December 2018), available at publiclawforeveryone.com/2018/12/14/the-supreme-courts-judgment-in-the-scottish-continuity-bill-case.

[35] *Miller 1* (n 18) [144].

[36] ibid [146].

[37] Aileen McHarg, 'Constitutional Change and Territorial Consent: the *Miller* Case and the Sewel Convention' in Elliott, Williams and Young (n 20) 174–77.

[38] Albert Venn Dicey, *Introduction to the Study of the Law of the Constitution* (Indianapolis, Liberty Fund, 1982) 26: 'There are many enactments … which Parliament never would and (to speak plainly)

efforts to make its intention to achieve certain legislative objectives unusually clear. Moreover, as Keith Ewing notes in respect of *Miller 1*, there 'seems something slightly odd about a court refusing to apply primary legislation in a decision which for all practical purposes is about reclaiming the sovereignty of Parliament'.[39]

Legislation Must be Capable of Being Effective

The final aspect of the developing doctrine of parliamentary effectiveness is potentially the most radical. Whereas the cases previously considered impose obligations on *other* constitutional actors in the name of parliamentary sovereignty, this part of the doctrine imposes limitations on Parliament itself. This is the idea that, in order for legislation to be effective, there may be certain conceptual limits on the content of legislation; specifically, Parliament may be unable to oust judicial review.

This idea appears to have originated in Laws LJ's speech in *Cart*, in which he said that:

> If the meaning of statutory text is not controlled by … a judicial authority, it would at length be degraded to nothing more than a matter of opinion. Its scope and content would become muddied and unclear. Public bodies would not … be kept within the confines of their powers prescribed by statute. The very effectiveness of statute law, Parliament's law, requires that none of these things happen. Accordingly … the need for such an authoritative judicial source cannot be dispensed with by Parliament. This is not a denial of legislative sovereignty, but an affirmation of it …[40]

A similar argument was made by Lord Reed in *UNISON*, who said in support of the importance of the principle of access to the courts:

> Without such access, laws are liable to become a dead letter, the work done by Parliament may be rendered nugatory, and the democratic election of Members of Parliament may become a meaningless charade.[41]

However, the issue received its most extensive consideration (albeit in *obiter dicta*) by the Supreme Court in *Privacy International*.[42] Dinah Rose QC, on behalf of the claimants, invited the court to accept the proposition that a provision purporting to oust the High Court's supervisory jurisdiction could not properly be upheld because it would conflict with the rule of law. However, in so doing, she emphasised that she did not seek to question the principle of parliamentary

never could pass. If the doctrine of Parliamentary sovereignty involves the attribution of unrestricted power to Parliament, the dogma is no better than a legal fiction'.

[39] Keith Ewing, 'Brexit and Parliamentary Sovereignty' (2017) 80 *MLR* 711, 723.

[40] *R (Cart) v Upper Tribunal* [2009] EWHC 3052 (Admin), [2010] 2 WLR 2012 [38]. This passage was cited with approval by Lady Hale in the Supreme Court: [2011] UKSC 28, [2012] 1 AC 663, [30].

[41] *R (UNISON) v Lord Chancellor* [2017] UKSC 51, [2020] AC 869.

[42] *R (Privacy International) v Investigatory Powers Tribunal* [2019] UKSC 22, [2020] AC 491.

sovereignty, but rather to 'explain its boundaries, and why the laws of a sovereign Parliament require an independent interpreter of unlimited jurisdiction to ensure those laws are faithfully implemented'.[43]

Although not necessary to dispose of the case, this proposition received endorsement from all seven members of the court, albeit in varying degrees. While Lord Lloyd-Jones was willing to 'wholeheartedly endorse' Laws LJ's dictum in *Cart*,[44] Lord Wilson did so only in respect of jurisdictional errors.[45] Lord Sumption (with whom Lord Reed agreed) was, however, only prepared to accept it 'up to a point'. He agreed that, if Parliament had intended to create a tribunal of legally limited jurisdiction, it was inconsistent with that intention for the courts to lack capacity to enforce those limits, and this was correctly described as giving effect to the sovereignty of Parliament, not limiting it. Nevertheless, he did regard it as conceptually possible for Parliament to create a legally unlimited body or one with unlimited discretionary power to determine its own jurisdiction, and 'a sufficiently clear and all-embracing ouster clause might demonstrate that Parliament had indeed intended to do that', though 'it would be a strange thing for Parliament to intend'.[46] By contrast, Lord Carnwath (with whom Lady Hale and Lord Kerr agreed), while implicitly accepting the conceptual argument,[47] seemed to go further in regarding the rule of law as placing a normative limit on Parliament's ability to oust judicial review.[48]

In justifying this claimed conceptual limit on parliamentary sovereignty, Laws LJ drew an analogy with the rule that Parliament cannot bind its successors:

> The old rule means that successive Parliaments are always free to make what laws they choose; that is one condition of Parliament's sovereignty. The requirement of an authoritative judicial source for the interpretation of law means that Parliament's statutes are always effective; that is another.[49]

But, once more, this analogy is far from compelling. The inability of Parliament to bind its successors derives directly from the unlimited legislative competence enjoyed by each successive Parliament. Parliament itself may choose to legislate compatibly or incompatibly with earlier legislation. Attempts at entrenchment are valid when enacted, but simply ineffective against a future Parliament which does not wish to be bound by them. By contrast, if ouster clauses can never have effect if they are deemed to be incompatible with the rule of law, this is an absolute limit on Parliament's legislative authority, enforced at the discretion of the courts.[50]

[43] ibid [114], [209].
[44] ibid [160].
[45] ibid [236].
[46] ibid [210].
[47] ibid [116], [122].
[48] ibid [132], [144].
[49] *Cart* (n 40) [38].
[50] In *Privacy International* (n 42), both Lord Carnwath ([131]–[144]) and Lord Sumption ([182]–[188]) accepted that it is for the Court to determine whether a particular ouster clause is compatible with the rule of law.

Indeed, by placing conditions on judicial obedience to statute, this supposed conceptual limit on parliamentary sovereignty appears to turn the doctrine on its head.

Moreover, while there is a certain intuitive appeal in the idea that legislation should be effective, this, again, has never been part of the traditional understanding of sovereignty. On the contrary, it has always been accepted that practical effect, in terms of enforceability or likelihood of obedience, is an entirely different question from legal validity,[51] as in Sir Ivor Jennings' famous example of legislation banning smoking in the streets of Paris.[52] Nor, as the Supreme Court's treatment of the statutory recognition of the Sewel convention demonstrates, is there any necessary assumption that legislation is intended to create legally enforceable rules.[53]

The Doctrine of Parliamentary Sovereignty: Formal or Substantive?

It should be clear from the discussion so far that these various invocations of the idea of parliamentary effectiveness involve extensions of the doctrine of parliamentary sovereignty, rather than simply drawing out implications that were always inherent in it. Moreover, they entail significant departures from constitutional orthodoxy, using sovereignty as a substantive principle to control the executive, the devolved legislatures, and potentially even Parliament itself. Nevertheless, to draw substantive implications from parliamentary sovereignty is not, in itself, necessarily novel. Elliott argues that sovereignty, like all principles, consists of a core and penumbra; hence 'the additional penumbral implication ascribed by the Court in [*Miller 2/Cherry*] … is wholly defensible, albeit that it is admittedly a step beyond the implications that the court had previously attached to the doctrine'.[54]

At the core of the doctrine are Dicey's positive and negative aspects of sovereignty: that 'Parliament … has … the right to make or unmake any law whatsoever' and that 'no person or body is recognised by the law … as having a right to override or set aside the legislation of Parliament'.[55] Hasan Dindjer usefully terms these the 'plenary authority' and 'legal supremacy' rules.[56] These two rules are not uncontroversial. The legal supremacy rule does not necessarily entail the plenary authority

[51] See *Manuel v Attorney-General* [1983] Ch 77, 95 per Sir Robert Megarry.

[52] Sir Ivor Jennings, *The Law and the Constitution*, 5th edn (London, University of London Press, 1959) 170–71.

[53] See, generally, David Feldman, 'Legislation Which Bears No Law' (2016) 37 *Statute Law Review* 212.

[54] Elliott (n 11) 630–31. See also Mark Elliott, 'Judicial Power in the United Kingdom's Changing Constitution' (2017) 36 *U Queensland LJ* 273.

[55] Dicey (n 38) 3–4.

[56] Dindjer (n 12).

rule,[57] and of course the questions whether Parliament is free of legal constraints, or whether its plenary authority is continuing or self-embracing, are matters of perennial debate. Equally, the plenary rule may permit Acts of Parliament to be overridden or set aside (for example the 'disapplication' of statutes incompatible with EU law, or the ability of Ministers via 'Henry VIII powers' or the devolved legislatures to amend or repeal them) provided that the authority to do so may itself be traced to an Act of Parliament. Nevertheless, the core of the doctrine of parliamentary sovereignty is relatively stable and received strong endorsement by the Supreme Court in *Miller 1*.[58]

Beyond the core, it is undoubtedly true that 'the reach and influence of the idea of parliamentary sovereignty can be seen throughout our constitutional arrangements'.[59] It shapes the nature of the UK constitution in profound ways: by ruling out entrenchment and strong-form constitutional review, as well as a federal division of powers, it contributes to the constitutional centrality of the Westminster Parliament,[60] and it lies at the heart of the theory of political constitutionalism.[61] However, it is important to recognise that the various penumbral implications of parliamentary sovereignty can and do take different forms.

In the first place, some of the most important constitutional implications of sovereignty – including the impossibility of entrenchment and the unitary (legal) character of the territorial constitution – are no more than logical out-workings of the core plenary authority and legal supremacy rules. Moreover, though important, their significance should not be overstated. For example, parliamentary sovereignty is (formally at least) compatible with weaker forms of constitutional review (whether under statute or at common law),[62] and with forms of political entrenchment, such as the protections for devolved autonomy provided by the Sewel convention and pre-enactment referendums. Similarly, Neil Walker has argued that the unitary conception of the constitution 'is actually a very flexible notion, capable of embracing a wide range of different constitutional structures

[57] Colin Munro, *Studies in Constitutional Law*, 2nd edn (Oxford, OUP, 1999) 132.

[58] *Miller 1* (n 18) [43].

[59] Roger Masterman and Colin Murray, *Constitutional and Administrative Law*, 2nd edn (Harlow, Pearson, 2018) 123.

[60] The constitutional centrality of Parliament also rests on the idea of responsible government, which, as Jeffrey Goldsworthy notes, is conceptually and practically different from parliamentary sovereignty: *The Sovereignty of Parliament: History and Philosophy* (Oxford, Clarendon Press, 1999) 9. The Supreme Court in *Miller 2/Cherry* recognised what it called parliamentary accountability as a distinct principle (at [46]), albeit it subsequently tended to conflate the two. Parliamentary privilege (which, as Dawn Oliver notes, reinforces, but is not a necessary incident of, parliamentary sovereignty: 'Parliament and the Courts: A Pragmatic (or Principled) Defence of the Sovereignty of Parliament', in Alexander Horne, Gavin Drewry and Jeff King (eds), *Parliament and the Law* (London, Bloomsbury Publishing, 2018) 296)) further contributes to the insulation of Parliament from judicial control.

[61] John Griffith, 'The Political Constitution' (1979) 42 *MLR* 1; Keith Ewing, 'The Resilience of the Political Constitution' (2013) 14 *German Law Journal* 2111; Michael Gordon, 'Parliamentary Sovereignty and the Political Constitution(s): From Griffith to Brexit' (2019) 30 *King's Law Journal* 125.

[62] cf Gordon (ibid) 134–35.

and visions', and that although certain fundamental limits are set by the unitary conception, these 'are less constraining than is often assumed'.[63]

Secondly, while other constitutional doctrines may *look like* they involve deriving substantive implications from parliamentary sovereignty, they may not in fact be incidences of sovereignty at all. The best examples here are legal controls over prerogative powers. The Supreme Court in *Miller 2/Cherry* stated that:

> Time and again, in a series of cases since the 17th century, the courts have protected parliamentary sovereignty from threats posed to it by the use of prerogative powers, and in doing so have demonstrated that prerogative powers are limited by the principle of parliamentary sovereignty.[64]

However, while the rules that prerogative powers cannot alter Acts of Parliament[65] and, by extension, cannot be used to frustrate the operation of statute,[66] follow more or less directly from the legal supremacy rule, other limitations on prerogative power do not. The rule that prerogative powers cannot be used to change the *common law*[67] (except to the extent that this is inherent in the prerogative power itself)[68] and the principle of dualism, which means that international treaties entered into by the executive cannot alter domestic law unless and until given effect by Act of Parliament,[69] confine the scope of the executive's law-making power beyond that strictly required to uphold the supremacy of statute. As Craig correctly notes, the courts could have upheld, but did not, 'a theory of parallelism, whereby statutory power and prerogative power existed in tandem, subject to the fact that Parliament could expressly curtail the prerogative if it wished to do so'[70] (similar to the treatment of common law rule-making and devolved legislation). Instead, prerogative powers were expressly confined, 'in order thereby to foster and support parliamentary sovereignty'.[71] The Supreme Court in *Miller 1* also viewed the dualist system as 'a necessary corollary of parliamentary sovereignty',[72] citing Campbell McLachlan as follows:

> If treaties have no effect within domestic law, Parliament's legislative supremacy within its own polity is secure. If the executive must always seek the sanction of Parliament in the event that a proposed action on the international plane will require domestic

[63] Neil Walker, 'Beyond the Unitary Conception of the United Kingdom Constitution' [2000] *Public Law* 384, 388.

[64] *Miller 2/Cherry* (n 1) [41].

[65] *Case of Proclamations* (1611) 12 Co Rep 74; Bill of Rights 1688, Arts 1 and 2; Claim of Right 1689, Art 2.

[66] *Attorney General v De Keyser's Royal Hotel Ltd* [1920] AC 508.

[67] *Case of Proclamations* (n 65).

[68] See *Miller 1* (n 18) [52]–[53].

[69] eg *JH Rayner (Mincing Lane) Ltd v Department of Trade and Industry* [1990] 2 AC 418.

[70] Craig (n 12) 258.

[71] ibid.

[72] *Miller 1* (n 18) [57]. And see also *R (SC, CB and 8 Children) v Secretary of State for Work and Pensions* [2021] UKSC 26, [2021] 3 WLR 428 [78].

> implementation, parliamentary sovereignty is reinforced at the very point at which the legislative power is engaged.[73]

But are these additional constraints on executive rule-making really justified by reference to parliamentary sovereignty? In fact, the constitutional basis of the dualist system has increasingly been questioned. Eirik Bjorge has argued that its traditional justification is one founded upon the separation of powers, in order to protect citizens against abuse of power by the executive,[74] and that this traditional view 'is once again gaining ground'.[75] This explanation has been accepted by both academics[76] and judges,[77] and indeed received its strongest endorsement from Lord Kerr in *R (SG) v Secretary of State for Work and Pensions*,[78] where he held (in dissent) that Article 3 of the United Nations Convention on the Rights of the Child had direct effect in domestic law. He justified this conclusion by saying that if it is right to characterise

> the rationale for the dualist theory as a form of protection of the citizen from abuses by the executive, the justification for refusing to recognise the rights enshrined in an international convention relating to human rights and to which the UK has subscribed as directly enforceable in domestic law is not easy to find. Why should a convention which expresses the UK's commitment to the protection of a particular human right for its citizens not be given effect as an enforceable right in domestic law?[79]

Bjorge sees the rule that the executive cannot override the common law as equally being grounded in the separation of powers.[80] Craig argues that the principal beneficiary of the rule laid down in the *Case of Proclamations* was Parliament, 'since the case concerned the extent of monarchical regulatory power independent from the legislature'.[81] However, the case was decided before parliamentary sovereignty in its modern sense was fully established, and served to control *the forum in which* the King could change the law, rather than to strip the Crown of law-making authority. In any case, as Goldsworthy notes, the legislative sovereignty

[73] Campbell McLachlan, *Foreign Relations Law* (Cambridge, CUP, 2014), [5.20]. See also Philip Sales and Joanne Clement, 'International Law in the Domestic Courts: the Developing Framework' (2008) 124 *LQR* 388, 389.

[74] Eirik Bjorge, 'Miller, Treaty-Making and the Rights of Subjects', in Elliott, Williams and Young (n 20) 100–04.

[75] ibid 99.

[76] eg McLachlan, writing after *Miller 1*, appears to have endorsed a separation of powers-based, rather than sovereignty-based rationale for dualism: 'The Foreign Relations Power in the Supreme Court (2018) 134 *LQR* 380, 394–95. But Sales and Clement are strongly critical of abuse of powers justification: see Sales and Clement (n 73).

[77] See Lord Steyn in *Re McKerr* [2004] UKHL 12, [2004] 1 WLR 807, [52]; Lady Hale in *Nzolameso v City of Westminster* [2015] UKSC 22, [2015] 2 All ER 942, [29].

[78] *R (SG) v Secretary of State for Work and Pensions* [2015] UKSC 16, [2015] 1 WLR 1499, [235]–[257].

[79] ibid [255]. See also Lady Hale (ch 2) and Gráinne McKeever (ch 7). But note the firm rejection of any domestic effect for unincorporated treaties in *SC* (n 72) [74]–[96].

[80] Bjorge (n 74) 107.

[81] Craig (n 24) 50.

of the Crown in Parliament is not incompatible with the independent authority of the Crown.[82]

Finally, though, parliamentary sovereignty does seem to have had – in the traditional constitution – a genuinely substantive penumbral effect in relation to another aspect of the separation of powers: the constitutional role of the judiciary. Roger Masterman and Se-shauna Wheatle describe a minimalist conception of the separation of powers attributable to the normative influence of parliamentary sovereignty, which prescribed the legally and constitutionally inferior or subservient role historically adopted by courts in the UK.[83] The influence of parliamentary sovereignty can be seen most clearly in the *ultra vires* model of judicial review, where it both provided the justification for the courts' role in policing the legality of decision-making by constitutionally inferior bodies, yet placed strict limits on that role, in order that the courts did not themselves usurp the intention of Parliament. This sovereignty-supporting version of the separation of powers also mandated an approach to statutory interpretation based on the primacy of legislative intent.

More generally, Dawn Oliver describes parliamentary sovereignty as a 'tenet of the constitution', by which she means that it is 'a proposition that serves as the foundation for a system of belief or behaviour'.[84] At the heart of this belief system is the understanding that responsibility for ensuring constitutionally appropriate behaviour is a *shared* endeavour, not one which lies solely with the courts.[85] Thus, alongside the limits on the constitutional role of the judiciary, it entails a belief in the *positive* merits of political modes of constitutional regulation, manifested in a reluctance to codify, in a preference for conventional rather than legal rules and in the insistence that aspects of constitutional behaviour ought to be beyond the reach of the courts.

It is, of course, a continued adherence to this traditional understanding of the substantive implications of parliamentary sovereignty that explains much of the criticism of the very different substantive use made of the doctrine in the cases discussed above, especially *Miller 1* and *Miller 2/Cherry*. For example, the more traditional account of control of the executive as a partnership between the courts and Parliament can be seen in the dissenting judgments in *Miller 1*,[86] and in dismay at the Supreme Court's dismissal in *Miller 2/Cherry* of political constraints on the abuse of the prorogation power as offering 'scant reassurance'.[87] As Gordon notes, there is little sense in the latter judgment that 'the responsibility of upholding the

[82] Goldsworthy (n 60) 9.

[83] Roger Masterman and Se-shauna Wheatle, 'Unpacking Separation of Powers: Judicial Independence, Sovereignty and Conceptual Flexibility in the UK Constitution' [2017] *Public Law* 469, 472–75. See also Elliott, 'Judicial Power' (n 54) 274–78.

[84] Oliver (n 60) 303.

[85] ibid 294.

[86] See Lord Reed at [240] and Lord Carnwath at [244]–[255].

[87] *Miller 1* (n 18) [43]. See, eg, Finnis (n 9) 12–13.

values and principles of our constitution and making them effective'[88] is a shared task with the political institutions.[89]

Parliamentary Sovereignty, Parliamentary Effectiveness and the Substantive Turn in UK Constitutional Law

The transformation of parliamentary sovereignty from a doctrine requiring judicial restraint into an active justification for judicial intervention in constitutional controversies is part of a more general substantive turn in constitutional adjudication. A key aspect of this substantive turn has been the development of the principle of legality,[90] which was explicitly relied upon in *Miller 1*[91] and *Privacy International*,[92] and was arguably implicit in *Miller 2/Cherry*.[93]

Varuhas has recently traced the development of the principle of legality from an interpretive principle protective of a narrow class of vested rights, to a broader principle concerned with the protection of a more general category of fundamental or constitutional rights, to an even broader tool encompassing a wider set of constitutional values and principles.[94] This last group now includes, to borrow Craig's term, 'structural' norms,[95] concerned with the allocation of power between the branches of state, as well as what might be termed 'content-based' norms, concerned with the substance of public decision-making. Varuhas explains that:

> The shift involved in recognising values as trigger norms [for the principle of legality] is that such values are elevated from the substrata that underpins legal norms to the surface level of the law, themselves now having the status of legal norms and, where engaged, having direct legal consequences.[96]

The broader the principle of legality becomes, and the more widely it is deployed as a technique of constitutional reasoning, the more it makes sense to subsume

[88] *Miller 2/Cherry* (n 1) [39].
[89] Gordon (n 13).
[90] *R v Secretary of State for the Home Dept, ex parte Simms* [2000] 2 AC 115, 131 per Lord Hoffmann.
[91] *Miller 1* (n 18) [87].
[92] *Privacy International* (n 42) [100]–[101], [165].
[93] Alison Young, 'Prorogation, Politics and the Principle of Legality' (*UK Const Law Blog*, 13 September 2019), available at https://ukconstitutionallaw.org/2019/09/13/alison-young-prorogation-politics-and-the-principle-of-legality; Elliott (n 11) 637–38. The Divisional Court held in *R (Elgizouli) v Secretary of State for the Home Dept* [2019] EWHC 60 (Admin), [2021] 3 All ER 247 that the principle of legality is limited to the statutory sphere. On appeal to the Supreme Court, only Lord Kerr was prepared to accept the existence of the common law right contended for (that it was unlawful for the state to facilitate the execution of the death penalty, in this case through the provision of mutual legal assistance in respect of a former British citizen detained in the United States on terrorism charges). In his view, however, the fact that the Home Secretary was exercising a prerogative power was immaterial to the application of the principle, citing in support the decision in *Miller 2/Cherry* (n 1), [142]–[143], [161].
[94] Varuhas (n 23) 580–82.
[95] Craig (n 24).
[96] Varuhas (n 23) 582.

the sovereignty of Parliament within it. In part, this is because an account of the principles of the UK constitution which did not include parliamentary sovereignty would be obviously incomplete. But in addition, in so far as the principle of legality is perceived to be *in competition with* parliamentary sovereignty, as in its stronger forms which do not merely supplement, but may appear to rewrite, statutory language,[97] its legitimacy is open to question. In the face of criticisms of illegitimate judicial activism,[98] couching judicial creativity in the language of parliamentary sovereignty offers significant presentational advantages. It suggests that the courts are engaged in an inherently conservative exercise of defending traditional constitutional values (albeit one that may necessitate drawing out hitherto unnoticed implications), rather than refashioning the constitution in wholly novel ways. Thus, for example, Craig rejects the criticism that the decision in *Miller 1* involved judicial usurpation of political power, since the case involved a zero-sum contestation between the legislature and the executive, 'and the result either way did not augment judicial power'.[99] Ewing agrees, since '[i]t seems unlikely to be both an assertion of parliamentary sovereignty and an expansion of judicial power'.[100]

However, for a number of reasons, this reassurance may be misplaced. First, to locate parliamentary sovereignty within the principle of legality is to subtly downgrade its constitutional status; no longer 'constitutional alpha and omega', but rather 'a constitutional principle that, while of critical importance, forms part of a network of fundamental principles'.[101] As Elliott points out:

> On this view, the very meaning of parliamentary sovereignty – and hence the degree of constitutional authority it ascribes to the legislative branch – is not an isolated matter, but is something that is informed by and must take account of the other fundamental principles with which it sits in relationship.[102]

Thus, for instance, we see the reimagining in *UNISON* and *Privacy International* of the relationship between parliamentary sovereignty and (a more than purely formal account of) the rule of law, not as antagonistic, but as mutually supportive, in turn entailing that a refusal to give effect to (even clear) statutory words is no longer seen as a contradiction of parliamentary sovereignty, but rather an affirmation of it.

Moreover, to treat parliamentary sovereignty, not as a legal *doctrine* with specific implications, but as a legal *principle* focuses attention on the underlying values that

[97] See Varuhas (n 23) 590–604, for discussion of different variants of the principle of legality.

[98] In particular from academics and commentators associated with the Judicial Power Project. For discussion, see Paul Craig, 'Judicial Power, the Judicial Power Project and the UK' (2017) 36 *U Queensland LJ* 355 and Richard Ekins and Graham Gee, 'Putting Judicial Power in its Place' (2017) 36 *U Queensland LJ* 375.

[99] ibid 359.

[100] Ewing (n 39) 724.

[101] Elliott (n 11) 645.

[102] ibid.

the principle is said to serve – in this case, representative democracy. While this, as has been discussed, has the potential to generate new legal rules which protect and enhance Parliament's constitutional status, it also has the potential to limit its authority. As Trevor Allan has argued, if the doctrine of parliamentary sovereignty 'articulates the courts' commitment to the current British scheme of parliamentary democracy', their continuing adherence to it 'must entail commitment to some irreducible minimum concept of the democratic principle'. Hence, if 'Parliament ceased to be a representative assembly, in any plausible sense of the idea, or if it proceeded to enact legislation undermining the democratic basis of our institutions' judges may no longer feel obliged to respect its legislative output.[103] Not only are the demands of democratic legitimacy inherently contestable, but if the Westminster Parliament's authority is based on a democratic rather than a purely institutional or historical claim, then it becomes vulnerable to democratic rivals. The 'authority Parliament derives from its representative character' is not, as Lord Hoffmann claimed in *Bancoult*, in fact 'unique'.[104] Rather, Westminster is one of four representative legislatures in the UK, each with their own – in some respects, arguably superior – democratic claims.[105] The direct democratic authority of the people acting in referendums, swept aside by the Supreme Court in *Miller 1*,[106] may also come to take on a greater constitutional significance.

Secondly, the uncertainty inherent in this new approach to parliamentary sovereignty – and hence the potential for further judicial creativity – can be seen in relation to each element of the developing doctrine of parliamentary effectiveness identified above. For example, as regards meaningful opportunities to exercise legislative authority, the UK government is obviously concerned about the potential for the decision in *Miller 2/Cherry* to be extended to dissolution as well as prorogation of Parliament. Consequently, its proposal to repeal the Fixed-Term Parliaments Act 2011 and 'revive' the dissolution prerogative has been accompanied by a comprehensive ouster clause[107] (with the potential to test the limits of judicial obedience to statute mooted in *Privacy International*). Similarly, while arguing that the constitutional scale argument played only a supporting role in *Miller 1*,[108] Gavin Phillipson suggests that it may have the potential to act as an independent limit on prerogative authority in a limited number of other situations, most notably in requiring statutory authorisation for a decision to withdraw from

[103] Trevor Allan, 'The Limits of Parliamentary Sovereignty' [1985] *Public Law* 614, 620, 624. And see *Moohan v Lord Advocate* [2014] UKSC 67, [2015] AC 901, [35] per Lord Hodge.

[104] *R (Bancoult) v Secretary of State for Foreign and Commonwealth Affairs* [2008] UKHL 61, [2009] 1 AC 453, [35].

[105] See *AXA General Insurance Ltd v Lord Advocate* [2011] UKSC 46, [2012] 1 AC 868, [46] and [49] per Lord Hope.

[106] *Miller 1* (n 18) [116]–[125].

[107] *Draft Fixed-Term Parliaments Act 2011 (Repeal) Bill*, CP 322 (2020) 6; Dissolution and Calling of Parliament Bill 2021–22, cl 3.

[108] Phillipson (n 27) 49, 56, 78–79. See also Jack Williams, 'Prerogative Powers after *Miller*: An Analysis in Four E's', in Elliott, Williams and Young (n 20) 53.

the European Convention on Human Rights.[109] But what of the broader potential of the idea that Parliament must have meaningful opportunities to legislate? Could this be extended from Parliament as an institution to individual members, as for example in relation to controversy over the impact of the ending of the coronavirus virtual Parliament arrangements on the ability of particular MPs to participate effectively,[110] or the availability of resources for Private Members' Bills? Such arguments would appear to be ruled out by Article 9 of the Bill of Rights, but this was given a narrow interpretation in *Miller 2/Cherry* and may be vulnerable to further reading down in the light of the principle of legality.

Similarly, the decision in the *Continuity Bill Reference* has created a new, and highly imprecise, limitation on devolved competence, which at the time of writing is being tested in another reference by the UK Law Officers of two Holyrood Bills to the Supreme Court.[111] These place Human Rights Act-style interpretive obligations in relation to, and duties on UK Ministers acting under, Westminster legislation in devolved areas, and may therefore be seen as conditioning the future exercise of Westminster's power to legislate for Scotland. However, no reference was made in relation to a duty under section 14(2) of the UK Withdrawal from the European Union (Continuity) (Scotland) Act 2021 on UK Ministers to 'have regard' to the environmental principles created by that Act. The idea that there must be access to the courts in order for legislation to be effective also begs the question what other conditions of effectiveness may be implied into statutes. It is, for example, but a short step from holding (as in *UNISON*) that access to the courts rules out unreasonable court fees, to a decision that it requires access to legal aid. In addition, it could permit the reading in of other rule-of-law-related conditions of legislative effectiveness. As Alexander Latham-Gambi notes, commenting on the implications of *Privacy International*, '[s]ince the nature of law is itself a controversial matter, this means that the frontiers of parliamentary sovereignty will themselves be controversial'.[112]

A final criticism of this expansive approach to parliamentary sovereignty concerns the appropriateness of the constitutional vision it embodies. For one

[109] Phillipson (n 27) 79–80. See also Gavin Phillipson and Alison Young, 'Would Use of the Prerogative to Denounce the ECHR "Frustrate" the ECHR? Lessons from *Miller*' [2017] *Public Law* (Brexit Special Issue) 150.

[110] See, eg, 'Coronavirus: Jacob Rees-Mogg Rules Out Return of Virtual Parliament' (*BBC News*, 15 October 2020), available at www.bbc.co.uk/news/uk-politics-54552690.

[111] The United Nations Convention on the Rights of the Child (Incorporation) (Scotland) Bill and the European Charter of Local Self-Government (Incorporation) (Scotland) Bill. See the letter from Alister Jack MP to John Swinney MSP, 24 March 2021, available at www.gov.uk/government/publications/alister-jack-letter-to-scottish-government-on-uncrc-bill-24-march-2021 and *UNCRC-ECLSG References – Written Case for the Attorney General and Advocate General for Scotland*, available at https://www.gov.uk/government/publications/supreme-court-case-no-20210079-and-20210080-written-submission.

[112] 'What is Parliament Doing When it Legislates? Legislative Intention and Parliamentary Sovereignty in *Privacy International*' (*UK Const Law Blog*, 20 April 2020), available at ukconstitutionallaw.org/2020/04/20/alexander-latham-gambi-what-is-parliament-doing-when-it-legislates-legislative-intention-and-parliamentary-sovereignty-in-privacy-international.

thing, although the Supreme Court in *Miller 2/Cherry* presented its decision as a vindication of constitutional orthodoxy, it was, of course, not neutral. The court gave a highly simplistic account[113] of what is in fact a complex, contestable – and in the context of that dispute, actively contested – relationship between Parliament and the executive.[114] Similarly, I have previously criticised the decision in *Miller 1* as presenting a partial – in both senses of the word – account of the constitutional issues and authority claims at stake in the decision to leave the EU.[115] In giving substance to parliamentary sovereignty, there is therefore a danger of entrenching a particular understanding of the constitutional order which constrains the constitutional flexibility which has always been a major part of its appeal. What is required to maintain the effectiveness of parliamentary sovereignty may thus be a more fundamentally contestable issue than is assumed in the developing doctrine discussed in this chapter.

[113] *Miller 2/Cherry* (n 1) [55].

[114] See David Howarth, 'Westminster *versus* Whitehall: What the Brexit Debate Revealed about an Unresolved Conflict at the Heart of the British Constitution' in Oran Doyle, Aileen McHarg and Jo Murkens (eds), *The Brexit Challenge for Ireland and the United Kingdom: Constitutions Under Pressure* (Cambridge, CUP, 2021); Loughlin (n 9) 15–18. For criticism of the court's attitude to executive power in *Miller 1*, see also Timothy Endicott, *The Stubborn Stain Theory of Executive Power: from Magna Carta to* Miller (London, Policy Exchange, 2017), available at policyexchange.org.uk/wp-content/uploads/2017/09/The-Stubborn-Stain-Theory-of-Executive-Power.pdf.

[115] McHarg (n 37) 179. See also Elliott (n 21) 281–84.

13

The Three Tiers of Executive Power in Northern Ireland

CONOR McCORMICK*

Introduction

Unitary analyses of executive power are deeply embedded in various doctrines of UK constitutional law, which tends to obscure the unique way in which executive power is structured in Northern Ireland. The main objective of this chapter is to examine the legal differences between Ministers of the Crown and Ministers in the Northern Ireland Executive, as well as the constitutional differences between those Ministers and the officials who staff their departments, in the light of some recent case law and legislation. After assessing several orthodox understandings of the Crown, which see it as a metaphor for the unitary nature of 'primary' executive power in the UK, among other things, it will be suggested that the law of Northern Ireland further recognises both a 'secondary' tier of executive power vested in devolved Ministers and a 'tertiary' tier of executive power vested in devolved departments. It will be argued that both the nature and the scope of these subordinate executive powers are not only different from those which flow more directly from the Crown, but also that they are partially different from (yet constitutionally dependent upon) each another.

Primary Executive Power

Throughout the UK, understandings of executive power are influenced strongly by the monarchical character of the UK constitution more generally. The concept of the Crown is one of the most obvious manifestations of this influence. In literal terms, the Crown is of course 'a piece of jewelled headgear under guard at the

* Gordon Anthony, Claire Archbold, Anurag Deb, Brice Dickson and Ben Yong each provided constructive feedback on a draft of this chapter. The author owes them many thanks, though of course the finished text is attributable only to him.

Tower of London', but it is also a symbol for 'the powers of government which were formerly wielded by the wearer' of the regalia.[1] The Crown, in this context, is widely understood in a metaphorical sense to mean one of two things, namely the monarch and the executive.[2]

When referring to the monarch, the Crown can be taken to mean either the monarch in a personal capacity or the monarch in an official capacity,[3] with only the latter being relevant for present purposes. This is because the Crown qua the monarch in an official capacity is perhaps the most accurate description of the legal repository for a small bundle of royal prerogative powers which continue to exist today, though they derive their authority from the status of the monarch in bygone times and are supposed to be exercised in accordance with strict constitutional conventions. The effect of those conventions is to eliminate most of the discretion of the monarch, in that (Prime) ministerial advice on how to exercise the powers in question has been proffered and accepted routinely since 1708.[4] It is on this constitutional basis that, formally speaking, the Queen retains the executive power to appoint Ministers, to dissolve Parliament, and to grant the Royal Assent to legislation, though those powers are invariably exercised in accordance with ministerial advice in practice.[5] In other words, where it is said that the Queen has given the Royal Assent to legislation, for instance, this will generally mean that the Government has advised the Queen to exercise the prerogative in this way. The continued involvement of the Queen in these executive affairs is presumably intended to draw on the symbolic dignity and authority of the monarchy as a marker of their constitutional significance.

When referring to the executive, the Crown is normally taken to represent 'a single body of ministers, making up Her Majesty's government',[6] which creates a veneer of unity, continuity and stability with respect to the various functions of the state.[7] Indeed, Daintith and Page have cautioned against underestimating the significance of this effect, given 'the pull' towards a plurality of governmental units in modern times.[8] With that said, the aspirational symbolism served by this understanding of the term is to be contrasted with the rather negligible value it holds as an institutional description of the government. Detailed empirical descriptions of

[1] *Town Investments Ltd v Dept for the Environment* [1978] AC 359, 397 (HL).

[2] *M v Home Office* [1993] UKHL 5, [1994] 1 AC 377, 395.

[3] Jason Allen, 'The Office of the Crown' (2018) 77 *Cambridge Law Journal* 298.

[4] 1708 is the year in which Queen Anne refused her assent to the Scottish Militia Bill. See Adam Tomkins, *Public Law* (Oxford, OUP, 2003) 63.

[5] See, eg, *R (Miller) v Prime Minister* [2019] UKSC 41, [2020] AC 373 for a judgment which formally turned on whether the government's advice to the Queen was unlawful.

[6] *R (BAPIO Action Ltd) v Secretary of State for the Home Dept* [2008] UKHL 27, [2008] 1 AC 1003, [33].

[7] Terence Daintith and Alan Page, *The Executive in the Constitution: Structure, Autonomy, and Internal Control* (Oxford, OUP, 1999) 27. Also see Martin Loughlin, 'The State, the Crown and the Law' in Maurice Sunkin and Sebastian Payne (eds), *The Nature of the Crown: A Legal and Political Analysis* (Oxford, OUP, 1999) 33–76.

[8] Daintith and Page (n 7) 27.

the relevant architecture can be read elsewhere.[9] For present purposes, the important point to emphasise is that although the vast functions of central government are in reality distributed along both horizontal and vertical lines – that is, between various Ministers and their officials – the executive powers which make that panoply of functions lawful are normally derived from or conferred upon the Crown.[10]

In fact, to be precise, the normal practice is for executive powers to be vested in the Crown by way of a custodian of the Royal seals, such as the Lord High Chancellor or one of Her Majesty's Principal Secretaries of State, though, as Simcock explains, there is only one Secretary of State recognised by the law in most circumstances.[11] In effect, this means that 'most of the statutory functions of government can be shifted between departments by administrative action'.[12] Indeed, such functions are transferred regularly from one ministry to another 'in the hope of achieving the elusive goal of greater overall coherence'.[13] Like the conceptual underpinnings of the Crown itself, this unitary arrangement has its origins in the monarchical history of the UK, in that the once powerful office of 'King's secretary' has evolved over time into a title shared by the highest ranking Ministers in the government, though it started out as a personal appointment made to trusted individuals responsible for looking after the monarch's signet. In short, and in so far as the executive powers of central government are concerned, all roads lead back to the Crown.

Pressure Points

Before turning to the relevance of these executive powers in Northern Ireland, and how they differ from the construction of devolved executive powers, it is important for comparative purposes to highlight two constitutional pressure points which arise from this unitary legal framework.

The first pressure point arises from an inevitable overlap between the departmental portfolios of Ministers in the UK Government. Those overlaps mean that it

[9] ibid; Mark Elliott and Robert Thomas, *Public Law*, 4th edn (Oxford, OUP, 2020) 132–52.

[10] Allen (n 3). There are three main sources of executive power at this level. The first is the royal prerogative, which is recognised as the basis for certain 'political' prerogative powers like declaring war and signing international treaties. Unlike 'personal' prerogative powers, exercisable by the Queen qua the monarch in an official capacity, as explained above, the Queen plays no part in the exercise of these powers. They are exercised by Ministers on behalf of the Crown. The second and most significant source of executive power at this level is statute, in that Parliament has conferred on the Crown limited powers for specified purposes in a wide range of contexts. The third source of executive power at this level, which is more controversial and ill-defined, is the common law. In effect, this source permits the Government to do anything which is not prohibited by the general law applicable to individuals, in addition to being permitted to do things which individuals cannot where statutory or prerogative powers allow it. See, generally, Elliott and Thomas (n 9) 152–77.

[11] AJC Simcock, 'One and Many – The Office of Secretary of State' (1992) 70 *Public Administration* 535, 546.

[12] ibid 553.

[13] See *BAPIO* (n 6) [33].

is possible for ministerial disagreements to occur about the appropriate direction in which to take a 'cross-cutting' government policy. It might be suggested that the work-around to this dilemma resides in the guiding influence of constitutional conventions, notwithstanding the looseness of their application in recent times.[14] In particular, it might be expected that the convention of individual ministerial responsibility for departmental affairs would succumb to the greater weight of the convention on collective Cabinet responsibility in the event of any conflict, particularly given that the unitary conception of executive power at this level provides some reinforcement to the latter. Indeed, the Ministerial Code contains a number of passages which reflect a view of this kind.[15] In practice, however, politically irreconcilable ministerial conflicts are not always prevented by this variant of constitutional idealism, and judicial opinions have differed about how those disputes ought to be resolved.

The leading case on this issue, *BAPIO*, concerned an overlap in the policy areas of immigration and NHS employment which resulted in a ministerial conflict between the Secretary of State for the Home Department and the Secretary of State for Health respectively.[16] The facts centred on the eligibility of international medical graduates for NHS training posts. The Health Secretary had asked the Home Secretary to amend the relevant immigration rules in a way which would have limited that eligibility so as to give priority to candidates educated in the UK or the European Economic Area, as it then was, but the Home Secretary refused to do so.[17] The Health Secretary sought to achieve her policy objective nonetheless – that is, without the agreement of the Home Office – by issuing 'guidance' to NHS employers which debarred international medical graduates from employment as junior doctors so as to keep those posts open for graduates who were UK or EEA nationals. Pursuant to a judicial review taken by a group of international medical graduates affected by the Health Secretary's guidance, a majority in the House of Lords reasoned that, in the words of Lord Mance, the Health Secretary 'as one emanation of the Crown was exercising her prerogative to give informal guidance inconsistently with the legitimate expectations generated … by another emanation of the Crown, the Home Secretary'.[18] This, Lord Mance said, was an inconsistency with effects so profound that it rendered the relevant guidance invalid.[19] Lord Rodger, who was also in the majority, regarded it as 'wrong' both as 'a matter of constitutional theory' and 'as a matter of substance' to put the 'powers, duties and responsibilities' of each Minister 'into a separate box' given that both

[14] On the nature and significance of constitutional conventions generally, see Elliott and Thomas (n 9) 63–76.

[15] 'Ministerial Code' (*Cabinet Office*), paras 2.2–2.4 and 4.4–4.5, available at www.gov.uk/government/publications/ministerial-code.

[16] See *BAPIO* (n 6) [12]–[15].

[17] ibid [9].

[18] ibid [60].

[19] ibid.

were 'formulating and implementing the policies of a single entity, Her Majesty's Government'.[20]

Significantly, however, the dissenting judgment of Lord Scott in *BAPIO* fastened upon a number of criticisms about the unitary conception of executive power adopted by the majority. Arguing that 'the constitutional theory of the indivisibility of the Crown is … no basis upon which an important issue as to the lawfulness of guidance given by a minister to institutions for which she has statutory responsibility ought to be decided', Lord Scott opted to base his judgment instead on the 'reality' that government departments exercised their 'quite separate statutory powers' independently of one another.[21] It followed, in Lord Scott's view, that the case should have been resolved in favour of the Health Secretary, and therefore to the disadvantage of the international medical graduates involved, by reference to the departmentalised reality of executive power rather than 'on the basis of an archaic constitutional theory that has become a legal fiction'.[22] Although Lord Scott's preferred conception of executive power at this level is reflected to some extent in legal doctrines deployed in other contexts – such as the *Lavender* principle which provides that a department should not exercise a discretionary power under the dictation of another department[23] – the unitary approach demanded by the Crown and favoured by the majority in *BAPIO* remains the most authoritative general statement of the law on this issue.[24]

The second constitutional pressure point arising from the unitary legal framework provided by the Crown relates to the idea that '[i]n British constitutional law, the civil service have no legal or constitutional personality separate from the Government or ministers'.[25] The legal basis for this arrangement is a wartime decision of the Court of Appeal in England and Wales, *Carltona*,[26] which has since become a metonym for the general but far-reaching principle of constitutional law noted above, namely that government officials do not require specific delegations of power to make decisions in the name of a Minister. As Lord Reed recently put it, 'a decision made on behalf of a minister by one of his officials is constitutionally the decision of the minister himself'.[27]

[20] ibid [34].

[21] ibid [28], citing Mark Freedland, 'The Crown and the Changing Nature of Government' in Sunkin and Payne (eds), *The Nature of the Crown* (n 7).

[22] ibid.

[23] See *H Lavender and Son Ltd v Minister of Housing and Local Government* [1970] 1 WLR 1231. For further examples of case law where the concept of indivisibility has not been applied, see SH Bailey, *Cases, Materials and Commentary on Administrative Law*, 5th edn (London, Sweet & Maxwell, 2018) 22.

[24] Debates about the consequences of an indivisible understanding of the Crown in matters connected to Overseas British Territories and the Commonwealth fall outside the scope of this article, though it can be noted that UK courts have continued to adhere to an indivisible concept of the Crown in such contexts, notwithstanding academic criticism. See Anne Twomey, 'Responsible Government and the Divisibility of the Crown' [2008] *Public Law* 742; Allen (n 3) 315–19.

[25] Harry Woolf et al, *De Smith's Judicial Review*, 8th edn (London, Sweet & Maxwell, 2018) 116.

[26] *Carltona Ltd v Commissioners of Works* [1943] 2 All ER 560. This case is given detailed consideration by Claire Archbold (ch 14).

[27] *R (Bourgass) v Secretary of State for Justice* [2015] UKSC 54, [2016] AC 384, [49].

Importantly, while some jurists have suggested that the *Carltona* principle should be regarded as an exception to the public law presumption against delegation which applies in respect of statutory office-holders,[28] the Supreme Court has clearly grounded it on a different construct altogether:

> An official in a government department is in a different constitutional position from the holder of a statutory office. The official is a servant of the Crown in a department of state established under the prerogative powers of the Crown, for which the political head of the department is constitutionally responsible. The holder of a statutory office, on the other hand, is an independent office-holder exercising powers vested in him personally by virtue of his office. He is himself constitutionally responsible for the manner in which he discharges his office. The Carltona principle cannot therefore apply to him when he is acting in that capacity.[29]

In other words, the relationship between Ministers of the Crown and their 'crown servants' is distinguishable from the relationship between statutory office-holders and their 'civil servants' in that the former are governed by a unitary legal framework which is consistent with the unitary conception of primary executive power demanded by the Crown. This distinguishing feature has been characterised as a constitutional pressure point because the modern realities of departmental government can give rise to a number of related tensions. Chief among these is the issue of scope in so far as the cross-departmental authority of officials acting in the name of a Minister is concerned, and in particular the question of whether an official affiliated to a particular department and serving under the Minister responsible for that department can exercise statutory powers which would normally fall under the authority of a different Minister. There has been case law to suggest that executive powers cannot be exercised in this way, even where the decision of an 'alien' official is rubber-stamped by the Minister in charge of the department which would normally exercise those powers.[30] A formal transfer of functions under the Ministers of the Crown Act 1975 would validate any such arrangement in most circumstances, but the need for such transfers demonstrates that there is a slightly fictional quality to the unitary nature of executive powers in this sense as well.

Furthermore, in *Adams*,[31] Lord Kerr himself applied some unexpected pressure to a number of the assumptions which have flowed from *Carltona* over the years, albeit in the specific context of a statutory decision taken by a junior

[28] For an analysis of the earlier authorities, see Jonathan Swift, 'Crown Proceedings' in Michael Supperstone, James Goudie and Paul Walker, *Judicial Review*, 6th edn (London, LexisNexis, 2017) paras 14.27–14.33.

[29] See *Bourgass* (n 27) [50].

[30] *R v Secretary of State for Trade, ex p Chris International Foods Ltd* [1983] Lexis Citation 1323. As this is an unreported judgment, a short synopsis may be usefully set out here. The Ministry of Trade passed its responsibility for banana licensing powers exercised by a Board of Trade to the Ministry of Agriculture, Fisheries and Food, such that the part played by the Trade Secretary's Department 'was no more than the rubber stamping of the Ministry of Food's decisions as to allocations of licences'. Hodgson J ruled that the Trade Secretary 'had no legal right to transfer to the Ministry of Food all the powers and discretions given to him by Parliament' in this context.

[31] *R v Adams* [2020] UKSC 19, [2020] 1 WLR 2077.

Minister rather than a crown or civil servant. Disclaiming the idea that *Carltona* should be presumed to apply by default in the absence of express statutory words to the contrary, Lord Kerr suggested that

> whether the *Carltona* principle should be considered to arise in a particular case depends on an open-ended examination of … [various factors] … namely, the framework of the legislation, the language of pertinent provisions in the legislation and the "importance of the subject matter", in other words, the gravity of the consequences flowing from the exercise of the power, rather than the application of a presumption.[32]

Much has been written about these obiter dicta already. It should be noted, in particular, that some commentators have been extremely critical of Lord Kerr's thinking.[33] Indeed, notwithstanding the provisional character of the remarks in question, critics have argued that this aspect of Lord Kerr's reasoning 'threatens the smooth workings of our whole system of government' by introducing 'unnecessary doubt into the relationship between a Secretary of State or another Ministerial departmental head and junior ministers and civil servants'.[34] Those who subscribe to this view insist that *Adams* must be reversed either by the Supreme Court itself or by primary legislation.[35] Others, meanwhile, have described Lord Kerr's proposal as 'a developed position that is more nuanced than the essentially binary choice suggested by the original *Carltona* decision'.[36]

Regional Relevance

The nature of the executive powers analysed in the foregoing paragraphs is of considerable constitutional significance to Northern Ireland, both historically and in the present day.

From 1921 to 1972, following the initial establishment of a devolved administration, the UK Government continued to exercise a range of executive powers which were not transferred to the new Government of Northern Ireland.[37] In addition, all executive power was vested in the Crown as represented by the Governor,[38] meaning that Northern Ireland's devolved government offices and departments formally owed both their creation and their internal organisation 'to the direct

[32] ibid [26].

[33] Richard Ekins and Stephen Laws, *Mishandling the Law: Gerry Adams and the Supreme Court* (London, Policy Exchange, 2020); Jonathan Sumption, 'Supreme Court's Gerry Adams Decision Has Left the Law in an Awful Mess' (*The Times*, 2 July 2020), available at www.thetimes.co.uk/article/supreme-courts-gerry-adams-decision-has-left-the-law-in-an-awful-mess-x09nltwqd.

[34] Ekins and Laws (ibid) 11.

[35] ibid 46.

[36] See Claire Archbold (ch 14).

[37] Government of Ireland Act 1920, s 9.

[38] See Donal Lowry, 'A "Supreme and Permanent Symbol of Executive Authority": The Crown and the Governorship of Northern Ireland in an Age of "Troubles"' in Harshan Kumarasingham (ed), *Viceregalism: The Crown as Head of State in Political Crises in the Postwar Commonwealth* (Switzerland, Palgrave Macmillan, 2020) 93–126.

exercise of the discretionary authority of the Crown as head of the executive'.[39] In 1972, for reasons too well known to recount here, the UK Government resumed full responsibility for all the functions of government in Northern Ireland.[40] Prior to that first instance of 'direct rule', centralised Northern Ireland matters had been the executive responsibility of the Home Secretary. On account of the increase in responsibilities resulting from the suspension of the devolved institutions at the time, however, a dedicated Secretary of State for Northern Ireland was deemed justified in order 'to exercise the executive functions of government, coordinate the administrative machinery and represent Northern Ireland in the Cabinet'.[41] By necessity, the Northern Ireland Office for which the new Secretary of State would become responsible was an unusually complex department, not least because it was forced to reorientate its practices around a number of unusual divides, including a geographical divide between London and Belfast, an administrative divide between two separate civil services, and a functional divide between devolved and non-devolved matters.[42] Although the Secretary of State was supported by a team of junior ministers in these endeavours, on top of the support provided by departmental officials and special advisers, the executive powers required to carry on the cross-cutting business of government for Northern Ireland remained vested exclusively in the Crown by way of the Secretary of State at all times. It is notable that the orthodox framework for understanding primary executive power proved capable of surviving even this set of constitutional pressures.

At various points since 1972, further variants of governance by direct rule have required the Secretary of State for Northern Ireland to exercise wide-ranging executive powers over Northern Ireland for extended periods of time.[43] Interestingly, in a judicial review application dismissed in 1996 by Kerr J, as he then was, it was actually argued that powers conferred on 'the Secretary of State' by section 42(2) of the Fair Employment (NI) Act 1976 were to be interpreted as conferring powers on the Secretary of State for Northern Ireland alone.[44] The case was brought by an individual who had been terminated from his employment as an administrative assistant in the UK passport agency in Belfast on the basis of a statutorily conclusive certificate issued by the Home Secretary, providing that that decision had been taken 'for the purpose of safeguarding national security and of protecting public safety and public order'.[45] Counsel for the applicant had argued, among other things, that the Secretary of State for Northern Ireland 'was clearly best

[39] Government of Ireland Act 1920, s 8; Arthur Quekett, *The Constitution of Northern Ireland: Part III – A Review of Operations Under the Government of Ireland Act 1920* (Belfast, HM Stationery Office, 1946) 130.

[40] Northern Ireland (Temporary Provisions) Act 1972.

[41] Derek Birrell, *Direct Rule and the Governance of Northern Ireland* (Manchester, Manchester UP, 2009) 21.

[42] ibid 69–70.

[43] See Brice Dickson, *Law in Northern Ireland*, 3rd edn (Oxford, Hart Publishing, 2018) 7–18.

[44] *Re Quinn's Application* [1996] NIJB 115, 117.

[45] ibid 116.

placed to judge what was required to safeguard national security or protect public safety or public order in a Northern Irish context'.[46] However, recalling that since 'the historical position is that the office of the Secretary of State is one', the learned judge showed no hesitation in ruling that 'any powers exercisable by "the Secretary of State" will, save in exceptional and unambiguously stated circumstances, be exercisable by any of Her Majesty's Secretaries of State'.[47] This is arguably the most context-specific illustration there is of the practical effects which can flow from having a unitary conception of primary executive power in Northern Ireland.

Today, of course, the UK Government plays a continuing role in various matters which have not been transferred to the Northern Ireland Executive under the terms of the Northern Ireland Act 1998 (NIA),[48] and in relation to any functions which it agrees to discharge by way of an arrangement.[49] Equipped with a broad understanding of the way in which those primary executive powers have evolved, and the unitary way in which they are treated by the courts when exercised by a plurality of ministers and officials alike, it is time to consider the remarkable extent to which this picture differs from the law on devolved executive powers.

Secondary and Tertiary Executive Power

Section 23 of the NIA provides that

> executive power in Northern Ireland shall continue to be vested in Her Majesty [and that] [a]s respects transferred matters, the prerogative and other executive powers of Her Majesty in relation to Northern Ireland shall … [subject to certain specific provisos] … be exercisable on Her Majesty's behalf by any Minister or Northern Ireland department.

Based on this statutory framework, it might reasonably be argued that the existence of devolution has done nothing to alter the unitary nature of executive power in the UK, in that while the range of executive power-holders has expanded as a consequence of devolution, the source of that power – the Crown – remains singular.[50] However, leaving to one side the political background to the statutory framework in question, and the idea that a Secretary of State in the UK Government 'is not competent to exercise prerogative or executive power under section 23',[51] to

[46] ibid 117.

[47] ibid 118.

[48] See Cathy Gormley-Heenan and Derek Birrell, *Multi-Level Governance and Northern Ireland* (Basingstoke, Palgrave Macmillan, 2015) ch 2.

[49] Northern Ireland Act 1998, s 28.

[50] The Court of Appeal has observed that this feature of the statutory framework is a 'variation' on the terms of the Belfast (Good Friday) Agreement, which envisaged that the Northern Ireland Assembly would be 'the prime source of authority in respect of all devolved responsibilities' and would exercise 'full legislative and executive authority'. See *Re Buick's Application* [2018] NICA 26, [34].

[51] *Re JR80's Application* [2019] NIQB 43, [125](h); approved by the Court of Appeal in so far as prerogative powers are concerned at [2019] NICA 58, [126](a).

accept this argument would be to overlook two fundamental changes in the constitutional qualities of the executive powers which inhere in devolved Ministers and departments by virtue of that provision. First, there is the markedly conditional nature of those devolved executive powers, which is to say that devolved Ministers and departments are subject to a host of universally applicable conditions on the exercise of their executive powers which do not apply to the UK Government in the same way. Second, there is the semi-siloed nature of the executive powers invested in devolved Ministers and departments, in that devolved Ministers and departments exist as separate entities with multilateral obligations between them, rather than as administrative units within a single executive office. The remainder of this chapter will be devoted to exploring these properties in further detail, together with the extent to which they differ as between devolved Ministers and departments. It will be suggested that because Ministers are subject to fewer conditions on the exercise of their executive powers than departments, they ought to be conceptualised as secondary executive power-holders, while departments should be conceptualised as tertiary executive power-holders.

Ministers

At the devolved level, a First and deputy First Minister must be elected by nomination on the basis of party-political strength in the Northern Ireland Assembly.[52] Together, the First and deputy First Ministers are jointly responsible for what is now called the Executive Office (formerly known as the Office of the First Minister and deputy First Minister)[53] and for a range of specific statutory functions. Among the most fundamental of these functions are the power to determine how many Ministers will be appointed to join the Executive Committee;[54] the power to determine which functions will be exercisable by the holder of each ministerial office,[55] as well as the power to assign or transfer functions between corresponding departments.[56] Most of these functions can be exercised only with cross-community support from the Assembly, which obviously limits the degree of discretion involved. Moreover, the First and deputy First Ministers do not have any substantive powers of ministerial patronage. This is because each ministerial appointment (other than Justice)[57] is determined by way of the d'Hondt formula,[58] though this does entitle the nominating officer for each political party to choose a Ministry (other than Justice) from the dwindling list open to them. This ensures that the composition of the Executive Committee is proportionate to the number

[52] Northern Ireland Act 1998, ss 16A–16C.
[53] Departments Act (NI) 2016, s 1(1).
[54] ibid s 17(1)(a).
[55] ibid s 17(1)(b).
[56] Departments (NI) Order 1999, SI 1999/283 (NI 1), art 8.
[57] Northern Ireland Act 1998, Sch 4A.
[58] ibid s 18.

of Assembly seats won by each party, which is in keeping with the consociational design of the devolved settlement as a whole.[59]

Although the Executive Committee 'has not and never has had executive power or the entitlement to exercise executive power' in its own right,[60] its original functions[61] have been refined and enlarged over the years, as will be explained further below. One of its most significant functions is to agree on and review a Programme for Government, namely 'a programme incorporating an agreed budget linked to policies and programmes, subject to approval by the Assembly, after scrutiny in Assembly Committees, on a cross-community basis'.[62] The underlying purpose of this function is to provide some 'glue' for a 'strained and unstable' centre, where Ministers are not bound by any formal expectations of collective responsibility or confidentiality, though the Executive Committee's effectiveness in this regard has been repeatedly questioned.[63]

Since the commencement of the Northern Ireland (St Andrews Agreement) Act 2006, the Executive Committee has also been responsible for discussing and agreeing upon '*any* significant or controversial matters' which arise before the Assembly has given its approval to a draft Programme for Government, as well as 'any significant or controversial matters *that are clearly outside the scope of that programme*' once the approval of the Assembly has been secured.[64] It must also discuss and agree upon 'significant or controversial matters that the First Minister and deputy First Minister acting jointly have determined to be matters that should be considered by the Executive Committee'.[65] Following the commencement of the Executive Committee (Functions) Act (NI) 2020, however, there are both specific and general caveats to be borne in mind here.

Specifically, nothing arising from the powers and duties outlined above prevents a statutorily delimited group of ministerial decisions from being made without recourse to the Executive Committee, namely (1) 'quasi-judicial decisions' made by the Justice Minister or her department, and (2) decisions, regulations or orders made under the Planning Act (NI) 2011 by the Infrastructure Minister or her department (except a function under section 1 of that Act).[66] Generally, nothing

[59] See Rick Wilford, 'Consociational Government: Inside the Northern Ireland Executive' in Rupert Taylor (ed), *Consociational Theory: McGarry and O'Leary and the Northern Ireland Conflict* (Abingdon, Routledge, 2009).

[60] *Re Solinas' Application* [2009] NIQB 43, [30].

[61] See the Northern Ireland Act 1998, s 20(3), which provides that '[t]he Committee shall have the functions set out in paragraphs 19 and 20 of Strand One of the Belfast Agreement'.

[62] Belfast (Good Friday) Agreement, Strand One, para 20.

[63] See Rick Wilford, 'Inside Stormont: The Assembly and the Executive' in Paul Carmichael, Colin Knox and Robert Osborne (eds), *Devolution and Constitutional Change in Northern Ireland* (Manchester, Manchester UP, 2007) 177–80; Wilford (n 59) 190–93. Wilford notes similar problems with the effective operationalisation of 'Executive Programme Funds', which were likewise designed to encourage cross-cutting work in the spirit of joined-up government.

[64] Northern Ireland Act 1998, s 20(4)(a)–(aa). Emphasis added.

[65] ibid s 20(4)(b).

[66] ibid s 20(6)–(7).

arising from these powers and duties 'requires a Minister to have recourse to the Executive Committee in relation to *any matter* unless that matter affects the exercise of the *statutory responsibilities* of one or more other Ministers *more than incidentally*'.[67] In addition, it should not be assumed that a Minister's statutory responsibilities are affected 'more than incidentally' only because there is a statutory requirement to consult that Minister.[68] The rationale for enacting the majority of these caveats formed the subject of a fairly heated political debate within unionist circles during the passage of the relevant Bill.[69] While some claimed that they were introduced merely to reverse some effects of the *Buick* case, which will be discussed further below, others claimed that they would go beyond what was necessary to accomplish that objective and thereby diminish 'the scope for ethno-national control within the Executive Committee'.[70] On account of these contested narratives, it seems likely that litigation over the meaning of the revised thresholds for referral to the Executive Committee may prove necessary in due course. Indeed, for an important judgment delivered just as this book was going to press, see *Re Safe Electricity A&T Ltd's Application* [2021] NIQB 93.

The Executive Committee's main functions as originally set out in the Belfast (Good Friday) Agreement also included questions of executive and legislative prioritisation,[71] which, in tandem with the responsibilities outlined above, have been further recognised by the Ministerial Code.[72] The Ministerial Code likewise designates the Executive Committee as the relevant forum for 'the discussion of, and agreement on, issues which cut across the responsibilities of two or more Ministers' and for 'recommending a common position where necessary'.[73] Beyond providing an itemised list of the functions for which the Executive Committee is responsible,[74] the Ministerial Code plays a key role in operationalising and enforcing those functions. This is because Ministers are under a statutory duty to 'act in accordance with the provisions of the Ministerial Code',[75] which includes a Ministerial Pledge of Office[76] and a Ministerial Code of Conduct.[77] Furthermore, the NIA stipulates that Ministers have 'no Ministerial authority' to take decisions which ought to have been brought to the Executive Committee for consideration.[78] As such, legal challenges may be taken against any Minister who falls foul of these requirements.

[67] ibid s 20(8). Emphasis added.
[68] ibid s 20(9).
[69] See, esp, Northern Ireland Assembly, Official Report, 21 July 2020; 27 July 2020; 28 July 2020.
[70] Gordon Anthony, 'The Quartet Plus Two: Judicial Review in Northern Ireland' in TT Arvind et al (eds), *Executive Decision-Making and the Courts* (Oxford, Hart Publishing, 2021) 277.
[71] Belfast (Good Friday) Agreement, Strand One, para 19.
[72] 'Ministerial Code' (*Northern Ireland Executive*), available at www.northernireland.gov.uk/topics/your-executive/ministerial-code.
[73] ibid para 2.3.
[74] ibid.
[75] Northern Ireland Act 1998, s 28A(1).
[76] 'Ministerial Code' (n 72) para 1.4.
[77] ibid paras 1.5–1.6. See the Northern Ireland (Ministers, Elections and Petitions of Concern) Bill 2021-22, cl 4, for recently proposed revisions to this Code.
[78] Northern Ireland Act 1998, s 28A(10); 'Ministerial Code' (n 72) para 2.4.

However, the last-mentioned duty to bring certain decisions forward for consideration by the Executive Committee is moderated by a number of related rules which provide ways of seeking a determination of the Executive Committee in circumstances where it is unclear to a Minister whether they ought to refer a particular matter to it,[79] together with some provisions catering for urgent ministerial decisions[80] and retrospective Executive Committee determinations.[81]

Once a particular matter has been referred to the Executive Committee – either by a Minister, or by the Presiding Officer of the Assembly[82] – the First and deputy First Minister are under an obligation to 'seek to secure' that its decisions 'are reached by consensus wherever possible'.[83] If consensus is impossible, however, the matter will be put to a vote which can be made to require cross-community support if any three members of the Executive Committee vote in favour of that requirement.[84] Critics have described this mechanism as a 'power-snaring' rather than a power-sharing arrangement because, in effect, it means that the DUP and Sinn Féin, as the only parties with at least three Ministers, can veto any matter which reaches the Executive Committee.[85] Indeed, when in November 2020 this veto power was utilised by the DUP in order to prevent the extension of coronavirus restrictions that had been proposed by the Health Minister, its effects gave rise to widespread concern about the constitutional stability of the devolved administration.[86]

Everything described in this sub-section so far has served to emphasise the highly conditional nature of the executive power invested in Northern Ireland Ministers individually. While statutory powers are normally conferred upon the departments for which individual Ministers are responsible, the creation of such executive functions must always be read against the above-mentioned duties to refer particular decisions to the Executive Committee for discussion and agreement. To the extent that these arrangements might be said to render such executive powers unitary in nature, it must be recalled and stressed that the orthodox understanding of primary executive powers vested in UK Government Ministers is based on an indivisible conception of the office of Secretary of State which simply has no parallel in Northern Ireland.[87] It is notable in this context that specific Ministers,

[79] ibid para 2.5.

[80] ibid para 2.14.

[81] ibid para 2.15. For some interesting discussion on an inappropriate use of this power, see *Belfast City Council v The Minister of Enterprise, Trade and Investment* [2017] NICA 28.

[82] Northern Ireland Act 1998, s 28(B).

[83] ibid s 28A(8)(a); 'Ministerial Code' (n 72) para 2.12.

[84] ibid s 28A(8)(c).

[85] Gormley-Heenan and Birrell (n 48) 58.

[86] 'Coronavirus: Stormont in deadlock over NI Covid restrictions' (*BBC News*, 11 November 2020), available at www.bbc.co.uk/news/uk-northern-ireland-54897748.

[87] Though detailed comparisons with Scotland and Wales are beyond the scope of this chapter, it is noteworthy that the majority of central executive power in those jurisdictions is framed as a unitary concept, which further emphasises the unique nature of the Northern Ireland position. See the Scotland Act 1998, esp ss 44–52, and the Government of Wales Act 2006, ss 45–52, 56–57. Some of the law officers' functions give rise to exceptions.

junior Ministers and political parties can be excluded from office if they no longer enjoy the confidence of the Assembly.[88] It should also be remembered that, in practice, Northern Ireland Ministers have been known to embark on 'solo runs' which push firmly against a unitary conception of their executive powers and give reinforcement to the semi-siloed understanding suggested above. Indeed, one of the main drivers for the changes enacted in 2006 was a unilateral decision to abolish primary-to-secondary school transfer testing by the then Education Minister.[89]

Furthermore, since the changes introduced in 2006 there has been a small but significant number of inter-ministerial/departmental legal challenges involving various aspects of the Executive Committee's role in central government affairs at the devolved level.[90] In 2016, for instance, the former Attorney General for Northern Ireland records having represented the Department of Culture, Arts and Leisure 'in an application for judicial review brought by the Minister of Justice in relation to a decision to make the draft Court Files Privileged Access Rules (Northern Ireland) 2016' in circumstances where the former had not referred the matter to the Executive Committee for discussion and agreement.[91] While that case was eventually withdrawn,[92] relieving the court of any need to hand down judgment, in 2013 a short judgment by Morgan LCJ was in fact issued pursuant to an urgent judicial review application taken by the Minister of Finance and Personnel in respect of a decision by the Minister of Agriculture and Rural Development.[93] The latter Minister had decided to transfer funds from one pillar of an agricultural funding scheme, which facilitated direct payments to farmers, to another pillar of the same scheme which provided funding for rural development projects. Ruling that the matter under dispute should have been brought to the attention of the Executive Committee on account of its significant and controversial nature, Morgan LCJ concluded that the relevant Minister had not complied with the Ministerial Code and therefore had no authority to take the decision in question.[94] Similarly, in 2016 the Minister for Enterprise, Trade and Investment successfully challenged a decision concerning the launch of a Belfast Metropolitan Area Plan (BMAP) which had been taken unilaterally by the Minister for the Environment.[95] Emphasising that 'a Minister has no power to take a decision in violation of the Ministerial Code relating to the obligation to bring to the attention of the Executive Committee any matter that requires to be considered by it for discussion and

[88] Northern Ireland Act 1998, s 30.

[89] Wilford, 'Inside Stormont' (n 63) 179.

[90] For an analysis of some prominent legal challenges taken by Ministers and others before this constitutional turning point, see John Morison and Marie Lynch, 'Litigating the Agreement: Towards a New Judicial Constitutionalism for the UK from Northern Ireland?' in John Morison, Kieran McEvoy and Gordon Anthony (eds), *Judges, Transition and Human Rights* (Oxford, OUP, 2007) 128–139.

[91] Attorney General for Northern Ireland, 'Sixth Annual Report – 2015/16', para 21, available at www.attorneygeneralni.gov.uk/sites/ag/files/media-files/AGNI%20Annual%20Report%202015-16_0.pdf.

[92] ibid.

[93] *Re the Minister of Finance and Personnel's Application* [2013] NIQB 137.

[94] ibid [7].

[95] *Re the Minister of Enterprise, Trade and Investment's Application* [2016] NIQB 26.

agreement by reason of being cross-cutting, significant or controversial',[96] Treacy J, as he then was, found that the Minister for the Environment had acted unlawfully 'by authorising and directing the Department to adopt the BMAP without informing the Executive until after the event and despite objections having been made by other Ministers'.[97]

While this inter-ministerial/departmental litigation is arguably the most constitutionally sensitive of the case law surrounding the Ministerial Code, a number of important challenges have been taken by private parties too. Successful cases have advanced arguments in respect of a ministerial decision to remove funding from a loyalist 'Community Transformation Initiative' without the full and proper approval of the Executive Committee;[98] a ministerial decision to uphold his department's policy of banning men who have had sex with men from donating blood without bringing it to the attention of the Executive Committee;[99] and a departmental decision to grant planning permission in the absence of a Minister, about which more will be said shortly.[100]

On the other hand, some private challenges have been relatively unsuccessful. In *Re Central Craigavon Ltd's Application*, for instance, Morgan LCJ held that although a planning policy had been adopted in breach of the Ministerial Code – as it had been a cross-cutting matter and should have been brought to the Executive Committee – the breach did not deprive the Environment Minister of executive power on account of its 'inadvertent' and 'technical' nature.[101] By the same token, in *Re Newry Chamber of Commerce and Trade's Application*, which concerned a decision to grant planning permission in respect of an out-of-city development which risked damaging the vitality and viability of Newry city centre, Treacy J held that the applicant's challenge was 'outside the material scope' of the relevant legislative provisions.[102] The court emphasised, in any event, that although the scale of the development and the existence of local objections were significant and controversial in a certain sense, when determining whether something is significant or controversial in the sense required for a contravention of the Ministerial Code it 'must refer to those matters which members of the Executive might believe to be so'.[103] Moreover, although a substantive breach of the Code was established

[96] ibid [36].

[97] ibid [37]. The remedial order granted by Treacy J was later overturned by the Court of Appeal, but his reasons for finding that the Minister had acted ultra vires were upheld: see *Belfast City Council* (n 81).

[98] *Solinas* (n 60).

[99] *Re JR65's Application* [2013] NIQB 101.

[100] See *Re Buick's Application* [2018] NIQB 43; *Re Buick's Application* [2018] NICA 26. Also see *Reference by the Attorney General for Northern Ireland of Devolution Issues to the Supreme Court pursuant to Paragraph 34 of Schedule 10 to the Northern Ireland Act 1998* [2020] UKSC 2.

[101] *Re Central Craigavon Ltd's Application* [2010] NIQB 73, [21]–[31]. The applicant appealed against this aspect of the High Court's decision, inter alia, but the Court of Appeal refused to rule on it because the issue was by then 'of academic interest': *Central Craigavon Ltd v The Department of the Environment for Northern Ireland* [2011] NICA 17, [16]–[19].

[102] *Re Newry Chamber of Commerce and Trade's Application* [2015] NIQB 65, [137].

[103] ibid [126]–[134], citing *Re Central Craigavon Ltd's Application* [2010] NIQB 73.

in *Re Neeson's Application*, the High Court was unwilling to quash the impugned decision in question on account of concerns in connection with 'the interests of good administration', among other things.[104]

It should now be clear that the executive power invested in devolved Ministers is subject to justiciable conditions which differentiates the nature of that power from its primary equivalent. If further support is needed to substantiate this claim, it should be recalled that everything said in this sub-section about the power-limiting provisions of the Ministerial Code must be read '[w]ithout prejudice to the operation of section 24' of the NIA,[105] which imposes a further set of justiciable limits on the exercise of executive power at this level. In addition to establishing the machinery for challenging subordinate legislation made by the Executive, section 24, as amended at the time of writing, provides in particular that Ministers and departments have 'no power to do any act' which (1) is incompatible with any of the Convention rights protected by the Human Rights Act 1998; (2) is incompatible with Article 2(1) of the Protocol on Ireland/Northern Ireland in the EU Withdrawal Agreement, which commits the UK to ensuring that no diminution of rights, safeguards or equality of opportunity is caused by its departure from the European Union; (3) discriminates against a person or class of person on the ground of religious belief or political opinion, or (4) aids or incites another person to discriminate against a person or class of person on that ground.

Departments

So far as the unique constitutional position of Northern Ireland departments is concerned, one thing seems relatively clear, while another seems regrettably unclear.

What is reasonably clear is that, in contrast with the relationship between UK Ministers and their departments, Northern Ireland departments are not treated as the alter egos of their Ministers.[106] Instead, Northern Ireland departments are regarded as separate legal entities with a unique constitutional relationship to their Ministers. More accurately, each department is 'a body corporate' capable

[104] *Re Neeson's Application* [2016] NIQB 58, [37](iii). The substantive breach arose from a ministerial decision to disapply a policy regarding the employment of individuals with conflict-related convictions.

[105] Northern Ireland Act 1998, ss 28A(1) and 28A(10).

[106] For some implicit statutory recognition of this distinction see, eg, the Functioning of Government (Miscellaneous Provisions) Act (NI) 2021, s 11, which requires a Minister '*and their department*' to supply information reasonably requested by an Assembly Committee. Similarly, s 13 of the same Act requires that '[t]he Minister in charge of a Northern Ireland department, *or the department*, must provide the relevant Assembly committee with a written or oral briefing on the department's submission to each monitoring round'. Emphasis added. Note, however, that there appears to be a discrete statutory deviation from this understanding contained in the Human Rights Act 1998, s 7(13), which, by way of clarifying a reference to 'The Minster' in s 7(12), states that '"The Minister" includes the Northern Ireland department concerned'.

of acquiring and holding land 'for the purposes of its functions',[107] though those functions must 'at all times be exercised subject to the direction and control'[108] of whichever Minister is 'in charge'[109] of the department concerned. In addition, the NIA requires the First and deputy First Ministers to 'ensure that the functions exercisable by those in charge of the different Northern Ireland departments … are exercisable by the holders of different Ministerial offices'.[110]

There are perhaps two key points to note about the historical background to this bifurcated arrangement.[111] The first point is that, under the Government of Ireland Act 1920, devolved executive powers were to be exercised 'by departments (headed by Ministers)' rather than simply 'by departments'.[112] In other words, executive powers were to be exercised 'through (not by) departments'.[113] The second and most important point is that, in contrast, most devolved executive powers have been assigned to or conferred directly upon Northern Ireland departments in the interests of constitutional continuity ever since direct rule was first introduced in 1972, though always overlain by a relationship of 'direction and control' either with the Northern Ireland Secretary or, as is the case today, with devolved Ministers.[114]

What is regrettably unclear, however, is the extent to which this unique constitutional status entitles Northern Ireland departments to exercise executive powers in the absence of any ministerial oversight or democratic accountability. The leading case on this question,[115] *Buick*,[116] concerned a senior civil servant's decision to grant planning permission for a waste incinerator in the absence of a Minister. The decision was challenged both on the basis that the civil servant, as a departmental official, had no power to make the decision without a Minister in place, and on the basis that the decision was unlawful because it should have been referred to the Executive Committee on account of its cross-cutting nature. At the time the decision was taken, there were no Ministers in place and no Executive Committee in being, on account of a seemingly intractable political impasse.[117] In the High Court, Keegan J (as she then was) ruled that the decision was ultra

[107] Departments (NI) Order 1999, art 5(1)–(2).

[108] ibid art 4(1).

[109] ibid art 2(2)(b).

[110] Northern Ireland Act 1998, s 17(3).

[111] For further details see Austen Morgan, *The Belfast Agreement: A Practical Legal Analysis* (Belfast, The Belfast Press, 2000) chs 4 and 12.

[112] ibid 47.

[113] ibid 46.

[114] ibid 211.

[115] For the other leading cases concerning departmental decision-making in the absence of Ministers, see *Hughes' (Brigid) Application* [2018] NIQB 30, [2020] NI 257; *JR80* (n 51) [2019] NIQB 43; *JR80* (n 51) [2019] NICA 58.

[116] See n 100 above.

[117] See Jess Sargeant and Jill Rutter, 'Governing Without Ministers: Northern Ireland Since the Fall of the Power-Sharing Executive' (*Institute for Government*, 25 September 2019), available at www.instituteforgovernment.org.uk/publications/governing-without-ministers-northern-ireland. Also see Adam Evans, 'Northern Ireland, 2017-2020: An Experiment in Indirect Rule' [2021] *Public Law* 471.

vires on a number of grounds.[118] The learned judge reasoned, inter alia, that to qualify the words of the statutory regime so as to permit the decision would be to devalue the constitutional importance of ministerial oversight and democratic accountability.[119] In the Court of Appeal, on the other hand, Morgan LCJ and Stephens LJ, as he then was, held that the statutory regime was 'ambiguous' on this point, in that it could be read to support the view that 'giving departments statutory, executive and prerogative powers was intended to facilitate the operation of government in the absence of Ministers'.[120] Treacy LJ dissented from this interpretation by endorsing the reasoning of the court below and by adding that any ambiguity ought to be construed consistently with established constitutional principles, including the accountability of civil servants to Ministers, and with the Belfast (Good Friday) Agreement.[121] Notwithstanding these differences in view, however, the Court of Appeal held that the department's decision was unlawful because it was cross-cutting, significant and controversial, which meant that it could not be lawfully decided without having been considered by the Executive Committee.[122]

While legislation was later passed to counteract some of the administrative consequences of the Court of Appeal's judgment in this case,[123] it is not necessary to explore those developments any further in order to reach a general conclusion with respect to the unique constitutional relationship between Northern Ireland Ministers and departments. Whether or not departments are able to exercise executive powers in the absence of Ministers, under normal circumstances the law requires all departmental powers to be exercised under the direction and control of Ministers. Fundamentally, that requirement amounts to an additional condition on the exercise of such powers, for which there is no parallel in respect of secondary executive power-holders. For that reason, and bearing in mind the underlying principles of democratic constitutionalism engaged by this interdependent dynamic, it is suggested that while the current statutory framework does not allow the executive power of Northern Ireland departments to be elided with that of their Ministers, they should be characterised as tertiary power-holders so that their decisions are scrutinised more carefully than those of their ministerial counterparts. Indeed, given that statutory powers are routinely conferred upon departments rather than Ministers in Northern Ireland (though there are various exceptions to this drafting convention),[124] the constitutional desirability of greater accountability over the exercise of departmental powers is compelling.

[118] *Buick* (n 100) [2018] NIQB 43, [42].

[119] ibid.

[120] *Buick* (n 100) [2018] NICA 26, [51].

[121] ibid [61]–[67].

[122] ibid [52]–[58].

[123] Northern Ireland (Executive Formation and Exercise of Functions) Act 2018; Northern Ireland (Executive Formation etc) Act 2019; Executive Committee (Functions) Act (NI) 2020. For more analysis on these developments, see Anthony (n 70), but note that some of them have been rendered redundant by the return of Ministers and their repeal is therefore envisaged by the Northern Ireland (Ministers, Elections and Petitions of Concern) Bill 2021–22, cl 6.

[124] See, eg, the Justice (NI) Act 2002, s 22(2) (which confers a power to appoint the Attorney General for Northern Ireland on the First and deputy First *Ministers*, acting jointly) and the Firearms (NI)

Conclusion

The regulation of executive powers in Northern Ireland is an important but neglected subject.[125] Though it could have been explored from a great variety of perspectives, ranging across both internal and external points of view,[126] the approach of this chapter has been to propose a conceptual framework for understanding the way in which those powers might be approached by a judicial mind. Taking into account the incrementalism of the common law method,[127] a three-tiered approach to executive power in Northern Ireland has been suggested by reference to the small but rich body of legislation and case law touching upon the subject to date. Whereas a three-tiered interpretation of that jurisprudence may be novel, the legal doctrines underpinning it have not been radically reformulated in the pursuit of constitutional or indeed conceptual idealism. It is a pragmatic proposal, grounded in an awareness of the idea that administrative law is rarely 'shaped by rational criteria or administrative needs', but by historical, political and typically incidental developments.[128] In summary, it has been contended that three tiers of executive power should be recognised in Northern Ireland. The first, relating to primary executive power, is vested in the UK Government and continues to be treated as a unitary concept notwithstanding the presence of some constitutional pressure points in the case law. Secondary executive power, by contrast, is vested in devolved Ministers on an individual basis and is best characterised as a semi-siloed and comparatively conditional form of power on account of the legal architecture arising from that fundamental difference. Tertiary executive power, which is held by departments, is different again in so far as it is moderated by greater conditionality than any of its superordinates and because it must be subjected to greater scrutiny for that reason. The balance of power between these tiers, while no less important than their qualitative differences, is for another day.

Order 2004, SI 2004/702 (NI 3), art 63(7C) (which confers a quasi-judicial power on the *Minister* of Justice to determine certain applications for the removal of firearms prohibitions).

[125] It has been said more generally that 'the modern executive remains relatively obscure in public law scholarship'. See Thomas Poole, 'The Executive in Public Law' in Jeffrey Jowell and Colm O'Cinneide (eds), *The Changing Constitution*, 9th edn (Oxford, OUP, 2019) 189.

[126] Daintith and Page (n 7) argue (at 12) that we should 'resist the easy assumption that the allocations of powers and functions *within* each of the organisational blocs identified by separation of powers doctrine are less significant to the protection of constitutional values than are the relations *between* those blocs'.

[127] See John Laws, *The Common Law Constitution* (Cambridge, CUP, 2014), Lecture I, for an authoritative analysis of 'the common law's fourfold method – evolution, experiment, history and distillation'.

[128] Matthias Ruffert, 'National Executives and Bureaucracies' in Peter Cane et al (eds), *The Oxford Handbook of Comparative Administrative Law* (Oxford, OUP, 2020) 505.

14

Beyond *Carltona: R v Adams*, Accountability and the Delegation of Powers

CLAIRE ARCHBOLD*

Introduction

The *Carltona*[1] doctrine is, on the surface, one of the easiest to grasp rules of public law. Handy in all kinds of situations, it is a small but important brick in the foundations of the UK's modern administrative state. The rule appears simple. A Minister in charge of a UK government department cannot personally take every decision which has to be taken in the running of a large department. So as a matter of necessity the law regards as valid decisions taken by their junior Ministers or civil servants without specific delegation.

However, if we look more closely at the principle, the rationale for its almost automatic devolution of decision-making in central government appears less clear, and later cases hint at a need for reconsideration. Judicial treatment has not consistently articulated the underlying rationale of *Carltona*. Dicta sometimes apparently conflict. In several leading cases the courts have sought to put boundaries on the doctrine and to assert the courts' right of review. However, one judge has tried to stretch its boundaries outside central government departments,[2] a move from which later courts have retreated. With touchpoint cases dealing with police powers and the liberty of the individual, the context of decisions makes clear the challenge of balancing the need for efficient government with the need for accountability for executive decision-making.

* Thanks are due to Professor Christopher McCrudden, Professor Brice Dickson and Dr Conor McCormick of Queen's University Belfast, Heather Stevens, Solicitor and Léonie McLaughlin of the Office of Legislative Counsel, for their insightful discussion and comments on a draft of this chapter, but the views expressed are the author's own. They do not represent the views of the Northern Ireland Civil Service or of any Northern Ireland Minister or department.

[1] *Carltona v Commissioners of Works* [1943] 2 All ER 560 (CA).

[2] Sedley LJ in the *Birmingham Justices* case, discussed below at n 62.

The *Carltona* judgment was given at the start of the growth of the modern administrative state in the UK. Since then, much ink has been spilled on accountability for executive decision-making in what has been called the 'sprawling and diverse' edifice of modern government, extending well beyond UK government Ministers and the great departments of state.[3] Significant power has been delegated to local government, arms-length bodies and the devolved institutions. This chapter explores whether *R v Adams*[4] should encourage us to look beyond a simple invocation of *Carltona* and to ask a different question when assessing where there should be delegation or devolution of power in any given situation. Would a clearer articulation of the principles and rationale for the devolution of executive decision-making provide a better lens through which legal practitioners, policy makers and commentators could focus on the underlying issues of transparency and accountability for executive decision-making?

The Exercise of Crown Power

The exercise and oversight of state power in the UK is famously regulated by an unwritten (or, perhaps more accurately, uncodified) Constitution operating in both the political and legal spheres. As McCormick sets out,[5] the constitutional architecture of the United Kingdom is that power flows down from the Queen-in-Parliament through statute law, or, for a small category of powers, directly from the Crown's residual prerogative and common law powers. The executive branch of the state is referred to as 'the Crown' and executive power[6] is most often exercised through Ministers, the most senior of whom are the Secretaries of State.

Generations of law students have wondered why statutes only infrequently give powers to named Ministers, but more often to 'the Secretary of State'. The Interpretation Act 1978 defines the term 'Secretary of State', seemingly tautologically, as 'one of Her Majesty's principal Secretaries of State'[7] and any Secretary of State is empowered to act for any other Secretary of State, including in relation to transfer of property and signing of contracts.[8]

This quirk of the Constitution arises from the historic origins of the office as a single clerk or private secretary to the monarch. The first appointment of two

[3] Mark Elliott and Robert Thomas, *Public Law*, 4th edn (Oxford, OUP, 2020) 38.

[4] *R v Adams* [2020] UKSC 19, [2020] 1 WLR 2077.

[5] See Conor McCormick (ch 13).

[6] The slipperiness of 'Crown' language is captured by Jason Allen, who says: 'Rules of attribution provide that any valid act by a minister shall count as an act of the Crown. But there need not be a relation of identity between the entities ['Minister' and 'Crown'] nor perfect symmetry between rules of attribution and liability that operate between them'. See Jason Allen, 'The Office of the Crown' (2018) 77 *CLJ* 298, 298–99.

[7] Interpretation Act 1978, Sch 1.

[8] Ministers of the Crown Act 1975, s 3.

concurrent Secretaries of State was by Henry VIII.[9] Brazier observes that the 'undivided office of "Secretary of State" has continued to the present, and in the eyes of the law there is only one Secretary of State'.[10] When exercising prerogative or common law powers of the Crown, Secretaries of State therefore do so directly.

Along with ministerial accountability to Parliament, the unity of the Crown and *Carltona* give conceptual coherence to the chain of accountability within government departments. Beneath the Secretaries of State sit junior Ministers. They may have statutory powers of their own, but in day-to-day business they do not exercise their own power but rather that of their Secretary of State under the *Carltona* principle. They are accountable to Parliament through their Secretary of State. This chain of accountability also covers civil servants within departments who exercise powers under *Carltona*. Civil servants are not employees engaged by way of a contract, but are Crown servants, appointed in an exercise of the prerogative. Like their Minister, they are exercising the power of the Crown, and are accountable to Parliament through that Minister for so doing.

The Rule against Sub-Delegation of Powers

Carltona stands as a striking exception to the general principle of both public and private law that, where a power has been conferred, it must be exercised by the person or body on whom it has been conferred. In public law, there is a presumption that sub-delegation is not permitted[11] and unlawful sub-delegation of a public law function is susceptible to challenge by judicial review.[12] A distinction is drawn between delegation and agency, and there is no difficulty in public bodies appointing agents to undertake preparatory work or support functions as they exercise their statutory powers, provided the officially designated decision-maker retains control of the decision.[13] The significance of delegation is demonstrated by the particularly strong reluctance in the courts to allow the delegation of judicial or quasi-judicial powers.[14] The case law also demonstrates a distinction, important in practice, between cases where the power has been given to the head of a hierarchical organisation, where it is to be expected that a lower official would take the decision, and cases where it has been given to an individual because of particular

[9] Rodney Brazier, *Ministers of the Crown* (Oxford, OUP, 1997) 9. In 1540, due to the increasingly varied and onerous duties of the office, Henry VIII appointed two office holders for the first time, Sir Thomas Wriothesley and Sir Ralph Sadler, each with a seal entitling him to exercise the whole of his power.

[10] ibid.

[11] Often expressed as the maxim *delegatus non potest delegare*.

[12] Harry Woolf et al, *De Smith's Judicial Review*, 8th edn (London, Sweet & Maxwell, 2018) (hereafter *De Smith*), para 5-159.

[13] ibid paras 5-165 to 5-169 and Peter Watts and Francis Reynolds (eds), *Bowstead and Reynolds on Agency*, 21st edn (London, Sweet & Maxwell, 2017) para 5-003.

[14] *De Smith* (n 12) para 5-161.

skill or knowledge they are likely to possess.[15] In the latter case, sub-delegation will be particularly frowned upon.

The so-called rule against sub-delegation is a strong presumption rather than a rule of statutory interpretation.[16] Additional or ancillary powers may be read into a statutory power, by necessary implication at common law,[17] or by the action of the Interpretation Acts,[18] to allow business to function. However, the courts will not be generous in finding a power of complete sub-delegation by implication.

A recent decision of the Northern Ireland Court of Appeal, *McKee v Charity Commission*,[19] upholding the decision of the court below,[20] illustrates clearly the limits of implied delegation in arms-length bodies.[21] The powers and functions of the Northern Ireland Charity Commission were set out in the founding statute and included delegation of some specific functions to employees. Functions of the Commission beyond those delegated by statute were routinely undertaken by employees, including the taking of decisions affecting individuals such as the fitness of persons to be charity trustees. The Commission argued that this delegation was a valid exercise of the power in the Interpretation Act (NI) 1954 for a body corporate to regulate its own procedure and business and to employ such staff as may be found necessary for the performance of its functions.[22] In the alternative it asked the court to imply a power to delegate. The judgment turned on Beatson J's reasoning in *Noon v Matthews*,[23] in particular the distinction between the conferral of power on a public officeholder because of that person's expected personal qualifications and experience and the situation where:

> the exercise of the power in question is not final or conclusive, where the power is given to the head of an organisation which is itself hierarchically structured, and where the responsibilities of the person or body named in the statute are such that the court considers delegation is inevitable, [in which cases] a less strict approach is taken and authority to delegate is likely to be implied.[24]

The Court in *McKee* applied a strict test to the question of whether delegation was 'inevitable' and could therefore be said to have been intended by the legislator. There was a paucity of evidence of a heavy workload. Rather, the statutory scheme appeared to countenance a situation where the Commission took the decisions necessary to the exercise of its statutory powers, duties and functions, while the staff undertook the research, information gathering, briefing advice and

[15] *Noon, River Manager, Conservators of the River Cam v Matthews* [2014] EWHC 4330 (Admin), [26] (Beatson J).

[16] *De Smith* (n 12) para 5-163.

[17] John Willis, 'Delegatus non potest delegare' (1943) 21 *Canadian Bar Review* 257.

[18] Interpretation Act 1978; Interpretation Act (NI) 1954.

[19] *McKee v Charity Commission* [2020] NICA 13.

[20] *McKee v Charity Commission* [2019] NICh 6.

[21] The first instance judgment of McBride J (ibid) contains a full review of the possible circumstances in which delegation would be permitted.

[22] Interpretation Act (NI) 1954, s 19(1)(a)(v) and (vi).

[23] See *Noon* (n 15).

[24] ibid [26].

recommendation.[25] The Court noted the significant consequences of its decision for the Charity Commission and suggested a legislative amendment to provide unambiguously the necessary power to the Commission as an appropriate resolution. The Charities Bill recently introduced to the Northern Ireland Assembly by the Minister for Communities seeks to address this issue accordingly.

Delegation and Ministers: The *Carltona* Principle

With this striking example in mind, the significance of *Carltona* for the smooth running of a large, busy department is clear. But is *Carltona* more than a pragmatic rule born of necessity? It is sometimes stated to be an exception to the presumption against sub-delegation, but may be better seen as different in kind: an *alter ego* principle[26] rather than a downward transfer of power.

To understand the significance of this distinction, it is worth interrogating the judgment of Lord Greene MR in *Carltona v Commissioners of Works*.[27] It is rarely mentioned that it is a war-time decision, taken in the context of a massive extension of state decision-making, and in an emergency situation.[28] Did this affect the court's decision?

The Commissioners of Works was a body which never met, but whose power was exercised by the First Commissioner, a role carried out by the Minister of Works and Planning. A senior official in the department requisitioned a factory using the sweeping power under regulation 18B of the Defence (General) Regulations 1939. The factory owners claimed that the official had failed to take into account the matters in the statute to which regard was to be had, and in any event had improperly exercised a power which sat only with the Secretary of State. Lord Greene said:

> In the administration of government in this country the functions which are given to ministers (and constitutionally properly given to ministers because they are constitutionally responsible) are functions so multifarious that no minister could ever personally attend to them … The duties imposed upon ministers and the powers given to ministers are normally exercised under the authority of ministers by responsible officials of the department. *Public business could not be carried on if that were not the case.*

[25] *Re Belfast Telegraph Newspapers Application* [2001] NI 178, 185 (Carswell LCJ).

[26] See David Lanham, 'The Harmless Fiction of the Alter Ego Principle' (1984) 100 *LQR* 587.

[27] *Carltona* (n 1).

[28] The 'regulation 18B' cases also include *Liversidge v Anderson* [1942] AC 206, in which the House of Lords' timid decision on whether the Home Secretary required objective reasons for his belief that an individual should be interned was the occasion for Lord Atkin's famous dissent based on the rule of law. The emergency context may strike a chord with readers considering judicial responses to the pandemic emergency of 2020–21. In cases at the height of the Covid-19 pandemic, such as *R (Dolan) v Secretary of State for Health and Social Care and Secretary of State for Education* [2020] EWCA Civ 1605, the courts initially gave a wide margin of appreciation to government in the unprecedented circumstances, but later cases have tested the proportionality of decisions taken which affected individual rights. See eg the judgment of Lord Braid in the Scottish case of *Philips and others (petitioners)* [2021] CSOH 32 (Court of Session Outer House).

> *Constitutionally, the decision of such an official is, of course, the decision of the minister. The minister is responsible. It is he who must answer before Parliament for anything that his officials have done under his authority, and, if for an important matter he selected an official of such junior standing that he could not be expected competently to perform the work, the minister would have to answer for that in Parliament.* The whole system of departmental organisation and administration is based on the view that ministers, being responsible to Parliament, will see that important duties are committed to experienced officials. If they do not do that, Parliament is the place where complaint must be made against them.[29]

The judgment is a creature of its time. By modern standards, it is short. It does not spell out the authorities behind its statements, but assumes a background knowledge of constitutional law and practice. Although there are prior decisions of a similar type,[30] it cites no authorities. But the highlighted paragraph can be seen to contain the seeds of four propositions:

1. Necessity – public business could not be carried on if officials did not exercise powers for Ministers.
2. The *alter ego* principle – 'Constitutionally, the decision of such an official is, of course, the decision of the minister'.
3. Parliamentary accountability – the Minister must answer to Parliament for the acts of his officials and 'Parliament is the place where complaint must be made'.
4. The Minister must select an experienced official or one of sufficiently senior standing to competently perform the duty in question.

Taken together, Lord Greene's four propositions suggest a limited scope for judicial oversight of the devolution of ministerial decisions. Poole suggests that the *alter ego* doctrine may turn a department into something of a 'black box' and 'prevent the development of suitably tailored principles designed to enhance good administration'.[31] Necessity and accountability to Parliament have received frequent reference in later cases, but the *alter ego* principle is more inconsistently referred to.[32]

Some later cases focus on the inclusion or exclusion of *Carltona* as a matter of statutory interpretation,[33] as well as reviewing on the basis of the requirement

[29] *Carltona* (n 1) 563 (emphasis added).

[30] See Willis (n 17).

[31] Thomas Poole, 'The Executive in Public Law', in Jeffrey Jowell and Colm O'Cinneide (eds), *The Changing Constitution*, 9th edn (Oxford, OUP, 2019) 188, 198.

[32] The *alter ego* principle is stated as the basis of the doctrine in, eg, *Lewisham Borough v Roberts* [1949] 2 KB 608, 629 (CA); *R v Skinner* [1968] 2 QB 700 (CA); *Re Golden Chemical Products Ltd* [1976] Ch 300, 307 (ChD); and see Lanham (n 26).

[33] In *R v Secretary of State for the Home Dept, ex parte Doody* [1994] 1 AC 531, Lord Mustill, at 566F–567A, characterised the rationale for *Carltona* as being 'without question' one which 'principally depends upon the interpretation of the statute' and said that 'through the statute book there are innumerable instances where powers are conferred on a minister, and where it is perfectly obvious that Parliament contemplated a delegation'. *Lewisham* (n 32) also uses the language of delegation and devolution interchangeably.

to select a sufficiently senior officer to take the decision.[34] This suggests a level of discomfort with the consequences of the principle that, as the editors of Supperstone, Goudie and Walker succinctly put it, 'decisions taken by [departmental] officials are in law decisions of the Minister'.[35]

The Boundaries of the *Carltona* Principle

The courts have been content that *Carltona* should apply to civil servants in executive agencies, as the Minister retains formal accountability for their work.[36] However, a leading case in this area, *R v Secretary of State for the Home Department, ex parte Oladehinde*,[37] also set boundaries to the application of *Carltona*, by exploring what Lord Greene meant by 'a suitably senior official'. Lord Griffiths was clear that failure to select a sufficiently senior decision-maker, so that the decision is 'suitable to their grading and experience,[38] could fall within the ambit of *Wednesbury* irrationality. This view was shared by Lord Phillips CJ in *DPP v Haw*.[39]

The courts have held that *Carltona* may be excluded by express words in a statute or by necessary implication.[40] There has been some inconsistency in the cases as to whether this is as a result of a presumption in favour of *Carltona*, the simple operation of statutory construction, a matter of delegation[41] or an exception to the *alter ego* principle. Recent Supreme Court cases, first *Bourgass*[42] and in particular *R v Adams*,[43] have moved the conversation on significantly.

In *R (Bourgass) v Secretary of State for the Home Department* the Supreme Court looked closely at the rationale for the question of who could decide to keep a prisoner in solitary confinement for over 72 hours. Prison Rules permitted a prison governor to take decisions on segregation for up to 72 hours. Beyond that, authorisation of the Secretary of State was required. This statutory scheme

[34] See, eg, *R v Secretary of State, ex parte Oladehinde* [1991] 1 AC 254.

[35] Supperstone, Goudie and Walker, *Judicial Review*, 6th edn (London, LexisNexis, 2017) para 14.30. Similarly, Forsythe says: 'Strictly speaking there is not even delegation in these cases. Delegation requires a distinct act by which the power is conferred upon some person not previously competent to exercise it. But the authority of officials to act in their ministers' names derives from a general rule of law and not from any particular act of delegation' (Wade and Forsythe, *Administrative Law*, 11th edn (Oxford, OUP, 2014) 266).

[36] *Oladehinde* (n 34); *R v Secretary of State for the Home Dept, ex parte Sherwin* (1996) 32 *BMLR* 1; *Castle v Crown Prosecution Service* [2014] EWHC (Admin) 587. For recent decisions on 'suitable officials', see *R (TM (Kenya)) v Secretary of State for the Home Dept* [2019] EWCA Civ 784, *R (Goloshvili) v Secretary of State for the Home Dept* [2019] EWHC 614 (Admin).

[37] See *Oladehinde* (n 34).

[38] ibid 285.

[39] *DPP v Haw* [2007] EWHC 1931, [2008] 1 WLR 379, especially at [29].

[40] Lord Donaldson, *Oladehinde* (n 34) 265: 'I have no doubt that there can be an implied limitation which can affect the *Carltona* principle' and see also Lord Kerr in *R v Adams* discussed below.

[41] For an example of both delegation and statutory construction reasoning, see *Doody* (n 33).

[42] *R (Bourgass) v Secretary of State for the Home Dept* [2015] UKSC 54, [2016] AC 384.

[43] *R v Adams* (UKSC) (n 4).

was held by Lord Reed, giving the judgment of the Court, to be intended to provide a safeguard to the prisoner, which was not met when a senior prison governor made the extension decision, claiming to be acting under the *Carltona* principle. *Carltona* is not, he said, the operation of either delegation or agency, but of the *alter ego* principle. The decision of the civil servant is constitutionally that of the Minister. He differentiated between this position and that of an independent statutory office holder, who had their own duties to carry out.[44] He concluded that:

> … the Secretary of State, having no authority to direct the governor in the exercise of his disciplinary powers, could have no constitutional responsibility for the governor's exercise of those powers (as distinct from his own supervisory functions), and that the rationale underpinning the *Carltona* principle would therefore be absent.

While giving its place to the *alter ego* principle, the express and detailed consideration of parliamentary intention in the architecture of the statutory scheme in *Bourgass* prefigures the approach of Lord Kerr on the next occasion on which the Supreme Court considered *Carltona*, in *R v Adams*.

The focus in *Adams* was squarely on the question of whether some decisions are so important that they cannot be delegated. The proposition was in some doubt. It could be said to be inconsistent with the premise of the *alter ego* principle, and the current (pre-*Adams*) edition of *De Smith* says, circumspectly:

> It may be that there are, however, some matters of such importance that the Minister is legally required to address himself to them personally, despite the fact that many dicta that appear to support the existence of such an obligation are at best equivocal. It is however possible that orders drastically affecting the liberty of the person … require the personal attention of the Minister.[45]

In the early 1970s, an Interim Custody Order (ICO)[46] had been made for the administrative detention of Gerry Adams, now the retired President of Sinn Féin. He had twice escaped from custody, been recaptured, and then convicted and sentenced for the escapes. The ICO had been signed by a junior Northern Ireland Office Minister. An opinion relating to the issue, by the then Senior Crown Counsel of Northern Ireland, Brian Hutton (a future Lord Chief Justice of Northern Ireland and Lord of Appeal), was later made public under the 30-year rule relating to the release of state documents. In it, Hutton cited an earlier edition of *De Smith*, which suggested in clearer terms that the decision to make an ICO should be made personally by the Secretary of State. The parties in the case accepted that the Secretary of State had never turned his mind to the ICO in respect of Mr Adams. After the release of the legal opinion, an appeal out of time was brought against the convictions for the escapes.

[44] *Bourgass* (n 42) [49]–[51].
[45] *De Smith* (n 12) para 5-187.
[46] Made under art 4(1) of the Detention of Terrorists (NI) Order 1972.

The Court of Appeal of Northern Ireland determined the modern position to be that there is a presumption that statutory powers can be exercised by a junior Minister or official, but that the presumption can be displaced by statutory or other evidence to the contrary.[47] The seriousness of the matter being decided was one factor, but not a determining factor, in this exercise. Weatherup J said that:

> The present case did not involve a decision of an official in the Department … the decision was taken by a Minister, appointed by the Crown, having the same advice and assistance from officials in the Department as the Secretary of State and also being answerable to Parliament.[48]

He held that the decision had been properly taken and was valid, and gave a clear restatement of the classic *Carltona* position, namely that the case

> is not one of delegation … [A] decision assigned by Parliament to, for example, a Secretary of State, when permissibly exercised by another Minister or by an appropriate official, is constitutionally the decision of the Secretary of State.[49]

Giving the unanimous decision of the Supreme Court,[50] Lord Kerr took the opposite view. In this case, the clear interpretation of the statutory scheme was that the decision should be made by the Secretary of State personally. While it was not necessary to reach a conclusion on whether *Carltona* amounted to a legal presumption rebuttable only by express words, Lord Kerr's provisional (and *obiter*) view was that it did not. While Parliament legislated against the background that the *Carltona* principle is well-established,

> the matter should be approached as a matter of textual analysis, unencumbered by the application of a presumption, but with the enjoinder of Lord Griffiths well in mind.[51] In this way, whether the *Carltona* principle should be considered to arise in a particular case depends on an open-ended examination of the factors identified by Coghlin LJ in *McCafferty*,[52] namely, the framework of the legislation, the language of pertinent provisions in the legislation and the 'importance of the subject matter', in other words, the gravity of the consequences flowing from the exercise of the power, rather than the application of a presumption.[53]

In reflecting on these factors, Lord Kerr focused on the fact that the functions of making and signing the ICO were deliberately separated by Parliament, the fact that the burden of dealing with a relatively small number of these orders would not be unduly onerous (so making devolution of the duty inevitable) and the 'momentous' nature of a power to detain without trial, potentially for an indefinite period.[54]

[47] *R v Adams* [2018] NICA 8.
[48] ibid [51].
[49] ibid [13].
[50] *R v Adams* (UKSC) (n 4).
[51] In *Oladehinde* (n 34) above, Lord Griffiths said that a power of a Minister may 'generally' be exercised by a member of the Minister's department.
[52] *McCafferty's Application for Judicial Review* [2009] NICA 59.
[53] *R v Adams* (UKSC) (n 4) [26] (footnotes added).
[54] ibid [36]–[38].

This judgment points to a developed position that is more nuanced than the essentially binary choice suggested by the original *Carltona* decision. Parliament, in legislating, will be aware of the principle and its constitutional underlay, but it creates a statutory scheme in awareness also of wider factors, including the gravity of the consequences of the decision being made. It is not fatal to the argument that the legislation does not expressly exclude *Carltona*. The threefold test of the framework of the relevant legislation, the language of the applicable provisions and the 'importance of the subject matter' (including the gravity of its consequences) must be considered in each case.[55]

What is the Impact of the Decision in *Adams*?

On the narrow view, *Adams* is a judgment dealing with a historical issue, a piece of legislation which has now been repealed, and is unlikely ever to trouble the courts again. It is readily distinguishable from most other decisions, as dealing with an exceptional factual situation of extra-judicial internment. Lord Kerr dwelt on the 'momentous' nature of the power and stated his wider remarks to be 'provisional'. They are *obiter* and clearly caveated. Arguably, his position is not that far from the one stated in the court below.

Nonetheless, there has been criticism from some commentators that the decision gives rise to uncertainty and creates a risk to an established and widely used government and drafting convention.[56] One public law expert, however, has already made a contrary case: that the case represents no great movement from established doctrine.[57]

It has yet to be seen whether the judgment in *Adams* gives rise to a string of cases testing the boundaries of *Carltona*. It may be distinguished and come to be seen as based on its own unusual facts. However, the judgment can be seen to be

[55] For discussion, see Neil Parpworth, 'Deprivation of Liberty and the *Carltona* Principle' (2020) 84 *Journal of Criminal Law* 497. See also Kark Laird, 'Statutory Powers: *Carltona* Principle: *R v Adams*' [2021] *Crim LR* 69; Neil Parpworth, 'Held to Account' (2020) 170 *New Law Journal* 19.

[56] Richard Ekins and Stephen Laws, *Mishandling the Law*, (London, Policy Exchange, 2020) 46, available at policyexchange.org.uk/wp-content/uploads/Mishandling-the-Law.pdf. David Horvath-Franco, in 'The Supreme Court's judgment in *Adams* and the missing step of statutory construction' (2020) 71 *NILQ* 503, makes a different argument, namely that, notwithstanding the invalidity of the order, the applicant's conviction for escaping from custody should be upheld, construing the offence as not dependent on the lawfulness of the custody.

[57] Paul Daly, University of Cambridge, blogging at www.administrativelawmatters.com. Daly cites as cases establishing the displacement of *Carltona* by necessary implication *CREEDNZ Inc v Governor-General* [1981] 1 NZLR 172, 183; *Attorney General (Quebec) v Carrières Ste-Thérèse Ltée* [1985] 1 SCR 831; *Re Patterson, ex parte Taylor* (2001) 207 CLR 391. MacMenamin J explained for the Irish Supreme Court in *WT v Minister for Justice* [2015] IESC 73 that: 'In law, the principle … is capable of being negatived or confined by express statutory provision to the contrary, or by necessary implication … In such cases, then, the test is whether it can be established that a statute clearly conveys that the *Carltona* principle is not to be recognised, or clearly implies such a conclusion'.

the culmination of a trend where cases invite us to look beyond a mechanistic invocation of *Carltona* in central government decision-making. It prompts us to ask whether, in the modern administrative state, *Carltona* is always a sufficient guarantee of good governance of the powers granted to Ministers by Parliament. Rather than solely carrying out an inquiry into parliamentary language, it locates that inquiry expressly in the context of the consequences of the decision.

In 2017, Gregson surveyed delegated decisions within and beyond central government and suggested statutory reform of *Carltona*.[58] His elegant solution proposes a presumption against implied delegation outside central government, and a presumption in its favour in relation to UK Ministers, provided in each case that the delegator has control over and is answerable for the delegate and that the delegate has the attributes required to exercise a discretionary power. In each case, the presumption could be rebutted by additional consideration of whether the requirements of 'swift administration or leadership' required the opposite outcome.

As Gregson identifies, there is a readily available alternate universe of decision-making in large public sector bodies outside central government which shows us what life without *Carltona* looks like. It is to this that we now turn.

The Wider Public Sector: Could *Carltona* Reach Beyond Central Government?

The orthodoxy is that the *Carltona* doctrine does not apply outside central government departments,[59] although its reach has been extended to executive agencies such as the Benefits Agency[60] and the Immigration Service,[61] provided that the Minister retains an accountability to Parliament for the decisions taken.

In *R (Chief Constable of West Midlands Police) v Birmingham Justices*,[62] Sedley LJ tried to use *Carltona* as the basis for creating more ease of delegation in the hierarchical and highly-pressured environment of policing. He said:

> Although the *Carltona* case is frequently cited as a source of the 'alter ego' doctrine, it can be seen that Lord Greene's reasoning is not predicated on this. It is predicated on the proposition that the departmental head is responsible for things done under his authority. The relevance of the alter ego doctrine is that Crown servants were at that time taken in law to hold their positions by grace and not by contract … [The Minister's] implied power to delegate functions depended, therefore, on two things; the conferment of a

[58] Rory Gregson, 'When should there be an implied power to delegate?' [2017] *Public Law* 408, 418.

[59] Wade and Forsythe (n 35) 267.

[60] *R v Secretary of State for Social Security, ex parte Sherwin* (1996) 32 *BMLR* 1, noted in Richard Moules, *Environmental Judicial Review* (Oxford, Hart Publishing, 2011) 192.

[61] In *Oladehinde* (n 34); immigration officers serve in an executive agency of the Home Office.

[62] *R (Chief Constable of West Midlands Police) v Birmingham Justices* [2002] EWHC 1087 (Admin).

> power in terms which implicitly permitted their delegation and the existence of persons to whom he could delegate them without parting with ultimate responsibility.[63]

Sedley LJ went on to outline as a rationale for *Carltona* the distinction between a power designated to an officer because he or she is at the apex of a hierarchically structured organisation, where delegation is permitted, and a power given by Parliament to an office holder because of his or her personal qualifications, where it is not, which is reminiscent of the exceptions to the rule against sub-delegation explored in the *McKee* judgment.[64]

Moules suggests that the *Birmingham Justices* case conflates the political accountability of a Minister to Parliament and the legal accountability of any holder of a statutory power to the courts,[65] but one can perhaps see in it an attempt to recast *Carltona* to solve the problem of when decisions can safely be delegated in state bodies beyond central government. Later police cases did not follow Sedley LJ's reasoning, but they solved the problem by finding a similar justification to delineate circumstances where the rule against sub-delegation would be inapt. In *DPP v Haw*, Lord Phillips used now-familiar words:

> Where the responsibilities of the office are such that delegation is inevitable, there will be an implied power to delegate unless the statute, expressly or by implication, provides to the contrary.[66]

The decision in *DPP v Haw*, like that of Lord Kerr in *Adams* and of the Northern Ireland courts in *McKee*, looks at the real-world context of the exercise of the power when it assesses the level of accountability which the legislature must have intended. Lord Phillips described the distinction between the reasoning which led him to find that delegation was permitted, and that which allowed devolution of decision-making to officials in *Carltona* as 'of only academic significance',[67] but looking at the extent of delegation/devolution with which the courts are comfortable in different circumstances emphasises the importance of the underlying principle of accountability and is a reminder to decision-makers that their power should be further delegated with care.

The World Beyond Whitehall: Permissible Sub-Delegation

The difference between delegation of ancillary functions and of full decision-making powers in non-departmental public bodies is starkly illustrated by the case

[63] ibid [9].
[64] See *McKee* (n 19).
[65] Moules (n 60) 193, and see Wade and Forsythe (n 35) 268–69.
[66] *DPP v Haw* (n 39) [33]. The reasoning in *Haw* was adopted in *R (Hamill) v Chelmsford Magistrate Court* [2014] EWHC 2799.
[67] *ibid.*

of *McKee*, discussed above.[68] While the case law has been clear that the *Carltona* principle does not apply in local government,[69] that is an area in which the courts have developed more extensive flexibility in the rule against sub-delegation to tackle the same practical problem, namely how to balance meaningful accountability for decision-making with the huge burden of work in local and regional authorities. It is not only in Whitehall that the person to whom power is given cannot reasonably be expected to take every decision requiring its exercise. While the courts remain unforgiving of sub-delegation in relation to judicial and quasi-judicial functions,[70] a more relaxed approach to sub-delegation in local government allows for a similar solution to that provided for by *Carltona*, while remaining doctrinally distinct.

The common law position was expressed by the House of Lords in relation to sub-delegation by a Council treasurer in *Provident Mutual Life Assurance Association v Derbyshire City Council*:

> Equally clearly, the performance of such duties as in consequence fall up on the respondents' treasurer could not possibly all be performed by him personally, and Parliament cannot possibly have intended that this should be so. The respondent's treasurer required staff to carry out the financial affairs which he is enjoined to administer.[71]

The assumption as to parliamentary intention here was specific to the statute, but more recently the Local Government Acts have put in place a comprehensive and clearly articulated statutory scheme of delegation, with the functions of a Council being delegated to the mayor, to committees or to officers.[72] The clarity and extent of this scheme of delegation may be seen as an explanation for the relaxed attitude to sub-delegation displayed in some of the local government case law and there has been an acceptance that the *Provident Mutual Life* principle applies generally to local government powers.[73] Such delegation could even be derived from common practice

> precisely because the Director of Environmental Services *in persona* alone could not handle the range of matters, large and small, which are delegated to him, and a further chain of delegating resolutions would be unnecessary in the light of those authorities. A certain amount of realism is called for in judging the probability of such authority having been given … I see no need for there to be an express statement on any particular document to the effect that that was what was being done, though clearly to do so would be wise.[74]

[68] See the text at n 19 above.

[69] See, eg, the Northern Ireland case of *Re Bell's Application* [2000] NI 245.

[70] 'It is well settled that certainly no person made responsible for a judicial decision can delegate his responsibility', per Lord Parker CJ in *R v Brixton Prison Governor, ex parte Enahoro* [1963] 2 QB 455, 465–66.

[71] *Provident Mutual Life Assurance Association v Derbyshire City Council* [1981] 1 WLR 173, 179 (Lord Roskill).

[72] In England and Wales, the main power to delegate is found in the Local Government Act 2000, s 9E; in Northern Ireland it is in the Local Government Act (NI) 2014, s 7.

[73] *Younger Homes (Northern) v First Secretary of State* [2003] EWHC 3058, upheld at [2004] EWCA Civ 1060; *R (Blow-up Media UK) v Lambeth LBC* [2008] EWHC 1912.

[74] *Younger Homes* (ibid) [30] per Ouseley J at first instance.

The cases also show, though, that this is not automatic. The courts will look for a course of dealing, and a degree of formality in the delegated decisions taken.[75] The search for parliamentary intention and for a clear course of dealing located in the real world of day-to-day business may both be seen as a way to balance the reality of the office with the need for assurance as to propriety, accountability and transparency in local authorities' decisions.

Delegation in the Devolved Administrations

The application or otherwise of *Carltona* in the devolved institutions indicates the consequences of the subtle differences between their institutional frameworks. In Scotland and Wales, the devolution legislation replicates the Westminster model, with a legislature and an Executive drawn from the largest party elected to it. Executive power is exercised by 'The Scottish Ministers' and 'The Welsh Ministers' exercising power jointly on a Cabinet model.[76] Two Scottish prison cases, *Somerville v Scottish Ministers*[77] and *Beggs v Scottish Ministers*[78] apply *Carltona* in the devolved context and make it clear that the doctrine, the position of the civil service[79] and the position of Scottish Ministers[80] are to be regarded as exactly equivalent to those of their Whitehall counterparts.

However, the position in Northern Ireland is quite different. Statutory powers in Northern Ireland are more frequently given to departments than to Ministers and a departmental power may be exercised by a Northern Ireland Minister or

[75] *R (Goodman and Hedges) v Lewisham LBC* [2003] EWCA Civ 140); see generally Moules (n 60) 186–90.

[76] Scotland Act 1998, s 53; Government of Wales Act 2006, s 58A.

[77] *Somerville v Scottish Ministers* [2007] UKHL 44, [2007] 1 WLR 2734.

[78] *Beggs v Scottish Ministers* [2007] UKHL 3, [2007] 1 WLR 455.

[79] In *Beggs* (ibid) Lord Hope said at [8]–[9]: 'In my opinion two points require to be made in the light of this background. The first is that the status of civil servants is different from that of employees or agents of a body such as a company or a trade union. Civil Servants are servants of the Crown, not of Ministers who are answerable to Parliament for the departments in which they serve; see *Carltona v Commrs of Works* [1943] 2 All ER 560. The status of civil servants in Scotland was not affected by the devolution settlement. The Scottish Ministers are answerable to the Scottish Parliament and to the court for any undertakings that they may give … for the actions of officials within the various branches of the Scottish Executive. But the officials are not their servants or agents. It is the fact that they perform their functions under direction and control of the Scottish Ministers that makes the Scottish Ministers answerable for what they do or fail to do. Ministerial responsibility for acts and failures of civil servants in their Departments cannot be delegated'.

[80] In *Beggs* (n 78), Lord Rodger said at [32]: 'The effect of section 53 of the Scotland Act 1998 was to transfer the functions specified in subsection (2) from Ministers of the Crown to Scottish Ministers, so far as the functions are exercisable within devolved competence … The overall intention and effect of these provisions is that, so far as matters are within devolved competence, the relevant powers are transferred from the Ministers of the Crown to the Scottish Ministers and so, in these respects, the Scottish Ministers are to be in the same position as the Ministers of the Crown'.

a senior official of the department. The operative provision is article 4 of the Departments (NI) Order 1999,[81] which provides that:

> 4(1) The functions of a department shall at all times be exercised subject to the direction and control of the Minister.
>
> …
>
> (3) Subject to the provisions of this Order, any functions of a department may be exercised by—
>
> (a) the Minister; or
> (b) a senior officer of the department.

The prerogative and other executive powers of the Crown are also exercised 'by any Northern Ireland Minister or Department'.[82] There is no collective cabinet responsibility in the mandatory coalition of Northern Ireland's devolved Executive Committee and each department is a corporation with separate legal personality.[83]

The implications of what might previously have seemed only a footnote to history were explored by the Northern Ireland courts in the context of the period of decision-making without Ministers between 2017 and 2020 (when the Northern Ireland Executive was suspended). What decision-making space was there for officials without Ministers in place, and what did accountability and transparency of decision-making mean in such an exceptional situation?

The question was first addressed by Sir Paul Girvan in *Re Brigid Hughes's Application*, a decision about the power to fund the programme of Troubles-related legacy inquests.[84] He stated the dilemma clearly. Without Ministers in place, he observed *obiter* that Northern Ireland was operating outside the normal Westminster convention that policy is made not by civil servants, but by Ministers accountable to the legislature. Instead, he said, there was

> a vacuum in which there are rudderless departments without ministers, the lack of a functioning Executive Committee and the absence of a sitting Assembly [which] produces an essentially undemocratic system of unaccountable government provided effectively by senior civil servants who, as the respondent's counsel conceded, find themselves in an uncomfortable situation.[85]

[81] SI 1999/283 (NI 1).

[82] Northern Ireland Act 1998, s 23. The use of 'any' in this section might be seen as importing the concept of the indivisibility of the Secretary of State into the Northern Ireland settlement, although it is absent from the exercise of statutory powers; see Stephens LJ, as he then was, in *Re JR80's Application* [2019] NICA 58. This model is carried over from s 8 of the Government of Ireland Act 1920, which was based on the model of government of nineteenth century Ireland; the section is a clear antecedent of the Northern Ireland Act 1998 and the Departments (NI) Order 1999.

[83] Departments (NI) Order 1999, art 5. This may be why Northern Ireland departments can sue each other, as seen in, eg, *Minister of Enterprise, Trade and Investment's Application* [2015] NIQB 65.

[84] *Re Brigid Hughes's Application* [2018] NIQB 30.

[85] ibid [68]–[69].

Although *Hughes* stated the dilemma succinctly, it dealt with a decision taken while Ministers were in place. The authoritative consideration of decisions taken without Ministers[86] was by the Court of Appeal in *Re Buick's Application*,[87] considered elsewhere in this volume by McCormick.[88] After some time without Ministers, a senior civil servant granted planning permission to a waste incineration plant, a decision of such significance that the court held it should have been taken by a Minister. The Lord Chief Justice contrasted *Carltona* with the position in Northern Ireland, where not only are statutory powers normally given to departments rather than Ministers, but where the statutory architecture envisages periods after elections of up to six weeks with no Ministers in place, compelling the inference that departmental powers can be exercised in the absence of Ministers.[89] Although the 'direction and control' requirement of the Departments (NI) Order[90] was therefore ambiguous,[91] decisions such as this one, which were significant, controversial or cross-cutting, were envisaged by the statutory scheme as needing to be put before the Executive Committee and so could not be taken by civil servants with no Executive in place.[92] Morgan LCJ said:

> We are reinforced in these views by our recognition of the constitutional position of civil servants. That role is to advise Ministers and be accountable to them. The appellant's submissions would effectively turn civil servants into Ministers. Such a remarkable constitutional change would require the clearest wording and we do not consider that the Northern Ireland Budget Act 2018 provides any basis for the implication of such a major departure from established constitutional principles.[93]

In *Buick*, having resolved the question as to whether there could be any decision-making power without Ministers, and without the *Carltona* framework, the court differentiated between routine decisions which Parliament had intended as appropriate for departments acting alone, and those which were so significant or controversial as to require the direction of elected Ministers and the oversight of the elected Assembly.

Moving Beyond *Carltona*?

The original and brief statement of the *Carltona* principle by Lord Greene, delivered in an emergency context and at an early stage in the expansion of the modern

[86] No discussion of the exercise of power in this period in Northern Ireland is complete without mention of Stephens LJ's decision in *Re JR80's Application* (n 82), which deals with the prerogative power to set up a statutory scheme to pay compensation to the victims of historical institutional abuse. While dealing with the exercise of and accountability for state power, it is not directly relevant to the subject of this chapter.

[87] *Re Buick's Application* [2018] NICA 26.

[88] See Conor McCormick (ch 13).

[89] *Buick* (n 87) [51].

[90] See Departments (NI) Order 1999, art 4(1).

[91] *Buick* (n 87) [51].

[92] ibid [54].

[93] ibid [55].

administrative state, gave a wide discretion to Ministers to devolve decision making throughout their department. 'Of course' the decision of the official was a decision of the Minister, and it was for Parliament, not the courts, to oversee the exercise of the functions. The classical expression of the *Carltona* principle does not lend itself to openness and transparency of delegation, or to meaningful judicial oversight.

While acknowledging the *alter ego* principle, the courts have over the years nudged the dial on *Carltona* towards greater judicial oversight of the devolution of ministerial powers. In particular, in searching for the intention of Parliament to apply *Carltona* or not in specific statutory schemes, the Supreme Court in *Bourgass*[94] and most strikingly in *Adams* might be said to have taken into account the significance of the real-world consequence of a decision in determining whether it is right that it should be devolved beyond the accountable decision-maker.

The importance of accountability is one side of the *Carltona* balance. The other is the need for administrative workability. *R (Chief Constable of West Midlands Police) v Birmingham Justices*[95] attempted to expand *Carltona* to create a doctrinal basis for this beyond central government; cases such as *DPP v Haw*,[96] the local government cases and the cases involving arms-length bodies such as *McKee*[97] show the courts using an implied power of delegation in a nuanced way to balance the need for workability and the imperative of accountability, weighing the decision using the 'inevitability' arguments and the text of the legislation. Even in Northern Ireland, dealing with the starkest challenge to decision-makers' authority where no Ministers were in place, the court in *Buick* interrogated the Northern Ireland Act 1998 to conclude that Parliament must have intended some circumscribed power to reside in departments, while balancing the need for accountability through the elected institutions in cases which were significant or controversial.

Almost 40 years ago, Lanham asked whether the *alter ego* principle was merely a harmless fiction.[98] The modern administrative state is a huge and diverse mechanism, and particularly in times of emergency decisions taken by individual officials may dramatically impact the rights of individuals. In 1996, Freedland asked whether the rule against delegation and the *Carltona* principle were both part of a coherent body of law, expressing the courts' concerns to ensure bureaucratic rationality.[99] A decade later, Gregson[100] proposed a set of statutory presumptions uniting the two doctrines as mirror images of each other: a presumption in favour of, and a presumption against delegation, each with an exception to ensure workability and appropriate safeguards. After *Carltona*'s seemingly wide embrace of executive discretion to devolve power, there has been a judicial search for coherent

[94] *Bourgass* (n 42) above.
[95] *Birmingham Justices* (n 62).
[96] *DPP v Haw* (n 39).
[97] *McKee* (n 19).
[98] Lanham (n 26) 587.
[99] Mark Freedland, 'The rule against delegation and the *Carltona* doctrine in an agency context' [1996] *Public Law* 19, 22–23.
[100] Gregson (n 58).

administrative practice, accountability for the use of power and judicial oversight of executive decisions.

In the stark factual situation of *Adams*, Lord Kerr's insistence on considering the statutory language, its context and its consequences is a reminder to courts, legislators and decision-makers that the law does not depend mechanistically on a presumption that a power can be devolved. Instead, the judgment encourages them to interrogate the exercise of delegated or devolved statutory power, assessing not only Parliament's use of language but also the context and impact of the decision in the real world. The judgment in *Adams* does not do away with *Carltona*; far from it. Whether it triggers statutory reform of the doctrine or further common law development, it provides an opportunity to move beyond the unspoken complexities of the original *Carltona* decision and ensure that the principle is fit for service in a world more complex even than the one in which it was given. The judgment is a fitting part of its author's legacy, with its focus on substantive justice, its insistence on questioning accepted doctrine, and its determination that government should be done well.

15

Protecting the Right to a Fair Trial in an Era of Criminal Justice Transformation

JOHN JACKSON

Introduction

Since the time when Lord Kerr began practising at the Bar in the early 1970s, criminal justice systems in many countries have undergone unprecedented change prompted by diverse influences such as the growth of 'penal populism', an increase in preventive justice and the development of new managerial models for the administration of criminal justice.[1] Although some have considered that this has necessitated a shift towards crime control away from due process,[2] one development that would seem to counteract such a shift has been an increasing emphasis on fair trial rights at least within Europe as the basis for promoting closer cooperation and trust between systems.[3] In the UK the fair trial rights in Article 6 of the European Convention on Human Rights (ECHR) were given greater prominence by the enactment of the Human Rights Act 1998, which requires public authorities to act compatibly with the Convention. Under section 3 of the Human Rights Act legislation must be read in a way which is compatible with the ECHR so far as it is possible to do so and under section 4 where this is not possible, the courts may make a declaration of incompatibility.

[1] Renaud Colson and Stewart Field, *The Transformation of Criminal Justice* (Paris, Harmattan, 2011); Valsamis Mitsilegas, Peter Alldridge and Leonidas Cheliotis (eds), *Globalisation, Criminal Law and Criminal Justice* (Oxford, Hart Publishing, 2015).

[2] See, eg, Yvonne Daly and John Jackson, 'The Criminal Justice Process: from Questioning to Trial' in Deirdre Healy, Claire Hamilton, Yvonne Daly and Michelle Butler (eds), *The Routledge Handbook of Irish Criminology* (Abingdon, Routledge, 2016) 280; Jacqueline Hodgson, *The Metamorphosis of Criminal Justice* (Oxford, OUP, 2020).

[3] See Andrea Ryan, *Towards a System of European Criminal Justice* (Abingdon, Routledge, 2014); John D Jackson and Sarah J Summers (eds), *Obstacles to Fairness in Criminal Proceedings: Individual Rights and Institutional Forms* (Oxford, Hart /Bloomsbury, 2018) ch 1.

It would seem an opportune time now, over 20 years since the Human Rights Act came into force, to take stock of how the judiciary has managed to preserve the right to a fair trial in the face of so many changes to criminal justice. The aim of this chapter is not to conduct an empirical analysis of how well this has been achieved in criminal cases on the ground. Nor is it to conduct a comprehensive analysis of the judgments of the highest courts on the right to a fair trial.[4] Instead, judicial approaches towards fair trial standards are considered in the light of certain landmark decisions where senior judges have had to wrestle with the challenge of determining what fairness requires in the face of sweeping changes to the processes of criminal justice. In this chapter we shall see that Lord Kerr has made a significant contribution in this area.

Three particular challenges will be considered. First, there has been the challenge of maintaining fundamental bedrock principles that have long been considered fundamental to a fair trial. Fundamental principles of natural justice such as the need for courts and tribunals to be independent and impartial and the right to know the case against one have their roots in the common law. Yet a particularly chilling phenomenon in recent times has been the extent to which governments have introduced legislation as part of their counter-terrorism strategy to enable secret intelligence evidence to be used against suspects who have no opportunity of knowing what such evidence is.

Secondly, there has been the challenge of maintaining longstanding principles associated with a fair criminal trial in the face of a shift in terms of the relationship between the state and the accused. Fifty years ago, it was accepted that those suspected of criminal offences could refuse to participate in police investigations, and in the presentation of cases against them when charged, without fear of being penalised or suffering adverse consequences. But suspects are now expected to cooperate actively with the police investigation and any subsequent court proceedings.[5] This has had far-reaching consequences for principles long associated with the common law such as the presumption of innocence, the right of silence, the privilege against self-incrimination, and the right not to cooperate in disclosing one's defence before trial.

Thirdly, there has been the challenge of interpreting standards of fairness that have themselves been undergoing change. According to Lord Bingham, the senior Law Lord at the time when the Human Rights Act came into force, fairness 'is a constantly evolving concept' and 'standards and perceptions of fairness may change, not only from one century to another but also sometimes from one decade to another'.[6] The European Court of Human Rights (ECtHR) in Strasbourg, whose judgments the courts must take account of under the Act, has considered that the

[4] See Brice Dickson, *Human Rights in the UK Supreme Court* (Oxford, OUP, 2013) ch 7.

[5] See Abenaa Owusu-Bempah, *Defendant Participation in the Criminal Process* (Abingdon, Routledge, 2017).

[6] *R v H* [2004] UKHL 3, [2004] 1 WLR 411, [11]. See also Tom Bingham, *The Rule of Law* (London, Penguin, 2010) 90–91.

ECHR is a 'living instrument which must be interpreted in the light of present day conditions' and domestic courts charged with interpreting the ECHR face a similar challenge.[7] In recent decades, two particular developments have highlighted the need for standards of fairness to change. Hand in hand with an expectation that defendants should actively participate at all stages of criminal proceedings, there has been a shift from the courtroom to the police station as the forum where the outcome of many cases is effectively decided. Over the same period, there has also been a shift at the other end of the criminal justice spectrum away from automatic early release for prisoners, towards procedures which require a risk assessment to be made before those considered dangerous when sentenced are eligible for release.[8] These pre-trial and post-trial procedures can determine outcomes that have immense consequences for the lives of those affected by them and courts have faced the challenge of considering what fairness requires in these circumstances.

Upholding Fundamental Fairness

One theme that has been prominent in much counter-terrorism scholarship has been the way in which exceptional measures can become normalised within legal processes.[9] The use of so-called 'closed material procedures' (CMPs), which have the effect of excluding parties from the proceedings and from knowing the case against them, began in the relatively obscure setting of the Special Immigration Appeals Commission (SIAC) but have since been exported to a wide range of other settings. Under the Justice and Security Act 2013 they may now be used in any proceedings other than in a 'criminal cause or matter'. Although CMPs cannot be used in criminal trials, they have been used to review measures such as control orders that have punitive effects on terrorist suspects.[10] SIAC's rules of procedure also provide that the Commission may receive evidence that would not be admissible in a court of law.[11] In a landmark ruling in *A v Secretary of State for the Home Department (No 2)*[12] the House of Lords unanimously held that, in the absence of express words to the contrary, this could not include the admission of evidence procured by torture inflicted by officials of a foreign state. A distinction was made by their Lordships between the (permissible) use of such evidence by the executive in making the initial decision to certify a particular individual as an international terrorist and the (impermissible) use of such evidence in a court of law which runs contrary to the common law and would damage the integrity of the proceedings.

[7] *Tyrer v UK* (1979–80) 2 EHRR 1, para 31.

[8] For a recent example, see the Terrorist Offenders (Restriction of Early Release) Act 2020.

[9] See, eg, David Bonner, *Executive Measures, Terrorism and National Security* (Aldershot, Ashgate, 2007).

[10] Lucia Zedner, 'Preventive Justice or Pre-Punishment? The Case of Control Orders' [2007] 60 *Current Legal Problems* 174.

[11] See Special Immigration Appeals Commission (Procedure) Rules 2003, SI 2003/1034, r 44(3).

[12] *A v Secretary of State for the Home Dept (No 2)* [2005] UKHL 71, [2006] 2 AC 221.

This expression of the senior judiciary's determination to prohibit the use of torture evidence in judicial proceedings has not been matched with an equal determination to prohibit the use of CMPs. Various judgments have drawn Kafkaesque parallels and expressed deep unease about them.[13] In *Al Rawi v The Security Service*,[14] which provided the trigger for the Justice and Security Act 2013, a majority of the Supreme Court took a strong stance against CMPs by holding that the courts had no 'inherent jurisdiction' to authorise a CMP in a civil claim at common law. But some Justices considered that a CMP might be more appropriate than an action having to be struck out altogether.[15] The appellants, the Security Service and other organs of the state, argued that placing before a judge all relevant material in a CMP was preferable to having to withhold potentially pivotal evidence. But in Lord Kerr's view the central fallacy of this argument lay in the unspoken assumption that once the judge sees everything he or she is bound to be in a better situation to reach a fair result. That assumption was misplaced. In resounding words that have since been frequently cited he stated:

> To be truly valuable, evidence must be capable of withstanding challenge. I go further. Evidence which has been insulated from challenge may positively mislead. It is precisely because of this that the right to know the case that one's opponent makes and to have the opportunity to challenge it occupies such a central place in the concept of a fair trial.[16]

Although the decision in *Al Rawi* was commendable in terms of expressing the Supreme Court's determination to hold the line as the guardian of fundamental fair trial principles which Lord Hope said it had done for centuries, the senior judiciary has not considered that legislation providing for CMPs is incompatible with the ECHR. In its Grand Chamber judgment in *Chahal v UK* the ECtHR considered that closed proceedings could be compatible with standards of fairness when it declared that there are 'techniques which can be employed which both accommodate legitimate security concerns about the nature and sources of intelligence information and yet accord the individual a substantial measure of procedural fairness'.[17] The reference in *Chahal* to the use of security-cleared lawyers in Canada as one such technique prompted the UK to deploy so-called 'special advocates' to represent the interests of excluded parties, first in the SIAC and then in a range of other CMPs.[18] In *Roberts v Parole Board*[19] a majority of the House of Lords considered that the Parole Board had the power to invoke the special advocate procedure, although they accepted that there could be cases where the procedure would not

[13] See, eg, *Roberts v Parole Board* [2005] UKHL 45, [2005] AC 738, per Lord Steyn at [95] and Lord Carswell at [126]. Lord Rodger, at [110], considered such references 'inapposite'.

[14] *Al Rawi v The Security Service* [2011] UKSC 34, [2012] 1 AC 531.

[15] See the judgments of Lord Clarke and Lord Mance (with whom Lady Hale agreed).

[16] *Al Rawi* (n 14) [93].

[17] *Chahal v UK* (1996) 23 EHRR 13, para 131.

[18] For a detailed analysis of this phenomenon, see John Jackson, *Special Advocates in the Adversary System* (Abingdon, Routledge, 2019).

[19] *Roberts v Parole Board* (n 13).

be sufficiently fair to be compatible with Article 5(4) of the ECHR, which requires that new deprivations of liberty must be reviewed by a court-like body. In *Secretary of State for the Home Department v MB and AF*[20] the Law Lords gave rather mixed signals as to whether the use of CMPs and special advocates were compatible with Article 6 when they were deployed in the review of control orders imposed on terrorist suspects under the Prevention of Terrorism Act 2005. Most of the Law Lords appeared to accept that the appointment of a special advocate would afford a sufficient and substantial measure of procedural protection to controlees in almost all cases. However, with the exception of Lord Hoffmann, they followed *Roberts* in considering that special advocates may not ensure a fair trial in every case and ruled that the CMPs should be given a Convention-compatible reading under section 3 of the Human Rights Act except where to do so would be incompatible with the right of the controlled person to a fair trial.

This was not a particularly helpful ruling for judges who had to decide in a particular case whether the procedures met the requirements of a fair trial. When AF's case was sent back to the House of Lords, a clearer and more robust response was given which was influenced greatly by a unanimous judgment of the Grand Chamber of the ECtHR in *A v UK*,[21] issued just before AF's case was due to be heard. *A v UK* concerned the procedural protections that were necessary when the applicants had been detained without trial under the Anti-Terrorism, Crime and Security Act 2001, which had been enacted as the government's response to the events of 9/11. The ECtHR ruled that the procedural requirements for Article 5(4), which in a case involving the lengthy deprivation of liberty must import 'substantially the same fair trial guarantees as Article 6 in its criminal aspect', were not satisfied unless detainees were provided with sufficient information about the allegations against them to enable them to give effective instructions to the special advocate.[22] In *Secretary of State for the Home Department v AF*[23] the Secretary of State argued that account could be taken of the fact that control orders were less severe than lengthy detention. But their Lordships did not think there was room for such a distinction and in the face of the ruling in *A v UK* did not feel they could take any other course but to follow it and to read down the relevant provisions of the 2005 Act under section 3 of the Human Rights Act, even though it meant substantially departing from their 'apparently absolute requirements'.[24]

Although the decision to take this course was unanimous, not all of the Law Lords were happy about following the Grand Chamber's decision, Lord Hoffmann going so far as to say that *A v UK* was 'wrong'.[25] The reservations about disclosing to controlees even a bare minimum gist of the case against them were based on the

[20] *Secretary of State for the Home Dept v MB and AF* [2007] UKHL 46, [2008] 1 AC 440.
[21] *A v UK* (2009) 49 EHRR 29.
[22] ibid [217], [220].
[23] *Secretary of State for the Home Dept v AF* [2009] UKHL 28, [2010] 2 AC 269.
[24] ibid [67].
[25] ibid [70].

fact that dangerous criminals who could not be prosecuted for fear of disclosing details that would jeopardise informants' lives or national security could not now be issued with control orders for the very same reasons. Lord Hoffmann's concern that the ruling might well destroy the system of control orders which was the state's defence against terrorism proved prophetic, as very few control orders were in fact issued after the ruling despite intelligence suggesting that in 2007 no fewer than 2,000 suspects posed a threat to national security.[26] But the answer to this problem was not, according to Lord Scott, to ask the courts to water down the requirements of a fair trial. If indeed national security demanded a tougher response, then it was up to government to face up to the political consequences and enact legislation that curtailed a fair trial even if this might be incompatible with the ECHR.[27] The courts would have to apply such legislation but such a curtailment would be at the behest of Parliament, not of the courts. Lord Hope also made a telling contrast, reminiscent of that made by their Lordships in *A v Secretary of State for the Home Department*, between the role of the executive and the role of the courts, when he said that, while the first responsibility of government was 'to protect and safeguard the lives of its citizens', the courts had another duty 'to protect and safeguard the rights of the individual'.[28] This differentiation in role explains the recent unanimous decision of the Supreme Court in *R (Begum) v Special Immigration Appeals Commission*[29] to respect the government's assessment that Ms Begum's return to the UK to appeal her deprivation of UK citizenship would present a risk to national security. While this meant that her case could not be fairly heard, a fair trial in these circumstances could not trump the safety of the public. What a court cannot be required to do, on the other hand, in the absence of the express will of Parliament, is to try a case unfairly.

In the end then, the House of Lords chose to build into CMPs the fundamental fairness requirement that excluded parties must know and be able to effectively test the gist of the case against them, although it took the ECtHR to lend its weight to this principle before doing so. Such a principle is nevertheless a far cry from the stringent requirements of what is required in a criminal trial and falls short of the common law requirement, long considered fundamental to a fair trial, that defendants are given knowledge of the *full* case against them. Lord Brown pointed out that the Strasbourg Court's solution represented a compromise that gave some weight to the demands of national security.[30] Despite the claim that it was importing substantially the same fair trial guarantees as Article 6(1) in its criminal aspect, *A v UK* did not require the disclosure of an accuser's identity or even the accuser's evidence, whatever difficulties that might pose for the suspect.

[26] Clive Walker, 'Terrorism Prosecution in the United Kingdom' in Fionnuala Ní Aoláin and Oren Gross (eds), *Guantánamo and Beyond: Exceptional Courts and Military Commissions in a Comparative Perspective* (Cambridge, CUP, 2013) 225, 247.

[27] *AF* (n 23) [97].

[28] ibid [76].

[29] *R (Begum) v Special Immigration Appeals Commission* [2021] UKSC 7, [2021] 2 WLR 556.

[30] ibid [120].

This brings us to the key guarantees that are mandated for a criminal trial. Article 6 of the ECHR stipulates that everyone charged with a criminal offence shall be presumed innocent until proved guilty according to law and shall be entitled to a number of minimum rights. But as we shall see in the following section, the senior judiciary, following the broad proportionality approach of the ECtHR, has watered down some of these key guarantees in the interests of bringing the guilty to justice.

Maintaining Fair Criminal Trial Standards

Although control orders, replaced now with terrorism prevention investigation measures (known as 'TPIMs'), have been one weapon in the government's arsenal to combat terrorism, the preferred approach of successive governments ever since the Diplock courts were established in Northern Ireland has been to deal with suspected terrorists through the criminal courts. This has meant abiding by the minimum requirements for a criminal trial set out in Article 6 of the ECHR. Article 6 has been considered a 'strong' right to be distinguished from Articles 8–11 of the ECHR by virtue of the fact that (apart from the public hearing requirement) it is not expressly qualified in the way that those rights are.[31] But in a landmark judgment after the Human Rights Act came into force Lord Bingham made it clear that, following the jurisprudence of the ECtHR, the UK courts would adopt a proportionality approach towards the constituent rights in Article 6, and in particular that limited qualification of them was acceptable if 'reasonably directed by national authorities towards a clear and proper public objective and if representing no greater qualification than the situation calls for'.[32]

While proportionality analysis has become a dominant technique in determining rights adjudication across the world,[33] and has been considered central by the ECtHR to the whole of the ECHR,[34] there has been a lack of clarity about the way in which the test propounded by Lord Bingham should be applied. First, there is uncertainty about the degree of deference that should be given to Parliament when it has decided to restrict any of the fair trial protections. In *DPP v Woolmington*[35] Lord Sankey famously declared that the principle that the prosecution must prove the guilt of the accused is the golden thread to be seen throughout the web of

[31] Andrew Ashworth, 'The Exclusion of Evidence Obtained by Violating a Fundamental Right: Pragmatism before Principle in the Strasbourg Jurisprudence' in Paul Roberts and Jill Hunter (eds), *Criminal Evidence and Human Rights: Reimagining Common Law Procedural Traditions* (Oxford, Hart Publishing, 2012) 145, 147.

[32] *Brown v Stott* [2003] 1 AC 681, 704.

[33] Alec Stone Sweet and Jud Mathews, 'Proportionality Balancing and Global Constitutionalism' (2008) 47 *Columbia Journal of Transnational Law* 24.

[34] See, eg, *Sporrong v Sweden* (1983) 5 EHRR 35, para 69, *Soering v UK* (1989) 11 EHRR 439, para 89.

[35] *Woolmington v DPP* [1935] AC 462, 481.

English criminal law. Despite this rhetoric, such a principle has always been subject to statutory exceptions and it has become increasingly common not only in terrorist offences but across a whole swathe of different types of offences for reverse onuses to be placed on defendants in relation to issues which would otherwise have to be proved by the prosecution.[36] One judicial approach towards reverse onuses has been to defer largely to Parliament on these issues, as it is Parliament, not the courts, which is charged with the primary responsibility for deciding what should be the constituent elements of a criminal offence.[37] But this approach has been questioned as it may lead the court to give too little weight to the presumption of innocence enshrined in Article 6(2) of the ECHR and the obligation imposed on the court by section 3 of the Human Rights Act.[38] It has been suggested that this issue could be resolved more clearly by distinguishing two strands of the proportionality test.[39] The first strand involves considering the policy grounds being pursued when imposing the restriction and deciding whether these are legitimate aims. Here the courts should be slow to question the policy behind the pursuit of a reverse onus. But the second strand, which involves considering whether the imposition of the reverse onus is proportionate to the achievement of the policy goal, is concerned with the procedure adopted to implement the policy, and here the courts have a valid claim to be more vigilant in their scrutiny, founded on their constitutional role to ensure procedural justice and the rule of law. This chimes well with Lord Hope's analysis of the proper role of the courts in *AF*, referred to above.[40]

The second area of uncertainty has concerned how exactly the proportionality test should be approached. In *Brown v Stott* Lord Bingham said that any restriction on an Article 6 right should be no greater than the situation calls for, but he then went on to say that the ECtHR has long recognised the need for a fair balance between the general interest of the community and the personal rights of the individual.[41] This can be regarded as adopting a balancing rather than a strictly proportionate approach to the interests concerned, involving a utilitarian analysis of the rights and public interest in question and giving no significantly greater weight to rights than to security or safety measures.[42] So in *Brown v Stott* itself, which concerned a restriction of the privilege against self-incrimination, a right

[36] Andrew Ashworth and Meredith Blake, 'The Presumption of Innocence in English Criminal Law' [1996] *Crim LR* 314, estimating that approximately 40% of indictable offences regularly prosecuted employ some form of reverse onus. For the use of reverse onuses in terrorist offences, see Walker (n 26).

[37] *R v Johnstone* [2003] UKHL 28, [2003] 2 Cr App R 493, [51] per Lord Nicholls.

[38] *Sheldrake v DPP; Attorney General's Reference (No 4 of 2002)* [2004] UKHL 43, [2005] 1 AC 264, [31] per Lord Bingham.

[39] Ian H Dennis, *The Law of Evidence*, 7th edn (London, Sweet & Maxwell, 2020) 465.

[40] See the text at n 28.

[41] *Brown* (n 32) 704, citing *Sporrong v Sweden* (n 34), paras [52]–[53] and *Sheffield v UK* (1998) 5 BHRC 83, para 52.

[42] See Benjamin Goold, Liora Lazarus and Gabriel Swiney, *Public Protection, Proportionality and the Search for Balance* (London, Ministry of Justice, 2007) 2.

recognised by the ECtHR as lying at the heart of the notion of a fair procedure under Article 6,[43] the Privy Council held that legislation requiring an individual to identify the person who had been driving his or her car was compatible with the ECHR on the ground that it was not a disproportionate response to the problem of maintaining road safety.

This does not mean that the courts have invariably held that restrictions in the public interest are proportionate. In relation to reverse onuses, the courts have been wary of simply accepting that reverse onuses are necessary on the ground that there is a strong public interest in combatting serious crime such as terrorism, drug dealing and organised crime, and in certain cases they have used section 3 of the Human Rights Act to read down such onuses to impose a mere evidential burden on defendants.[44] In one such case Lord Bingham declared that security concerns do not absolve Member States from their duty to ensure that basic standards of fairness are observed.[45] But there have been other cases involving serious offences with high penalties where the reverse onus has been upheld.[46] According to Dennis, it ought to be the case that the more serious the offence, the more compelling should be the justification for a reverse onus but the application of such a principle has been 'patchy' to say the least.[47] Uncertainty as to how reverse onuses should be construed led him to conclude that the case law resembles a forensic lottery and the underlying principles at stake remain unclear.[48]

Critics have pointed out that the broad balancing approach adopted by the ECtHR and the UK courts can be contrasted with the stricter approach taken in Germany, where the Federal Constitutional Court has frequently invoked the important idea of the 'core' of the right when considering whether Articles of the Basic Law relating to a fair trial have been violated.[49] A strict proportionality requirement would strike a proper balance between the purpose of any restriction of the right and the individual right in question. Dennis has argued that there are both epistemic and non-epistemic dimensions of an Article 6 right that need to be considered before any restriction for the achievement of a legitimate aim is justified.[50] Restrictions must not be such as to diminish the likelihood of achieving the correct verdict. So, for example, the presumption of innocence has a vital epistemic dimension in requiring the prosecution to prove the truth of its allegation

[43] *Saunders v UK* (1997) 23 EHRR 313, para 68.

[44] See Andrew Ashworth, 'Four Threats to the Presumption of Innocence' (2006) 10 *International Journal of Evidence and Proof* 241.

[45] *Sheldrake v DPP* (n 38) [21].

[46] *R v Johnstone* (n 37).

[47] Dennis (n 39) 470.

[48] ibid 473–74.

[49] See Goold, Lazarus and Swiney (n 42) 33. For further discussion of approaches to the notion of proportionality in criminal justice matters, see Emmanouil Billis, Nandor Knust and Jon Petter Rui (eds), *Proportionality in Crime Control and Criminal Justice* (Oxford, Hart Publishing, 2021).

[50] Ian Dennis, 'The Human Rights Act and the Law of Criminal Evidence' (2011) 33 *Sydney Law Review* 333, 348–49.

that the defendant committed the offence charged. But the presumption also has non-epistemic functions as it gives effect to a person's moral and political claim to fair treatment by the state, which requires that it treats its citizens as law abiding until it proves otherwise. Similar non-epistemic arguments pertaining to the relationship between the state and the individual may be made in relation to the privilege against self-incrimination.[51] It can be argued that at its core the privilege expresses the principle that if accused persons are to be treated as if they are innocent until proved guilty they should not be required or expected to actively assist the state in proving guilt.

While the core of these rights hinges upon the accused's non-participation in the criminal process, the core of the right to examine witnesses provided in Article 6(3)(d) of the ECHR hinges upon the accused's right to participate positively in the proceedings. A somewhat different calibration comes into play here as the interests of witnesses have to be taken into account as well as those of the accused and the state. Witnesses subjected to cross-examination are entitled to fair treatment as well as the accused.[52] But when the government introduced legislation under section 41 of the Youth Justice and Criminal Evidence Act 1999 severely restricting the ability of defendants to examine complainants about their sexual history and potentially preventing an accused putting forward relevant evidence which might be central to the defence, the House of Lords unanimously held in *R v A (No 2)*[53] that it was possible under section 3 of the Human Rights Act to read the section as subject to an implied provision that evidence which is required to ensure a fair trial should not be treated as inadmissible. Although reading in such a requirement was a dramatic departure from the ordinary language of the statute, the decision can be seen as an expression of the vital epistemic need for defendants to, as Lord Steyn put it, 'put forward a full and complete defence by advancing truly probative material'.[54] A similar need to give priority to epistemic considerations underlay the decision in *R v Davis*[55] some years later, when the House of Lords unanimously held that anonymous witness orders made to protect the identity of witnesses who claimed the defendant had been involved in a fatal shooting had deprived him of a fair trial as they had clearly handicapped the defence's cross-examination, which depended upon investigating the witnesses' motives for giving what was alleged to be a lying conspiratorial account.

In *Davis* the House of Lords placed particular emphasis on the long-established common law principle that the accused should be confronted by his or her accusers in order that the accused may cross-examine them and challenge

[51] See Owusu-Bempah (n 5) 84–87. See also Mike Redmayne, 'Rethinking the Privilege Against Self-Incrimination' (2007) 27 *OJLS* 209.

[52] See Ian Dennis, 'The Right to Confront Witnesses: Meanings, Myths and Human Rights' [2010] *Crim LR* 255.

[53] *R v A (No 2)* [2001] UKHL 25, [2002] 1 AC 45.

[54] ibid [45].

[55] *R v Davis* [2008] UKHL 36, [2008] 1 AC 1128.

their evidence. But a number of their Lordships also referred to a line of Strasbourg authorities to the effect that no conviction should be based solely or to a decisive extent upon the statements or testimony of anonymous witnesses.[56] The ECtHR had developed a similar 'sole or decisive' rule in relation to the use of hearsay statements, but one year after *Davis* a bench of seven judges in *R v Horncastle*[57] in the newly constituted Supreme Court unanimously held that no such limitation should be placed on hearsay statements and also questioned whether any such limitation should apply to the use of anonymous evidence. What seemed to explain this apparent *volte face* was that in contrast to *Davis*, where there were no counter-balancing safeguards to protect the accused from being convicted upon anonymous statements, in *Horncastle* the accused had been protected by a carefully 'crafted code' in the Criminal Justice Act 2003 governing the admission of hearsay, with safeguards to give protection from the risk of an unsafe conviction.[58] Lord Phillips, who gave the leading judgment, made the telling criticism that the ECtHR had formulated the sole or decisive rule without discussion of the principle underlying it or full consideration of whether there was justification for imposing the rule as an overriding principle applicable equally to continental and common law jurisdictions.[59] But their Lordships' dismissal of the rule can itself be criticised for failing to give full consideration to the rationale for it. The Court's objection was that the 'sole or decisive' rule made no allowance for the fact that sole or decisive hearsay statements of unavailable witnesses could be perfectly reliable and their exclusion risked acquitting guilty defendants; however, this gave insufficient attention to the fact that fairness cannot be understood as being synonymous with reliability and a fair verdict is more than simply a reliable verdict.[60]

This is not to say that there should not be limits to the right to examine witnesses. But arguably non-epistemic requirements again need to be built into the proportionality analysis as well as epistemic ones. It can be argued that the value of defence participation in a criminal trial extends beyond simply fair treatment for the accused. The legitimacy of the criminal trial and the verdict that results from it turn upon the prosecution and defence being able to operate within a position of institutional equality so that the public can be properly assured of the trier of fact's impartiality.[61] The more a case rests upon the inculpatory evidence of a witness whom the state authorities have been able to question, the more important it is that the defence is given an opportunity to counteract such evidence by

[56] See the judgments of Lord Reed at [25], Lord Carswell at [59] and Lord Mance at [89].

[57] *R v Horncastle* [2009] UKSC 14, [2010] 2 AC 373.

[58] ibid [36].

[59] ibid [14].

[60] Laura Hoyano, 'What is Balanced on the Scales of Justice? In Search of the Essence of the Right to a Fair Trial' [2014] *Crim LR* 4.

[61] See John D Jackson and Sarah J Summers, 'Seeking Core Fair Trial Standards across National Boundaries: Judicial Impartiality, the Prosecutorial Role and the Right to Counsel' in Jackson and Summers (n 3) 99, 106–7.

also questioning the witness. Although Lord Kerr was a member of the Supreme Court in *Horncastle* (and defended the decision extra-judicially),[62] in *Home Office v Tariq*[63] he emphasised the importance of equality of arms in the different context of a claim of unlawful discrimination, where the respondent argued that Article 6 required *AF*-type gisting. Giving the sole dissenting speech in favour of the respondent, he said that if the respondent were denied the essence of the case against him as a result of the majority decision, then one party would have exclusive access to the judgment seat and the system of justice could not fail to be tainted in consequence.[64]

To conclude this section on the way in which the highest courts have approached the fair trial criminal standards in Article 6, we have seen that they have been willing to use the tool given under the Human Rights Act to read the standards into their interpretation of legislation and have done so even when such an interpretation departs from its clear terms where they have considered it necessary to do so. The criticism that can be made, however, is that there has been a failure to articulate fully the underlying significance of these standards and this has tended to skew the proportionality exercise that has to be carried out when restrictions have been placed upon them. The following section will consider how the courts have reacted to claims that the standards themselves need to evolve to keep pace with criminal justice developments.

Keeping up with Evolving Standards

One of the dramatic changes that has taken place over the last 40 years has been the increasing use of pre-trial and post-trial procedures to affect outcomes that have far-reaching consequences for individuals and the need therefore to ensure that they operate fairly. As regards pre-trial procedures, we have seen that there has been a shift in favour of encouraging suspects to cooperate with the authorities from the beginning of a police investigation. One important safeguard for suspects in such an environment is the right to have access to legal advice when they are questioned by the police. When such a right was enacted under section 58 of the Police and Criminal Evidence Act 1984 (PACE), the Court of Appeal hailed it as 'one of the most important and fundamental rights of a citizen'.[65] But the code of practice governing the questioning of terrorist suspects in Northern Ireland originally made no reference to suspects having a right to have a solicitor present

[62] Lord Kerr, 'The Conversation between Strasbourg and National Courts – Dialogue or Dictation?' (2009) 44 *Irish Jurist* 1.

[63] *Home Office v Tariq* [2011] UKSC 35, [2012] 1 AC 452.

[64] ibid [110].

[65] *R v Samuel* [1988] QB 615, 630.

when they were questioned, even when legislation was enacted permitting courts in certain circumstances to draw inferences from an accused's silence under police questioning.[66] In *Murray v UK* the ECtHR considered that in a situation where the applicant was faced with the possible consequences of inferences being drawn from silence, it was of 'paramount importance' that the applicant had access to a lawyer at the initial stages of police questioning.[67] But a question that did not have to be decided in *Murray* – as the applicant was denied *any* access to legal advice up to 48 hours from his detention – was whether terrorist suspects should also be allowed to have a solicitor present during police questioning. In *R v Chief Constable of the Royal Ulster Constabulary, ex parte Begley and Williams*,[68] the House of Lords refused to recognise such a right on the ground that it was impermissible to develop the law in a direction that was contrary to the expressed will of Parliament, which was what the House was being asked to do. While it is fair to acknowledge that in this pre-Human Rights Act era there were limits to what could be achieved by the judiciary in developing the law when they had to operate within a system of parliamentary sovereignty,[69] the decision was criticised on the ground that it failed to recognise the changed context in which questioning was taking place after the curtailment of the right of silence.[70]

After the passage of the Human Rights Act the senior judiciary seemed prepared to take a more dynamic approach towards evolving standards, particularly when the ECtHR had already pointed the way forward. In *Salduz v Turkey*[71] the ECtHR issued its landmark Grand Chamber judgment that the suspect's right to a fair trial under Article 6 of the ECHR requires that access to a lawyer should be provided when suspects are first questioned by the police. This went beyond *Murray* by recognising that suspects required the protection of access to a lawyer in *every* case when they are questioned by the police, as any evidence obtained during this stage determines the framework in which the offence charged will be considered at trial. Although PACE legislation in England and Northern Ireland made provision for a right of access to a lawyer from when suspects were first questioned, there was no such right in Scots law, which permitted suspects to be questioned for six hours without access to a lawyer.[72] In *Cadder v HM Advocate*[73] the Supreme Court unanimously endorsed *Salduz* and rejected the Scottish system. Lord Hope observed that *Salduz* had been followed repeatedly in subsequent cases

[66] See Criminal Evidence (NI) Order 1988, SI 1988/1987 (NI 20).

[67] *Murray v UK* (1996) 22 EHRR 29, para 66.

[68] *R v Chief Constable of the Royal Ulster Constabulary, ex parte Begley and Williams* [1997] 4 All ER 833.

[69] See Brice Dickson, 'The House of Lords and the Northern Ireland Conflict – A Sequel' (2006) 69 *MLR* 383, 386.

[70] Sean Doran and John Jackson, *All ER Annual Review 1997* (London, Butterworths, 1998) 218–19.

[71] *Salduz v Turkey* (2009) 49 EHRR 19.

[72] Criminal Justice (Scotland) Act 1980, s 2.

[73] *Cadder v HM Advocate* [2010] UKSC 43, [2010] 1 WLR 2601.

in the ECtHR and that the majority of those Member States which prior to *Salduz* did not afford a right to legal representation at interview were now recognising that their legal systems should do so.[74]

While the Supreme Court's recognition of the need to follow a 'clear and constant' jurisprudence of the ECtHR hastened the need to keep up with Strasbourg's development of fair trial standards, it posed a question that has never been altogether satisfactorily resolved, which is whether the Court should be free to develop evolving standards *further* than Strasbourg has gone. In *R (Ullah) v Special Adjudicator*,[75] Lord Bingham declared that the duty of national courts is to keep pace with the Strasbourg jurisprudence as it evolves over time: 'no more, but certainly no less'. This cautious approach was reflected in post-*Cadder* jurisprudence.[76] Thus in *Ambrose v Harris*[77] the accused was questioned at the roadside by police and, although cautioned that he need not reply to questions, made admissions without legal advice about driving when he was under the influence of alcohol. The majority judgment engaged in an extensive review of the Strasbourg authorities to reach the conclusion that it would be to go further than Strasbourg had gone to hold that his right of access had been breached. In the majority's view, the ECtHR had not said, or at least had not said with sufficient clarity, that a person who has become a suspect and is not in custody must as a rule have access to a lawyer.[78] The same kind of reasoning was used in *McGowan* v *B*[79] to reject the argument that any valid waiver of the *Salduz* right required the suspect first to receive legal advice before deciding whether to exercise the right. According to the Justices, there was no rule to this effect that had been identified by the Strasbourg Court. The task of the Court was primarily, by examination of Strasbourg jurisprudence, to identify as best it could the requirements which the Strasbourg Court had set for waivers to be effective.[80]

In his dissenting judgments in both these cases, however, Lord Kerr challenged this cautious approach. In his view, the domestic court could not simply wait until Strasbourg had pointed the way. The domestic court had a duty not only to ascertain where the jurisprudence of the Strasbourg Court clearly shows that it currently stands but to resolve the question of whether the claim to a Convention right is viable, even where the Strasbourg jurisprudence has not yet disclosed a clear view:[81] 'If the much vaunted dialogue between national courts and Strasbourg is

[74] ibid [47]–[49].
[75] *R (Ullah) v Special Adjudicator* [2004] UKHL 26, [2004] 2 AC 323, [20]. See also *R (Al-Skeini) v Secretary of State for Defence* [2007] UKHL 26, [2008] 1 AC 153, [106] per Lord Brown.
[76] See Robin M White and Pamela Ferguson, 'Sins of the Father: The "Sons of Cadder"' [2012] *Crim LR* 357.
[77] *Ambrose v Harris* [2011] UKSC 43, [2011] 1 WLR 2435.
[78] ibid [64] per Lord Hope. See also [82] per Lord Brown, [95] per Lord Dyson.
[79] *McGowan* v *B* [2011] UKSC 54, [2011] 1 WLR 3121.
[80] ibid [5] per Lord Hope, [78] per Lord Hamilton.
[81] *Ambrose* (n 77) [129].

to mean anything, we should surely not feel inhibited from saying what we believe Strasbourg ought to find in relation to those arguments.'[82]

The '*Ullah*-type reticence' to go beyond Strasbourg, as Lord Kerr called it,[83] has not been reflected to the same extent when it has come to evolving standards of fairness in parole procedures established to determine whether prisoners should be released. The Grand Chamber decision of the ECtHR in *Stafford v UK*[84] provided the momentum for the landmark ruling in the House of Lords case of *R v Secretary of State for the Home Department, ex parte Anderson*[85] that decisions about the actual term of imprisonment to be served by convicted murderers sentenced to mandatory life imprisonment should be made by independent courts or tribunals and not by the Secretary of State for the Home Department, a member of the executive. In the later decision in *R (Smith) v Parole Board; R (West) v Parole Board*[86] the House of Lords held that under Article 5(4) of the ECHR prisoners had a right to have their detention reviewed by a judicial body when a new situation arose, as it did in cases where their licences were revoked and they were recalled to prison. But the House relied on the common law requirements of procedural fairness when it decided how such a body should conduct its proceedings. As Lord Hope put it, the introduction of human rights into domestic law required a minimum standard of human rights protection but it did not restrict any other right or freedom and this is where the common law was able to step in and impose those conditions of procedural fairness that it requires of a court.[87] The House of Lords held that while the common law duty of procedural fairness did not require the Parole Board to hold an oral hearing in every case where prisoners were seeking release after recall, they should have the benefit of a procedure which fairly reflects the importance of what is at stake for them. Given that the liberty of the prisoner is a matter on which there is much at stake, the ruling gave a more expansive interpretation of what procedural fairness required than had been considered necessary in previous rulings.[88]

In *R (Osborn) v Parole Board*[89] the Supreme Court further shifted the balance in favour of oral hearings when it held that in order to comply with common law standards of fairness, the Parole Board should hold an oral hearing before determining the application of *any* prisoner seeking release whenever fairness to the prisoner requires such a hearing in the light of the facts of the case and the importance of what is at stake. Giving the judgment of the Court, Lord Reed considered

[82] ibid [130].

[83] ibid.

[84] *Stafford v UK* (2002) 35 EHRR 32.

[85] *R v Secretary of State for the Home Dept, ex parte Anderson* [2002] UKHL 46, [2003] 1 AC 837.

[86] *R (Smith) v Parole Board; R (West) v Parole Board* [2005] UKHL 1, [2005] 1 WLR 350.

[87] ibid [74].

[88] John Jackson, 'Human Rights, Criminal Justice and the Future of the Common Law' (2006) 57 *NILQ* 352, 360–1.

[89] *R (Osborn) v Parole Board* [2013] UKSC 61, [2014] AC 1115.

that the purpose of holding an oral hearing is not only to assist the Parole Board in its decision making, but also to reflect the prisoner's legitimate interest in being able to participate in a decision with important implications for him, where he has something useful to contribute.[90] This proved to be a significant decision in a number of respects. First, it led to a profound change in the willingness of the Parole Board and the Northern Ireland Parole Commissioners to hold oral hearings. Second, more broadly, it re-set the relationship between the ECtHR and the domestic courts on the question as to who should have the ultimate responsibility for setting fair trial standards. Lord Reed stated that the Convention could not be treated as if it were 'Moses and the prophets'; on the contrary, the ECtHR had often referred to the 'fundamentally subsidiary role of the Convention'.[91] The Human Rights Act gave domestic effect to the guarantees described as Convention rights but it did not supersede the protection of human rights under the common law or statute, or create a discrete body of law based upon the judgments of the ECtHR. Thirdly, Lord Reed's judgment set out in clear terms that the purpose of a fair hearing is not just to reach the right decision; it has at least two further values, namely to avoid a sense of injustice which the person who is the subject of the decision will otherwise feel, and to uphold the rule of law.[92] The reference to these values was a welcome retreat from the position that fairness is only necessary to ensure correct decision making.

Conclusion

Three observations can be made about the approach that senior judges have taken towards the right to a fair trial in the criminal justice system from this retrospective overview of leading decisions. First, against the background of government attempts to limit fair trial rights, the highest courts have not been slow to use the powerful interpretative tool that was given to them by the Human Rights Act to read legislation in a manner that has reinforced fundamental fair trial processes such as the right to challenge the case against oneself, and fair trial rights long associated with the criminal trial such as the presumption of innocence. The requirement to take account of the judgments of the ECtHR has encouraged the domestic courts to safeguard the rights of the defendant in the criminal process and to keep up with evolving standards where a clear and constant jurisprudence has emerged from the ECtHR. All of this contrasts with the pre-Human Rights Act era, where there was a tendency for the Law Lords to feel constrained from developing fair trial rights by the need to defer to the will of Parliament.

Second, however, there was a tendency when the Human Rights Act came into force to let the ECtHR take the lead on the approach to be taken when governments

[90] ibid [2].
[91] ibid [56].
[92] ibid [68].

restricted fair trial rights. It has been argued that this encouraged an insufficiently rigorous approach when determining to what extent restrictions may justifiably be placed upon fair trial rights. Strasbourg also took the lead in developing the scope of evolving rights such as the right of access to a lawyer when suspects are questioned by the police.

The third observation is that in the last decade there are signs that the UK's highest court is treating the development of fair trial rights as primarily a matter for domestic law. Lord Kerr was one of the judges who took the lead in deprecating '*Ullah*-type reticence' which had the effect of inhibiting the courts from giving full effect to Convention rights. In *Osborn* Lord Reed gave full expression to the view that just because an issue falls within the ambit of a Convention right, the legal analysis of the problem should begin and end with Strasbourg case law. Dickson has argued that one of the unintended consequences of the Human Rights Act has been a growing reluctance to use the common law to achieve the same goals as the Act.[93] As noted above, a number of the fair trial rights have strong roots in the common law and, notwithstanding the passage of the Human Rights Act, judges did on occasions use the common law to justify their reasoning. In *Osborn*, however, a shift of emphasis seemed to take place in favour of basing decisions on the common law. Lord Reed cited a number of post-Human Rights Act authorities where the common law provided the basis for the decision, including *Smith and West*, and then went on to decide the cases in *Osborn* on this basis. This was a welcome recognition of the fact that as fair trial rights are rooted in domestic law, they can be regarded as already domesticated and can be developed on this basis.

This chapter began by alluding to the immense changes that have taken place in criminal justice in recent decades and, with a Royal Commission on Criminal Justice promised in the 2019 Conservative manifesto, there is likely to be no waning in the pace of change. Whether the Human Rights Act will survive as a powerful interpretative tool for the courts in applying fair trial standards is impossible to say. What will remain unchanged will be the continuing need for the courts to safeguard and develop fair trial standards as circumstances change to ensure a proper balance of power in the criminal process between the state and the individual.

[93] Dickson (n 4) 34.

16

A Dialogue on Discrimination and Equality: The UK Supreme Court and Article 14 of the ECHR

RORY O'CONNELL*

This chapter examines how UK courts – especially the Supreme Court and earlier the House of Lords – have interpreted and applied Article 14 of the European Convention on Human Rights (ECHR), the non-discrimination provision. UK courts have developed an extensive case law on Article 14. They have considered questions about the rights of same sex partners to succeed to housing rights and the rights of unmarried partners to receive pensions; they have also considered discrimination in relation to sentencing and detention regimes; and they have decided discrimination cases in the context of high policy on national security and social and economic matters. This extensive case law has facilitated a healthy dialogue with the European Court of Human Rights (ECtHR) in Strasbourg as to the scope and application of the right to non-discrimination.

The chapter focuses on two themes. First, there is the dialogue between the UK courts and the ECtHR. UK judges have sometimes commented on the complexity of the non-discrimination case law[1] and have made 'heavy weather' of some aspects.[2] Despite this, the dialogue has been productive, in that it has produced more detailed understanding of several aspects of the non-discrimination right. Second, there is the debate about different notions of formal and substantive equality. Article 14 might be inapt to address serious structural disadvantage. Colm O'Cinneide highlights the stark contrast between the proclamations of equality in UK law and the reality of endemic fatal inequality as manifest in the Grenfell fire.[3]

* I am grateful to Dr Shauna Page, Professor Brice Dickson and Dr Conor McCormick for feedback on drafts of this chapter.

[1] *R (DA) v Secretary of State for Work and Pensions* [2019] UKSC 21, [2019] 1 WLR 3289 (*Second Benefit Cap case*), [20] where Lord Wilson referred to the 'unnecessarily cumbersome and complicated' judicial discussions in the benefit cap cases.

[2] *Siobhan McLaughlin's Application for Judicial Review* [2018] UKSC 48, [2018] 1 WLR 4250, [20] per Lady Hale.

[3] Colm O'Cinneide, 'Grenfell and the Limited Reach of Equality within the UK Constitutional Order' (2019) 5(2) *Queen Mary Human Rights Law Review.*

One response might be to develop Article 14 to promote more substantive models of equality. Meghan Campbell, Sandra Fredman and Aaron Reeves, for instance, argue for a model of equality that is:

> multidimensional, simultaneously redressing disadvantage; addressing stigma, stereotyping prejudice and violence; facilitating participation; and accommodating difference and the need for structural change.[4]

Arguments for substantive equality have found favour, at least on occasion, with courts in South Africa[5] and Canada.[6] The Article 14 jurisprudence has often been more formalist, though more substantive readings are possible.[7] Recently these have included arguments that the ECtHR attaches importance to the vulnerability of groups and the menace of stereotyping.[8]

This chapter sets out the terms of Article 14 and the four elements of the Article 14 inquiry used by UK courts. It then examines how the case law has addressed each of those elements. The chapter concludes with comments on the dialogue between UK courts and Strasbourg and on what the Article 14 case law reveals about the opportunity for a more substantive approach to equality.

As might be expected, Lord Kerr has made important contributions to the Article 14 case law, writing unanimous judgments in *Steinfeld*[9] and *Brewster*,[10] as well as authoring notable dissents, including a radical argument for an exception to the UK's dualist approach to international treaties for human rights conventions.[11]

[4] Meghan Campbell, Sandra Fredman and Aaron Reeves, 'Palliation or Protection: How Should the Right to Equality Inform the Government's Response to Covid-19?' (2020) 20 *International Journal of Discrimination and the Law* 183; see also Sandra Fredman, 'Substantive Equality Revisited' (2016) 14 *International Journal of Constitutional Law* 712; Meghan Campbell, 'The Austerity of Lone Motherhood: Discrimination Law and Benefit Reform' (2021) *Oxford Journal of Legal Studies* 1.

[5] Anne Smith, 'Equality Constitutional Adjudication in South Africa' (2014) 14 *African Human Rights Law Journal* 609; Catherine Albertyn, 'Contested Substantive Equality in the South African Constitution: Beyond Social Inclusion Towards Systemic Justice' (2018) 34 *South African Journal on Human Rights* 441.

[6] Jena McGill and Daphne Gilbert, 'Of Promise and Peril: The Court and Equality Rights' (2017) 78 *Supreme Court Law Review* 235; Ruth Rubio Marin, *Gender in the History of Global Constitutionalism and the Construction of Women's Citizenship* (Cambridge, CUP, forthcoming) ch 3.

[7] Rory O'Connell, 'Cinderella Comes to the Ball: Article 14 and the Right to Non-discrimination in the ECHR' (2009) 29 *Legal Studies* 211; Sandra Fredman, 'Emerging from the Shadows: Substantive Equality and Article 14 of the European Convention on Human Rights' (2016) *Human Rights Law Review* 273; Charilaos Nikolaidis, *The Right to Equality in European Human Rights Law: The Quest for Substance in the Jurisprudence of the European Courts* (Abingdon, Routledge, 2015).

[8] Alexandra Timmer, 'Toward an Anti-Stereotyping Approach for the European Court of Human Rights' (2011) 11 *Human Rights Law Review* 707; Alexandra Timmer and Lourdes Peroni, 'Vulnerable Groups: The Promise of an Emerging Concept in European Human Rights Convention Law' (2013) 11 *International Journal of Constitutional Law* 1056; Oddný Arnardóttir, 'Vulnerability under Article 14 of the European Convention on Human Rights' (2017) 4 *Oslo Law Review* 150.

[9] *R (Steinfeld and Keidan) v Secretary of State for International Development* [2018] UKSC 32, [2020] AC 1.

[10] *In the matter of an application by Denise Brewster for Judicial Review* [2017] UKSC 8, [2017] 1 WLR 519.

[11] *R (SG) v Secretary of State for Work and Pensions* [2015] UKSC 16, [2015] 1 WLR 1449 (*First Benefit Cap case*), [254]. In *R (SC, CB and 8 children) v Secretary of State for Work and Pensions* [2021] UKSC 26 (*the SC case*) [74]–[96], the Supreme Court held that the courts had no role in determining whether the UK had breached obligations in an unincorporated international treaty.

Article 14 of the ECHR

Article 14 is the non-discrimination clause in the ECHR. The English text reads:

> The enjoyment of the rights and freedoms set forth in this Convention shall be secured without discrimination on any ground such as sex, race, colour, language, religion, political or other opinion, national or social origin, association with a national minority, property, birth or other status.

The equally authoritative French text differs in some respects:

> La jouissance des droits et libertés reconnus dans la présente Convention doit être assurée, sans distinction aucune, fondée notamment sur le sexe, la race, la couleur, la langue, la religion, les opinions politiques ou toutes autres opinions, l'origine nationale ou sociale, l'appartenance à une minorité nationale, la fortune, la naissance ou toute autre situation.

Note that Article 14 is not a free-standing non-discrimination guarantee; rather, it is accessory to or parasitic on the other Convention rights. As such it applies only within the 'ambit' or 'scope' of the other Convention rights. In this way it is different from Article 26 of the International Covenant on Civil and Political Rights (ICCPR) or Protocol 12 to the ECHR (P12). P12 provides for a free-standing non-discrimination right; it applies to 'any right set forth by law' and prohibits discrimination by 'any public authority'. The UK has not ratified P12.

The French text of Article 14 differs from the English in specifying that the enjoyment of the Convention rights must be assured without any 'distinction' whereas the English text says 'discrimination'. Article 14 has a list of prohibited grounds of discrimination (or distinction) drawn from Article 2 of the Universal Declaration of Human Rights 1948. The list includes sex, race, colour, religion but also other terms not familiar from UK anti-discrimination laws such as language, political or other opinion, national or social origin, association with a national minority, property and birth. The list of grounds is open-ended ('any ground such as' / 'fondée notamment sur le') and includes 'other status'; the French text is more open, referring to 'toute autre situation'.

Article 14 ECHR does not explicitly include a limitations clause such as those found in Articles 8 to 11 of the ECHR. The ECtHR has ruled that distinctions can be justified if they are for a legitimate reason and are proportionate.[12]

One of the contributions of UK courts to the dialogue on Article 14 has been the structured way they apply the provision. In the *Second Benefit Cap case*, Lady Hale identified four key inquiries:

> In deciding complaints under Article 14, four questions arise: (i) Does the subject matter of the complaint fall within the ambit of one of the substantive Convention rights? (ii) Does the ground upon which the complainants have been treated differently from

[12] *Belgian Linguistic case* (1967) 1 EHRR 252, para 10.

> others constitute a 'status'? (iii) Have they been treated differently from other people not sharing that status who are similarly situated or, alternatively, have they been treated in the same way as other people not sharing that status whose situation is relevantly different from theirs? (iv) Does that difference or similarity in treatment have an objective and reasonable justification, in other words, does it pursue a legitimate aim and do the means employed bear 'a reasonable relationship of proportionality' to the aims sought to be realised (see *Stec v UK* (2006) 43 EHRR 47, para 51)?[13]

These four questions are not always apparent from the ECtHR's own jurisprudence, which sometimes adopts a more 'broad brush' or 'holistic' approach.[14] Nevertheless, they provide a helpful framework and a convenient structure for this chapter. When we come to the objective and reasonable justification element, we will also look at the intensity of the review and the application of the justification test in the UK. But first, the ambit requirement.

Ambit

The case law demonstrates a flexible approach to deciding whether a situation is within the 'ambit' or 'scope' of a Convention right. This does not mean that the other Convention right must have been violated, nor even that there must have been an interference with the other Convention right[15] or an adverse impact on the right.[16] Article 14 can be brought into play where the state, even though it has no obligation to do so, has provided rules to protect specific aspects of the right.[17] So, for instance, there is no obligation for states to create a system of early release from prison, but if they do so then this policy is within the ambit of Article 5 of the ECHR (personal liberty).[18]

UK cases on the ambit requirement have provided an opportunity for the ECtHR to clarify the ambit of the right to property in Article 1 of the First Protocol to the ECHR (P1-1). UK courts, relying on comments in *Gaygusuz*[19] and other cases had suggested that P1-1 applied only to social security payments where these were contribution-based. In *Stec v UK*, the ECtHR convincingly explained that this could not be a sensible limitation on the ambit of P1-1 and that both contributory and non-contributory benefits were within the ambit for the purposes of Article 14.[20]

[13] *Second Benefit Cap case* (n 1) [136].

[14] *R (RJM) v Secretary of State for Work and Pensions* [2008] UKHL 63, [2009] 1 AC 311, [30] per Lord Neuberger.

[15] Lord Wilson rejected a government argument in the *Second Benefit Cap case* that seemed to rest on this, based on Lord Reed's judgment in the *First Benefit Cap case*: *Second Benefit Cap case* (n 1) [36].

[16] *Steinfeld* (n 9) [18] per Lord Kerr.

[17] Described as 'one of the modalities of the exercise of the right guaranteed' in *McLaughlin* (n 2) [17] per Lady Hale.

[18] *R (Clift) v Secretary of State for the Home Dept* [2006] UKHL 54, [2007] 1 AC 484. See also *A and B v Criminal Injuries Compensation Authority* [2021] UKSC 27 [39].

[19] *Gaygusuz v Austria* (1996) 23 EHRR 364.

[20] *Stec v UK* (2005) 41 EHRR SE18 (GC) (admissibility), paras 47–53.

Subsequently the UK courts have applied this approach. In *RJM* the House of Lords considered whether a homeless claimant was entitled to a disability premium. The relevant rules explicitly denied the benefit to the claimant. The House of Lords accepted that homelessness was a status and rejected an argument that it should refuse to follow *Stec* and *Gaygusuz*.[21] In the *Second Benefit Cap case*, the Supreme Court considered the effects of the reduced benefit cap introduced by the Conservative government after the 2015 general election. The case concerned six lone parents – all mothers – and their 12 children. Lord Wilson identified different possible effects of the benefit cap: a family might be forced to move home, for example, or fall behind on rent, or decide to cut back on food or turn off heating; these impacts brought the situation within the ambit of Article 8's right to respect for private and family life.[22]

The ambit requirement, even if flexible, still has some relevance. In the *First Benefit Cap case*, claimants invoked the UN Convention on the Rights of the Child (UNCRC) to assist in an argument that discrimination was unjustified. As the cases concerned P1-1 and not Article 8 the claimants' argument failed, there being no link between the rights of the child and the property rights of the adult claimants.[23] In *McLaughlin*, Lady Hale devoted some attention to establishing that widowed parent's allowance fell within the ambit of both the right to property (P1-1) and the right to respect for private and family life (Article 8).[24] She noted that there was still some uncertainty in the case law about how close a situation had to be to a Convention right to be within its ambit.[25]

Status

Article 14, as we have seen, is open-ended, concluding with the phrase 'or other status'. This section focuses on the definition of 'other status' but some of the listed grounds in Article 14 could also benefit from further scrutiny. Notably there are the references to discrimination based on 'property', 'birth' and 'social origin', which Benito Sánchez suggests could include discrimination on grounds of socio-economic disadvantage or class.[26] In *RJM*, Lord Neuberger suggested 'property' could cover homelessness.[27] Courts have identified different grounds as falling under the heading of 'other status': among others, sexual orientation,[28] being

[21] *RJM* (n 14) [32]–[33] per Lord Neuberger.
[22] *Second Benefit Cap case* (n 1) [37] per Lord Wilson.
[23] *SG* (n 11) [146] per Lord Hughes.
[24] *McLaughlin* (n 2) [16] per Lady Hale.
[25] ibid [22].
[26] Juan Carlos Benito Sánchez, 'Towering Grenfell: Reflections around Socioeconomic Disadvantage in Antidiscrimination Law' (2019) 5(2) *Queen Mary Human Rights Law Review*. See also Mel Cousins, 'The European Convention on Human Rights, Non-discrimination and Social Security: Great Scope, Little Depth?' (2009) *Journal of Social Security Law* 120.
[27] *RJM* (n 14) [44].
[28] *Steinfeld* (n 9) [16], among others.

married or unmarried,[29] residence[30] and disability (including caring for a child with a disability).[31] The term 'other status' could cover socio-economic status, though this has received limited attention in Strasbourg.[32]

While there is a long list of different recognised statuses, it is not certain how status is to be defined. Is it limited, for instance, to grounds similar to those explicitly listed? To 'personal characteristics'? To grounds that are immutable? Or something else? Or does any distinction qualify as a status?

The UK courts have discussed this aspect of Article 14, in some instances limiting Article 14 claims by denying that a status was involved. Sometimes respondents have proposed narrow interpretations of status. In the *Second Benefit Cap case* the Supreme Court rejected the government's argument that a status had to be permanent and accepted that being a lone parent with children under a certain age could be a status.[33] The Court also rejected the even odder argument that because the claimants were women, they could not also claim another status.[34] On some occasions UK courts have taken a narrow approach to the grounds of status. The House of Lords corrected one lower court which rejected a claim by an unmarried couple on the grounds that being unmarried was not a status; if being married constituted a status then so did being unmarried.[35]

The UK courts insist that status must have some meaning.[36] The House of Lords considered this issue at length in *Clift*.[37] Clift was a prisoner serving an 18-year sentence for crimes including attempted murder; under the law at the time prisoners serving fewer than 15 years were freed if the Parole Board recommended release. For those serving more than 15 years, the Secretary of State had to confirm the release. The House of Lords ruled that, even though 'status' should be given a 'generous meaning',[38] being a prisoner serving more than 15 years was not a status in the sense understood in Article 14. The ECtHR disagreed when the case came to Strasbourg: it found that there was a violation of Article 14.[39] In several respects it rejected the efforts of the UK courts to limit Article 14 by defining the concept of status. Subsequent ECtHR cases confirm that 'status' in

[29] *McLaughlin* (n 2) [31] per Lady Hale.

[30] *Carson v UK* (2010) 51 EHRR 13 (GC).

[31] *JD and A v UK*, App Nos 32949/17 and 34614/17, judgment of 24 October 2019, para 82.

[32] Benito Sánchez (n 26) cites *Garib v Netherlands*, where two judges dissented, finding a violation of Art 14 where discrimination was based on socio-economic disadvantage: App No 43494/09, judgment of 6 November 2017 (GC).

[33] *Second Benefit Cap case* (n 1) [38] per Lord Wilson.

[34] ibid [131] per Lady Hale.

[35] *In re G (Adoption: Unmarried Couple)* [2008] UKHL 38, [2009] 1 AC 173 (the case was named *Re P* in the lower courts, which were in Northern Ireland).

[36] *R (Stott) v Secretary of State for Justice* [2018] UKSC 59, [2020] AC 51, [209] per Lady Hale, [228] per Lord Mance.

[37] *Clift* (n 18).

[38] ibid [48] per Lord Hope.

[39] *Clift v UK*, App no 7205/07, judgment of 13 July 2010.

Article 14 should be given a wide meaning and should not be limited to 'innate' or 'inherent' characteristics.[40]

The Supreme Court has recognised the ruling in *Clift* for the most part and applied it in *Stott*.[41] Stott had been convicted of multiple sexual offences including raping an 8-year-old child. He received an extended determinate sentence of 21 years in custody. Being on an extended determinate sentence meant that he was eligible for parole only after serving two-thirds of his sentence, whereas other prisoners were eligible after serving half their sentence. The Divisional Court had been bound by the House of Lords ruling in *Clift* to find that there was no Article 14 status in the *Stott* case. The Supreme Court accepted that Stott could rely on the extended determinate sentence as a status.[42]

While the Supreme Court has largely complied with the *Clift v UK* ruling on status, there is still some scope for disagreement.[43] In *Stott*, Lady Hale defended the proposition that a claimant cannot invoke the specific distinction being made as itself the status for Article 14 purposes; the status must be independent of the distinction.[44] Having said that, she endorsed the view in *Clift v UK* that:

> whether there is a difference of treatment based on a personal or identifiable characteristic in any given case is a matter to be assessed taking into consideration all of the circumstances of the case and bearing in mind that the aim of the Convention is to guarantee not rights that are theoretical or illusory but rights that are practical and effective.[45]

Lord Carnwath dissented on this point, arguing that the UK courts should not follow *Clift v UK*. He questioned the reasoning in *Clift v UK*; he acknowledged the long list of cases where the ECtHR had found violations on grounds that do not resemble the core explicit grounds, but thought the ECtHR judgments disclosed no clear rationale and that the point about status had not been argued in many of them.[46] He noted that *Clift v UK* was a section judgment rather than a Grand Chamber judgment, and that he would need a Grand Chamber judgment and convincing reasons to persuade him to depart from the Law Lords' reasoning in *Clift*.[47] Lord Carnwath was the lone dissenter on that point in *Stott*; he did not refer to the Grand Chamber judgments in *Biao v Denmark* or *Khamtokhu v Russia*, both cited by other judges.[48]

[40] *Biao v Denmark* (2016) 64 EHRR 1 (GC), para 89.

[41] *Stott* (n 36).

[42] ibid [70]–[81] per Lady Black. Lady Black had difficulty with the argument that an Art 14 status had to have an 'independent existence' from the discriminatory treatment. See also [184]–[185] per Lord Hodge.

[43] Gerards regards the ECtHR case law as lacking in consistency and being capable of different readings: Janneke Gerards, 'The Discrimination Grounds of Article 14 of the European Convention on Human Rights' (2013) 13 *Human Rights Law Review* 99.

[44] *Clift* (n 36) [210] per Lady Hale. See also the *SC case* (n 11) [69]–[71]; *A and B* (n 18) [66].

[45] ibid [212] per Lady Hale.

[46] ibid [175].

[47] ibid [179].

[48] See *Biao* (n 40) and *Khamtokhu*, App No 60367/08, judgment of 24 January 2017 (GC).

In the *Second Benefit Cap case*, Lord Carnwath (Lord Reed and Lord Hughes agreeing) accepted that lone parenthood was a status but he was diffident about some of the other ways of classifying the claimants.[49] Lord Hodge (Lord Hughes agreeing) adopted a similar approach. He was willing to accept there was a relevant status in the case but on the broader issue of status he anticipated 'future dialogue with the ECtHR'.[50]

Lord Walker has an insightful paragraph on status in *RJM*, where the House of Lords accepted that homelessness could be a status for the purposes of Article 14.[51] Lord Walker suggested that status should be thought of as a series of concentric circles. The inner circle included the 'innate, largely immutable' characteristics. Next were characteristics that could be acquired but were fundamental to an individual's personality. Further circles included other acquired characteristics. The main point to this analysis was that the nature of the status was relevant to the intensity of the scrutiny required. Distinctions based on grounds such as sex, race or ethnicity, sexual orientation, disability, religion, nationality or birth require very weighty reasons.[52] Other distinctions require some justification, but the standard is much less.

This approach follows from the accessory nature of the Article 14 right. By definition, Article 14 applies only in the enjoyment of fundamental rights. The ECtHR should require justification for any difference in the enjoyment of a Convention right, but the standard of justification is very different depending on the nature of the status, the importance of the effect on the right[53] and the subject matter. Distinctions in the enjoyment of fundamental rights, especially ('notamment') on the listed grounds, require justification. That Article 14 is concerned with non-discrimination in the enjoyment of fundamental rights is precisely why 'if the alleged discrimination falls within the scope of a Convention right, the Court of Human Rights is reluctant to conclude that nevertheless the applicant has no relevant status'.[54] In *Stott* Lord Mance suggests that Article 14 is not about guaranteeing 'complete equality of treatment',[55] but the example he gives relates to private businesses offering services to consumers, not to the state regulating fundamental rights. There should not be room for any 'indefensible anomaly'[56] when the state is regulating Convention rights.

[49] *Second Benefit Cap case* (n 1) [108].
[50] ibid [131]. Lord Hodge would also welcome more guidance from Strasbourg: *Stott* (n 36) at [185].
[51] *RJM* (n 14) [5].
[52] Arnardóttir (n 8) 155.
[53] In *Clift v UK* (n 39), the ECtHR noted the importance of the early release system to the central purpose of Art 5.
[54] *Mathieson v Secretary of State for Work and Pensions* [2015] UKSC 47, [2015] 1 WLR 3250, [22] per Lord Wilson.
[55] *Stott* (n 36) [235] per Lord Mance.
[56] The term is Lord Bingham's in *Clift* (n 18) [33].

Different Treatment or Differential Impact Compared to an Analogous Situation

The original formulations of the four questions in an Article 14 inquiry referred to different treatment.[57] Lady Hale's more recent formulation also addresses indirect discrimination. This reflects the evolution in the ECtHR case law which historically had downplayed indirect discrimination arguments but then recognised their force in the landmark case of *DH v Czech Republic*.[58]

The analogous situation requirement has caused some difficulties. Judges have noted that this is not the same as the 'arid'[59] comparator requirement in domestic anti-discrimination case law.[60] The comparator requirement is based on a formalist notion of equality that does not adequately promote equality.[61] Judges, when they get involved in reviewing the analogous situation requirement, often fall into the traps inherent in formalist approaches to equality. Formalist approaches are based on the Aristotelian principle that like cases must be treated alike and different cases differently in proportion to their difference.[62] The problem is that it is always possible to identify both similarities and differences between any two situations.[63] The disagreement between the majority and the dissent in *McLaughlin* demonstrates this. Is the survivor of an unmarried couple in an analogous situation to the survivor of a married couple (or a couple in a civil partnership) in respect of widowed parent's allowance? The majority thought yes, because she was left to care for the children of the relationship. Lord Hodge, in dissent, thought no.[64]

It can be complicated to decide who is the appropriate person in the analogous situation. In the *Second Benefit Cap case*, Lord Wilson identified three possible comparators.[65] He pointed out that the claimants could claim that they were being treated differently from others in a similar position and at the same time being treated in an identical way to others in a relevantly different position.[66]

In *Stott*, the comparison between prisoners sentenced to different types of punishment was not straightforward as each sentencing regime had different properties. In some ways, prisoners receiving an extended determinate sentence were worse off but in other ways they were arguably better off; for instance, a prisoner

[57] See, eg, *McLaughlin* (n 2) [15] per Lady Hale.
[58] *DH v Czech Republic* (2008) 47 EHRR 3 (GC).
[59] *Hurley v Secretary of State for Work and Pensions* [2015] EWHC 3382 (Admin), [59] per Collins J.
[60] *McLaughlin* (n 2) [24] per Lady Hale.
[61] Sandra Fredman, *Introduction to Discrimination Law* (Oxford, OUP, 2002) 96–102.
[62] The dissent of Judges Pejchal and Wojtyczek in *JD and A v UK* (n 31), refers to the Aristotelian underpinnings of the Art 14 case law.
[63] Peter Westen, 'The Empty Idea of Equality' (1982) 95 *Harvard Law Review* 537.
[64] *McLaughlin* (n 2) [73]–[80] per Lord Hodge.
[65] *Second Benefit Cap case* (n 1) [46] per Lord Wilson.
[66] ibid [42]–[43] per Lord Wilson.

sentenced to life could be released but would remain on licence for the rest of his or her life.[67] Lady Black elided the discussion on analogous situations and justification, while Lord Hodge thought there were differences in the situations of the different types of prisoners. The discussion in *Stott* demonstrates that the analogous situation discussion can be complicated but also illustrates a fundamental problem with the formal equality approach: it is not logical to say that because the situation is different it is therefore acceptable to inflict less favourable treatment on the claimant. That requires something more – namely, justification.

Unsurprisingly therefore, the analogous situation discussion elides into the justification discussion[68] and judges suggest that if there is no obvious answer to the analogous situation query then it is best to turn to justification.[69] If there is a justification, after all, there is no unlawful discrimination. Furthermore, a fundamental relevant difference might provide the justification. More radically, Dickson suggests the analogous grounds inquiry is otiose in light of the justification requirement.[70] Considering the complications and the tendency to fall into the trap of formal equality, there is much to be said for this position. The Supreme Court of Canada's substantive equality jurisprudence, for instance, does without such a requirement and steers away from the 'treating like cases alike' model of formal equality.[71]

Objective and Reasonable Justification

The fourth question on Article 14 of the ECHR refers to the justification test. According to the ECtHR, 'discrimination means treating differently, without objective and reasonable justification, persons in relevantly similar situations.'[72] The ECtHR approach to discrimination and proportionality means that justification is often the most substantive part of any discrimination inquiry. Justification requires a legitimate aim and a 'reasonable relationship of proportionality'.[73] As UK judges have noted, the ECtHR approach is helpful in clarifying that there is no concept of 'justified discrimination'; that is to say, 'justification negatives the very existence of discrimination'.[74] UK judges have been generally clear that it is the

[67] *Stott* (n 36) [147] per Lady Black.

[68] Lady Black commented that the ECtHR sometimes moves 'almost seamlessly' between the status, analogous ground and justification discussions: *Stott* (n 36) [43]. Later, she also moves from discussion of the analogous situations point to a more integrated discussion of that and justification at [137]. See also Lord Hodge at [200].

[69] *Stott* (n 36) [148] per Lady Black, [213]–[214] per Lady Hale. See too *McLaughlin* (n 2) [26] per Lady Hale.

[70] Brice Dickson, '*Stott*, Status and Stare Decisis' (2019) 70 *Northern Ireland Legal Quarterly* 283, 286.

[71] *R v Kapp* 2008 SCC 41, 294 DLR (4th) 1, [15]–[22].

[72] *DH* (n 58) para 175.

[73] *Carson* (n 30) para 61.

[74] *Second Benefit Cap case* (n 1) [48] per Lord Wilson.

distinction or the difference in treatment that has to be justified, rather than the overarching policy at issue.[75] In indirect discrimination cases the focus is slightly different; there the measure, not the discriminatory impact, must be justified.[76]

UK judges have specified four different parts of the justification inquiry. There must be a legitimate aim; the distinction must be rationally related to (or appropriate to) the legitimate aim; it must be the least intrusive way to achieve the aim; and there must be a fair balance between the different interests in play.[77] However, before we look at the justification test, we need to consider the preliminary question of just how intense the scrutiny should be when considering justification.

Intensity of Review

The question of the intensity of the review is crucial in proportionality or justification inquiries. The intensity of the review depends on several factors: the ground of discrimination in play, the importance of the right and the subject matter.

In principle, UK judges do not directly apply the ECtHR's margin of appreciation.[78] Lord Kerr offered robust guidance on this in *Steinfeld.* The case concerned the anomalous situation that arose following the recognition of same-sex marriage whereby persons in same-sex relationships could choose to become married or to become civil partners, but opposite-sex couples could not choose to become civil partners. While the respondent emphasised the margin of appreciation Strasbourg had shown in this area, Lord Kerr rejected this approach:

> It follows that a national court must confront the interference with a Convention right and decide whether the justification claimed for it has been made out. It cannot avoid that obligation by reference to a margin of appreciation to be allowed the government or Parliament (at least not in the sense that the expression has been used by the ECtHR). The court may, of course, decide that a measure of latitude should be permitted in appropriate cases.[79]

As the last sentence indicates, even if the UK judges do not apply the margin of appreciation, they recognise that some matters are more appropriately the concern of the legislature or executive. That the ECtHR regards some matters as within the margin of appreciation allows the domestic courts to decide how to approach those questions domestically, but they could decide to follow the ECtHR lead.[80]

[75] ibid [53] per Lord Wilson.

[76] ibid [134] per Lady Hale.

[77] ibid [61] per Lord Wilson; *R (Tigere) v Secretary of State for Business, Innovation and Skills* [2015] UKSC 57, [2015] 1 WLR 3820, [33] per Lady Hale.

[78] *In re Recovery of Medical Costs for Asbestos Disease (Wales) Bill* [2015] UKSC 3, [2015] AC 1016, [54]; *McLaughlin* (n 2) [34] per Lady Hale.

[79] *Steinfeld* (n 9) [29] per Lord Kerr. See also Lady Hale (ch 2).

[80] *Second Benefit Cap case* (n 1) [118] per Lord Carnwath, Lord Reed and Lord Hughes agreeing; [125] per Lord Hodge, Lord Hughes agreeing.

The case law sometimes provides conflicting principles on this question.[81] On the one hand, social and economic policies are for the government and the legislature.[82] At the same time, the courts have a role to play when human rights and especially equality rights are involved:

> In a constitution which respects and protects fundamental rights, it is the role of the courts to protect individuals from unjustified discrimination in the enjoyment of those fundamental rights. There are no 'no go' areas.[83]

This tension is also evident in *Stott*, where Lady Black and Lord Hodge refer to the wide margin of appreciation given to the legislature in matters of sentencing policy, while at the same time recognising that in some cases courts need to exercise close scrutiny.[84]

The approach to the level of scrutiny will depend on how the executive or the legislature has considered a particular issue. In *Steinfeld*, for instance, Lord Kerr reviewed the Strasbourg cases where a margin of appreciation had been recognised in relation to matters of equal marriage, but he concluded that they were very different from the situation where Parliament, in the Marriage (Same Sex Couples) Act 2013, had deliberately created a new distinction.[85]

In the Northern Ireland cases on same sex marriage, the Court of Appeal drew attention to the way in which the Northern Ireland Assembly had most recently rejected a proposal to legislate for same sex marriage. The majority of the Assembly had supported same sex marriage, but the motion was defeated because a petition of concern had triggered the requirement for cross-community support.[86] This meant that even though a majority of the Assembly supported the proposal, it had failed because it did not get 60 per cent support nor the support of sufficient numbers of unionists. In this circumstance the Court of Appeal held that greater scrutiny was called for, when a petition of concern had thwarted the will of the Assembly on a matter concerning sexual orientation.[87]

One aspect of the intensity of review issue deserves closer attention, which is the 'manifestly without reasonable foundations' (MWRF) approach. This term originates in *James v UK*[88] and was adopted by the ECtHR in *Stec* for the Article 14

[81] For instance, when dealing with sex discrimination in social rights cases: Mark Simpson, Gráinne McKeever and Ann Marie Gray, *Social Security Systems Based on Dignity and Respect* (London, Equality and Human Rights Commission, 2017) 32.

[82] *Second Benefit Cap case* (n 1) [133] per Lady Hale.

[83] ibid.

[84] In *Stott* (n 36) [153], Lady Black accepted that because Strasbourg would apply a margin of appreciation in relation to prisoners and penal status, the domestic courts should 'respect the policy choices of Parliament in relation to sentencing'. See also Lord Hodge at [198]. In light of other comments on the margin of appreciation this needed rather more discussion; an argument could be made for sentencing policy as falling within the judges' area of expertise.

[85] *Steinfeld* (n 9) [36].

[86] Assembly rules provide that 30 Members of the Legislative Assembly can require a vote to be taken on a cross-community basis.

[87] *Close's Application for Judicial Review* [2020] NICA 20, [54].

[88] *James v UK* (1986) 8 EHRR 123.

inquiry there.[89] The UK courts have now applied it, not without controversy, in social security cases. In *Humphreys*, Lady Hale wrote that the normal requirement for weighty reasons to justify sex discrimination 'gives way' in the area of state benefits, but this did not mean that distinctions in this area should escape 'careful scrutiny'.[90] In the *Bedroom Tax case*, the Supreme Court affirmed that the MWRF test was the right one to apply when faced with 'a question of economic and social policy, integral to the structure of the welfare benefit system'.[91]

While a deferential test, the MWRF test does not mean distinctions in social security always survive scrutiny.[92] In the *Bedroom Tax case*, the Supreme Court found there was no reasonable justification for a policy that accorded an exception for a carer of an adult but not of a child, nor where there was an exception for a child whose disability meant they could not share a bedroom but no such exception for an adult.[93] The Supreme Court did reject the claims of most of the claimants and we will return to some of them later when looking at the ECtHR case of *JD and A v UK*.[94]

In the *Second Benefit Cap case* the Supreme Court discussed the MWRF test at length, and whether it applied to all the elements of the justification test. Lord Wilson noted how some judicial comments suggested that the MWRF test applied to only the first three elements of the justification inquiry but not to the final, fair balance element.[95] He then repudiated his own earlier comments to that effect and ruled that the MWRF test should apply to all four parts of the justification test.[96] Lord Carnwath explicitly rejected the efforts of the dissenters to cast doubt on this.[97] The dissenters (Lady Hale and Lord Kerr) were open to supporting the differentiated approach, noting it was not clear that Strasbourg applied the MWRF test to all parts of the justification inquiry.[98]

The risk with the MWRF approach is that it has the potential to 'effectively nullify the potential of using' Article 14 to challenge the allocation of resources.[99] The MWRF test does not apply to all areas of state decision-making, and it rests on an uncertain legal foundation. The Court of Appeal of Northern Ireland has

[89] *Stec v United Kingdom* (2006) 43 EHRR 47 (GC) (merits) at para 52.

[90] *Humphreys v Commissioners for Her Majesty's Revenue and Customs* [2012] UKSC 18, [2012] 1 WLR 1545, [22] per Lady Hale.

[91] *R (MA) v Secretary of State for Work and Pensions* [2016] UKSC 58, [2016] 1 WLR 4550 (*Bedroom Tax case*), [36] per Lord Toulson; Lords Neuberger, Mance, Sumption and Hughes agreed with this judgment. See also Lady Hale (ch 2).

[92] Collins J has suggested that close scrutiny is especially appropriate when the claimants are vulnerable and the legislature has not specifically considered their situation: *Hurley* (n 59) [69].

[93] *Bedroom Tax case* (n 91) [46] per Lord Toulson.

[94] *JD and A v UK* (n 31).

[95] *Second Benefit Cap case* (n 1) [61]–[65].

[96] ibid [65] per Lord Wilson. Lord Carnwath (Lord Reed and Lord Hughes agreeing) reaffirmed this at [110]. Lord Hodge (Lord Hughes agreeing) also confirmed this at [125].

[97] ibid [117]–[118].

[98] ibid [148] per Lady Hale, [176] per Lord Kerr. See also Lady Hale (ch 2).

[99] O'Cinneide (n 3) 13.

rejected an argument by the Attorney General of Northern Ireland that the MWRF approach applies outside the social security context. In *Close*,[100] the Attorney argued that that the MWRF test should apply to the Northern Ireland Assembly's refusal to legislate for same sex marriage. The Court of Appeal rejected this – the MWRF test was developed in a long line of social security cases and could not be applied to this different problem.

The MWRF test does not rest on as secure a basis as is assumed. The UK cases frequently cite the *Stec* case and Lady Hale's judgment in *Humphreys* on the MWRF test. Cited much less often, however, is a portion of Lady Hale's judgment where she notes specific features of the *Stec* and *Runkee* judgments.[101] In this passage she draws attention to the fact that those cases concerned historic attempts to address economic disadvantage of women in the workplace and consequently in pension arrangements. It is understandable that courts should tread lightly when legislatures are trying to address systemic widespread and pervasive disadvantage affecting women and subsequently trying to reform pension and social security systems to address the changing nature of employment. In *Humphreys* the claimant was a man who argued that the policy of not splitting child tax benefit but rather paying it to the primary carer was indirectly discriminatory against men. This was undoubtedly the case, and so the court understandably applied the deferential MWRF test. The arguments for a deferential approach in that situation do not apply when the legislature or executive adopts a policy that reinforces the vulnerability of people who have been historically disadvantaged.[102] The MWRF test was also referred to by the Grand Chamber in the *Carson* case,[103] but this concerned discrimination on grounds of residence and age; unlike grounds like race or sex, distinctions based on residence and age do not require weighty reasons for justification.

In *JD and A v UK*, the ECtHR confirmed this narrower reading of the MWRF test. The Court noted that while it had accorded a wide margin of appreciation in relation to P1-1 standing alone, where the state was considering 'general measures of economic or social strategy'[104] a different approach was required when there was an allegation of discrimination. The ECtHR ruled that a wide margin of appreciation could not justify discrimination and specifically limited the MWRF test to circumstances where 'an alleged difference in treatment resulted from a transitional measure forming part of a scheme carried out in order to correct an inequality'.[105]

[100] *Close* (n 87) [44].

[101] *Humphreys* (n 90) [19] and [22], referring to *Runkee v UK*, App No 42949/98, judgment of 10 May 2007, [2007] 2 Family Court Reporter 178.

[102] Vulnerability here refers to socially constructed patterns of disadvantage, not to an essentialist understanding: Timmer and Peroni (n 8); Arnardóttir (n 8).

[103] *Carson* (n 30) para 33.

[104] *JD and A* (n 31) para 87.

[105] ibid para 88.

The Supreme Court in the recent *SC* case has reviewed the *JD* case somewhat critically; while finding some of the ECtHR's reasoning unconvincing the Supreme Court has agreed there is no mechanical rule that domestic decisions should be respected unless manifestly without reasonable foundation, and that very weighty reasons are required to justify distinctions based on sex.[106] The Supreme Court criticised some of the language of Lady Hale in *Humphreys* where she referred to the MWRF test, and highlighted her invocation of the need for 'careful scrutiny' as being more consistent with the more nuanced Strasbourg jurisprudence.[107] Instead of being a test, the courts should treat the phrase 'manifestly without reasonable foundation' as indicating there is a wide margin of appreciation.[108]

The Justification Test

Having considered the question of the intensity of review, this section discusses the four different elements of the justification test considered in UK cases. These elements are not always differentiated in practice.

It is normally straightforward for the state to articulate a legitimate aim and for this to be accepted as legitimate by the courts. In the *Second Benefit Cap case* the respondent identified three aims for the benefit cap: to improve the fairness of the system and the public's confidence in its fairness; to make savings; and to incentivise non-working parents to work.[109] Legitimate aims in *Stott* included public protection and maintaining public confidence in the sentencing framework, though Strasbourg had expressed some doubt on the latter aim.[110] The promotion of marriage and now civil partnership has also been held to be a legitimate aim.[111]

While it is normally straightforward, sometimes state authorities struggle to identify a legitimate aim. In *Brewster*, the claimant sought a survivor's pension in a statutory occupational pension scheme. She had not been married to her partner and the regulations required unmarried persons to complete a nomination form to designate a beneficiary; the beneficiary further had to prove cohabitation. This nomination requirement had been copied from regulations in England and Wales and was retained even when the regulations in England and Wales had dropped it. The respondent offered a post hoc justification for the requirement imposed on unmarried couples. According to Lord Kerr, a post hoc justification required closer scrutiny.[112]

[106] *SC case* (n 11) [142].
[107] ibid [151]–[153], [158].
[108] ibid [160].
[109] *Second Benefit Cap case* (n 1) [7] per Lord Wilson.
[110] *Stott* (n 36) [152] per Lady Black.
[111] *McLaughlin* (n 2) [36] per Lady Hale.
[112] *Brewster* (n 10) [50], [61]–[62], [64].

While the courts, both in Strasbourg and in the UK, have generally accepted the existence of a legitimate aim, this has not always been the case. In *Steinfeld* the respondent argued that the legitimate aim was the need for time to figure out how to resolve the anomaly created by the 2013 Act whereby opposite sex couples could not avail of civil partnerships. Lord Kerr denied this could be a legitimate aim, distinguishing it from cases where legislatures needed time because a distinction had historically been thought to be justified but was no longer justified.[113]

If there is a legitimate aim, the next question is whether the distinction is rationally related (or appropriate) to the distinction. While the rational connection test might seem straightforward, judges can differ significantly on this. The *Second Benefit Cap case* furnishes an example. The majority accepted that the revised benefit cap was justified, but Lady Hale concluded it was barely rational: it could not achieve fairness between those in and outside of work, nor could it make any significant savings.[114] In *Steinfeld* Lord Kerr thought the distinction introduced by the 2013 Act did not satisfy any of the four elements of the justification test, and noted that there had been several less intrusive means open to Parliament in 2013 rather than the choice to introduce a new distinction into the law. Also, in *Brewster*, Lord Kerr considered that the requirement of a nomination did not have a rational connection to the purported legitimate aim and failed the less intrusive means and fair balance parts of the test.[115]

To legislate requires making distinctions, and both European and UK judges recognise this. There is no requirement for individualised judgments to be made in every situation where the state makes a distinction. But the existence of bright-line rules alongside individualised assessments may create problems. Lady Hale dissented in *Stott* partly because of this. In *Stott* prisoners serving extended determinate sentences had to serve two-thirds of their sentence before being considered for parole. This was different from other prisoners, including those serving life sentences. Lady Hale accepted that the protection of the public was a legitimate aim, but the differential policy was not a proportionate way of achieving it as prisoners in Stott's situation still had to satisfy a Parole Board as to their suitability for release. That existing individualised procedure rendered the distinction unnecessary.[116]

The degree of rationality expected in the MWRF test is not always clear. In the *Second Benefit Cap case*, the judges disagreed on the application of the justification test. The majority accepted the cap was justified under the MWRF test, with several majority judges uncomfortable with the role of evaluating the evidence before them.[117] On the other hand, Lady Hale found that the weight of the

[113] *Steinfeld* (n 9) [46] per Lord Kerr.
[114] *Second Benefit Cap case* (n 1) [153].
[115] *Brewster* (n 10) [67].
[116] *Stott* (n 36) [220] per Lady Hale. See also Lord Mance's dissent at [246].
[117] *Second Benefit Cap case* (n 1) [91] per Lord Wilson, [123] per Lord Carnwath, Lord Reed and Lords Hughes agreeing.

evidence suggested the risk of real harms to lone parents and their children, while the benefits were largely minimal or speculative.[118] Lord Kerr also found there to be a lack of proportionality, although his analysis also suggests the policy lacked rationality: he rejected the argument about incentivising parents to work since that was not really a viable option.[119] It does seem odd that the Supreme Court regarded as rational the application of the reduced benefit cap to lone parents with young children even though government policy recognised that it was difficult and undesirable for lone parents of young children to work.[120]

Even when dealing with payments in the social security system, the courts do sometimes find violations. In *McLaughlin* Lady Hale (with three judges agreeing) found that there was no proportionality shown in a policy of denying widowed parent's allowance to the unmarried survivor of a relationship.[121] Indeed, she seemed to doubt that the distinction satisfied the rationality requirement.

As noted above, in *JD and A v UK* the ECtHR clarified that the MWRF test does not necessarily apply in social security cases. The ECtHR applied a higher degree of scrutiny to the situation of two of the claimants than the majority of the Supreme Court had done in the *Bedroom Tax case*.[122] The ECtHR accepted that the application of the restriction to the first applicant was justified: she and her severely disabled daughter lived in specially adjusted accommodation but did not have a need for an extra bedroom. However, the ECtHR reached this conclusion on the basis that discretionary housing benefit, along with legal protections in the Human Rights Act 1998 and Equality Act 2010, provided sufficient justification.[123] This was a somewhat more robust standard than in the majority judgments of the Supreme Court. The ECtHR found that there was unjustified discrimination in respect of the second applicant, who was living in her specially adapted house under the Sanctuary Scheme. The purpose of the Sanctuary Scheme was to enable people to remain in their own homes. The purpose of the housing benefit reduction was to incentivise people to leave their homes. These aims were contradictory and there was no explanation as to why the latter aim predominated, especially in the context of the state's positive obligations to protect people from unlawful violence.[124]

Conclusions

The Article 14 case law demonstrates a healthy and respectful dialogue between UK courts and the ECtHR. UK courts have sometimes gone beyond the ECtHR; at

[118] ibid [156].
[119] ibid [190].
[120] This was part of the claimants' argument: ibid [51] per Lord Wilson.
[121] *McLaughlin* (n 2) [39] per Lady Hale.
[122] *Bedroom Tax case* (n 91).
[123] *JD and A* (n 31) para 102.
[124] ibid paras 104–105.

other times the ECtHR has found a violation where the domestic courts have not. In this interplay the key concepts in Article 14 have been clarified.

When UK courts have gone further than the ECtHR this reflects the fact that the domestic courts are national authorities and so the margin of appreciation does not apply to them in the way that it applies to an international court with a jurisdiction spanning 47 states. In particular, the domestic courts have gone further than Strasbourg in finding violations based on marital status and in finding, in Northern Ireland, that the refusal to recognise same sex marriage breaches the Convention.

At the same time, the ECtHR has found Article 14 violations where the domestic courts did not. This was notably the case in *Stec*, *Clift* and, more recently, *JD and A*. For the most part the domestic courts have accepted the ECtHR jurisprudence in *Stec* and *Clift*. There is still some diffidence in relation to the ruling in *Clift*, with some UK judges saying that the dialogue on the meaning of 'status' continues.

More importantly though, the extensive discussion in these cases has enabled the Supreme Court and the ECtHR to clarify the nature of the obligations in Article 14. The *Stec* case may be the clearest and most important example of this. The dialogue continues and several of the recent Supreme Court cases discussed in this chapter are under consideration in Strasbourg, notably *Stott*[125] and the *Second Benefit Cap case*.[126]

As noted at the beginning of this chapter, there is a risk that the Article 14 case law may be inadequate to deal with serious structural inequality which disadvantages particular groups. While UK judges have been willing to go beyond Strasbourg in cases focusing on matters of status inequality (direct discrimination on sexual orientation or marital status), they have been extremely deferential when matters of economic inequality come before them.[127] The Article 14 case law is not toothless, but judges could develop it to give greater protection to the most vulnerable, drawing on some of the more assertive Strasbourg case law and academic writing on substantive equality.[128]

The MWRF test needs reconsideration in the light of the ECtHR ruling in *JD and A v UK*; indeed, the Supreme Court has already indicated a more nuanced approach is required (*SC case*). As suggested above, the UK courts adopted the MWRF test too readily as the test appropriate for social security cases. The courts have at least made clear that it should not be adopted for all cases involving social policy.[129] Within the social security sphere the test has been adopted on the basis of the *Stec* and *Runkee* judgments without giving due weight to the fact that those

[125] *Stott v UK*, App No 26104/19.

[126] *DA and RA v UK*, App No 46692/19. There is also a case on the different levels of childcare provided to working parents and non-working parents: *LT v UK*, App No 8786/20.

[127] On the interconnection between status inequalities and economic inequalities see Campbell, Fredman and Reeves (n 4) 190, and Campbell (n 4).

[128] See also Kathryn McNeilly (ch 3).

[129] *In re G* (n 35); *Close* (n 87).

cases involved very special circumstances, specifically the historic attempts of the legislature to address the de facto sex inequalities concerning employment and the vulnerabilities created for women as a consequence. This is a very different circumstance from policies that deliberately inflict hardship on groups of people, predominantly women. That the adult claimants in the *Second Benefit Cap case* were all women and lone parents should have triggered more anxious scrutiny; the sex discrimination argument had been addressed in the *First Benefit Cap case*, but received less attention in the *Second Benefit Cap case*.[130] In the *Second Benefit Cap case* Lord Wilson accepted that it was likely the benefit cap reduced 'a family well below the poverty line';[131] this 'planned misery'[132] should trigger more anxious scrutiny rather than the MWRF approach.

In applying this more anxious scrutiny, judges need also to pay attention to the context in which the claimants find themselves, and the risk of being exposed to stigmatisation and deprivation. Judges could more consistently describe and attach importance to the specific contexts in which claimants experience inequality. They could give closer attention to the ways in which people are disadvantaged, made vulnerable and suffer hardship.[133] Some judges – Collins J[134] and Lady Hale – have done this. Lady Hale, for example, in her dissent in the *Second Benefit Cap case*, depicted the difficult challenges facing lone parents of young children. The claimants faced the challenges of how best to provide for the material and psychological needs of their children while the support that would enable them to do so – 'good, stable and consistent alternative care arrangements' – were in 'short supply and very expensive'.[135] Campbell, Fredman and Reeves highlight the cruel absurdity of capping benefits to incentivise people to find work during the Covid-19 pandemic.[136] Campbell highlights that the social security cases involving lone mothers tend to focus on the economic discrimination aspect and so downplay other types of harm such as gender stereotyping including negative stereotypes about lone mothers.[137] The recent *SC case* continues this trend.[138]

[130] Lord Carnwath suggested at [114], [122] that the claimants in the *Second Benefit Cap case* were groups 'more distant' from the core groups such as sex. See Campbell, Fredman and Reeves (n 4) above at 193.

[131] *McLaughlin* (n 1) [33] per Lord Wilson.

[132] Susan Marks, 'Human Rights and Root Causes' (2011) 74 *MLR* 57, 59.

[133] According to O'Cinneide (n 3) 13, the dominant model of equality in the UK 'assumes individual self-sufficiency and participative capacity to be the default norm rather than something that (for so many people) has to be generated, supported and maintained by proactive state intervention'.

[134] In *Hurley* (n 59).

[135] *Second Benefit Cap case* (n 1) [144]. See also Kathryn McNeilly (ch 3).

[136] Campbell, Fredman and Reeves (n 4) above at 189. See also Gráinne McKeever (ch 7).

[137] Campbell (n 4).

[138] The judgment identifies some harms, that the children could not have birthday parties in commercial venues or attend summer clubs: *SC case* (n 11) [12], [33]. The Supreme Court judgment omits mentioning that one of the adult claimants had long term health conditions, that the second adult claimant had been in an abusive relationship, and that the children could not get their choice of food: *R (SC, CB and 8 children) v Secretary of State for Work and Pensions* [2019] EWCA Civ 615, [2019] 1 WLR 5687, [13]–[14].

The courts have applied aspects of Article 14 with some degree of flexibility, in particular the ambit requirement and the status requirement. In so doing the principle of non-discrimination can be deployed across different spheres of activity and to groups not envisaged in the text of the 1950 Convention. There is at least some awareness that the analogous situation element of the approach is problematic. The recognition that some types of distinction call for weighty reasons is welcome and important. At the same time, the courts have not fundamentally moved from a formal understanding of equality to embrace a substantive conception that challenges structural discrimination and the harms it inflicts on particular groups. For Article 14 not to be a fairy tale, UK and European judges need to adopt a contextual analysis that identifies the specific ways in which people are made vulnerable and how structural factors contribute to hardship.

17

The Next Chapter: Siblings after Adoption

SARAH HANSEN

Introduction

This chapter considers post-adoption contact between siblings who are adopted from public care.[1] There is a particularity about the sibling relationship in part because of its potential longevity, spanning the lifetime of the parties, but in addition because it is a relationship which children themselves often see as important.[2] A further, latent reason why sibling relationships may give rise to different considerations from those relating to contact arrangements for adults is the lack of culpability or responsibility for the position the siblings find themselves in when separated by adoption.[3] While sibling relationships have a role in the decision about whether a child should be adopted at all, the interaction between rights and welfare in the adoption decision itself have been eloquently and insightfully elucidated and debated elsewhere.[4] Here the focus is on the rights and welfare considerations arising when decisions are being made about relationships between siblings after adoption has been determined for a child. The aim is to prompt deeper examination of a subject which may seem small when it sits in the shadow of the overall adoption decision but which is anything but small in the lives of those affected.

[1] Contact after adoption can take many forms and has many names. Here the term 'direct contact' will be used to refer to face-to-face meetings between an adopted child and a birth relative and 'indirect contact' will be used as an umbrella term to encompass all contact which is not face-to-face, which may include the provision of information, photographs, letters, phone calls etc. Indirect contact may or may not involve the adopted child directly.

[2] Caroline Boyle, 'What is the Impact of Birth Family Contact on Children in Adoption and Long-Term Foster Care? A Systematic Review' (2017) *Child & Family Social Work* 22, 28.

[3] See also, in relation to adults and culpability, Andrew Bainham, 'Swimming Against the Tide: Challenging Contact Arrangements in Public Law Proceedings' [2015] *Family Law* 1356, 1364; Brid Featherstone, Anna Gupta and Sue Mills, *The Role of the Social Worker in Adoption – Ethics and Human Rights: An Enquiry* (London, BASW, 2018) 12.

[4] See, eg, Samantha M Davey, *A Failure of Proportion: Non-Consensual Adoption in England and Wales* (Oxford, Hart Publishing, 2020) and Judith Pepper, 'Siblings in Care Proceedings: Together and Apart' [2020] *Family Law* 1333.

Research on Post-Adoption Contact and the Statutory Framework for Decisions

Research Findings on Post-Adoption Contact

The move towards adoption being more 'open' arose from research into the impact of 'relinquishment' adoptions, particularly the identity issues experienced by children who were raised without knowledge of their adoptive origins.[5] Since then, research has moved on to look at the benefits and difficulties of post-adoption contact in the context of adoption from public care.[6] While the research methodologies, contexts and participants differ and the general adage of family law that 'every case is different' applies, Neil has helpfully summarised some of the key messages from the extensive research which she, and others, have carried out.[7] The benefits, in broad terms, of post-adoption contact for adopted children are that it may assist with feelings of loss or rejection and contribute to a family environment in which the adoption can be discussed. For adopters it may be a source of information, while for birth relatives the benefit may be to help them through the feelings of grief and loss experienced. All involved can find the contact emotionally straining and therefore Neil suggests that contact plans should be individualised, taking into account both the risk of harm or potential harm through contact and the potential benefits of contact in each case.[8]

Maintaining sibling contact has in the past been feared as something which might put prospective adopters off – a sweeping and perhaps unfair assumption about prospective adopters.[9] In a number of studies into direct post-adoption contact, there have been adopters who expressed support for continuing sibling contact and recognised the benefits of it, even when that contact was not straightforward.[10] It may be that recruitment for such studies necessarily screens

[5] John Triseliotis, *In Search of Origins: The Experiences of Adopted People* (London, Routledge & Kegan Paul, 1973).

[6] See, generally, John Triseliotis, 'Maintaining the Links in Adoption' (1991) *The British Journal of Social Work* 21, 401; Carole Smith and Janette Logan, *After Adoption: Direct Contact and Relationships* (London, Routledge, 2004); Elsbeth Neil, Mary Beek and Emma Ward, *Contact After Adoption: A Longitudinal Study of Post-Adoption Contact Arrangements* (London, CoramBAAF, 2015); Mandi MacDonald, *Connecting or Disconnecting? Adoptive Parents' Experiences of Post Adoption Contact and their Support Needs* (Belfast, Health and Social Care Board NI, 2017); Sarah Meakings, Amanda Coffey and Katherine Shelton, 'The Influence of Adoption on Sibling Relationships: Experiences and Support Needs of Newly Formed Adoptive Families' (2017) 47 *The British Journal of Social Work* 1781.

[7] Elsbeth Neil, 'Rethinking Adoption and Birth Family Contact: Is There a Role for the Law?' [2018] *Family Law* 1178.

[8] ibid.

[9] Bainham (n 3) 1361; see also Christine Jones, Mandi MacDonald and Rebecca Brooks, *Post-Adoption Contact and Adoptive Parents' Receptiveness to Direct Contact in the Four Nations of the UK* (University of Strathclyde, 2020) 3.

[10] See, eg, Smith and Logan (n 6) 150, where 33 of the 34 children in the subsample who had post-adoption contact with siblings were satisfied with it; Meakings, Coffey and Shelton (n 6) 1793;

out those who may feel less favourably disposed towards the maintenance of contact but certainly it does not support a general proposition that adopters are against it; indeed quite the opposite.

Notwithstanding a commitment to achieving it, research findings show that direct contact with siblings is not without its difficulties. These include the concerns adoptive parents have about sensitive information passing between siblings, particularly if one half of the sibling relationship retains contact with other birth relatives.[11] Another difficulty is that the carers for different siblings may have differing views on what is best for the children and the complex networks of relationships may lead to practical difficulties in making arrangements for contact.[12] The relationships can be changeable in nature, described as having an ebb and flow to them, with different siblings wanting or needing different things from their sibling relationships across their childhood and with their age, stage and personal characteristics contributing to what they may benefit from in terms of a relationship.[13] The intensity of the relationship sought may be changeable but a key finding from research studies is that children themselves value the relationships they have with siblings.[14]

The increased focus from research studies on openness in adoption, in particular for siblings, has been reflected in practice guidance, which suggests that siblings who are not placed together should have contact where it is in their best interests.[15] There is also international recognition of the importance of the sibling relationship for children who are not in the care of their parents.[16] Practitioners and the judiciary are alert to and concerned by the potential loss of sibling relationships following adoption.[17] There are no UK-wide statistics on the levels of contact occurring after adoption between siblings. It is possible to get an idea of the levels of contact from studies that have been carried out, but it is not always clear from such studies what the reasons are for a lack of contact between some children and their siblings. In the Wales Adoption Study, 87 per cent of the 374 children whose records were considered had at least one sibling. There were 256 case records for children placed

Julie Doughty, Sarah Meakings and Katherine Shelton, 'Rights and Relationships of Children Who Are Adopted from Care' (2019) 33 *International Journal of Law, Policy and The Family* 1, 18.

[11] Jeanette Cossar and Elsbeth Neil, 'Making Sense of Siblings: Connections and Severances in Post-Adoption Contact' (2013) 18 *Child & Family Social Work* 67, 72.

[12] ibid.

[13] Christine Jones, 'Sibling Relationships in Adoptive and Fostering Families: A Review of the International Research Literature' (2016) 30 *Children & Society* 324, 329 see also Meakings, Coffey and Shelton (n 6) 1796.

[14] Smith and Logan (n 6) ch 8; June Thoburn, 'The Risks and Rewards of Adoption for Children in the Public Care' [2003] *Child and Family Law Quarterly* 391, 397.

[15] Department for Education, *Adoption: National Minimum Standards* (2014) para 8.2.

[16] UN General Assembly, 'United Nations Guidelines for Alternative Care of Children' 24 February 2010 (reissued 13 April 2010) Res 64/142, para 17, though note this refers to siblings for whom there is an existing bond.

[17] Daniel Monk and Jan Macvarish, *Siblings, Contact and the Law: An Overlooked Relationship* (London, Birkbeck, 2018); Andrew McFarlane, 'Holding the Risk: The Balance Between Child Protection and the Right to Family Life' [2017] *Family Law* 610, 615.

for adoption who had at least one sibling who was not with them in their adoption placement. Of those children, sibling contact was planned for 70 per cent of them but only 21 per cent had plans for direct contact.[18] In another study which considered contact between siblings while in public care and moving towards permanent placement, the numbers of siblings having contact significantly reduced over time despite practice advice and government guidance encouraging contact.[19] Of those children who do have direct contact after adoption, a recent study suggests it is predominantly happening with siblings rather than other relatives.[20] Overall, it is hard to get a full picture of what is happening with sibling contact across the UK and why, and this is an area where improved central statistics might assist.

The Statutory Framework for Post-Adoption Contact

In England and Wales, a placement order may be made upon application to the court; it places a child for adoption and allows the parental responsibility of the child's parents to be restricted.[21] This can be followed by an application for an adoption order by the prospective adoptive parent or parents which, if granted, extinguishes the parental responsibility of the biological parents.[22] At the making of a placement order, the court may make an order for contact with a specified individual, either upon an application or on its own initiative.[23] At the making of the adoption order and at any time thereafter, the court upon an application has the power to make an order for post-adoption contact with an individual. While it can make an order to *prevent* contact on its own initiative it cannot make an order *for* contact without an application.[24]

In Scotland, a child's route from public care to adoption is likely to be via a 'permanence order', with authority granted to place the child for adoption and thereby extinguish the parental rights of the birth parents.[25] Thereafter an adoption order may be sought by the adopters and this can contain any conditions that a court sees fit, including a condition for post-adoption contact.[26] After an adoption order has been made, an application by a parent whose parental rights have been

[18] Doughty, Meakings and Shelton (n 10) 16. See also Cossar and Neil (n 11) 71: in a sample of 45 children separated from birth siblings, 19 had contact with all their siblings, 20 with some and 6 with none.

[19] Christine Jones, Gillian Henderson and Ruth Woods, 'Relative Strangers: Sibling Estrangements Experienced by Children in Out-of-Home Care and Moving Towards Permanence' (2019) 103 *Children and Youth Services Review* 226, 232–33.

[20] Jones, MacDonald and Brooks (n 9) 3.

[21] Adoption and Children Act 2002 (hereafter 'ACA 2002' or 'the 2002 Act'), ss 21 and 25.

[22] ACA 2002, ss 46–51.

[23] ACA 2002, s 26.

[24] ACA 2002, ss 51A and 51B. See generally Brian Sloan, 'Post-Adoption Contact Reform: Compounding the State-Ordered Termination of Parenthood?' (2014) 73 *CLJ* 378.

[25] Adoption and Children (Scotland) Act 2007, ss 80–87.

[26] ibid, s 28, see generally *AB v LM* [2019] SAC (Civ) 19, [2019] Fam LR 60.

extinguished by adoption requires leave of the court.[27] Recent amendments confirm that contact orders can also be made in favour of a child for contact with another.[28]

In Northern Ireland, where the process of 'freeing' for adoption remains, an application to free a child for adoption has the effect of extinguishing the parental responsibility of the parents and a further application for an adoption order must be made to transfer parental responsibility permanently to the adoptive parent or parents.[29] The court has the power at both the freeing order and the adoption order stages to make an order for contact under the Children (NI) Order 1995 or, at the point of an adoption order, to make the adoption order itself conditional.[30] The proposed Adoption and Children (NI) Bill, on which there were consultations in 2017 and which may imminently be debated by the Northern Ireland Assembly, would bring the adoption process closer to that in England and Wales should it be enacted.

In each of the three UK jurisdictions, contact falls to be considered at each stage of the adoption process and the courts have the power to give contact a legal form, even if the form itself varies. Despite the similarity of the powers and mechanisms for achieving contact, as far as can be ascertained, the numbers of children having contact with birth family members after adoption varies by jurisdiction.[31] The way in which these powers have operated in practice will be revisited at the end of this chapter, but mechanisms exist within the legal framework for post-adoption contact between siblings.

Siblings Separated by Adoption – How are Decisions About Post Adoption Contact Made?

The simple answer is that the welfare considerations set out within legislation should guide decisions on whether contact with a sibling will be in a child's best interests.[32] The relevant legislative provisions are broadly drafted to allow the vast array of possible factual circumstances to be included in the decision-making. Such a welfare analysis may be assisted by social work assessments.[33]

[27] Children (Scotland) Act 1995, s 11.
[28] Children (Scotland) Act 2020, s 15.
[29] Adoption (NI) Order 1987, arts 16, 18, 17(3) and 12.
[30] Children (NI) Order 1995, arts 10, 8 and 8(4)(e); Adoption (NI) Order 1987, art 12(6). See also *Re NI and NS* [2001] NIFam 7 and *Re J (Freeing without consent)* [2002] NIFam 8. Northern Ireland retains the term 'contact order' rather than 'child arrangements order'.
[31] Jones, MacDonald and Brooks (n 9) 2.
[32] ACA 2002, s 1 in England and Wales; Adoption and Children (Scotland) Act 2007, s 14 in Scotland; Children (NI) Order 1995, art 3 in Northern Ireland.
[33] An assessment which may be made with the assistance of research-based frameworks such as Elsbeth Neil and David Howe, 'Conclusions: a transactional model for thinking about contact' in Elsbeth Neil and David Howe (eds), *Contact in Adoption and Permanent Foster Care: Research, Theory and Practice*, (London, BAAF, 2004). See generally Shelagh Beckett, *Beyond Together or Apart: Planning for Assessing and Placing Sibling Groups* (London, BAAF, 2021).

However, a number of issues arise. As Doughty and others aptly note, without balancing the rights of those involved you cannot assume you have properly assessed the welfare of the child.[34] Additionally, the child to whom the proceedings relate, often referred to as the 'subject child', is not the only child with an interest; the rights of the sibling also raise legitimate issues. What follows is an attempt to map out the types of rights issues which arise and which courts ought to grapple with and balance explicitly.[35] These include rights under the European Convention on Human Rights (ECHR) and the United National Convention on the Rights of the Child (UNCRC) for the subject child and the mirror rights for non-subject children, as well as, for both sets of children, the general public law principles which apply to decision making – in particular, the duty to give reasons for a decision.

The Rights of the 'Subject Child'

Where close personal ties exist between siblings they will attract, prior to adoption, the protections of Article 8 of the ECHR: the right to respect for private and family life.[36] These include a positive obligation to allow the relationship to be developed, with discretion given to individual states (a wide margin of appreciation) and a requirement not to interfere with that right unless it is in accordance with law, necessary and proportionate.[37] It has been argued that adoption with contact may tip the balance on whether the interference represented by adoption is proportionate within the protections afforded by Article 8.[38] Therefore the contact issue becomes a factor in whether the adoption itself is proportionate. Though this argument has been applied to the parent-child relationship, where the relationship between siblings engages Article 8 it may also be valid. Whether or not it forms part of the adoption decision, the decision about post-adoption contact must consider the Article 8 rights of the siblings and, regardless of whether the contact is direct or indirect, any interference with their relationship must be not only the least necessary but also proportionate to the legitimate aim the restriction is seeking to achieve.

On the question of whether sibling contact ought to be direct or indirect, once again that will fall to be considered on the facts of the individual case, taking into account the rights of the siblings. When post-adoption contact with parents is discussed, the purpose is often said to be to assist an adopted child in understanding his or her identity. However, there have been suggestions that the purpose of

[34] Doughty, Meakings and Shelton (n 10) 20.

[35] Kirsty Hughes and Brian Sloan, 'Post-adoption Photographs: Welfare, Rights and Judicial Reasoning' (2011) *Child and Family Law Quarterly* 393.

[36] *ABC v Principal Reporter* [2020] UKSC 26, [2020] 1 WLR 2703. Of course most of the ECHR was effectively incorporated into UK law by the Human Rights Act 1998.

[37] For positive obligation see *ABC v Principal Reporter* [2020] UKSC 26, [2020] 1 WLR 2703, [29].

[38] Davey (n 4) 165–67.

contact between siblings after adoption may go beyond that to include the maintenance of relationships, for which direct contact is more appropriate.[39] Clarity on the purpose of contact is not only an important element of social work planning but a key part of the legal reasoning when considering whether a measure restricting contact is proportionate to the aim sought and, as such, amounts to an acceptable interference with Article 8 of the ECHR.

There is a statutory right of the child, and a corresponding duty on the court, to give consideration to the ascertainable wishes and feelings of the subject child.[40] This is bolstered by the child's right under Article 12 of the UNCRC both to express views on matters relating to him or her and to have those views heard in proceedings relating to him or her. Given the age profile of the children subject to compulsory adoption from public care, it may be that it is only in a limited number of cases that it will be possible to ascertain children's views on sibling contact after adoption, but where it is possible there is a strong legal basis for ensuring it forms part of the decision making. The voice of the child in proceedings in Scotland has been explicitly strengthened through recent amendments to legislation, which require the court to give the child the opportunity to express views in the way the child prefers and to have regard to those views.[41]

Fenton-Glynn sets out the right to be heard under Article 12 of the UNCRC and points out that, while adoption may involve very young children, all children have a right to be heard even if the weight afforded to their views varies with age. Further, she observes the ways in which the views of very young children, who are often the subject of adoption, might be gleaned from behaviour and non-verbal indicators.[42] Three persuasive reasons are given by her for ensuring that the child is heard: first, one cannot determine a child's best interests without at least understanding what he or she has to say on the subject; second, engaging the child will assist with the child's understanding of the process and potentially lead to a better outcome; and finally, symbolically taking the time to hear a child recognises that the child is not an object – the child is not 'subject' to the proceedings but rather is a participant with rights.

For the child who is the subject of proceedings the court needs to consider all the welfare factors in the case, including the ascertainable wishes and feelings of the child, with thought given to how those views are expressed and the weight to be given to them in order to give meaning to Article 12 of the UNCRC. There is also, among the rights of others, the right to respect for the private and family life of the child's siblings and whether any proposed interference with those rights is

[39] House of Lords, Select Committee on Adoption Legislation, *Second Report of Session 2012–2013*, HL Paper 127 (2013) para 266.

[40] ACA 2002 s 1(4)(a); Children (NI) Order 1995, art 1(3)(a).

[41] Children (Scotland) Act 2020, s 2, amending the Adoption and Children (Scotland) Act 2007, s 14(4A).

[42] Claire Fenton-Glynn, 'The Child's Voice in Adoption Proceedings' (2014) 22 *International Journal of Children's Rights* 135.

proportionate. Further, the manner in which the court and public authority go about taking decisions will need to involve the child sufficiently in proceedings to comply with the procedural requirements of Article 8, again taking into account the age and understanding of the child.[43] An added complexity for the court is that the way in which the rights of the child are argued by adults – whether parents, guardians ad litem or local authorities – adds a filter to them. Regard must also be had to the rights and interests of the non-subject sibling.

The Rights of the Non-Subject Sibling

A consideration for courts in making any decision in relation to adoption, including that of contact, is the wishes and feelings of the child's relatives – which includes siblings.[44] Siblings who are not the subject of the proceedings still have a statutory basis for having their views considered. This is bolstered for siblings who are themselves children by Article 12 of the UNCRC, which articulates a right for children to express their views on matters concerning them and also to be heard in proceedings affecting them. There are also procedural implications of Article 8 for siblings. Overall, they should have sufficient involvement in the process to protect their interests.[45] Despite these strong imperatives to take into account the views of non-subject children, the risk remains that siblings who are not subject to the proceedings will be missed in the decision-making process.[46]

The right to respect for private and family life under Article 8 of the ECHR exists around a relationship and so where it is engaged for the subject child it is a right which is shared with the non-subject sibling. Another reason that a distinct consideration of the rights of those involved is important is that it is the welfare of the subject child which is paramount, not the welfare of all children affected by the decision.[47] Considering whether a decision to restrict the sibling *relationship* is proportionate to the aim pursued would help to ensure that non-subject child's substantive rights are respected alongside the welfare of the subject child. A frequent concern is the potential risk of contact between an adopted child and a sibling who remains in contact with or in the care of the birth family, with whom the adopted child is not intended to have contact. It may be that asking the proportionality question regarding any intended restrictions on the relationship could assist in the difficult situation where a sibling relationship is considered important but there is risk to be managed from the other relationships which the non-adopted sibling maintains.

[43] Art 6 of the ECHR was not thought to add anything to the procedural requirements under Art 8 for siblings in *ABC v Principal Reporter* [2020] UKSC 26, [2020] 1 WLR 2703, [27].

[44] ACA 2002, s 1(4)(f)(iii).

[45] *ABC v Principal Reporter* [2020] UKSC 26, [2020] 1 WLR 2703, [30].

[46] Monk and Macvarish (n 17) 87.

[47] *Re D-O'H (Parenting Assessment)* [2011] EWCA Civ 1343, [2012] 2 FLR 713, [35].

There are also practical considerations for the court to bear in mind. One such consideration is that a non-subject sibling must know about the proceedings, something that led Jones and Jones to suggest that in Scotland there should be a requirement to notify siblings of the adoption proceedings so that they might express their views on contact.[48] The non-subject child may him- or herself have been adopted or be awaiting adoption and as such may have a right to respect for a private and family life with an adoptive family.

A Duty to Give Reasons

A concerning finding from research studies into this subject is the inability to ascertain from the child's local authority notes why contact is not taking place between siblings.[49] This is despite the importance, emphasised in research, of children knowing and understanding the decisions made about contact in order to help them manage feelings of loss.[50] As well as the need for reasons being linked to the welfare of children, it is possible to argue that these decisions fall within the category of decision making that affects such a substantial interest in their lives as to attract a duty to give reasons as a matter of procedural fairness in law.[51] Further to that, such a duty may arise under Article 6 of the ECHR, as the question of contact falls within the ambit of civil rights and obligations.[52]

Recent changes in Scottish law will include a requirement, in some circumstances, to ensure court decisions are explained to the child unless it is not in the child's best interests.[53] Though this seems like something that should be par for the course, prioritising it and ensuring there is a responsibility that it occurs recognises the legal status of a child as a holder of rights and harks back to the very purpose of rights – to recognise human dignity – a basic tenet of which is to have decisions about your life explained to you so that you can in turn exercise any right you may have to express a view or take action in relation to those decisions. Ensuring that siblings know and understand the reasons for decisions about their relationships ought to be a key issue for practitioners in the range of disciplines which adoption crosses.

[48] Fiona Jones and Christine Jones, *Prioritising Sibling Relationships for Looked After Children* (Edinburgh, Clan Childlaw, 2018) 1.

[49] Jones, Henderson and Woods (n 19) 233; Doughty, Meakings and Shelton (n 10) 16.

[50] Cossar and Neil (n 11) 74.

[51] See, generally, *Dover District Council v CPRE Kent* [2017] UKSC 79, [2018] 1 WLR 108, [50]–[60]; *R (Hasan) v Secretary of State for Trade and Industry* [2008] EWCA Civ 1321, [2009] 3 All ER 539; *R v Secretary of State for the Home Dept, ex p Doody* [1994] 1 AC 531.

[52] See, eg, *Hentrich v France* (1994) 18 EHRR 440; *Ruiz Torrija v Spain* (1994) 19 EHRR 553.

[53] Children (Scotland) Act 2020, s 20.

Siblings Born after Adoption: Who Decides What and How?

Adoption may sever the legal ties between a child and their birth family but it does not stop that family growing and changing or new siblings being born.[54] Siblings born after adoption raise a number of practical and perhaps also moral issues. The complex and sometimes large sibling networks of adopted children have led to adopters expressing concern about the possibility of children inadvertently commencing relationships with relatives as they grow older, particularly in smaller jurisdictions.[55] The rise of DNA ancestry sites and social media also increases the chances of information about wider family being discovered in an unintended or accidental way rather than in a planned and considered manner. The question of who decides, and when and how, that a child should know about or have contact with siblings born after adoption is not straightforward.

The role of the state in this scenario highlights the ongoing tension between an adoptive family as a new legal relationship which itself ought to be free from unjustified interference, and recognition of the adopted child's (and corresponding siblings') potential rights to have knowledge of their identity and to be able to develop their relationships. Rather than seeing the continued role of the state as an interference in the life of adoptive families, it can be reconceptualised as a difference in treatment of adopted children: children entering the public care system with the same childhood issues may potentially receive different levels of support or treatment depending on their placement type.[56] This can lead to suggestions that there is discrimination based on status as an adopted child if the practices and procedures around identification and facilitation of relationships with birth siblings differ from those applicable to children in other placement types. That difference in the role of the state again boils down to the conception of adoption as a process which puts an end to state intervention in the life of the child and recognition that an adoptive parent has all the legal entitlements of a parent to make decisions about what is in the best interests of his or her child. This can be further complicated if adoptive parents wish to develop a relationship between an adopted child and a new sibling but local authorities are unsupportive.[57] There is a difficult balance to be struck between ensuring adoptive family autonomy on the one hand and identifying what falls within the state's duty to support an adopted child on the other.

[54] It is with gratitude to two participants in my own research that I consider this issue which, while discussed in abstract terms here, in their lives is a very real and emotive matter.

[55] MacDonald (n 6) 14.

[56] Doughty, Meakings and Shelton (n 10) 10.

[57] Sarah Meakings, Amy Paine and Katherine Shelton, 'Birth Sibling Relationships After Adoption: Experiences of Contact with Brothers and Sisters Living Elsewhere' (2020) *British Journal of Social Work* 1, 11.

The courts can also play a role, as the statutory framework permits contact applications to be lodged after the making of the adoption order. This would be the means through which knowledge about or contact with subsequent siblings could be pursued, but it requires the adults or children involved to play an active, and what might be perceived as provocative, role.[58] It further requires the parties involved to have knowledge of the birth of siblings and to know that such a mechanism for seeking contact exists.[59] If an application for contact is brought by a birth or adoptive parent, or by a child, the rights of those involved may differ where there has been no previous relationship.

It has been held in England and Wales that an adoption order brings to an end any Article 8 rights that exist between a child and their birth parents and siblings.[60] This approach has been questioned on the basis of ECtHR case law.[61] The argument is that the lack of an existing relationship is outside of the control of the children and has some parallels with the reasoning applied to unmarried fathers in the past, for whom Article 8 ties have been deemed to exist even in the absence of legal ties and on the basis of limited relationships. The question of the engagement and protection of Article 8 between birth siblings after adoption feels like an unfinished chapter in the development of the rights of siblings but, on the basis of the current law, Article 8 may not provide much protection. If it were engaged it would entail a positive obligation on the state to facilitate the relationship. Any such right would also have to be balanced against the right to respect for private and family life engaged between the adopted child and his or her adoptive family or the sibling and his or her family depending on where the application originated. Beyond the engagement of Article 8, any contact application for a sibling born after adoption would fall to be determined according to the welfare criteria as applied to a contact application and the rights of the children involved to be protected from harm.

It seems there is a situation, the extent of which is unknown, where adopted children have siblings with whom they have no contact and potentially no or limited knowledge about. In any individual case the reason for that may lie with birth parents, adopters, local authorities or the courts, but it seems to be a situation that simply occurs rather than being planned. From the perspective of children, if or when they find out, whether in childhood or in adult life, how will that knowledge affect them, and whose responsibility will it have been? In Northern Ireland, a lengthy statutory inquiry into abuse in state-funded institutions for alternative

[58] ACA 2002, ss 51A and 51A(4)(b); in Northern Ireland, the Children (NI) Order 1995, art 10 (requiring leave of the court); in Scotland, the Children (Scotland) Act 1995, s 11.

[59] Daniel Monk and Jan Macvarish, 'Siblings, Contact and the Law: An Overlooked Relationship? [2019] *Family Law* 180, 184.

[60] *Re A (A Child) (Adoption: Human Rights)* [2015] EWHC 2609 (Fam), [2016] Fam 171 and *Re TJ (Relinquished Baby: Sibling Contact)* [2017] EWFC 6. Compare *In the matter of Re B (A Child)* [2011] EWCA Civ 509, [2011] 2 FLR 1179 [9].

[61] Sarah Hansen, 'Birth Relationships After Adoption – Is There a Role for Article 8? (2019) 31 *Child and Family Law Quarterly* 211.

care of children considered evidence that siblings were at linked institutions without knowledge of one another. Though an extreme example of siblings being unaware of one another and in close proximity, the finding of the inquiry was that the concealment of siblings – which, it is noted, was contrary to government guidance even then – was 'a cruel and unjustified practice, and one which was a serious and systemic form of emotional abuse'.[62] The outworking of adoption is not easy and the roles and responsibilities of those involved can be undefined, but the issue of subsequent siblings is deserving of reflection in order to prevent the system sleepwalking into repeating old mistakes.

Contact with Siblings after Adoption: The Role of the Courts

As outlined at the start of this chapter, there are a number of occasions when the question of contact comes before the court in the proceedings that lead to adoption. The courts have the power to make a court order for contact. They might influence plans in ways which fall short of a court order, through expressing an opinion or encouraging further discussion between parties, but ultimately the currency of a court is court orders. Although researchers have emphasised that direct contact might be something that should be thought about in more cases, rather than relying on a default position of indirect contact, the other message which comes across is that direct contact works best when there is trust in adoptive parents and flexibility in the plans.[63] This is sometimes seen as incompatible with a court order setting out contact, with some cautioning that, due to the varying nature of the contact needs of children, making fixed court orders may not be the solution.[64]

If adoption is the placement decision of the court and post-adoption contact is deemed to be in children's best interests, the imposition of a court order on adopters can be viewed as overstepping the mark and trespassing on the exercise of the adopters' parental responsibility. The cases have to grapple with the court having a responsibility to determine what is best for a child and how that responsibility is translated into existence. While research has identified that many adoptive parents are supportive of post-adoption contact for siblings, and perhaps more are open to direct contact than is assumed by professionals, reported cases also contain examples where contact that was considered by the court as in children's best interests has been stopped without clear indications as to why.[65]

[62] Historical Institutional Abuse Inquiry, *Report of the Historical Institutional Abuse Inquiry* (2017), vol 2, ch 5, Sisters of Nazareth, Derry/Londonderry, paras 73–74.

[63] Neil (n 7) 1182.

[64] Doughty, Meakings and Shelton (n 10) 20.

[65] Jones, MacDonald and Brooks (n 9) and *Re P (Children) (Placement Orders: Parental Consent)* [2008] EWCA Civ 535, [2008] 2 FLR 625, [14].

The courts have retained the position articulated by the House of Lords in 1989 in a case in which they did make post-adoption contact a condition of the adoption order. The oft cited passage from Lord Ackner is as follows:

> It seems essential to me that, in order to safeguard and promote the welfare of the child throughout his childhood, the court should retain the maximum flexibility given to it by the Act and that unnecessary fetters should not be placed upon the exercise of the discretion entrusted to it by Parliament … The cases rightly stress that in normal circumstances it is desirable that there should be a complete break, but that each case has to be considered on its own particular facts. No doubt the court will not, except in the most exceptional case, impose terms or conditions as to access to members of the child's natural family to which the adopting parents do not agree. To do so would be to create a potentially frictional situation which would be hardly likely to safeguard or promote the welfare of the child. Where no agreement is forthcoming the court will, with very rare exceptions, have to choose between making an adoption order without terms or conditions as to access, or to refuse to make such an order and seek to safeguard access through some other machinery, such as wardship. To do otherwise would be merely inviting future and almost immediate litigation.[66]

There was a brief moment when it was thought this approach might be changing. In *Re P* the Court of Appeal, considering an order for contact between siblings where the sibling relationship was particularly important while a child was subject to a placement order, said that it was a matter for the court, not the local authority and prospective adopters, to consider contact not only at the placement stage but at the point of an adoption order. Considering the provisions of the 2002 Act (prior to amendment by the Children and Families Act 2014), the Court observed that if Parliament conferred on courts the power to make orders and required them to consider contact and the welfare of the child throughout the child's life then the 2002 Act 'envisages the court exercising its powers to make contact orders post adoption, where such orders are in the interests of the children concerned'.[67]

The moment was not long lived. In *Re J* the position in *Re P* was distinguished from the situation where an application was made for contact after the adoption order had been made (another case decided before the 2014 amendments).[68] *Re B*, the most recent case to consider the matter, arose after the 2014 amendments to the 2002 Act conferred a specific power to make orders for post-adoption contact rather than going through the Children Act 1989. In that case the view was endorsed, harking back to the House of Lords in 1989, that it would be extremely unusual to make such orders against the will of adopters.[69] McFarlane LJ went further to say that any move towards more direct contact in open adoption should

[66] *Re C (A minor) (Adoption Order: Conditions)* [1989] AC 1, 17.

[67] *Re P (Children) (Placement Orders: Parental Consent)* [2008] EWCA Civ 535, [2008] 2 FLR 625 [154].

[68] *Re J (A Child) (Adopted Child: Contact)* [2010] EWCA Civ 581, [2011] Fam 31, [9], [36]. See also *Re T (A Child) (Adoption: Contact)* [2010] EWCA Civ 1527, [2011] 1 FLR 1805, [22].

[69] *Re B (A Child) (Post-Adoption Contact)* [2019] EWCA Civ 29, [2019] Fam 389, [59].

come from practice and evidence presented to the courts on an individual basis rather than from the courts themselves, thereby defining the issue as one of welfare rather than of law.[70]

In contrast with the approach of the courts in England and Wales sits a striking judgment by Kerr LCJ when sitting in the Court of Appeal of Northern Ireland.[71] The case concerned a child who had been adopted by a maternal family member and a contact application by a grandmother. It was agreed that the relationship between the grandmother and the child was important and in the child's best interests to maintain. The objection to contact stemmed from the adopter and was said to be such as to have the potential to impact the child.[72] Lord Kerr departed, explicitly, from Lord Ackner's view in *Re C*, stating:

> It is now recognised that contact with a natural grandparent is generally in the interests of the child. This calls for a radically different approach from that suggested by Lord Ackner. It appears to us that where such contact is likely to benefit the child, it should only exceptionally be denied, especially where the basis on which it is resisted is opposition from the adoptive parent. In such circumstances it seems to us that, generally, contact should only be refused when it can be shown that this is likely to harm the child.[73]

Through focusing on what the court determined was best for the child, a court order was made, in spite of the argument, often raised against the use of court orders, that if the adopter did not agree to the contact, forcing it through a court order could have a negative impact on the child.[74] Perhaps a case which turned on its own unique facts, it is nonetheless a demonstration of Lord Kerr's willingness to challenge the status quo. It did not instigate a practice of making court orders for contact in Northern Ireland, where instead a practice has developed of having an arrangement with input from the parties which the court may give a view on and will check at the adoption hearing but is not usually incorporated in a court order nor made a condition of the adoption or freeing order.[75]

In relation to sibling contact, aside from the issues around the appropriateness of a court order, there is the question of children's access to such an order. A court in England and Wales cannot make the order of its own initiative and therefore must have an application before it. Given that many of the children involved in adoption proceedings will themselves be below the age of competency to bring legal proceedings, it leaves the issue of contact between siblings in the hands of the adults involved and restricts the court's ability to make an order on the matter.

Two issues arise from the perspective of the children involved. The first is that deferring to the adults who care for them to carry out what has been determined

[70] ibid.
[71] *Re L-P* [2004] NICA 34.
[72] ibid [17].
[73] ibid [16].
[74] ibid [17].
[75] *ZH v H and H* [2016] NIFam 6, [34]–[37].

by a court to be in a child's best interests is a position which is not taken in other areas of family law.[76] It may be that the difference can be justified by reference to the unique nature of the adoption situation but, if it cannot be, it puts adopted children in a different position from children in other family forms when it comes to the protection of their sibling relationships.

The second issue is, if court orders are too blunt an instrument to carry out these arrangements, what is the effective way to convey the court's assessment of what is in a child's best interests, to protect that conclusion for the child and to adapt to future changes? It has been identified as a difficulty that there is no chance to review plans for contact.[77] A tentative suggestion emerged that the courts might use their powers under section 51A of the 2002 Act to review the issue of contact after a period of time.[78] It has also been suggested that the requirement under section 1 of the ACA 2002 to consider children's welfare throughout their lives might require adoption plans to have a review built in through which the issue of contact might be considered.[79] Once again this invokes the balance between, on the one hand, the state and the court's responsibility to children who have been adopted from the public care system and, on the other hand, the recognition of the adoptive family as a new legal family for the child. The tensions that emerge from the issue of post-adoption contact for siblings, the rights involved and the role the court plays allow for reflection on the concept of modern adoption itself.

Conclusion

Running through welfare considerations and the balancing of rights in decisions about post-adoption contact between siblings are a number of underlying issues which relate to broader questions about modern adoption. There is an ongoing tension between adoption as a mechanism for creating a new, secure legal family versus recognition that not all pre-adoption relationships a child had were necessarily harmful and that some might remain of value to the child. The concerns about confidentiality in adoption permeate into consideration about sibling relationships where a sibling remains in contact with his or her birth family. Pulling against that is a sympathy for siblings who find themselves in different placements for reasons outside their control, which is something that some children who participated in research identified themselves as unfair.[80] Added to it all are

[76] McFarlane (n 17) 616.
[77] Cossar and Neil (n 11) 73.
[78] McFarlane (n 17) above at 616.
[79] Doughty, Meakings and Shelton (n 10) 8.
[80] Monk and Macvarish (n 17) 95–96.

advances in modern technology both as a resource for contact arrangements and a potential method of circumventing them.[81]

There is nothing straightforward about the question of post-adoption contact between siblings nor the role of the courts in such decisions. It engages the rights of children and adults in different and at times conflicting ways. It raises untold welfare issues which may be weighted differently by different adults involved and which are met in their complexity by the welfare issues of the other side of the sibling equation in question. The difficult situations which sibling relationships raise for practice also lead to questions about what modern adoption means, what constitutes continued interference in the lives of adopted children, and the extent to which any interference in the lives of adopted children is merited, justified or necessary. None of this is easy for any of those involved but, though it may feel like the decision to place a child for adoption is the most pressing and important one before decision makers, it is hoped that the issues raised here have highlighted how the decisions that follow on from that point are no less challenging, particularly for siblings.

[81] Elsbeth Neil, Ruth Copson and Penny Sorensen, *Contact During Lockdown: How are Children and their Birth Families Keeping in Touch?* (Nuffield Family Justice Observatory, 2020) 28 and Mandi MacDonald and Dominic McSherry, 'Constrained Adoptive Parenthood and Family Transition: Adopters' Experience of Unplanned Birth Family Contact in Adolescence' (2013) 18 *Child & Family Social Work* 87.

INDEX

www.ingramcontent.com/pod-product-compliance
Lightning Source LLC
LaVergne TN
LVHW020139280526
839948LV00003B/492